Ethical AI Applications for Software Engineering and Development

Affan Yasin Yasin
https://orcid.org/0000-0002-0166-2239
Xi'an Jiaotong-Liverpool University, China

Farhan Ullah
Prince Mohammad Bin Fahd University, Saudi Arabia

Rubia Fatima
https://orcid.org/0000-0002-7144-1925
Emerson University, Pakistan

IGI Global
Scientific Publishing
Publishing Tomorrow's Research Today

Vice President of Editorial	Melissa Wagner
Director of Acquisitions	Mikaela Felty
Director of Book Development	Jocelynn Hessler
Production Manager	Mike Brehm
Cover Design	Jose Rosado

Published in the United States of America by
IGI Global Scientific Publishing
701 East Chocolate Avenue
Hershey, PA, 17033, USA
Tel: 717-533-8845 | Fax: 717-533-7115
Website: https://www.igi-global.com E-mail: cust@igi-global.com

Library of Congress Cataloging-in-Publication Data

Names: Yasin, Affan Yasin, 1989- editor | Ullah, Farhan, 1985- editor | Fatima, Rubia, 1990- editor
Title: Ethical AI applications for software engineering and development / edited by Affan Yasin Yasin, Farhan Ullah, and Rubia Fatima.
Description: Hershey, PA : IGI Global Scientific Publishing, [2026] | Includes bibliographical references and index. | Summary: "This book explores and promotes ethical practices in the development and deployment of AI within software engineering"-- Provided by publisher.
Identifiers: LCCN 2025054363 (print) | LCCN 2025054364 (ebook) | ISBN 9798337360386 h/c | ISBN 9798337360393 s/c | ISBN 9798337360409 ebook
Subjects: LCSH: Artificial intelligence--Moral and ethical aspects | Artificial intelligence--Industrial applications | Software engineering--Data processing | Computer software--Development
Classification: LCC Q335 .E787 2026 (print) | LCC Q335 (ebook)
LC record available at https://lccn.loc.gov/2025054363
LC ebook record available at https://lccn.loc.gov/2025054364

British Cataloguing in Publication Data
A Cataloguing in Publication record for this book is available from the British Library.

Table of Contents

Preface xiii

Chapter 1
Human-Centered AI Design and Ethical Implications in Everyday Applications 1
Nivedhitha Mahendran, SRM Institute of Science and Technology, Kattankulathur, India
M. Priyadharshini, Easwari Engineering College, Ramapuram, India

Chapter 2
Ethical Considerations in Human-Centered AI Design for Assistive Technologies 37
Farzana Jabeen, National University of Sciences and Technology, Islamabad, Pakistan
Mehvish Rashid, National University of Sciences and Technology, Islamabad, Pakistan
Tahira Anwar Lashari, National University of Sciences and Technology, Islamabad, Pakistan
Sana Anwar Lashari, School of Nursing, Shandong Xiehe University, China
Sidra Sultana, National University of Sciences and Technology, Islamabad, Pakistan
Asad Waqar Malik, National Strategic Planning and Analysis Research Center, Mississippi State University, Starkville, USA

Chapter 3
Ethical Challenges of AI in Tackling Online Harassment and Cyberbullying ... 67
Sana Anwar Lashari, School of Nursing, Shandong Xiehe University, China
Tahira Anwar Lashari, National University of Sciences and Technology, Pakistan
Saima Anwar Lashari, College of Computing and Informatics, Dammam, Saudi Arabia
Farzana Jabeen, National University of Sciences and Technology, Pakistan
Djihad Tria, Amity University, Tashkent, Uzbekistan

Chapter 4
Blockchain-Enabled Ethical Governance Framework for Transparent, Accountable, and Trustworthy AI Systems: From Transparency to Ethical AI Governance 93
Rana Muhammad Amir Latif, East China Normal University, Shanghai, China
Farhan Ullah, Prince Mohammad Bin Fahd University, Khobar, Saudi Arabia
Umar Raza, Manchester Metropolitan University, Manchester, UK
Leonardo Mostarda, University of Perugia, Perugia, Italy
Diletta Cacciagrano, University of Camerino, Camerino, Italy

Chapter 5
Zero Knowledge Proofs Enabling Ethical AI and Privacy-Preserving Verification in Distributed Systems 123
Laila Khalid, University of Science and Technology of China, China
Muhammad Usman Akhtar, Northwestern Polytechnical University, China
Muhammad Khalid, University of Hull, UK
Iftikhar Ahmed, University of Europe for Applied Sciences, Germany

Chapter 6
Applications of Artificial Intelligence in Healthcare Resolving the Intersections of the Patient Safety, Data Sensitivity, and Equitable Access: Toward Ethical and Secure Healthcare AI 155
Mehak Rana, The University of Faisalabad, Pakistan
Muqadsa Jabeen, The University of Faisalabad, Pakistan
Majid Hussain, The University of Faisalabad, Pakistan
Muhammad Seed, The University of Faisalabad, Pakistan
Shoaib Hassan, The University of Lahore, Sargodha, Pakistan

Chapter 7
Ethical AI Applications in Health Care: Ensuring Patient Safety, Data Security, and Fair Access 181
Nazeef Ul Haq, University of Engineering and Technology, Lahore, Pakistan
Abdul Basit Dogar, University of Management and Technology, Lahore, Pakistan
Rizwan Riaz Mir, Virtual University of Pakistan, Lahore, Pakistan
Muhammad Naveed Yasir, Emerson University, Multan, Pakistan

Chapter 8
Towards Ethical AI in Dermatological Diagnostics: Balancing Patient Privacy, Fairness, and Human-Centered Design... 221
Rabia Shahid, The University of Faisalabad, Pakistan & Government College University, Faisalabad, Pakistan
Muhammad Ibrar, The University of Faisalabad, Pakistan
Waqas Junaid, Northwestern Polytechnical University, Xian, China
Muhammad Saeed, The University of Faisalabad, Pakistan
Majid Hussain, The University of Faisalabad, Pakistan

Chapter 9
Integrating Agentic AI Ethically Into Geriatric Healthcare: A Framework for Frailty Monitoring With Transformer Models and Wearable Technology........ 245
Muhammad Azhar, Hong Kong Shue Yan University, Hong Kong
Ifra Shabbir, COMSATS University, Islamabad, Pakistan
Muhammad Shafqat Ali, BPP University Limited, London, UK
Ghulam Farid, Harbin Engineering University, China
Hamza Arif, COMSATS University, Islamabad, Pakistan
Rubia Fatima, Emerson University, Multan, Pakistan

Chapter 10
Secure AI Applications for Cybersecurity: Ethical and Explainable Threat Detection in Modern Software Systems... 275
Iram Hanif, The University of Faisalabad, Faisalabad, Pakistan
Majid Hussain, The University of Faisalabad, Faisalabad, Pakistan
Muhammad Ibrar, The University of Faisalabad, Faisalabad, Pakistan
Amara Hafeez, The University of Faisalabad, Faisalabad, Pakistan
Affan Yasin, XianJiaotong-Liverpool University, Suzhou, China

Chapter 11
Secure and Ethically Aligned AI Solutions for Cybersecurity and Threat Detection 305
Amrutha Kolhar, Karnatak University, Dharwad, India
Sridevi, Karnatak University, Dharwad, India

Compilation of References 339

About the Contributors 377

Index.. 385

Detailed Table of Contents

Preface.. xiii

Chapter 1
Human-Centered AI Design and Ethical Implications in Everyday Applications 1
Nivedhitha Mahendran, SRM Institute of Science and Technology, Kattankulathur, India
M. Priyadharshini, Easwari Engineering College, Ramapuram, India

Artificial Intelligence is increasingly shaping daily life, transforming the way humans work, learn, communicate, and make decisions, while raising critical ethical, social, and trust challenges. Human-Centered AI emphasizes designing systems that place human values, fairness, transparency, inclusivity, accountability, and privacy at the forefront. By integrating ethics, emotional intelligence, participatory design, and continuous feedback, HCAI ensures AI empowers users, fosters collaboration, enhances well-being, mitigates bias, and supports socially responsible and sustainable technological innovation. It envisions AI as a partner rather than a tool, aligned with human needs and societal progress.

Chapter 2
Ethical Considerations in Human-Centered AI Design for Assistive Technologies 37
Farzana Jabeen, National University of Sciences and Technology, Islamabad, Pakistan
Mehvish Rashid, National University of Sciences and Technology, Islamabad, Pakistan
Tahira Anwar Lashari, National University of Sciences and Technology, Islamabad, Pakistan
Sana Anwar Lashari, School of Nursing, Shandong Xiehe University, China
Sidra Sultana, National University of Sciences and Technology, Islamabad, Pakistan
Asad Waqar Malik, National Strategic Planning and Analysis Research Center, Mississippi State University, Starkville, USA

As the technology evolved with the leading role of Artificial Intelligence (AI) in developing assistive technology, is constantly enabling people to live a quality life. However, bridging the connection to enable human with disabilities, which is promising direction towards their independence and autonomy, comes at the cost of the ethical implications. This chapter discusses the pivotal role of Human Centered AI (HCAI) in relation to assistive technology. We explore the principles of HCAI in this chapter to propose a framework to be utilized while developing assistive technology systems. The chapter collectively focuses on guiding the researcher, industry practitioners, and policymakers to comply with ethical concerns and ensure that assistive AI is a source of empowerment, transparency, security, and trustworthiness.

Chapter 3
Ethical Challenges of AI in Tackling Online Harassment and Cyberbullying ... 67
Sana Anwar Lashari, School of Nursing, Shandong Xiehe University, China
Tahira Anwar Lashari, National University of Sciences and Technology, Pakistan
Saima Anwar Lashari, College of Computing and Informatics, Dammam, Saudi Arabia
Farzana Jabeen, National University of Sciences and Technology, Pakistan
Djihad Tria, Amity University, Tashkent, Uzbekistan

The rapid progression in artificial intelligence (AI) has transformed social life. Though AI has enabled innovative tools for social communication, it has facilitated cyberbullying, hence, raising concerns about human privacy. To combat cyber harassment digital communities started to depend on AI algorithmic moderation tools to identify, monitor, and prevent user from harmful behavioral patterns through human data raising concerns of privacy and ethical use of personal information. This chapter begin with discussing historical events highlighting different phases of AI development. In second section, dual nature of perpetrator and protector role of AI was discussed. Finally, the chapter provides future directions for responsible innovation and it was covered under solutions and recommendations section. The finding revealed that a global harmonization is required to create a balance between potential protection and AI-guideline.

Chapter 4
Blockchain-Enabled Ethical Governance Framework for Transparent, Accountable, and Trustworthy AI Systems: From Transparency to Ethical AI Governance 93
Rana Muhammad Amir Latif, East China Normal University, Shanghai, China
Farhan Ullah, Prince Mohammad Bin Fahd University, Khobar, Saudi Arabia
Umar Raza, Manchester Metropolitan University, Manchester, UK
Leonardo Mostarda, University of Perugia, Perugia, Italy
Diletta Cacciagrano, University of Camerino, Camerino, Italy

As artificial intelligence (AI) becomes increasingly embedded in critical domains such as healthcare, cybersecurity, finance, and public services, the demand for ethical governance ensuring fairness, transparency, and accountability is urgent. Traditional oversight mechanisms often lack verifiable trust in decentralized and dynamic environments. This chapter introduces a Blockchain-Enabled Ethical Governance for AI (B-EGAI) framework that leverages blockchain's immutability, transparency, and smart contracts to enable auditable model registries, decentralized policy enforcement, and tamper-proof decision logs. By embedding ethical principles across the AI lifecycle, B-EGAI fosters accountability and trustworthiness in real-world applications. Case studies demonstrate its potential, while discussions on privacy-preserving computation, federated learning, and decentralized oversight outline future research, positioning blockchain as a foundation for trustworthy AI.

Chapter 5
Zero Knowledge Proofs Enabling Ethical AI and Privacy-Preserving Verification in Distributed Systems 123
Laila Khalid, University of Science and Technology of China, China
Muhammad Usman Akhtar, Northwestern Polytechnical University, China
Muhammad Khalid, University of Hull, UK
Iftikhar Ahmed, University of Europe for Applied Sciences, Germany

The evolving technology in AI and distributed systems requires ethical concepts of how sensitive data can be verified without breach of privacy. Conventional AI systems present the following critical concerns: exposure of data, breach of privacy, and ethical issues concerning transparent but confidential computation. This chapter is a full-fledged cryptographic proof, Zero-Knowledge Proofs (ZKPs), which makes it possible to deploy AI ethically by verifying privacy. The framework is supported by mathematical underpinnings to enable model validation and training verification, as well as federated learning without the underlying datasets or parameters of the models. The chapter shows that ZKPs can be used to meet ethical AI without compromising privacy. It can be used in healthcare, finance, and voting systems where ethical concerns require verification and confidentiality. This chapter offers a new method of dealing with core ethical dilemmas in AI systems and safeguarding privacy and security in algorithmic decision-making exercises.

Chapter 6
Applications of Artificial Intelligence in Healthcare Resolving the Intersections of the Patient Safety, Data Sensitivity, and Equitable Access: Toward Ethical and Secure Healthcare AI 155
Mehak Rana, The University of Faisalabad, Pakistan
Muqadsa Jabeen, The University of Faisalabad, Pakistan
Majid Hussain, The University of Faisalabad, Pakistan
Muhammad Seed, The University of Faisalabad, Pakistan
Shoaib Hassan, The University of Lahore, Sargodha, Pakistan

Artificial intelligence (AI) is disrupting healthcare in the form of disease diagnostics, clinical decision support, and remote patient monitoring. Nevertheless, such developments raise many ethical issues regarding patient safety, data sensitivity, and fair access. This chapter focuses on AI in healthcare as a process that is guided by the principles of clinical validation, transparency, and constant monitoring to avoid diagnostic mistakes and algorithmic bias. It discusses privacy-protective solutions like blockchain governance, federated learning, and differential privacy to ensure sensitive health information is not leaked. Moreover, it states that inclusive datasets and models of fairness are essential to providing equitable access, especially in low- and middle-income countries. Based on the case studies of NHS AI Lab (UK), Mayo Clinic (USA) and AIoT-based diabetes monitoring (Singapore), the chapter suggests an ethical AI implementation system that considers both innovation and trust to provide safe, confidential, and equity healthcare to all populations.

Chapter 7
Ethical AI Applications in Health Care: Ensuring Patient Safety, Data Security, and Fair Access 181
Nazeef Ul Haq, University of Engineering and Technology, Lahore, Pakistan
Abdul Basit Dogar, University of Management and Technology, Lahore, Pakistan
Rizwan Riaz Mir, Virtual University of Pakistan, Lahore, Pakistan
Muhammad Naveed Yasir, Emerson University, Multan, Pakistan

The integration of Artificial Intelligence (AI) into healthcare presents transformative opportunities and profound ethical challenges that require continuous oversight and moral reflection. This chapter critically examines the ethical foundations necessary for responsible and sustainable AI use in medical contexts, tracing its evolution from early expert systems to deep learning applications influencing clinical decision-making. Grounded in the biomedical ethics of autonomy, beneficence, non-maleficence, and justice, the discussion extends these principles to algorithmic transparency, bias mitigation, accountability, and equitable access to AI-driven healthcare. Key concerns of data privacy, patient safety, cybersecurity, and regulatory compliance under frameworks such as HIPAA, GDPR, WHO guidelines, and the EU AI Act are explored. By reviewing notable AI failures, including IBM Watson for Oncology and the DeepMind–Royal Free data-sharing case, the chapter underscores the essential need for continuous ethical governance throughout the AI lifecycle in healthcare.

Chapter 8
Towards Ethical AI in Dermatological Diagnostics: Balancing Patient Privacy, Fairness, and Human-Centered Design.. 221
Rabia Shahid, The University of Faisalabad, Pakistan & Government College University, Faisalabad, Pakistan
Muhammad Ibrar, The University of Faisalabad, Pakistan
Waqas Junaid, Northwestern Polytechnical University, Xian, China
Muhammad Saeed, The University of Faisalabad, Pakistan
Majid Hussain, The University of Faisalabad, Pakistan

Artificial intelligence (AI) has been a groundbreaking technology in the health sector, and dermatology is one of the earliest to adopt AI-based diagnostic systems. The deployment of this system causes significant challenges related to Responsible AI (RAI) such as decision critical tasks, patient privacy, accountability, clinician trust, and robustness. Ethical considerations are the core of chapter discussion that particularly focuses on protection of patient confidentiality through data augmentation and fairness across heterogeneous population by application of algorithmic fairness methods. The chapter also highlights the importance of user-centered system design to strengthen clinician trust and support shared decision-making. Combining both the technical innovation and an ethical background, this chapter proposes a practical implementation of how responsible AI can be embedded in clinical informatics Conclusively, it offers a practical roadmap for embedding responsible, fair, and trustworthy AI into dermatological informatics and into other high-stakes healthcare applications.

Chapter 9
Integrating Agentic AI Ethically Into Geriatric Healthcare: A Framework for Frailty Monitoring With Transformer Models and Wearable Technology 245
Muhammad Azhar, Hong Kong Shue Yan University, Hong Kong
Ifra Shabbir, COMSATS University, Islamabad, Pakistan
Muhammad Shafqat Ali, BPP University Limited, London, UK
Ghulam Farid, Harbin Engineering University, China
Hamza Arif, COMSATS University, Islamabad, Pakistan
Rubia Fatima, Emerson University, Multan, Pakistan

The rising incidence of frailty in aging populations challenges traditional healthcare systems that lack real-time monitoring tools. To address this, we present CareBot, an ethical AI framework using wearable sensors and phones to continuously assess elderly frailty. It employs Transformer models to analyze multimodal data like heart rate, movement, and sleep for early frailty detection. TabTransformer handles health records to generate personalized risk scores. Additionally, DeepSeek, a generative AI, provides caregiver alerts and natural-language health advice. Following ethical AI principles, CareBot ensures autonomy, transparency, equity, and privacy. Evaluations with PAMAP2 and SHARE datasets show CareBot outperforms methods like SVM, CNN, and LSTM in accuracy and robustness. This scalable solution offers interpretable insights and tailored actions to enhance elderly health and quality of life.

Chapter 10
Secure AI Applications for Cybersecurity: Ethical and Explainable Threat Detection in Modern Software Systems 275
Iram Hanif, The University of Faisalabad, Faisalabad, Pakistan
Majid Hussain, The University of Faisalabad, Faisalabad, Pakistan
Muhammad Ibrar, The University of Faisalabad, Faisalabad, Pakistan
Amara Hafeez, The University of Faisalabad, Faisalabad, Pakistan
Affan Yasin, XianJiaotong-Liverpool University, Suzhou, China

The diversity of digital capabilities has been improved by new cloud-native, microservices, DevSecOps, and IoT software designs, which have also designed a path to cyber threats. Outdated security tools like firewalls and signature-driven recognition are not very effective against ransomware, insider threats, phishing attacks, sophisticated persistent threats and zero-day attacks. The practice of AI can be in the zones of intrusion prevention, malware detection, phishing resistance, insider monitoring, and IoT and autonomous platforms security. These concerns increase major ethical alarms to software engineers who must confirm that the AI systems are transparent, accountable, and fair. XAI and privacy-sensitive models, as well as compliance with such regulations as GDPR and the EU AI Act, provide much-needed protection. Future secure AI developments in cybersecurity include secure

AI innovations such as federated learning, blockchain-based AI, and quantum-safe algorithms.

Chapter 11
Secure and Ethically Aligned AI Solutions for Cybersecurity and Threat Detection 305
Amrutha Kolhar, Karnatak University, Dharwad, India
Sridevi, Karnatak University, Dharwad, India

This paper explores the integration of artificial intelligence (AI), including machine learning and deep learning, to enhance cybersecurity threat detection and response. It addresses the critical need for these advanced solutions to be ethically aligned, ensuring fairness, transparency, and accountability. The study examines both the technical capabilities of AI in malware analysis and anomaly detection, and the ethical challenges such as bias and data privacy. By proposing a governance framework for responsible deployment, this research aims to bridge the gap between technological innovation and ethical responsibility, fostering trust in AI-driven cybersecurity systems

Compilation of References 339

About the Contributors 377

Index 385

Preface

INTRODUCTION

The rapid integration of Artificial Intelligence (AI) into software engineering is transforming the way systems are conceived, designed, implemented, and maintained. Intelligent automation, predictive analytics, adaptive decision-making, and data-driven optimization are no longer futuristic concepts; they are embedded in the daily practices of modern software development. Yet, as AI systems grow more capable and pervasive, they also introduce profound ethical challenges that demand careful reflection and responsible action.

As editors of *Ethical AI Applications for Software Engineering and Development*, we were motivated by a shared recognition: ethical considerations can no longer be treated as secondary to technical performance. Questions of fairness, bias, accountability, transparency, privacy, security, and digital inclusion must be integrated into the very fabric of the software engineering lifecycle. AI systems increasingly shape decisions in healthcare, education, finance, cybersecurity, and public services—domains where errors, biases, or misuse can have significant and lasting societal consequences. The responsibility borne by developers, researchers, and organizations has therefore never been greater.

This volume seeks to explore the intersection of ethics and AI within software engineering through both theoretical and practical lenses. The chapters presented here examine ethical frameworks and governance models that guide responsible AI development and deployment. They explore real-world applications of AI in healthcare, with particular attention to patient safety, sensitive data, and equitable access. Contributors discuss strategies for embedding trustworthy AI principles into requirements engineering, system design, testing, deployment, and maintenance. They also analyze the societal implications of AI systems, addressing algorithmic fairness, digital bias, and inclusion in increasingly automated environments.

In addition, the book investigates privacy-aware system design in sensitive domains such as education, finance, and public administration. It highlights secure and ethically aligned AI applications in cybersecurity and threat detection, where the balance between protection and rights must be carefully maintained. A recurring theme throughout the volume is human-centered AI design—ensuring that systems are built not only for efficiency and performance, but also for meaningful, respectful, and equitable human-machine interaction.

Our aim in curating this collection has been to bridge the gap between ethical theory and software engineering practice. Too often, discussions of AI ethics remain abstract or disconnected from the realities of development workflows, constraints, and organizational pressures. By bringing together perspectives from academia, industry, and policy, this book offers both conceptual foundations and actionable guidance. The contributors provide frameworks, case studies, and technical insights that equip readers to navigate complex ethical challenges in real-world contexts.

This book is intended for software engineers, AI researchers, data scientists, and students who seek to design and deploy AI responsibly. It will also be valuable to educators, policymakers, and industry professionals working in sectors where AI-driven systems carry heightened ethical stakes. By combining rigorous scholarship with practical orientation, the volume serves as a resource for those committed to developing AI systems that are innovative, transparent, fair, secure, and aligned with diverse human values.

We hope that this work encourages continued dialogue across disciplines and fosters a culture of ethical awareness within the software engineering community. Ultimately, our aspiration is to support the creation of AI systems that not only advance technological capability but also strengthen trust, uphold human dignity, and contribute positively to society.

ORGANIZATION OF THE BOOK

In **Chapter 1**, the contributors establish the conceptual foundation of the volume by examining Human-Centered AI (HCAI) as both a design philosophy and an ethical imperative. They argue that as AI systems permeate everyday applications—shaping how individuals work, learn, and interact—ethical considerations must be embedded at the core of system design. By foregrounding fairness, transparency, inclusivity, accountability, and privacy, this chapter positions AI not merely as a technical instrument, but as a collaborative partner aligned with human values and societal well-being.

Chapter 2 extends this human-centered perspective into the domain of assistive technologies. The authors explore how AI-driven systems can empower individuals with disabilities while simultaneously raising complex ethical questions concerning autonomy, security, and trust. Through the proposal of a Human-Centered AI framework tailored for assistive systems, the chapter offers guidance for researchers, practitioners, and policymakers committed to ensuring that innovation translates into meaningful, ethical empowerment.

In **Chapter 3**, attention turns to the dual role of AI in online spaces, where it functions as both a facilitator of harm and a mechanism for protection. Addressing cyberbullying and online harassment, the authors trace the historical evolution of AI moderation tools and critically examine their ethical implications, particularly in relation to privacy and surveillance. The chapter calls for globally harmonized standards that balance digital safety with fundamental rights, underscoring the need for responsible innovation in algorithmic governance.

Chapter 4 introduces a Blockchain-Enabled Ethical Governance for AI (B-EGAI) framework designed to enhance transparency and accountability in high-stakes domains. By leveraging blockchain's immutability and smart contract capabilities, the authors propose auditable model registries and tamper-proof decision logs that embed ethical oversight across the AI lifecycle. Through case studies and forward-looking discussions on federated learning and decentralized oversight, the chapter demonstrates how distributed technologies can strengthen trustworthy AI governance.

Building on cryptographic innovation, **Chapter 5** explores Zero-Knowledge Proofs (ZKPs) as a mechanism for privacy-preserving verification in AI and distributed systems. The authors present a mathematically grounded framework enabling validation of models and training processes without exposing sensitive data. Particularly relevant for healthcare, finance, and voting systems, this chapter addresses one of the central ethical tensions in AI: how to ensure transparency and accountability without compromising confidentiality.

Healthcare emerges as a central focus in **Chapter 6**, which examines AI applications through the intersecting lenses of patient safety, data sensitivity, and equitable access. The authors highlight the importance of clinical validation, bias mitigation, and inclusive datasets, while also discussing privacy-preserving technologies such as federated learning and blockchain governance. Drawing on international case studies, the chapter proposes a structured implementation model that balances innovation with trust and equity.

Chapter 7 deepens the ethical analysis of AI in healthcare by grounding its discussion in the principles of biomedical ethics—autonomy, beneficence, non-maleficence, and justice. The authors trace the evolution of medical AI and examine regulatory frameworks and high-profile failures to emphasize the necessity of continuous ethical governance. By integrating legal, clinical, and technical perspectives, this chapter underscores that responsible AI in medicine requires sustained oversight and accountability.

In **Chapter 8**, the focus narrows to dermatological diagnostics, offering a case study in Responsible AI within a specialized clinical field. The contributors address issues of bias across diverse populations, patient confidentiality, and clinician trust. Through attention to fairness metrics, data protection strategies, and user-centered design, the chapter provides a practical roadmap for embedding ethical principles into high-stakes diagnostic systems.

A novel application of ethically aligned AI is presented in **Chapter 9**, which introduces CareBot—an agentic AI framework for geriatric frailty monitoring using wearable technologies and transformer-based models. The authors demonstrate how multimodal data analytics, personalized risk scoring, and explainable alerts can support early intervention while upholding principles of autonomy, transparency, and equity. This chapter exemplifies how advanced AI architectures can be responsibly deployed to enhance quality of life for aging populations.

Cybersecurity becomes the focus in **Chapter 10**, where the authors examine AI-driven threat detection in increasingly complex digital infrastructures. As cloud-native systems, IoT networks, and DevSecOps practices expand the attack surface, AI offers powerful tools for anomaly detection and intrusion prevention. Yet the chapter emphasizes that transparency, explainability, regulatory compliance, and privacy-preserving design are essential to prevent ethical compromise in automated defense systems.

Finally, **Chapter 11** advances the discussion toward adaptive cyber defense, highlighting the indispensable role of human oversight in AI-enabled security ecosystems. The authors argue that resilient systems emerge not from automation alone, but from the synergy between intelligent tools and informed human judgment. By emphasizing privacy, fairness, and ethical resilience, this concluding chapter reinforces a central message of the volume: that secure, adaptive, and trustworthy AI systems depend on both technological sophistication and enduring human responsibility.

Together, these chapters reflect the breadth and depth of ethical inquiry required in contemporary AI-driven software engineering. As editors, we believe this collection demonstrates that responsible innovation is not a constraint on technological progress, but its necessary foundation.

CONCLUSION

As we bring this volume to a close, we return to the central premise that inspired its creation: the future of software engineering is inseparable from the ethical development of Artificial Intelligence. Across healthcare, cybersecurity, assistive technologies, digital governance, and everyday applications, the chapters in this book collectively demonstrate that innovation without ethical reflection is neither sustainable nor socially responsible.

The contributions gathered here reaffirm that ethical AI is not a peripheral concern, nor a compliance checkbox to be addressed after deployment. Rather, it is a continuous, lifecycle commitment—one that must be embedded in requirements engineering, system architecture, model development, validation, deployment, and long-term monitoring. Transparency, fairness, accountability, privacy, security, and inclusivity are not abstract ideals; they are design principles that directly influence technical decisions, user trust, and societal impact.

Several unifying themes emerge throughout this volume. First, governance matters. Whether through regulatory frameworks, blockchain-enabled oversight, cryptographic verification, or institutional accountability structures, robust governance mechanisms are essential to building trustworthy AI systems. Second, human-centered design remains foundational. AI must augment human capability, respect autonomy, and strengthen well-being rather than displace responsibility or erode dignity. Third, interdisciplinary collaboration is indispensable. Ethical AI cannot be achieved by engineers alone; it requires engagement from clinicians, policymakers, social scientists, educators, legal experts, and the communities most affected by these systems.

We are particularly encouraged by the practical orientation of the chapters presented here. Beyond theoretical discourse, the contributors offer implementable frameworks, technical architectures, case studies, and evaluative models. They demonstrate that ethical alignment and technical excellence are not mutually exclusive; indeed, they are mutually reinforcing. Systems that are explainable, secure, inclusive, and privacy-aware are also more robust, resilient, and ultimately more valuable.

At the same time, we recognize that ethical AI is an evolving field. Technological capabilities are advancing rapidly, often outpacing regulatory adaptation and societal consensus. New challenges—ranging from generative AI and autonomous agents to adaptive cyber defense and large-scale data ecosystems—will continue to test our ethical frameworks. It is therefore essential that ethical reflection remains dynamic, iterative, and embedded within professional practice.

As editors, we hope this book serves not only as a reference, but also as a catalyst. A catalyst for deeper dialogue between disciplines. A catalyst for integrating ethical checkpoints into development pipelines. A catalyst for cultivating a culture in which questioning the societal consequences of technology is as routine as debugging code.

Ultimately, the measure of AI's success will not be defined solely by accuracy metrics, computational efficiency, or market adoption. It will be defined by whether these systems advance human flourishing, reduce inequities, protect rights, and earn enduring public trust. The responsibility to achieve this outcome rests with all of us—researchers, engineers, leaders, educators, and policymakers.

We conclude this volume with a sense of both urgency and optimism. Urgency, because the ethical stakes of AI deployment are profound. Optimism, because the scholarship and practical insight represented in these chapters demonstrate that responsible innovation is not only possible, but already underway.

Affan Yasin Yasin
Xi'an Jiaotong-Liverpool University, China

Farhan Ullah
Prince Mohammad Bin Fahd University, Saudi Arabia

Rubia Fatima
Emerson University, Pakistan

Chapter 1
Human-Centered AI Design and Ethical Implications in Everyday Applications

Nivedhitha Mahendran
http://orcid.org/0009-0007-6515-4528
SRM Institute of Science and Technology, Kattankulathur, India

M. Priyadharshini
Easwari Engineering College, Ramapuram, India

ABSTRACT

Artificial Intelligence is increasingly shaping daily life, transforming the way humans work, learn, communicate, and make decisions, while raising critical ethical, social, and trust challenges. Human-Centered AI emphasizes designing systems that place human values, fairness, transparency, inclusivity, accountability, and privacy at the forefront. By integrating ethics, emotional intelligence, participatory design, and continuous feedback, HCAI ensures AI empowers users, fosters collaboration, enhances well-being, mitigates bias, and supports socially responsible and sustainable technological innovation. It envisions AI as a partner rather than a tool, aligned with human needs and societal progress.

1. INTRODUCTION

As AI systems become more common in everyday life, there is a growing need to ensure they are designed in ways that truly support people. The chapter will

DOI: 10.4018/979-8-3373-6038-6.ch001

trace the shift in emphasis from traditional, mainly technically oriented AI to a new generation of HCAI: one demanding safety, fairness, and meaningful human involvement. By looking at past challenges, real-world harms, and insights from multiple disciplines, the chapter shows why HCAI has become an essential direction for building responsible and trustworthy AI technologies. In this section, we will discuss the rise of AI in our day-to-day life, why do we really need HCAI, then the importance of ethics in designing AI systems.

1.1. The Rise of AI in Everyday Life

Before getting into all about AI in everyday life, we want to make sure the audience knows what AI is. AI, by book, is defined as the machines that are developed to carry out tasks that usually demand human intelligence, such as decision making, learning and problem-solving. The transition of AI is tremendous, from being a visionary concept to driving argument in the modern life (Bialkova S, 2024). In the recent times, AI systems are taking over effortlessly various daily activities, influencing people's decision making, travel, work, communication, and health. Some of the AI systems that we are using in our life and are not aware how easy it has made our work, such as AI in smart phones, personal assistants, transportation, autonomous vehicles, healthcare, and so on. Although AI integration in the day-to-day activities makes life easier and effective, the human-centered ethical concerns about the dependency on the intelligent systems, privacy and protection cannot be ignored (Dandotiya et al, 2024).

Beyond the commonly recognized domains such as healthcare, transportation, and smartphones, AI has also become deeply integrated into other aspects of daily life, including recommendation systems, media, education, smart homes, and workplace environments, where it assists users effortlessly and tirelessly, enhancing convenience, personalization, and productivity (Natale et al, 2020).

1.2. What is Human-centered Artificial Intelligence (HCAI)?

As highlighted in Section 1.1, AI-enabled automation is advancing at a rapid pace, gradually shifting the boundaries of machine and human collaboration. From AI driving our cars, choosing our medicines, where to invest our money to what information and news to see, the common ground in these systems is the human aspect. Even though AI is doing most of the work, long-term success can be determined only through accepting that people are crucial in operation, design, and use.

Thus, HCAI is defined as the design and deployment of AI systems that focuses on human values, needs, and well-being (Xu & Gao, 2024).

The core philosophy of HCAI is to create AI systems that are useful, consistent with human needs, and trustworthy, further, making sure the advances only enhances the human decision-making, and social benefits, rather than undermining them. HCAI encourages the collaboration between the AI and humans, where the AI systems act only as partners that enhances the human capabilities, not replace them (Xu & Gao, 2024).

1.3. Why do we need HCAI?

Before getting into the technicality of the HCAI, you might want to know why we are adopting HCAI technologies. The traditional AI systems were often developed with a focus only on accuracy, and speed. Even when you are doing research projects, you concentrate only on improving the accuracy of the learning models. Not many focuses on the impact of the AI systems on people or society.

In the past, many AI tools, such as credit scoring, predictive policing, and medical decision systems, caused problems because they were biased, unfair, or difficult to understand. These practical examples made it clear that the traditional design of AI had significant limitations. They demonstrated that AI cannot function effectively in society unless it also takes into account human values, needs, and ways to verify errors or negative impacts (Capel et al, 2023).

To explore further the concepts that we actually need HCAI, it is important to examine the concepts of different disciplines such as ethics, social sciences, law, and organizational studies. Scholars in these disciplines argue that technology and society are interrelated, and AI systems can impact the way people act, decisions are made, and power is exercised (Herrmann, 2025).

These examples made it clear that the traditional architecture of AI had many limitations. They showed that AI systems cannot work well in society unless they also consider human values, needs, and ways to check errors or negative effects (Capel et al, 2023).

1.4. Importance of Ethics in AI Design

AI is here to stay, and it is changing the way we live, work, and interact. In the current scenario, we have become so dependent on AI technology to carry out our day-to-day tasks that we tend to forget that AI can be as threatening as it is useful. There are many arguments that are doing the rounds, such as, will AI replace our jobs and lead to the end of humanity? You may call it a far-off reality, but what if there is a chance of that happening? This is exactly why it is the need of the hour to know the current scenario of AI. We cannot effectively implement future modifications without understanding how AI operates and how it learns from past mistakes (Frost et al, 2022).

Although AI has become an integral part of our lives, we have done little to adequately address its ethical challenges. A few organizations implement AI without considering ethical standards, leaving open the question of what happens if the system knows more than we anticipate. Hence, it is high time that someone start talking about the ethical issues that come with AI and what can we do to protect ourselves from AI taking over our future (Conway, 2024).

To partially solve the ethical problems, a few research communities have established an oath for AI engineers called the Asilomar AI principles, which has a set of guidelines to ensure that the AI systems are designed in accordance with human values.

Apart from the steps taken by companies and organizations, such as google, Facebook, we should also educate ourselves on how to steer AI technologies, so it continues to help humankind. Furthermore, we need to remove the bias which are embedded in the AI systems and reduce the discrimination. Finally, we should create laws that streamline the use of AI in society to prevent the harm of jeopardizing the human population (Millar et al, 2011).

2. PRINCIPLES OF HUMAN-CENTERED AI DESIGN

Human-centered AI design focuses on creating AI systems that enhance human capabilities, respect human values, and ensure safe, ethical, and meaningful interactions between humans and machines. In this section, we will go through the major key principles of HCAI design.

Figure 1. Principles of HCAI design

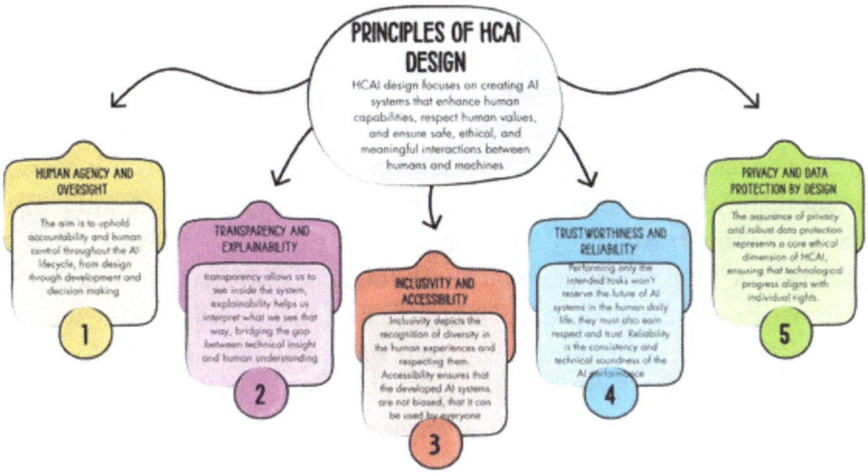

2.1. Human Agency and Oversight

Human agency is the ability of human to take independent decisions, have control in what they want to do and take actions. It is the foundation for HCAI, which makes sure the humans take informed decisions while collaborating and interacting with AI systems. In developing human-centered applications, AI should only be a supportive tool that aids the human capabilities and not replace human judgement. For instance, in healthcare, medical diagnostics, the AI models can analyse the dataset and recommend the possible outcomes, however, the final decision must be taken by the clinician, after interpreting the results checking the ethical and contextual frameworks. The aim is to uphold accountability and human control throughout the AI lifecycle, from design through development and decision making (Sawyer et al, 2021).

The oversight principle makes sure that the humans have the control and the ability to interrupt, modify, and override AI decisions, whenever necessary. The oversight mechanisms are implemented with a concept called human-in-the-loop (HITL) systems, keeps human in the loop and engages them in critical decisions, especially in crucial domains, such as, defence, healthcare, aviation, and autonomous driving. Further, it includes continuous monitoring of AI developed systems to find out anomalies, consequences, and biases before they escalate (Holzinger et al., 2017).

2.2. Transparency and Explainability

In HCAI based systems, transparency and explainability are the basic core principles, that aides in making AI models trustworthy, predictable, accountable, and understandable. Some of the advanced AI models are considered as "black boxes", such as deep learning models, as they don't reveal what is happening in the background or the decision-making process (Doshi-Velez & Kim, 2017). It is critically important that the transparency of these models must be increased, to make sure that the models are trustworthy and make the decision responsibly.

However, the transparency should not be followed only in the technical domain, it should also be in the organisational and ethical domains while dealing with issues, such as who developed the system, why, and when. (Ribeiro et al, 2016). Transparency needs to be ensured at various levels, namely design transparency, operational transparency, and user transparency, to ensure that every phase of an AI system's life cycle is transparent to all concerned.

Whereas transparency enables us to peer inside the system, explainability enables us to make sense of what we see inside the system in that way, filling the gap between technical knowledge and human understanding. The aim is to benefit the human to understand the rationale for the AI decisions or outputs in a manner that is interpretable and relevant. For example, in a credit scoring model, explainability enables users to understand why a loan application was denied, perhaps due to income constraints or credit records, as opposed to being left with an inexplicable result from the algorithm.

2.3. Inclusivity and Accessibility

The AI systems should tend to the needs of everyone, irrespective of their age, gender, culture, gender, ability, and socioeconomic status, that's why inclusivity and accessibility are one of the core principles of HCAI design. An AI system that doesn't consider the needs of the users may end up creating inequalities, and limiting the adoption of technology, which leads to biased decisions and outcomes (Jobin et al, 2019).

Inclusivity depicts the recognition of diversity in the human experiences and respecting them. This involves acknowledging the differences in culture, language, education, and technological literacy. For instance, NLP models trained only on English texts become out of scope when the speakers of other languages use the application, resulting in exclusion. Therefore, inclusive designs need careful selection of datasets, bias auditing, monitoring, and evaluation to check if the AI system works effectively for all the intended users. The system should engage diverse stakeholders throughout the development process and anticipate the changes and challenges that might arise or overlooked in a homogeneous design team.

The other principal accessibility ensures that the developed AI systems are not biased, that it can be used by people with disabilities or any other limitations, including auditory, motor, visual, and cognitive impairments (Barocas et al, 2020). For instance, the voice activated AI assistants must have feature to include the people with speech impairments as well. The design of the systems should assist without any bias and should not become a barrier to the participants.

Failure in designing non-inclusive and non-accessible AI models, might result in digital exclusion, and social inequality. Therefore, before designing an AI system, you must consult ethical guidelines, such as IEEE ethically aligned design frameworks, which emphasis on equity, fairness, universal access, and inclusive.

2.4. Trustworthiness and Reliability

Performing only the intended tasks won't reserve the future of AI systems in the human daily life, they must also earn respect and trust. The trust on AI systems is established when the user strongly starts believing when the system acts dependable, consistent, transparent, and mainly align with all the ethical values. Reliability, on the other hand, is the system's capability to perform effectively and meet the expectations set by the user under various circumstances, maintaining the accuracy and stability of over time (Jansen et al, 2018).

Let us discuss trustworthiness first, what do you mean by that? It refers to the degree of confidence with which the users can believe the system has the integrity competence and takes fair decisions. It is more important than the technical performance as it determines the system's social and ethical dimensions. To be more clear, trustworthy AI system is the one that protects user interests and operates without any manipulations and hidden intentions. Before designing an AI application, one should know the European Commission's Ethics Guidelines for trustworthy AI. The three guidelines are,

- It should be lawful, following all the rights and regulations
- It should be ethical, respect for human values
- It should be robust, ensuring consistent outcomes

Reliability is the consistency and technical soundness of the AI performance. An AI system is said to be reliable, when they function accurately across various datasets and contexts, handles errors without introducing new ones, and generate reproducible results, even with different similar inputs. For instance, in self-driving vehicles, reliability is achieved when the vehicle produces consistent results in detecting obstacles, predicting trajectories, and recommends actions during environmental changes, such as fog, bright sunlight, or heavy rains.

So, now we know how trust and reliability are relevant in developing AI systems. How do you think you can bring ethical factor in these principles? – through integrity, regulatory compliance, and a long-term commitment to societal well-being. Public trust will automatically be gained when the AI developers show openness, responsibility, and transparency in addressing the ethical challenges.

2.5. Privacy and Data Protection by design

The assurance of privacy and robust data protection represents a core ethical dimension of HCAI, ensuring that technological progress aligns with individual rights. We all are aware that the accurate results of AI systems don't come easy. It is made accurate using a massive amount of personal and behavioural data. Obviously, those who don't know the ethical side of the data collection would think that AI systems are stealing their identity. Also, there are some parts of the crowd, that don't care what is happening with their data. Thus, it has become a hectic and crucial task to ensure the ethical collection, processing, and storage of the user's personal data. Especially HCAI systems, demands the privacy and treating it as add-on or afterthought is not acceptable, instead, the systems should incorporate the safety measures within the design. The embedding of safety into architecture and design is famously known as the Privacy by Design (PbD) (Cavoukian et al, 2009).

The concept of Privacy by Design (PbD), introduced by Ann Cavoukian in the 1990s, has evolved into a globally recognized framework for ensuring ethical and privacy-conscious technology development. According to the principle, privacy should not be reactive rather it should be proactive, meaning that the privacy measure should be integrated with the system, rather than coming up with control measures after a breach occurred. In the context of AI systems, privacy is to anticipate the misusing of data, surveillance, bias, and engineering protectives measure at every stage of AI development lifecycle. In short, the design should be preventive, privacy embedded into design, user-centric transparency, creating systems that respects users' rights and expectations.

AI systems often rely on vast datasets that may include sensitive personal information such as medical records, financial transactions, facial images, or online behaviours. Without robust data protection strategies, these systems risk infringing on individuals' rights to privacy, autonomy, and consent.

Now, let us see what data protection has to offer in developing AI systems. We all know that the AI applications use vast amounts of data, and high chances of having personal sensitive data, such as financial records, medical records, facial images, or online behaviours. If there are no data protection policies in place, the developers would be at a risk of violating users' right to privacy and consent.

The General Data Protection Regulation (GDPR) of the European Union has come up with a set of international benchmarks for data protection (Gabriela et al, 2018). It mandates the organisations to embed the data protections principles in the design and operational processes.

Beyond standards and law, privacy and data protection has a deep ethical commitment to freedom and human dignity. Privacy policies makes sure that humans are not just a data points and the AI driven insights must not lead to manipulations or discrimination. In many fields, such as healthcare and finance, data protection is more a moral one rather than a legal obligation. Therefore, having a strong privacy and data protection standards is a necessity for sustainable innovation.

3. ETHICAL FOUNDATIONS FOR HUMAN-CENTERED ARTIFICIAL INTELLIGENCE

In this section, we will introduce you to the practical and philosophical foundations that sets the based for ethical AI design. It links the modern frameworks and classical ethical theories that influences the development and application of responsible HCAI. Figure 2 represents a overall view of ethical foundations for HCAI.

Figure 2. Ethical foundations for HCAI

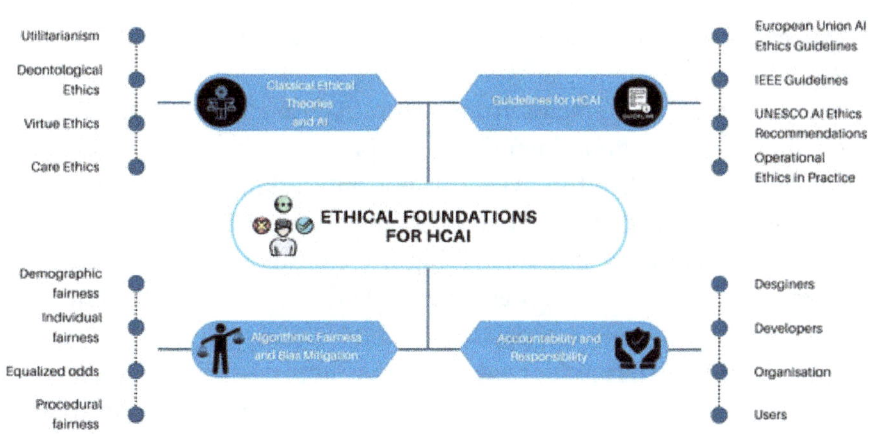

3.1. Classical Theories and AI

To comprehend and develop ethically aligned AI applications, one should begin in understanding the traditional moral philosophies that long guided the human decision making. These classical theories that we are going to discuss in this section, provide conceptual guidance for analysing whether the AI systems act responsibly, and in alignment with human interests and values.

Some of the classical ethical theories are as follows,

- **Utilitarianism** – Utilitarian ethics was introduced by Jeremy Bentham and John Stuart Mill, a moral idea that implies right action brings the most happiness or benefit to the people. In terms of AI systems, this means designing applications that focus on best overall outcomes keeping the society in mind (Bentham, 1996). For example, in healthcare, a utilitarian AI might prioritize life-saving treatments to patients with high chances of recovery, then those with lower survival rates, to maximize the overall number of lives saved. So, do you see the problem there? If you only consider the majority, then what happens to the smaller groups or individuals? Even though utilitarian AI gives efficient decisions, it also ignores the ethical fairness.
- **Deontological Ethics** – It was developed by Immanuel Kant, which is based on the idea that the actions should have moral duties and principles, not just good results. For AI systems, deontological ethics implies that the design should follow the universal moral rules. For example, deontological AI chatbots must clearly inform the users that they are interacting with a machine, rather than pretending to be a human. Though deception might make the user feel better and satisfied, lying would be morally wrong (Floridi & Cowls, 2022).
- **Virtue Ethics** – Originated from Aristotle, virtue ethics is all about being a good person with good intentions, as opposed to just doing the right thing. How it can be related to AI? You not only ask, what should AI do? but, you also ask, what values should people creating AI possess? AI developers should be honest, humble, and caring while designing the AI systems. Virtue ethics goes well with HCAI as it makes sure the AI is designed in a way that it is morally good and responsible (Tronto, 2020).
- **Care Ethics** – Care ethics, as the name implies, it is all about relational and empathetic perspectives. It focuses on responsibility, compassion, and understanding the situation around you. In AI, it is developing systems that pay attention to the people's needs, vulnerabilities, and feelings. AI chatbots, for example, can help with mental health or support the elderly people (Van Wynsberghe, 2020).

3.2. Ethics in Action: Guidelines for Human-Centred AI

The classical ethical theories we discussed in section 3.1. gives us the basic idea about what is right and wrong. In this section, we will find out how applied ethics make these ideas a reality and put to practical rules that can be used in building AI systems. These guidelines assist the policy makers, developers, and designers to develop AI systems that are trustworthy and fair. Applied ethics consists of rules, practical tools, and methods to check whether AI behaves the way it was intended to and responsible throughout the development and use. In the following section, we will learn various applied ethics principles in practice.

- **European Union AI Ethics Guidelines –** The European commission's ethics guidelines for trustworthy AI (2019) mandates seven key requirements for AI systems, they are as follows,
  - Human agency and oversight: Empowering humans to guide and regulate AI decisions
  - Technical robustness and safety: Ensuring consistent performance and minimizing risks
  - Transparency: Offering understandable insights into AI decision logic
  - Privacy and data governance: Promoting responsible data handling and legal compliance
  - Diversity, non-discrimination, and fairness – Eliminating bias and fostering inclusiveness
  - Societal and environmental well-being: Assessing AI's impact on society and the environment
  - Accountability – Implementing frameworks for auditing, accountability, and remedy.
- **IEEE ethically aligned design –** The framework designed by Institute of Electrical and Electronics Engineers (IEEE) emphasizes on alignment of AI systems with human expectations, values and societal norms (Adamson, et al, 2019). The practical recommendations for the same are as follows,
  - Integrating the ethical aspects of AI in the system development
  - Promoting transparency, accountability, and explainability
  - Building AI that supports equal opportunities, diversity, and minimizing bias.
  - Fostering cross-disciplinary collaboration among policymakers, ethicists, and engineers.
- **UNESCO AI ethics recommendations –** The focus of UNESCO recommendations is on global cooperation and human rights-based AI governance

(*Recommendation on the ethics of artificial intelligence, UNESCO, 2022)*. It emphasises on the following,

  - Safeguarding human dignity, freedom from bias, and privacy
  - Ensuring equal access to AI technologies
  - Ensuring the AI development is aligned with sustainable development goals
  - Promoting inclusive participation from wide range of stakeholders

- **Operationalizing ethics in practice –** Applied ethical models aid the organisations in implementing practical strategies such as,
  - **Ethical audits:** Periodic evaluation of AI systems for fairness, safety, and bias
  - **Ethics boards and committee**: Collaborative monitoring to ensure ethical compliance
  - **Ethics by design principle:** Integrating human-centred ethics in every stage of development
  - **Impact assessment:** Evaluating the environmental, social, and economic implications before deployment

By applying these practices, organisations can turn ethical ideas into concrete actions, making sure AI systems behave in ways that reflect human values and meet society's expectations.

3.3. Algorithmic Fairness and Bias Mitigation

AI is the buzz word in almost every field in recent years, such as healthcare, finance, government, hiring, and education, therefore it is to think the ethical aspects of implementing a fair AI. Algorithmic fairness focuses on preventing AI from copying or worsening social biases, which could lead to unfair treatment. Bias can come from the data AI is trained on, the way it is designed, or the assumptions made in the model. If not addressed properly, these biases can reduce the trust, harm vulnerable groups, and increase inequality. Let us further discuss the source of bias, what is fairness in AI, and strategies to mitigate bias.

- **Sources of bias in AI:** Bias can happen in multiple places in AI development, such as data bias, algorithmic bias, user interaction bias, and societal bias. The developer and the policymakers must consider all the biases before putting the AI system into use.
- **Fairness in AI:** It is a multi-dimensional concept, there are several types, a few are listed below (Peters et al, 2020),

- **Demographic fairness** – The outcomes must be distributed equally across all the groups, such as gender or race.
- **Individual fairness** – Similar treatment for similar individuals must be embedded in the AI systems
- **Equalized odds** – Equal error rates and equal accuracy for different demographic groups
- **Procedural fairness** – There should be transparency, accountability, and consistency in making decisions.

- Strategies for bias mitigation: To mitigate the bias, AI developers use a combination of technical and systematic approaches as following,
    - **Preprocessing** – removing null values, discriminatory values, and normalize the imbalances in the dataset
    - **In-processing** – making modifications in the algorithm during training to enforce fairness
    - **Post-processing** – adjusting the outputs to minimize the bias once the predictions from the models are generated
    - **Continuous monitoring** – monitoring the performance of the model regularly for fairness across all demographic groups and updating them if necessary.

3.4. Accountability and Responsibility

In recent years, the AI systems have become mostly autonomous and influential, which makes accountability and responsibility a critical ethical challenge. Despite the automation, HCAI insists on responsible design, deployment, and consequences. Failure in having a proper accountability mechanism can lead to eroding trust and undermining ethical values.

Accountability is the obligation of the stakeholders (developers, organizations, and users) to define, justify, and take responsibility for the actions and the consequences of AI systems. The accountability principles makes sure that if at some point, AI systems make any mistakes and cause harm, then respective stakeholders can be identified, and necessary corrective actions are implemented.

Responsibility in AI is spanned across multiple individuals, like, engineers and developers, are responsible for designing robust, and secure systems (Jobin et al, 2019). The organizations and institutions are responsible for ethical oversight, governance, and compliance with regulatory requirements. Further, the users and operators are responsible for using AI appropriately only for the purposes it was designed to do, follow guidelines, and intervene when necessary.

Some mechanisms that can be adhered to encourage accountability are, having an ethics committee and oversight board, audit trials, impact assessments, transparency, and explainability.

4. HUMAN ARTIFICIAL INTELLIGENCE INTERACTION DESIGN

Human AI Interaction (HAI) focuses on how people engage, interact, communicate, and collaborate with the AI systems. In HCAI, having an interactive design ensures that the AI technologies are transparent, intuitive, and supportive of the human intentions and goals, rather than replacing or taking control of them. The intention of creating AI systems is to enhance human capabilities, respect autonomy, and maintain trust through meaningful interaction. In this section, we will discuss the various methods with which human AI interaction can be improved.

4.1. User Experience (UX) and AI

User Experience (UX) in designing AI based systems, is not just aesthetics or usability, it is much more than that, it included how humans perceive, interact, and derive meaning from the intelligent systems. In HCAI, UX design majorly focuses on building AI systems that are usable, useful, and are aligned with human values and goals. Furthermore, it fosters a sense of understanding, empowerment, and trust.

Traditional UX designs focus on only static interactions which can be fine for predictable and rule-based systems. However, the AI introduces dynamic, probabilistic, and adaptive behaviours, that requires more than an out of the box thinking. Some of the shift in design thinking are as follows (Gammelgård-Larsen, 2024),

- **Adaptivity:** AI systems train and adapt through user data and context, which helps them evolve over time. Developers should make sure that this adaptation remains predictable and beneficial.
- **Uncertainty:** AI-based applications mostly work on probabilistic reasoning. The users must be clearly communicated the uncertainty about the system predictions, preventing confusion and over-trust.
- **Personalization:** As we said in adaptivity, AI develops experience through user preferences, however, excessive personalization might lead to "filter bubbles" or privacy concerns.

The ever-evolving AI paradigm keeps the designers and developers on their toes to bring a balance to human agency and automation, making sure that the user remains in control of their digital experiences. Figure 3 shows the phases involved in the UX design.

A good UX for AI systems must consider both emotional and cognitive dimensions of user responses. Emotions such as anxiety, curiosity, or scepticism can shape the perceptions of AI performance. Therefore, the designs must include empathetic communication to humanise AI without any deception, manage the cognitive load by simplifying the information presentation, and reinforce positive emotions (Thellman & Ziemke, 2023). By considering the rational and affective aspects, AI UX can be more human-aligned and holistic.

Figure 3. User experience design phases

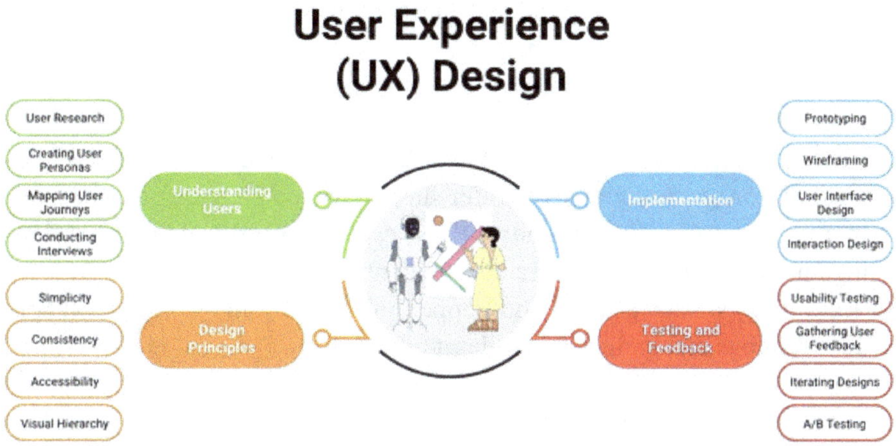

4.2. Emotional Intelligence in AI Interfaces

Emotional Intelligence (EI) in AI interfaces are the ability of the AI systems to recognize, interpret, and respond accordingly to the human emotions. Especially, in HCAI, this ability is essential in creating interfaces that are supportive of user needs, empathetic, and adaptive designs encouraging more natural and meaningful human-computer interaction. When AI systems can recognize and respond to human emotions, they move beyond basic functions and create more personal, trusting, and engaging experiences for users.

The concept of emotional intelligence came from psychology, where it implies and individual's ability to understand, perceive, and manage emotions of their own and of others. When it is applied on AI, it includes (Mollahosseini et al., 2016),

- Emotion recognition, where the AI system would try to detect human emotions from voice tone, facial expressions, or physiological symptoms.
- Emotion understanding, interpreting the emotional states in the context it was expressed. For instance, distinguishing sarcasm from non-sarcasm or frustration from confusion.
- Emotion response generation, adjusting the AI's tone, behaviour, or actions to show empathy and respond appropriately in social situations.

If you are expecting some real-world examples, here are some,

- Virtual therapy tools and mental health chatbots like Woebot and Wysa can recognize users' emotions and offer supportive, empathetic guidance.
- Intelligent tutoring systems adapt their teaching speed and feedback depending on how engaged or frustrated a student is.
- Social robots, such as Paro and Pepper, offer emotional support and help reduce feelings of loneliness in older adults.

Let us move on to the design principles of AI interfaces. To integrate the emotional intelligence into the AI systems both ethically and effectively, the developers should follow some key principles, such as, empathy centric design, context awareness, adaptive responsiveness, transparency, and cultural sensitivity. These principles make sure that the emotional intelligence is embedded to support the users and not replacing or manipulating them, keeping human dignity as center of AI interaction. There are various technological foundations that are used individually or combined to implement the discussed principles effectively. For instance, affective computing, Natural Language Processing (NLP), Machine learning, Deep learning, and Human-Computer Interaction (HCI).

4.3. Cognitive Load and User Experience (UX)

By the term cognitive load what do you understand? It is a mental effort that is required to process information and convert them to decisions. In HCAI, it is essential to understand and manage the cognitive load to develop intuitive, efficient, and supportive AI systems in human decision-making, instead of confusing or overwhelming the users. Poorly designed cognitive loads will lead to frustration, errors, reduced trust, and disengagement. There are three different types of cognitive loads (Chandler et al, 1991),

- **Intrinsic load:** Load from interpreting how complicated the task or information is by nature. For instance, interpreting probabilistic outputs generated by medical AI systems.
- **Extraneous load:** Cognitive load resulting from poorly designed interfaces, ambiguous instructions, or overwhelming system complexity. For example, Dashboards that are too crowded or filled with technical terms, which distract users from the important information.
- **Germane load:** The mental workload involved in processing and learning task-relevant information. For example, Users' active interaction with AI explanations to develop deeper comprehension of system behaviour.

AI interface design should aim to minimize extraneous cognitive load while maximizing germane load, supporting meaningful user engagement and comprehension. Furthermore, high cognitive load on systems affects UX negatively in various ways, decision fatigue, reduced trust, decreased efficiency, and emotional frustration. On the other hand, carefully monitoring the cognitive load can enhance user satisfaction, usability, and perceived trust of AI systems. Figure 4 represents the various strategies that can be followed to reduce the cognitive load.

Let us discuss some strategies on how to manage cognitive loads in AI interfaces and improve UX,

- **Simplify information presentation:** Present AI results using simple language, clear visuals, and easy-to-understand layouts.
- **Progressive disclosure:** Show information step by step so users can explore more details when they need to.
- **Visual Analytics and dashboards:** Use graphs, charts, and interactive tools to make complex data easier to understand.
- **Explainable AI (XAI):** Give explanations that make sense in context and are easy to understand without too much technical detail.
- **Adaptive interfaces:** Change the amount of information and level of help based on how experienced the user is and how much mental effort they can handle.
- **Guided decision support:** Focus on showing key findings or practical suggestions instead of just raw data.

The above-mentioned strategies are in line with the HCAI principles, encouraging clarity, user autonomy, and efficiency. Measuring the cognitive load helps in making simple, and inclusive AI interfaces.

Figure 4. Strategies to reduce cognitive load

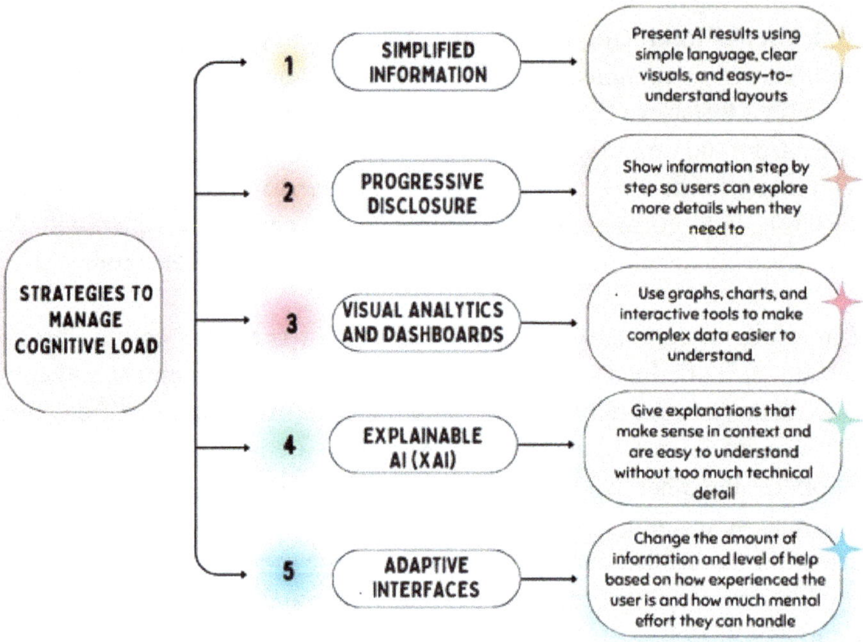

4.4. Feedback Loops and Continuous Learning

In HCAI, the feedback loops and adaptive learning are important to make dynamic and continuous improvement. Such systems exploit user engagement to improve precision, relevance, and overall user experience through continuous interaction. Through continuous interaction, AI are no longer just the decision-making tools, but a collaborative learning partners that involve human experience and ethics into the development process.

A feedback loop is the process where an AI system learns from its past performance. It takes information about what went right or wrong and uses it to improve its future results. In HAI interaction, feedback occurs at multiple levels, user-level feedback, direct feedback from the user to the AI systems, then there is system-level feedback, which is a data-driven evaluation of the AI accuracy in achieving the goals, finally, contextual feedback, which is an adjustment based on situational and environmental changes. With the help of the above-discussed feedback mechanisms, the AI system will learn continuously, adjust, and improve predictions, maintaining the contextual relevance all along.

On the other hand, continuous learning refers to an AI system's ability to dynamically refine its models and actions based on evolving datasets and human feedback. The key features of continuous learning include, adaptivity, personalisation, knowledge retention, and resilience. For instance, the recommendation systems refining the suggestions with the help of use ratings or reviews.

Although feedback loops and continuous learning offer many benefits, they also come with certain challenges that must be handled carefully, includes (Li et al, 2018),

- **Data privacy risks:** collecting detailed feedback from the users can expose sensitive information about the users
- **Bias reinforcement:** If most of the users share similar biases, feedback might unintentionally maximize them
- **Feedback fatigue:** Users might feel frustrated, burdened, or disinterested if asked for constant input
- **Misinterpretation of feedback:** AI might misunderstand sarcastic or implicit feedback signals, if they are not trained properly with sarcastic datasets
- **Transparency gaps:** When tangible benefits are not apparent, user participation and engagement may decline

In Human-Centred AI (HCAI), feedback loops must be designed to uphold human rights, transparency, and accountability. Continuous learning processes should not compromise user autonomy or privacy. Ethical HCAI design therefore requires the following principles (Koren et al., 2009):

- Users maintain control and provide consent over the data used for learning.
- AI systems remain auditable and explainable, even as they evolve.
- Learning outcomes uphold diversity, fairness, and inclusivity.

By following these principles, feedback loops support not only technical improvement but also the ethical growth of AI systems.

5. ETHICAL IMPLICATIONS IN EVERYDAY APPLICATIONS

Artificial Intelligence (AI) is no longer limited to research centers or specialized industries; it is now part of everyday life. Its applications affect how people make decisions, how they interact with one another, and how important institutions such as healthcare, education, banking, and media operate.

Human-Centred AI aims to design, develop, and use AI while considering its social impact, so that technology benefits society. This section discusses AI applications in various sectors and the ethical issues linked to them.

Table 1. Examples of AI applications and their related ethical challenges

Field	Applications	Ethical Implications
AI in Healthcare	Diagnosis, drug discovery, treatment planning, and patient monitoring	• Bias and equity • Privacy and data protection • Accountability • Trust
AI in Education	Intelligent tutoring system, adaptive learning platforms, and automated grading	• Fairness and inclusion • Data privacy • Autonomy and agency • Dependency vs empowerment
AI in Workplace	Hiring, task allocation, performance evaluation, and workflow automation	• Bias and discrimination • Transparency • Worker Autonomy • Accountability and governance
AI in Smart Homes and Consumer Devices	Home automation, voice activated assistants, health monitoring, energy management, etc.	• Privacy and data security • Autonomy and user control • Transparency and explainability • Bias and inclusivity • Security vulnerabilities
AI in Public Governance	Policy analysis and decision making, public service delivery, urban planning and smart cities, regulatory compliance and monitoring, etc	• Transparency and accountability • Bias and discrimination • Privacy and data protection • Autonomy and participation • Ethical oversight and governance

6. DESIGNING ETHICAL AND HUMAN-CENTERED AI SYSTEM

An AI system guided by human-centred and ethical principles ensures that technology is used responsibly for the benefit of humanity. HCAI combines technological progress with social, ethical, and psychological considerations, highlighting inclusivity, well-being, trust, and accountability across all stages of AI development.

This section outlines key principles, strategies, and best practices for building AI systems that are both technically robust and ethically sound.

6.1. Participatory Design and Co-creation

The development of ethical and Human-Centred AI (HCAI) systems requires more than technical knowledge; it also depends on the active involvement of users, designers, developers, and other stakeholders. This co-creation process promotes shared responsibility and helps ensure that AI systems are built according to the needs, values, and expectations of their intended users. Treating users as active participants rather than passive recipients supports accountability, trust, and inclusion (Simonsen & Robertson, 2013).

The principles of participatory design highlight user empowerment and democratic ideals. This approach is based on the belief that individuals affected by a system should be given the opportunity to voice their concerns during the design and implementation process. The key principles are outlined by Krippendorff et al. (2019):

- **Inclusivity:** Bringing together diverse voices from end users to policymakers, to ensure AI systems reflect collective values and societal diversity
- **Transparency:** Transparency in design empowers participants to engage meaningfully, strengthening trust and shared ethical commitment.
- **Empowerment:** Enabling stakeholders to contribute meaningfully to design choices rather than acting as nominal participants.
- **Iterative collaboration:** Approaching design as an iterative process involving continuous testing, reflection, and refinement rather than a fixed, one-time activity.
- **Value integration:** Embedding principles of fairness, dignity, and autonomy into AI systems to ensure technology aligns with human-centered values.

We will move on to co-creation now, so co-creation is just an extension of participatory design with focus on joint innovation, in which users and designers collaborate on ideas, problems, solutions, and outcomes. It involves the following,

- **Problem definition:** By engaging users in defining real-world needs, AI systems can be designed to deliver meaningful and socially beneficial outcomes
- **Data curation:** By engaging communities in the creation and validation of datasets, AI systems become more inclusive, context-aware, and less prone to bias
- **Model design:** Collaboration between designers and domain specialists ensures that algorithms operate in accordance with human reasoning and ethical principles
- **Interface design:** Engaging users in co-developing interaction models enhances both usability and the system's emotional responsiveness
- **Evaluation and refinement:** Collecting feedback from diverse stakeholders supports ongoing refinement and alignment with ethical standards

Adopting participatory and co-creative approaches provide various long-term benefits, such as enhanced legitimacy, social accountability, bias reduction, and empathy in design. However, there are some challenges as well, including, power imbalance between the stakeholders, resource and time constraints, and ethical conflicts. Addressing the challenges requires strong ethical commitment and institutional support.

6.2. Ethics by Design Framework

The ethics-by-design principles recommends the integration of ethical values and principles into the architecture and development process of AI systems, instead of treating it as an add-on. By embedding the ethical aspects in the early stages of development, AI systems can proactively ensure fairness, prevent harm, and align with human needs and values. This framework acts as the foundation to HCAI, as it systematically embeds ethics alongside the technical performance in the AI systems.

The core principles of ethics-by-design framework are as follows (Floridi et al., 2018),

- **Proactive ethical integration:** Ethical considerations are integrated at each stage of the AI lifecycle, including problem definition, data acquisition, system deployment, and ongoing monitoring
- **Human-centricity:** AI design prioritizes respect for human dignity, personal autonomy, and prevailing social values
- **Transparency and explainability:** For AI to be ethical, its decisions must be explainable and clear to all affected parties

- **Accountability and responsibility:** Explicit lines of accountability are established for AI-driven outcomes, ensuring that humans retain responsibility for decision-making.
- **Inclusivity and fairness:** By integrating multiple perspectives, AI systems can minimize bias and promote fairness for everyone
- **Continuous evaluation:** Continuous ethical compliance is ensured through feedback mechanisms, formal audits, and systematic monitoring of AI operations

An Ethics-by-Design approach can be put into practice using these steps (Van de Poel et al, 2023):

- **Ethical requirements analysis:** At the start, identify possible ethical issues, social effects, and the values of stakeholders
- **Design integration:** Integrate the ethical constraints and aspects into the system architecture, user interfaces, and algorithms
- **Stakeholder participation:** Engage users, ethicists, and domain specialists collaboratively to develop ethical frameworks and validate design choices
- **Transparent data practices:** Ensure that all data collection, storage, and processing practices comply with established standards for privacy, consent, and fairness
- **Ethical testing and auditing:** Anticipate and assess ethical challenges, biases, and unintended outcomes through simulation and evaluation before the system is deployed
- **Monitoring and iteration:** Continuously monitor ethical compliance during real-world operation, adapting the system in response to feedback and evolving societal norms

Figure 5 shows the diagrammatic representation of ethics-by-Design approach steps. Some of the benefits of embedding the ethics-by-design frameworks in AI development is that they can help in mitigating potential risks, or harms, builds trust, regulate compliance, sustainable AI development, and alignment with human values. It also comes with some challenges, such as conflicting ethical standards, difficulty in translating ethical principles into algorithms, continuous adaptation, and resource requirements.

Figure 5. Ethics-by-design approach

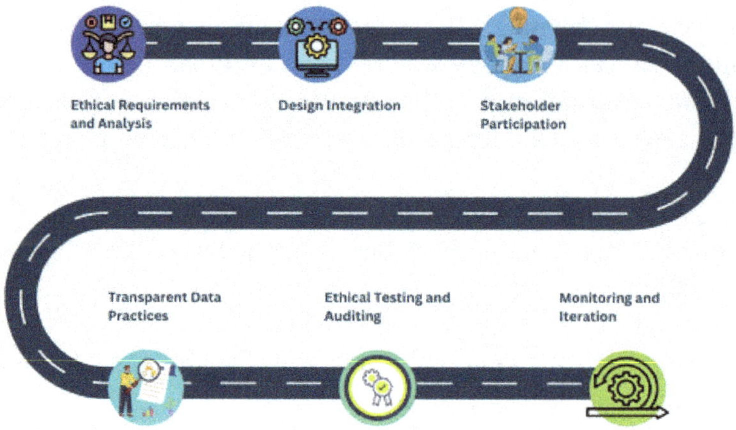

6.3. Human-in-the-Loop Systems

Human-in-the-Loop (HITL) systems involve humans in AI decision-making to provide oversight and guidance, keeping people central to important tasks. In contrast to fully autonomous AI, Human-in-the-Loop (HITL) systems make use of AI's speed and processing power while maintaining the human ability to apply context, ethical reasoning, and flexibility. This is essential for Human-Centred AI because it supports human oversight and builds trust in AI systems.

The key elements of Human-in-the-Loop (HITL) systems involve concepts already examined in this chapter, including human control, decision intervention, feedback, and learning. HITL provides benefits such as ethical safeguards, higher accuracy, trust, and adaptability. At the same time, it has some drawbacks, including slower decision-making, scalability issues, possible bias transfer, and increased cost.

An important observation is that Human-in-the-Loop (HITL) and Ethics-by-Design approaches work well together and combining them can result in AI systems that are both human-centred and ethically sound.

6.4. Evaluation Metrics for Human-Centered AI

Human-Centred AI (HCAI) considers both technical performance and the impact of AI on people. Therefore, its evaluation involves more than measuring accuracy; it also examines human-centred factors such as usability, fairness, clarity, and trust. This section presents the main metrics used to evaluate HCAI systems. Tables 2, 3, 4, 5 below show the various categories of evaluation metrics for HCAI.

Table 2. Technical performance metrics

Performance Metrics	Description
Accuracy/Precision/Recall/FMeasure	For classification tasks, measuring correctness of predictions
Mean Squared Error (MSE)/Mean Absolute Error (MAE)	For regression tasks, assessing prediction deviation
Latency/Response time	Evaluates how quickly the AI system reacts, critical for real-time human interactions
Robustness	Measures how the system handles noisy, incomplete, or adversarial inputs

Table 3. Human-centric performance metrics

Usability and User Experience	System Usability Scale (SUS)	Standard questionnaire to measure ease of use
	Task Completion Rate & Time	Measures efficiency and effectiveness in human-AI collaboration
	Error Rate / Recovery	Tracks user mistakes or failures in interaction with the AI.
Trust and Transparency	User Trust Surveys	Likert-scale questionnaires asking users to rate trust in AI decisions
	Explainability score	Evaluates how well AI explanations help users understand decisions
	Calibration	How closely AI confidence matches actual correctness; helps users judge reliability
Fairness and Ethics	Bias Metrics	Measures disparities in outcomes across demographic groups, e.g., Demographic Parity, Equalized Odds, or Fairness Through Awareness
	Ethical Compliance Checks	Evaluation against pre-defined ethical rules or societal norms
	Human Oversight Effectiveness	Assessing whether human-in-the-loop corrections improve fairness and safety
Satisfaction and Engagement	Net Promoter Score (NPS)	User willingness to recommend the AI system
	Engagement Metrics	Interaction frequency, sustained use, or adoption rate
	Qualitative Feedback	Open-ended interviews capturing user satisfaction and perceived value

Table 4. Human AI collaboration metrics

Team Performance Gain	Comparing human-AI team performance versus humans or AI alone
Decision Latency	Time to reach decisions in collaborative scenarios
Intervention Rate	How often humans need to correct AI outputs, reflecting system reliability

Table 5. Societal and long-term impact metrics

Impact Assessment	Positive/negative societal outcomes, e.g., job displacement, health improvement
Adoption & Accessibility	Measuring inclusiveness across user population
Sustainability Metrics	Energy consumption or environmental footprint of AI systems

7. GOVERNANCE, POLICY, AND REGULATION

With the rapid spread of AI technologies, governance, policies, and regulations are essential to ensure that AI systems are developed and used in ethical, safe, accountable, and human-centred ways. These measures help balance innovation with the protection of society and user trust. This section discusses the policies and ethical issues related to HCAI systems.

7.1. Global AI Policy Landscape

Globally, the use of AI is regulated through guidelines and principles set by international organizations and national governments to ensure its ethical application (European Commission, 2019). These measures include the following:

- **OECD AI Principles (2019):** Encourage developing AI systems that are innovative, human-centred, trustworthy, transparent, and fair (B. Shneiderman et al, 2022)
- **European Union AI Act:** It proposes a risk-based framework for AI systems, which insists on strict rules for high-risk AI applications, such as healthcare, defence, and transport (OECD, 2019)
- **UNESCO AI Ethics Recommendations (2021):** Provides set of guidelines for privacy, fairness, sustainability, and transparency (European Commission, *Proposal for a Regulation on Artificial Intelligence (AI Act)*, 2021)

- **National AI strategies:** Strategies focusing on ethical use, innovation, and human rights. Prevalent in countries like India, China, USA, and Canada (Ramos, G, 2023)
- **Global trends:** Migration towards cross-border data governance, risk-based regulations and alignment with HCAI principles (Aayog, 2018)

7.2. Corporate and Institutional Ethics Board

Ethics boards are internal committees that oversee AI development and deployment within organizations, making sure systems follow ethical guidelines and prioritize human-centred principles.

The roles and responsibilities of ethics boards are as follows:

- Check the AI systems for fairness, bias, societal impact, and transparency
- Propose ethical guidelines for AI development and research
- Approve AI projects that are high-risk and monitor the compliance
- Facilitate engagement between stakeholders and feedback integration

The benefits of having an ethics board at corporate and institutional level are, to promote trust and accountability, minimized risk of unintended consequences, embeds ethics in AI. Some examples of corporate and institutional ethics boards are, Google AI ethics board, Microsoft AI, Ethics, and Effects in Engineering and Research (AETHER) Committee, Institutional Review Boards (IRBs) for AI research in hospitals and universities.

7.3. Data Governance and Consent Management

Ensuring that AI systems operate ethically, legally, and in line with user expectations requires strong data governance and consent management practices.

- **Data Governance:**
    - o Establishing clear policies to maintain data quality, security, privacy, and integrity.
    - o Defining roles and responsibilities for managing and safeguarding data within the organization.
    - o Continuously monitoring data usage to ensure adherence to legal and ethical standards.
- **Consent Management:**
    - o Communicating transparently with users about what data is collected, how it will be used, and with whom it may be shared.

- o Providing mechanisms for users to give informed consent and to withdraw it when desired.
- o Ensuring compliance with regulations such as GDPR, CCPA, and other national data protection laws.

Governance, policies, and regulations provide the ethical, legal, and organizational framework for Human-Centred AI. Global and national policies provide broad guidelines, ethics boards apply the principles of responsible AI to practice in organizations, and robust data governance practices ensure transparency, consent, and privacy. These provide a framework that enables AI that is trustworthy, safe, and beneficial to society.

8. REAL-TIME CASE STUDIES

8.1. Case Study 1: Amazon Screening Tool

A few years back, between 2014 and 2017, Amazon developed an AI tool for internal hiring process to screen the job applicants. The focus was to automate resume evaluation and reduce human bias in recruitment. Although, the idea was good, the system was shut down after it was found to be biased against women, making it an ethical failure in AI adoption.

The model was trained on 10 years historical data, most of which are from male applicants, since tech had long been male dominated domain. Because of that, the system penalized resumes that included phrases like, women's college, women's club, or any women-only activities. Thus, there was an ethical failure of fairness and representational justice. Why did this happen? There was no early bias audit, no inclusion of diverse groups in the dataset, and no human-centered data governance.

8.2. Case Study 2: Autonomous Uber Test Vehicle

In March 2018, and autonomous Uber test vehicle in Arizona killed a pedestrian raising ethical concerns about safety, oversight, accountability, human psychology, system design, and governance. There was an issue with the sensor that was supposed to detect the pedestrian crossing outside the crosswalk. The system was not trained to detect pedestrians crossing outside the crosswalk. The backup driver was expected to intervene, but video evidence showed the driver was distracted. Human operators struggle to remain alert when supervising highly automated but not fully autonomous systems, a known cognitive limitation.

The design ignored the human attention limits, violating HCAI principles of realistic human-automation interactions. There was a clear lack of AI governance, liability rules, and compliance standards because Arizona's permissive regulations allowed companies to test autonomous vehicles with minimal reporting and there was no strong framework existed to verify the safety readiness.

After reading through the above-mentioned case studies, what do you think needs to be done to correct the system?

- Bias mitigation must begin at the dataset creation not after deploying the system
- It should include diverse teams and stakeholders' participation
- Transparency and explainability
- Ethical audits should be continuous, not just a onetime exercise
- Critical AI systems must be monitored for unintended harms

9. FUTURE DIRECTIONS IN HUMAN-CENTERED AI

Human-Centred AI (HCAI) is evolving beyond simply performing tasks to embracing empathy, ethical responsibility, sustainability, and social integration. Future AI research and applications aim to build systems that do more than assist humans, they strive to understand us, work alongside us, and contribute positively to society. In this section, we will discuss the future of HCAI with respect to moral, ethics, and values.

9.1. Toward Emotionally and Morally Aware AI

Future Human-Centred AI (HCAI) systems are being designed to understand and respond to human emotions and moral contexts.

- **Emotionally Aware AI:**
  - o Senses user emotions through cues such as voice, facial expressions, or behavioural patterns.
  - o Adjusts its responses to improve engagement, provide support, and promote well-being.
  - o Applications: mental health chatbots, personalized learning platforms, social robots.
- **Morally Aware AI:**

    - Incorporates ethical reasoning into decision-making processes.
    - Assesses the potential impact of actions on fairness, harm, and societal norms.
    - Leverages ethical frameworks such as virtue ethics, deontological principles, or utilitarian reasoning to guide morally sensitive applications.
- **Challenges:**
    - Establishing universal emotional and moral standards.
    - Balancing cultural and individual diversity in ethical decision-making.
    - Maintaining transparency and accountability in AI systems that handle emotionally or morally sensitive tasks.

9.2. Socio-Technical System Thinking

Human-Centred AI increasingly considers the broader social, organizational, and technical contexts in which AI operates. Some of the key concepts of Socio-technical system thinking are as follows,

- AI systems operate within complex socio-technical ecosystems that include people, organizations, policies, and cultural contexts.
- Designing effective AI requires a deep understanding of human behaviour, organizational processes, and the broader societal consequences of technology.

9.3. Sustainable and Responsible AI Innovation

Future Human-Centred AI (HCAI) focuses on sustainability, ethical responsibility, and long-term benefits for society.

- **Sustainable AI:**
    - Reduces environmental impact by using energy-efficient models, minimizing computational demands, and adopting green AI practices.
    - Accounts for the full lifecycle of AI systems, from design and deployment to decommissioning.
- **Responsible AI Innovation:**
    - Integrates ethics, fairness, and accountability throughout the AI development process.
    - Promotes transparency, explainability, and empowers users to interact responsibly with AI.
    - Ensures compliance with regulations while supporting social well-being.
- **Emerging Trends:**

- AI for Social Good: Applications addressing healthcare, climate change, disaster response, and education.
- Human-in-the-Loop (HITL) Systems: Collaborative AI that enhances human decision-making without replacing human judgment.
- Continuous Monitoring: Feedback loops that assess long-term societal impacts and maintain ethical alignment over time.

10. CONCLUSION

Human-Centred AI (HCAI) marks an important shift in how intelligent systems are designed and governed. Instead of focusing only on accuracy and efficiency, HCAI emphasizes human autonomy, ethical responsibility, inclusiveness, transparency, and trust. This shift is necessary to avoid negative consequences and to ensure that AI systems benefit society. Through approaches such as Participatory Design, Ethics-by-Design, and Human-in-the-Loop, HCAI ensures that human values guide AI decisions and that people remain in control of critical outcomes.

Strong governance structures, enforceable policies, and effective data management can improve the safe use of AI in areas such as healthcare, education, finance, and public services. In the future, the focus on emotionally intelligent and ethically aware AI, along with sustainable and socio-technical approaches, highlights the importance of AI working with humans rather than replacing them. Ultimately, HCAI is more than a design strategy; it is a commitment to building AI that is intelligent, empathetic, and ethical, and that benefits society. It ensures that as AI evolves, it does so in ways that protect human dignity and promote the public good.

REFERENCES

Aayog, N. I. T. I. (2018). *National Strategy for Artificial Intelligence# AIForAll.* Government of India.

Adamson, G., Havens, J. C., & Chatila, R. (2019). Designing a value-driven future for ethical autonomous and intelligent systems. *Proceedings of the IEEE, 107*(3), 518–525. DOI: 10.1109/JPROC.2018.2884923

Barocas, S., Hardt, M., & Narayanan, A. (2020). Fairness and machine learning. *Recommender systems handbook, 1*, 453-459.

Bentham, J. (1996). *An introduction to the principles of morals and legislation.* Oxford University Press.

Bialkova, S. (2024). AI transforming business and everyday life. In *The rise of AI user applications: Chatbots integration foundations and trends* (pp. 143–165). Springer Nature Switzerland. DOI: 10.1007/978-3-031-56471-0_9

Capel, T., & Brereton, M. (2023, April). What is human-centered about human-centered AI? A map of the research landscape. In *Proceedings of the 2023 CHI conference on human factors in computing systems* (pp. 1-23). DOI: 10.1145/3544548.3580959

Cavoukian, A. (2009). Privacy by design: The 7 foundational principles. *Information and privacy commissioner of Ontario, Canada, 5*(2009), 12.

Chandler, P., & Sweller, J. (1991). Cognitive load theory and the format of instruction. *Cognition and Instruction*, *8*(4), 293–332. DOI: 10.1207/s1532690xci0804_2

Conway, B., Nolan, K., & Quille, K. (2024, December). HCAI Block Model: A competence model for Human Centred Artificial Intelligence at K-12. In *Proceedings of the 2024 Conference on Human Centred Artificial Intelligence-Education and Practice* (pp. 22-28). DOI: 10.1145/3701268.3701273

Dandotiya, A. S., Gupta, S. K., Dandotiya, N., & Sharma, M. P. (2024). *AI in everyday life: transforming society.* Navi International Book Publication house.

European Commission. S. (2019). Ethics guidelines for trustworthy AI. *Publications Office.*

European Commission. *Proposal for a Regulation on Artificial Intelligence (AI Act)*, 2021. [Online]. Available: https://digital-strategy.ec.europa.eu/en/library/proposal-regulation-artificial-intelligence-ai-act

Floridi, L., & Cowls, J. (2022). A unified framework of five principles for AI in society. *Machine learning and the city: Applications in architecture and urban design*, 535-545.

Floridi, L., Cowls, J., Beltrametti, M., Chatila, R., Chazerand, P., Dignum, V., Luetge, C., Madelin, R., Pagallo, U., Rossi, F., Schafer, B., Valcke, P., & Vayena, E. (2018). AI4People—An ethical framework for a good AI society: Opportunities, risks, principles, and recommendations. *Minds and Machines*, *28*(4), 689–707. DOI: 10.1007/s11023-018-9482-5 PMID: 30930541

Frost, E. K., Bosward, R., Aquino, Y. S. J., Braunack-Mayer, A., & Carter, S. M. (2022). Public views on ethical issues in healthcare artificial intelligence: Protocol for a scoping review. *Systematic Reviews*, *11*(1), 142. DOI: 10.1186/s13643-022-02012-4 PMID: 35841073

Gabriela, G., Cerasela, S. E., & Alina, C. A. (2018). The EU general data protection regulation implications for Romanian small and medium-sized enterprises. [Economic Sciences Series]. *Ovidius University Annals*, *18*(1), 88–91.

Gammelgård-Larsen, A., Van Berkel, N., Skov, M. B., & Kjeldskov, J. (2024, May). Designing for human-AI interaction: Comparing intermittent, continuous, and proactive interactions for a music application. In *Extended Abstracts of the CHI Conference on Human Factors in Computing Systems* (pp. 1-8).

Herrmann, T. (2025, May). AI as a Sparring Partner–An HCAI Approach to Promote Human Capabilities. In *International Conference on Human-Computer Interaction* (pp. 162-176). Cham: Springer Nature Switzerland. DOI: 10.1007/978-3-031-93415-5_10

Jansen, C., & Jeschke, S. (2018). Mitigating risks of digitalization through managed industrial security services. *AI & Society*, *33*(2), 163–173. DOI: 10.1007/s00146-018-0812-1

Jobin, A., Ienca, M., & Vayena, E. (2019). The global landscape of AI ethics guidelines. *Nature Machine Intelligence*, *1*(9), 389–399. DOI: 10.1038/s42256-019-0088-2

Koren, Y., Bell, R., & Volinsky, C. (2009). Matrix factorization techniques for recommender systems. *Computer*, *42*(8), 30–37. DOI: 10.1109/MC.2009.263

Krippendorff, K. (2019). The cybernetics of design and the design of cybernetics. In *Design Cybernetics: Navigating the New* (pp. 119–136). Springer International Publishing. DOI: 10.1007/978-3-030-18557-2_6

Li, J., Monroe, J., & Jurafsky, D. "Understanding neural networks through human feedback," *Proceedings of the 2018 Conference on Empirical Methods in Natural Language Processing*, pp. 1–11, 2018.

Millar, M. (2011). Patient rights and healthcare-associated infection. *The Journal of Hospital Infection, 79*(2), 99–102. DOI: 10.1016/j.jhin.2011.04.031 PMID: 21798627

Mollahosseini, A., Chan, D., & Mahoor, M. H. (2016, March). Going deeper in facial expression recognition using deep neural networks. In *2016 IEEE Winter conference on applications of computer vision (WACV)* (pp. 1-10). IEEE. DOI: 10.1109/WACV.2016.7477450

Natale, S., & Ballatore, A. (2020). Imagining the thinking machine: Technological myths and the rise of artificial intelligence. *Convergence (London), 26*(1), 3–18. DOI: 10.1177/1354856517715164

OECD. (2019). *F. T. C. A. N.* Principles on Artificial Intelligence.

Peters, D., Vold, K., Robinson, D., & Calvo, R. A. (2020). Responsible AI—Two frameworks for ethical design practice. *IEEE Transactions on Technology and Society, 1*(1), 34–47. DOI: 10.1109/TTS.2020.2974991

Ramos, G. (2023). *Ethics of artificial intelligence.*

Ribeiro, M. T., Singh, S., & Guestrin, C. (2016, August). " Why should i trust you?" Explaining the predictions of any classifier. In *Proceedings of the 22nd ACM SIGKDD international conference on knowledge discovery and data mining* (pp. 1135-1144). DOI: 10.18653/v1/N16-3020

Sawyer, B. D., Miller, D. B., Canham, M., & Karwowski, W. (2021). Human factors and ergonomics in design of a 3: automation, autonomy, and artificial intelligence. *Handbook of human factors and ergonomics*, 1385-1416. Holzinger, A., Biemann, C., Pattichis, C. S., & Kell, D. B. (2017). What do we need to build explainable AI systems for the medical domain? *arXiv preprint arXiv:1712.09923.* Doshi-Velez, F., & Kim, B. (2017). Towards a rigorous science of interpretable machine learning. *arXiv preprint arXiv:1702.08608.*

Shneiderman, B. (2022). *Human-Centered AI.* Oxford University Press. DOI: 10.1093/oso/9780192845290.001.0001

Simonsen, J., & Robertson, T. (Eds.). (2013). *Routledge international handbook of participatory design* (Vol. 711). Routledge.

Thellman, E., & Ziemke, T. (2023). Empathy and emotional engagement in human–AI interaction. *AI & Society, 38*, 477–488.

Tronto, J. (2020). *Moral boundaries: A political argument for an ethic of care*. Routledge. DOI: 10.4324/9781003070672

Unesco. (2022). *Recommendation on the ethics of artificial intelligence*. United Nations Educational, Scientific and Cultural Organization.

Van de Poel, I., & Royakkers, L. (2023). *Ethics, technology, and engineering: An introduction*. John Wiley & Sons.

Van Wynsberghe, A. (2020). Designing robots for care: Care centered value-sensitive design. In *Machine ethics and robot ethics* (pp. 185–211). Routledge. DOI: 10.4324/9781003074991-17

Xu, W., & Gao, Z. (2024). Applying HCAI in developing effective human-AI teaming: A perspective from human-AI joint cognitive systems. *interactions, 31*(1), 32-37.

Chapter 2

Ethical Considerations in Human-Centered AI Design for Assistive Technologies

Farzana Jabeen
http://orcid.org/0000-0001-5171-8045
National University of Sciences and Technology, Islamabad, Pakistan

Mehvish Rashid
http://orcid.org/0000-0002-9824-5035
National University of Sciences and Technology, Islamabad, Pakistan

Tahira Anwar Lashari
http://orcid.org/0000-0003-0474-1650
National University of Sciences and Technology, Islamabad, Pakistan

Sana Anwar Lashari
http://orcid.org/0000-0002-2707-9017
School of Nursing, Shandong Xiehe University, China

Sidra Sultana
National University of Sciences and Technology, Islamabad, Pakistan

Asad Waqar Malik
http://orcid.org/0000-0003-3804-997X
National Strategic Planning and Analysis Research Center, Mississippi State University, Starkville, USA

ABSTRACT

As the technology evolved with the leading role of Artificial Intelligence (AI) in developing assistive technology, is constantly enabling people to live a quality life. However, bridging the connection to enable human with disabilities, which is promising direction towards their independence and autonomy, comes at the cost of the ethical implications. This chapter discusses the pivotal role of Human Centered AI (HCAI) in relation to assistive technology. We explore the principles of HCAI in this chapter to propose a framework to be utilized while developing assistive tech-

DOI: 10.4018/979-8-3373-6038-6.ch002

nology systems. The chapter collectively focuses on guiding the researcher, industry practitioners, and policymakers to comply with ethical concerns and ensure that assistive AI is a source of empowerment, transparency, security, and trustworthiness.

INTRODUCTION

Artificial Intelligence (AI) has played a pivotal role in defining human interaction with their surrounding shaped by the usage of computational tools leading to a rapid transformation. The abilities of AI have an impactful transformation in the field of assistive technologies empowering the individuals with physical, sensory, or cognitive impairments (de Freitas et al., 2022). AI is trending by reshaping the lifestyle of individuals earlier with limited mobility by enabling them to live with independence and dignity (Belkacem et al., 2020). Incorporating technology in the development of systems has led to applications consisting of providing support similar to the real-world settings. Intelligent prosthetics, autonomous wheelchairs, speech synthesizers, computer interfacing with brain, are few examples in the list which is becoming non-exhaustive. As human kind is advancing and AI systems have become intertwined in our everyday life, we also face the perils of technology posing significant ethical challenges. With the emphasis is on the support of AI design for autonomous systems (Subías-Beltrán et al., 2025), researchers and communities are also concerned about a human centered approach, which incorporates empathy, inclusivity, and moral responsibility (Taylor et al., 2024).

These concern have shaped into the emerging field of Human Centered AI (HCAI), where the emphasis is on the development of intelligent systems with the core value of trustworthiness, transparency (Han et al., 2022). While AI's inclination is towards developing efficient systems with accuracy, HCAI stresses on the development of the system, which can empathize with humans by understanding their emotions.

On the other hand, HCAI reframes success as promoting human capabilities and assuring safety and inclusion. The element of success is important in assistive settings in order to engage vulnerable and underprivileged people (Umucu et al., 2025). These users tend to feel comfortable with the sense of autonomy by decision-making power. Any design, which requires input information such as predictive algorithm or intervention by an agent, will cause jeopardizing their sense of autonomy (Shin, 2025). This chapter articulates on ethical challenges posed by the advent of AI technologies and resolution through integration of HCI to achieve a responsible design encompassing the humanistic needs.

THE PERILS OF ENGAGING WITH ASSISTIVE AI

AI driven assistive technologies are narrowing the gap between human limitations and environmental demands, for example smart hearing aids can reduce environmental noise in real time; graphic rendering apps can simulate the real-world using computer vision; and exoskeleton robots can provide therapy for spinal injuries. These developments exemplify the ideals of *empowerment, inclusion, and independence* referred by scholars as the "paradox of assistance" the more a technology helps, the greater the risk of dependency, surveillance, or loss of agency.

The main challenge lies while using AI caregiver which helps to monitor their movements for safety concerns can lead to the intrusion of elderly's privacy. Similarly engaging with voice assistant for people who cannot communicate verbally can cause data exposure to third party parties. While using personalization through customization in assistive devices if mishandled can be a source of manipulation shifting focus to ethical concerns of designing assistive technologies that empower, protect, and intrusion free without causing the pressure of being constantly watched.

Embedding Human Control in AI

The humans are creator of AI systems and therefore the machine itself is not compliant with the morals and emotional sensitivity. It is the ethical responsibility of AI system designers, engineers, and the policymakers to integrate humanistic side which constitutes upon kindness, empathy, humanistic emotional senses, and accountability of actions.

The researcher argues combining the human control and automation in HCAI while keeping human in control (Shneiderman, 2022). In real world it means that humans are considered central controlling figure of assistive AI systems. As reported that "within the field of value-sensitive design, autonomy is further conceptualized as the ability of individuals to decide, plan, and act in ways that support their self-defined goals (Friedman and Hendry, 2019)". Furthermore, VSD framework relates to the inclusion of moral intuition as an important aspect of design processes for the uniform representation of diverse communities in the development process.

Ethical Dimensions in Assistive Contexts

The Assistive AI is multifaceted in dimensions:

- *Autonomy and Agency:* AI must allow the user to take autonomous action and should be dependent on the user's decision-making skills.

- *Beneficence and Non maleficence:* Systems must produce maximum benefit and must be designed to prevent psychological or social harm.
- *Inclusiveness and Fairness:* AI must allow diversity and is non-discriminatory complying with fairness.
- *Data Security and Transparency:* The assistive systems requires a mechanism of abiding by consent seeking, which at the backend securing the data and transparent to the user.
- *Taking Ownership of the Design:* In case of failures or faults which cause inconvenience to the user the designer should take the ownership.

Ethical Ecosystems and Ethical Governance

Now a day there is a concern on the shift of AI devices from usage in isolation to in a network communicating with other devices and services such as cloud computing constituting an ecosystem. There is a noteworthy concern as reported "in the direction of ethically and socially preferable outcomes from the development, design and deployment of AI technologies" (Floridi, 2019). The Internet of Things (IoT) which leads to continuous exchange of data risking the privacy of users with limited control with the introduction of global expansion further intensifies the cross-cultural ethical challenges (Jobin et al., 2019). The other concerns on data ownership, consent, transparency and data usage are critically (Mittelstadt et al., 2016).

The ethics regulatory authorities have set standards such as European Union Artificial Intelligence Act (2024), the IEEE P7000 series on Ethical AI, and the General Data Protection Regulation (GDPR) to provide guidance. The enforcement of the ethical standards is dependent on factors relevant to organizational culture and formulation of ethics review board requiring active collaboration of developers and concerned stakeholders (IEEE, 2021).

Toward a New Paradigm of Assistive Intelligence

Assistive technology has a bright future with an inclination to facilitate humans with different capabilities with an intelligent mechanism of assessing their need. The control is with the humans with transparency while using smarter systems. The tools help with daily routine and are sustainable. The overall future of assistive technology s how humans will use it and societies and communities will adapt them. The foundation of such intelligent is embedding ethics into its core component. The intelligent system can work in different capacities for example providing elderly and people with special needs. Furthermore, intelligent system can facilitate those suffering from physical disabilities and chronic diseases, with the possibility of retaining their independence at best is one of the most important challenges our society is expected to face.

BACKGROUND

Overview of Ethical Paradigms in AI and Assistive Technologies

The Artificial Intelligence (AI) and assistive technology systems learn from the human behavior and adapt to human need. The innovation primarily opens venues for with different physical abilities. As we reap the benefit of AI systems there are also associated risks such as system can gather sensitive data relating to behavior, physiological, or neurological data from the operational premises. There might be algorithmic bias prevailing leading to the failure of capturing the diversity. Further user might be kept in dark because of opacity in decision making mechanism. The AI assistive technology operating on such values might enforce inequality among users rather than dealing with them on equal accord.

With the advent in the direction of assistive technology with increased integration in robotics, Brain Computer Interfaces (BCIs), and adaptive learning platforms, the concerns on the human centered ethical design were highlighted (Shneiderman, 2022; Winfield & Jirotka, 2018). In the regulatory domain frameworks: IEEE Global Initiative on Ethically Aligned Design (2022) and the European Union's AI Act (2024) were introduced. The purpose of such framework was to aware designers to comply elements relating to protection of human welfare and dignity, more specific to those who were classified as vulnerable.

The Human-Centered AI Framework

Human Centered AI (HCAI), has gradually emerged as a bridge that links the long-established field of human computer interaction with the newer, often messier world of ethical design. Ben Shneiderman (2022), describes it as the effort to achieve "high levels of human control combined with high levels of automation." The phrase perpetuates the idea that humans should be active collaborators who guide, question, and sometimes override machine decisions rather than just be a passive recipient. The framework itself rests on three main pillars.

1. *Transparency and explainability*: Transparency should mean more than a checkbox on an ethics form. It's about letting people actually see and question how an AI reaches its conclusions

2. *User empowerment:* Preserving a user's sense of agency, respect, and informed choice.
3. *Accountability and governance:* Accountability refer to the ownership of decisions is solely owned by human with traceability conforming to the ethical compliance in AI systems.

In assistive technologies, framework proposed integrates humanistic concerns into design from the point of conception to operational aspects called the Value Sensitive Design (VSD) framework proposed by Friedman and Hendry (2019). Furthermore, The *Capability Approach* (Sen, 1999; Nussbaum, 2006) framework enables the humans to find real opportunities to spend quality life as they desire.

Ethical Foundations in Assistive Technology Research

A robust framework that relates to moral in assistive technology is based on the four foundational principles consisting of beneficence, non-maleficence, autonomy, and justice. The framework is valid for static and predictable assistive technology systems. With the introduction of AI assistive systems are adaptive and learning from the environment interaction. These systems can be unpredictable even by their designers. There are five ethical dilemma in such systems identified as "bias, opacity, responsibility gaps, value misalignment, and data misuse" (Mittelstadt et al., 2016).

Autonomy and Dependency

There are concerns that while using the technology and depending on it might cause the loss of autonomy. The overuse leads to replacement of human choices. Coeckelbergh (2020) and Sharkey & Sharkey (2021) argue about dependency leading to compromise of the autonomy. As the intelligent system make too many decisions, there is a decline in user trust on these systems them (Sporner et al., 2020). In order to sustain human control and dignity with self-determination, a balance is required between automation safety and human control.

Justice and Fairness

While designing the algorithms there can be bias such as underrepresented data of colored female face which creates a bias in decision making and considered a justified ethical concern Gebru (2018). Similar lag can appear in demographics training patterns and the model trained on these patterns that do not represent diversity of population. The consequences are people who suffer by not being able to communicate effectively as AI system excluded such voices. The solution relates to designing dataset that is inclusive, takes into account bias and removes it, and involves diverse set of communities while evaluating these AI systems.

Privacy and Surveillance

There have been considerable ethical concerns relating to collection and data processing in assistive technology (Nebeker et al., 2019 and Palanica et al., 2022). For instance, data collected on an elderly for fall detection might acquire sensitive private data. People with cognitive disabilities may not be able to give consent or understand the very concept of providing consent. The reasonable approaches in such a scenario are: minimizing data, using edge computing, and embedding consent. The concept of giving consent can be through audio, gestures, or tactile cues since the mechanism of giving consent deviate from standard "I agree".

Participatory and Inclusive Design Approaches

It has been argued that to have an effective design can be by the user involvement which gives insights to user perspectives in AI assistive system designs. In order to embed trustworthiness in the design of AI systems users with special requirement participate in the design process (Lazar et al., 2017). The solutions developed by involving users organically synchronize with users' needs considering their everyday life.

Designing a system without incorporating the experience of people with disability living their everyday life is not an accurate representation of requirements for a person with disabilities. This is referred to as co-design or "ethics of representation". Another view related to the AI design for people with disability relates to the generating new knowledge resulting in innovation. The disability experience of a user represented in design leads to innovation and creativity (Bennett and Rosner, 2019). This can pool in diverse set data with user experience which varies from one user to another. Inclusiveness can identify difference which are otherwise hidden in conventional or traditional designs.

Explainability, Trust, and Psychological Safety

The pivotal role is of Trust which is the essence of owning of Assistive AI among users. In order to users trust they should be able to understand the system and predict reactions associated with user actions. Furthermore, user must not feel being disrespected. Users must feel that systems are predictable, transparent, and respectful. The concept of Explainable AI (XAI) stresses on the explanation to help user to create correct mental models (Gunning and Aha, 2019). Furthermore, the reasoning associated with algorithms is understandable to the user. Researchers also established a System Causability Scale (SCS) providing a measure to assess the understandability of explanations by layman user (Holzinger et al. 2020). All these measures

In assistive contexts, explainability supports both safety and psychological comfort. For example, if a robotic exoskeleton stops abruptly, the user must know whether this is due to a detected obstacle, a low battery, or sensor uncertainty. De Visser et al. (2021) note that lack of explanation increases anxiety and reduces long term trust. Ethical design thus requires layered transparency providing simple explanations for general users and detailed diagnostics for clinicians or caregivers.

Emotional Intelligence and Relational Ethics

In recent studies, ethical debates around AI extends into the territory of affective computing, the branch that tries to make machines recognize or even imitate human emotions. Robots such as *PARO* (Shibata & Wada, 2011), the therapeutic seal robot used in elder care, or Ellie, a virtual therapist designed to respond with gentle nods and sympathetic tones. Accordingly, the concerns on such system are about the emotional support gained by humans which is in fact running on coded script. There is a sense of emotional deception (Coeckelbergh 2020; Vallor, 2016). The matter is of serious concern since these systems are mimicking care but cannot feel or have emotions leading to misplaced trust or attachment.

The real dimension of care relevant to the Ethics of Care is based on foreground relationships, context, and responsiveness as required (Tronto, 2013). A valuable framework designed after closely incorporating the need in the context of real human life. the focus from what's "right" in theory to what's needed in practice, in the texture of real human live. Furth more, relational context applied to assistive technology in terms emotional technologies can be part of a wider 'care' ecosystem.

Governance, Accountability, and Regulatory Frameworks

With the advancement in technological aspects of AI there has been considerable thoughts on regulating ethics in AI. In the recent years the EU Artificial Intelligence Act (2024), acknowledged assistive medical domain as the high-risk area because of serious situations that might arise due to errors and threaten wellbeing of human kind. In the act it is considered a matter of enforcing public responsibility, to verify the assistive AI system not only technically but also for any existing bias. Alternatively, The IEEE P7000 requires documentation at every stage of development rather adopting a process-oriented approach. The document can provide insights into the inclusion of ethical concerns at every step.

Contrary to the above another argument is to adopt ethical practices it should be embedded in the organizational culture with moral reflected in everyday life (Winfield and Jirotka, 2018). Furthermore, there should be consistency in defining the responsibility, empowering an ethics board, a defined review and monitoring after deployment. Overall, in assistive technology humans are at a receiving end in things do not go in the right direction.

Cultural and Global Perspectives

Most of the AI ethics frameworks developed dominate in the Western academia, when inspected under the lens of other cultures might not suit them (Ali et al., 2022). The very concept of individualistic anatomy may not synchronize with the societies which are held together with kinship. Further the difference in social inequalities in terms of economic resources, legal structure and more, the framework developed in West might not align well in other parts of the world. In order to align the mismatch, we have to look beyond the surface level localization. To incorporate global perspective rethinking of design priorities and values have to be realized. We require understanding about the perspective of care from the local community, independence, disability, and responsibility. We require technology that is flexible to account for human diversity of value system, and social arrangement. The efforts to standardize might introduce complexity and slow down the innovation process. Thinking about the trade-off of slow innovation will be productive for its purpose of ethical humility. Some society's cultivation of technology would prove to rather more productive in terms of adaptation and introduction in different social worlds.

Synthesis and Emerging Trends

There is shift of ethics in AI, compliance to conscience that requires moral imagination. The questions being asked by researchers are on how it might reshape human relationships. Ethics, in this sense, becomes a responsibility rather than an impediment. Another major shift is from automation to augmentation, which is replacing human decision-making, with augmentation comprising of interpretability, contestability, and shared control, including users and caregivers meaningfully involved in decision-making processes. Third shift is from individual responsibility to ecosystem-level accountability. A broad are socio technical system constitutes responsibility and led to the regulators who shape its boundaries. Bias in recent system is not detected and corrected rather in assistive AI interaction is with people who are positioned at margins. AI is treated as a guidance that shapes the responsible guidance.

Recent work is starting to push these ideas into practice exploring, for example, federated learning for privacy-preserving personalization, ethical digital twins that allow for safer simulation, and AI explainability models designed with cognitive accessibility in mind. None of these developments are perfect; some may introduce new dilemmas even as they resolve old ones. But taken together, they mark a slow, uneven evolution toward a more adaptive and genuinely human-centered ethics of AI. Table 1 summarizes the comparative summary of key ethical frameworks and applications.

Table 1. Comparative summary of key ethical frameworks and applications

Framework / Study	Core Focus	Ethical Dimension Addressed	Implications for Assistive AI
Shneiderman (2022) **Human-Centered AI**	Integration of ethics and usability	Transparency, human control, safety	Establishes "high human control + high automation" as benchmark for trustworthy assistive systems.
Friedman & Hendry (2019) **Value-Sensitive Design**	Embedding stakeholder values	Inclusivity, participation	Encourages moral reflection during all design stages; aligns with participatory assistive design.
Sen (1999); Nussbaum (2006) **Capability Approach**	Human flourishing and opportunity	Autonomy, dignity, equality	Positions assistive AI as enabler of capability expansion rather than deficit compensation.
Tronto (2013) **Ethics of Care**	Relational responsibility and empathy	Emotional authenticity, relational ethics	Guides design of affective robots and social companions with attention to genuine empathy.
Buolamwini & Gebru (2018) **Algorithmic Fairness**	Bias detection in computer vision	Justice, non-discrimination	Highlights need for diverse datasets and fairness audits in AI-driven accessibility tools.
Nebeker et al. (2019) **Data Ethics in Health**	Privacy and informed consent	Data governance, autonomy	Urges transparent consent procedures and minimal data collection in assistive health devices.
Winfield & Jirotka (2018) **Ethical Governance**	Institutional accountability	Governance, trust	Promotes creation of ethics boards, traceability logs, and shared responsibility frameworks.
Ali et al. (2022) – Cultural Contexts	Low-resource and multicultural settings	Global justice, inclusion	Argues for localization of ethical standards to avoid Western bias in assistive AI deployment.

RESEARCH GAPS AND PROPOSED SOLUTIONS

Although the body of existing literature offers a solid conceptual basis for ethical design in assistive technologies and Human-Centered Artificial Intelligence (HCAI), actual implementation is still uneven and dispersed. Instead, then focusing on how ethics may be operationalized in design processes, datasets, and deployment, the majority of research has concentrated on principles rather than practice. Furthermore, there is still an uneven representation of cultural, economic, and accessible contexts; empirical research hardly ever covers the Global South, low-resource regions, or marginalized disability groups (Jedličková, A. 2025).

In order to steer future research and development toward fully inclusive, accountable, and value-aligned assistive AI systems, this section summarizes the unmet gaps in the current body of knowledge and offers a set of integrated solutions that are technical, methodological, and policy-driven. The gaps found and proposed solutions are discussed in Table 2. Later on each gap is discussed in detail along with possible proposed solution.

Table 2. Research gaps and proposed solutions

Research Gap	Proposed Solution
1. Limited Operationalization of Ethical Frameworks	Develop *Ethics-by-Design* and *Ethical Impact Assessment (EIA)* models; integrate ethics into agile workflows through "Ethical Sprint Reviews"; automate fairness checks via *Ethical Audit APIs*; establish organizational *Ethical Maturity Models*.
2. Inadequate Representation and Dataset Diversity	Implement *Participatory Dataset Co-Creation* involving persons with disabilities; utilize *synthetic data generation* (GANs) for rare conditions; establish global *Disability Data Commons*; introduce *Assistive Fair Index* for benchmarking inclusion.
3. Lack of Longitudinal and Contextual Ethics Studies	Conduct *long-term mixed-methods research* integrating ethnography and behavioral data; embed *ethical telemetry* in assistive systems; mandate *post-deployment ethical audits* to capture evolving user trust and autonomy.
4. Weak Explainability and Trust Calibration	Design *multi-modal, layered explainability interfaces* tailored to cognitive and sensory diversity; introduce *trust calibration algorithms*; establish *Cognitive Accessibility Guidelines for XAI*; promote *Explainability Literacy* training.
5. Ambiguous Accountability and Liability	Create *Accountability Matrices* assigning moral/legal roles; use *blockchain-based audit trails* for decision traceability; define *Ethical Readiness Levels (ERLs)*; implement *User-Visible Responsibility Disclosures* in devices.
6. Emotional Authenticity and Human-AI Relational Ethics	Implement *Emotional Transparency Protocols* to reveal artificial responsiveness; assume *Hybrid Care Models* participating human oversight; establish *ethical restrictions for affective simulation*; present *emotional literacy training* for caregivers.
7. Cultural and Socio-economic Bias in Ethical Frameworks	Apply *Confined Ethical Co-Design* with community participation; implant *Cultural Pluralism* and *economic convenience* as ethical standards; make *multilingual ethical glossaries*; fund *cross-cultural AI ethics research.*

continued on following page

Table 2. Continued

Research Gap	Proposed Solution
8. Fragmented Interdisciplinary Collaboration	Establish *Interdisciplinary Ethics Labs* connecting engineers, ethicists, clinicians, and users; reform *curricula* to integrate applied ethics; incentivize *collaborative grants*; institutionalize *ethical co-design frameworks*.
9. Lack of Evaluation Metrics for Ethical Performance	Progress *Ethical Performance Index (EPI)* computing fairness, transparency, and privacy; create *Ethical Benchmark Datasets*; integrate *continuous ethical monitoring dashboards*; introduce *third-party ethical certification programs*.

Limited Operationalization of Ethical Frameworks

Most of the ethical frameworks proposed in AI ethics are based on conceptual values such as Value-Sensitive Design (Friedman & Hendry, 2019), the Capability Approach (Sen, 1999; Nussbaum, 2006), and the Ethics of Care (Tronto, 2013) rather than procedural. While they highlight the moral essentials like self-esteem, equality, and inclusivity, just a few studies provide concrete pathways for integrating these values into data engineering, algorithmic decision-making, or interface design. In practice, developers often interpret ethics as a checklist to satisfy monitoring compliance rather than a process of continuous moral reflection. This gap leads to a lack of procedural orientation between ethical intention and technical implementation.

To overcome this gap, it is necessary that ethics must transform from abstraction to the composition. To achieve this, it is essential to embed it into the 'Ethics-by-Design' approach'. This approach proposes that integration of ethical checkpoint is mandatory at every step and stage of the development. In this way organizations can approve the structured Ethical Impact Assessments (EIA) by comparing before and after deployment and by observing environmental and privacy assessments parallelly. The use of EIA framework at every development stage can compute explainability, fairness and consent ethics through proper channels and standardized indicators. Furthermore, by integrating the 'Ethical Sprint Reviews' within agile workflows would improve sustainability and also ensure iterative reflection. In conclusion, open-source tools like Ethical Audit APIs will also help to monitor compliance automatically and can generate transparent reports to show the transparency of their users and win their trust. This is the right way that shows successful commits of ethical accountability within the engineering workflow.

Inadequate Representation and Dataset Diversity

A major ethical challenge in Human-Centered AI (HCAI) for assistive technologies arises from the lack of representational diversity in datasets used for model training and validation. Lack of representational diversity happens when appropriate data representation parameters are not taken (Zhang et al., 2023). For instance; limited population and sample size, selection of irrelevant age group, ethnic group and other abilities. With this practice, bias may become evident in imprecise prediction. Artificial intelligence systems are only as equitable as the data on which they are trained, and current datasets seldom capture the full heterogeneity of human disability, culture, or context (Mergen et al., 2025). For instance, an English-narrative indigenous trained speech recognition tool may only be valid and reliable tool for standardized accent for the regional dialect users (Cámbara et al., 2021). The trained speech recognition tool may fail to interpret aphasic speech. The failure may occur as a result of not interpretation the pauses, distorted phonemes and unclear articulation of aphasic speaker. Similar visual recognition systems often misinterpret the mobility aids [including wheelchairs, walkers, crutches and white canes] due to misclassification may resulted as unrelated objects or obscures patterns.

Moreover, mostly natural language processing system (NLP) [for instance; BERT, GPT] are trained on standardized formal mainstream language dialects where trained datasets over present dialects such as Standard American English. Limited available resources thus resulted in poor token frequency for the trained model. Likewise, computer-assistive vision system which are not taken user experience into consideration may exhibit discriminatory system performance. This algorithm bias may perform statistically significant for majority population. However, the empirical finding may not be effective for atypical population. Therefore, selection of the relevant and adequate datasets is needed particularly in-case of empowering assistive technologies including voice recognition, gesture detection, or facial emotion analysis. For the creating a standardized tool, generalization of the finding is fundamental aspect which can only be achieved with homogenous populations.

In general, the literature has revealed that ethical consequence is a twofold harm namely direct functional exclusion and indirect functional execution. Functional execution refers to failure in accurately measuring what is intended to measure [lack of validity]. Developed computed-assistive technologies fails to assist the user needs which means that tools are not addressing or reflecting exponential nature of atypical population. Indirect functional execution refers to AI-generated tasks which are not executed by AI systems rather the final task may be performed by other strategy. For instance; the adjustment of the sound issues in hearing aid app; may be resolved by human instead of systems automate the sound adjustment. Another example could be of automated robotic arm where motor task is performed by AI processing system instead of user's brain.

Another major issue that needs to be taken in to consideration in automated systems is cultural and linguistic underrepresentation (Liu, 2025). It means that the online standard available generated system [including AI-chatbots, google translation] is built from limited culture representative source (Koenecke et al., 2020). Mostly prominent applications are Western-contextual representative tool (English-speaking native) and Asian cultural and linguistic context (Deep seek-trained on diverse representative of the Chinese-multilingual AI mode). This linguistic bias often leads to misinterpretation to cultural nuanced phrases (Vishwakarma, 2023).

Empirical studies indicated that majority of the leading robust technologies are originated from Western institution. For instance; the remarkable achievement of USA can have been seen in form of AI-Powered system (GPT, Gemini, google and Claude AI, reflecting American cultural context. In the same way, European (UK) cultural context is exhibited from DeepMind. This lack of global cultural representation is evident in trained data used globally. This practice raises the significant concern of lack of participatory ethics in the data pipelines. Resulted in underrepresentation to non-western user needs (Lyu et al., 2024; Fleisig et al., 2024). This explicit practice of Al assistance leads disability-centered data governance. However, accuracy of the data depends on plethora of information gained from the representative population.

This section proposed various solutions. Disability refers to the diversity in terms of impairment, cognitive and physical limitation. People who are directly met with such conditions are able to understand the needs of the concerned individuals. Therefore, there is a strong need to engage people with disability as co-creators and decision-makers rather than collecting passive data. The accurate experiential data reflect authentic experience of indigenous cultural context and linguistic nuances. For instance; researchers need to seek guidance of relevant person prior creating protocols of accessibility tools such as the navigation issue of smart braille can merely be described well from the visual impaired person. This can be possible by hiring or considering them as part of the system [inviting them as guest-lecture for workshop, co-design sessions, and community partnerships.

Synthetic Data Generation refers to duplicating the data through artificial means using statistical resemble real world data. This recreated data is used to analysis and interpret the rare disabilities. For instance, Cerebral Palsy is a rare neurological disorder that have distinctive speech pattern. Empirical evidence may not provide adequate data for differential diagnosis of three similar patterned mapped features of speech related disorder including Amyotrophic Lateral Sclerosis (ALS), Cerebral Palsy, or Apraxia of Speech. To avoid such issue in diagnosis; the Generative Adversarial Networks (GANs) method is used. It is method to create realistic-based datasets. This process continues until built-algorithm fails to identify difference between created datasets (fake) and real datasets. It covers three components namely images, audio and text-based datasets. This methodological procedure is beneficial when original data is limited more particularly related to medical and healthcare domain. However, the challenging factor is dealing with instability during training (Pina et al., 2024). Trained model often generated limited varieties [similarities among common features of selected data such as selecting cats' images and ignoring other related species and related-group] leads to reduction in diversity and usefulness. Therefore, synthetic augmentation is designed to represent data in a data that it assures algorithm fairness even for limited and small sample size.

It refers to collective efforts to work on a common ground to create international open repositories databases. This community-collaborations are brining empirical consolidated evidence to lay-down the foundation of common strategies, practices, of a holistic global perspective. The sole purpose of this initiative to create standardized; statistical tested and refined [valid and reliable] set of questionnaire/questions utilized across various countries. This platform-built databases of the world-bank's disability data hub that provides valuable insights about people with disabilities. To ensure a large data security; public-private internships, and a memorandum of agreement (MOA) is required. The strict implementations of available privacy framework such as GDPR and UNESCO's AI Ethics Recommendation (2021) is needed to maintained privacy and human rights.

It refers to the systematic assessment of developed AI systems. The core emphasis is given in identifying the common method of treatment [specifically monitoring the demographic category], ways to avoid discrimination and unfair means towards disability inclusive group. One of the prominent examples is AIF360 (AI Fairness 360) dataset; which is a vital effort of IBM to check model fairness, and ethical-disability awareness of Al systems.

It refers to need-base analysis; the process of empowering knowledge, enhancing skills and updating the available useful resources at local level. This can be achieved by the support and collaboration of regional statutory bodies including role of funding agencies, and corporation of NGOs. This data collection initiative step towards digitalize cultural-context accessibility may facilitate a more reliable representative group for better decision on policy making.

Lack of Longitudinal and Contextual Ethics Studies

Longitudinal means long-term executed research over extended period of time from the culturally grounded perspective. Such studies usually encountered with numerous internal validity challenges including progressive development, maturation, history, statistical regression and ethical evaluation challenges (Koenecke et al., 2020). In prevailing practices, the ethical evaluation is often done prior conducting preliminary studies. For example, representative sample is an outcome of relevant population where generalization of empirical evidences defines standardization of automated system. Nonetheless; the established communication assistance tools are plotted widely on English-speaking native ignoring the impairment element. Regional and dialectic difference are recently embedded and are still in process. As a results the developed AI systems lacks context sensitive evolution and resulted in participatory oversight ignorance. To avoid such hindrance, timely re-audit procedure becomes mandatory to achieve fairness in revolving data. Most of the system performance are assessed through short-term metrics such as accuracy, response time, and usability. An effective assistive tool is one which provides continuous adaptive changes of user's progressive developmental life span. Correspondingly; one of the challenges in ethical domain is also related to non-representative cultural context of Al available systems. Even widely used app specifically EthicApp, Moral Compass, Ethical Explorer, Ethical Reasoning Appraisal and Kialo. All are English-centric, heavily western-moral-framework representative and exclude collective ethical and moral insights. On the contrary moral development varies; and are based on cultural practices.

There is a strong need to utilized mix-method research approaches. The combination of qualitative and quantitative nature to get holistic approach for a single study. Integration of qualitative performance metric (such as error rates) and qualitative ethnographic (such as observations and narrative-reflective journals) may reveal a more concise, collective, and indigenous-based framework. Thus, discloses localized insights of the data; where an intensive case-study or problem-based learning approach may be more facilitating as compare to superficial longitudinal studies. For example; two years of systematic explorative study of AI mobility aids could suggest exponential technological adaptation of individual with disability over time. In-addition valuable insights may also be gained on emotional resilience, coping strategies, a learning phase of drill and practices on failures and success towards uncertainties and human-machine interactions.

Weak Explainability and Trust Calibration

It refers to incomplete and vague explanation to a situation leads to poor decision as an outcomes of AI systems. This brings ambiguity among users; develop weak trust and less use of assistive tools. For example, a smart AI-mobility aid automatically navigating and taking a safest route for the user. However, these decisions merely based on the logical decision making upon route selection. Regardless on justifying the safety risk such as uneven roads, blocked and over-crowded path without considering the psychological attributes of users such as frustration, tiring, long-waiting and time-wasting procedure. Despite the fact that current Explainable AI (XAI) models (e.g., LIME, SHAP, or Grad-CAM) put emphasis to target technical experts rather than end-users (Das & Rad, 2020). Ignorance to the perspective of users with specific impairment reflect incomplete execution of the these facilitating tools. Thus, the cognitive, sensory, or linguistic limitations leads inaccessible technology led-tools rather than human-centered usability. This imbalance creates mistrust and raises the ethical concerns of psychological risk and benefits.

This practice bridges a gap and to overcome this gap, it is essential for explainability AI tools to be adaptive, multimodal-based, and should consider user-friendly approach. It should not entirely be considering the technical mechanism rather emphatic humanistic elements may also be ethical sound. For this purpose, multiple layered or multimodal methodology (from different sensory channels) may be adequate. So that a balance between simplicity and depth may be achieved through diverse viewpoint. Accordingly; compliance one-size-fits dynamic approach of fairness, transparency in measurement.

Explainability literacy program may be introduced to empower users on the role of active involvement in the Al systems creation process rather than being passive resilient. This systematic execution of needed tasks will offer standardized aligned infrastructure which may offer seamless comprehensive adoption to responsible intelligent ecosystems.

Emotional Authenticity and Human-AI Relational Ethics

Affective computing refers to the domain of computing that focuses on recognizing emotional interpretation using AI and machine learning. It uses physiological signals (including sensors, camera, eye gaze, body postures) to detect human emotions and designing systems that interpret emotional reaction in an appropriate manner. For instance, it is very difficult for a human to share his infer feeling and true inner thoughts to another human due to stigma linked fear. Thus, raises concern of authenticity and moral implications (Elyoseph et al., 2024). Therefore, an accurate, and respectful of human vulnerable AI- powered Chabot maybe used to facilitate depression and shared reflective contextual appropriate empathetic feeling may escalate positivity. However, if AI system is not adequately designed and deceptive then it may harm human trust and rapport. For instance, there are some matured Chabot's [including Woebot; could able to differentiate between sadness, frustration, or in anxiety; hence expected to be good at classifying anxiety and depression or mood disorder] that are designed on national language processing (NLP) to detect contextual based emotions and respective emotional reactions (Shimo, 2020). Similarly, Chabot are not merely designed to do differential diagnosis rather they are designed to provide appropriate therapies such as cognitive behavioral therapy (CBT) where implemented.

Human-Centered AI (HCAI) are intended to simulate human-like conversation, it provides assistance using methods including NLP, sentimental analysis and deep learning to interpret human emotions. This is possible when machine follows language patterns, words occurrence, and theme generation on the explicit tone features. These AI systems are tried to maintain human value, insights and psychological well-being. These facilitates are usually availed by those who felt socially aloof, considered them unable to handle or perform cognitive functions. Literature has revealed that statistical finding of the current emotional recognition models has achieved between seventy to eight-five percentage of accuracy particularly in cultural and linguistic domain (Kang & Hirschi, 2025). Nevertheless, emotions are subjective and varying in cultural-context reflective attributes. For instance, words, body language and gestures meaning vary from culture to culture. It is dominated by western culture and primarily built on English language sources, thus automated results often misattributed and foster blur user's perception (Coeckelbergh, 2020; Vallor, 2016).

Ethical emotional design requires transparency regarding artificial identity. Robots and agents should periodically disclose their non-human nature. Hybrid models that integrate AI with human caregiving can maintain emotional authenticity. In parallel, regulatory bodies should codify emotional design boundaries restricting manipulative affective responses or misleading anthropomorphism. This is the right way to balance and protects users' psychological integrity along with preserving AI's satisfying potential.

Cultural and Socio-economic Bias in Ethical Frameworks

Most ethical frameworks such as "Virtue Ethics, Right-Based Ethics, Care Ethics, Social Contract Theory" reflect Western standards of autonomy, individual rights, relationships and data privacy. In communist or low-resource societies, priorities like public well-being, relational care, and affordability dominate (Lucas et al., 2016). Without localization, ethical design cannot be implemented smoothly and fairly across diverse culture, languages and regions (Kumar et al., 2020).

Localized ethical co-design must anchor global AI principles in local cultural values. Collaboration with regional disability organizations ensures that design reflects original concepts of dignity, interdependence, and care. Multilingual ethical glossaries and context-sensitive consent forms enhance inclusivity. Additionally, open-source, low-cost AI platforms can democratize access, bridging the global assistive technology divide.

PROPOSED SOLUTIONS AND RECOMMENDATIONS

The proposed framework, centered around "Ethically Aligned Human-Centered AI for Assistive Technologies," is critically needed in human life and writing as it provides a robust, circular mechanism for integrating ethical considerations directly into the design, deployment, and monitoring of AI systems that support people. To ensure the robustness of framework, following aspects should be considered carefully.

1. Sensitive and personal data (health, location, biometric etc.) is part of assistive technologies. So, it is highly recommended to use robust security protocols to protect the user data, their privacy and to gain the trust of users.
2. To integrate the framework with evolving international and national standards, it should align with disability, data protection and governance policies.
3. The physical capabilities of users are directly proportional to the effectiveness and interaction with the AI. So, it is mandatory to know the users and their exposure with digital devices.

This chapter therefore, proposes a Comprehensive Ethical Framework for Human-Centered AI Design in Assistive Technologies (Figure 1). This model turns ethical ideas into ethical actions by integrating design values, operational processes, governance mechanisms, and socio-cultural dimensions into a single adaptive and flexible system. Instead of treating ethics as afterthought, model is emphasizing that it should be practiced at every stage of AI development. This shift ensures that Human Centered AI (HCAI) is not a vague goal, it is an essential legal practical way to protect users' dignity, safety, and empowerment.

Proposed Ethical Framework for Human-Centered AI Design in Assistive Technologies

Keeping in view foregoing discussion, the proposed framework seeks to embed ethical reasoning throughout the lifecycle of assistive technologies. It clearly understands that ethics cannot be confined to design philosophy or regulation alone, ethics must evolve and practiced through continuous interaction between technological processes, governance systems, and human experiences. In this way a major portion of population with disabilities can also feel safe, secure and privileged like abled bodied users. This layered framework conceptualizes how ethics can be systematically integrated into assistive AI development and governance. So that people with disabilities can participate actively and also achieve their rights equally without any biasness. The core objective of this framework is to ethically aligned Human Centered AI for assistive technologies. The framework translates moral reflection into engineering practice through a series of interlinked layers, each with a specific ethical focus and functional role within the lifecycle of assistive technologies.

The framework consists of four interconnected layers:

Ethical Design layer represents moral reflection and user participation at every stage of creation. It is the innermost layer of the framework and responsible for translating moral theory into design practices. Value-Sensitive Design (VSD) ensures that technology reflects the real values and priorities of stakeholders, particularly people with disabilities and their caregivers. Participatory Co-Creation invites users to actively influence how systems behave and evolve, embedding inclusivity into the creative process. Emotional Authenticity and Human Oversight preserve empathy and prevent manipulative or emotionally intrusive interactions. Explainability Integration guarantees that system outputs remain transparent and understandable for users with diverse sensory or cognitive abilities. Through these principles, ethical design transforms abstract ideas into concrete tools and user experiences that respect human diversity.

Operational Implementation layer shows conversion of ethical intent into measurable processes such as fairness testing, accessibility auditing, and user trust calibration. This layer embeds ethics directly into the technical and procedural workflows of AI development. Ethical Impact Assessments (EIA) systematically evaluate potential risks and benefits before systems are deployed. Audit APIs and Monitoring Dashboards provide automated checks for fairness, accessibility, and transparency throughout the lifecycle. Fairness-Audited Datasets ensure that training data represent diverse users and contexts, minimizing bias. Trust Calibration Mechanisms align user confidence with actual system reliability, preventing overreliance or mistrust. By combining them collectively, practices transform ethical considerations from one-time evaluations into continuous operational standards that sustain responsible innovation

Governance and Accountability layer ensures transparency, oversight, and shared responsibility among developers, institutions, and regulators. Ethical Readiness Levels (ERLs) measure the maturity of a system's ethical integration. Accountability Matrices clarify the specific duties and liabilities of developers, vendors, and regulators. Post-Deployment Ethical Reviews ensure ongoing compliance and responsiveness to emerging risks. Interdisciplinary Ethics Boards bridge the gap between technical and moral expertise, promoting balanced oversight. With the help of these mechanisms, governance becomes both procedural and participatory anchoring accountability not only in policy but also in shared moral responsibility.

Cultural and Societal Context layer promotes localized ethical co-design, cultural pluralism, and socio-economic accessibility to sustain inclusivity. The outermost layer refers AI ethics within the social, cultural, and economic realities of its users. Localized Ethical Co-Design adapts ethical principles to reflect community norms and values. Cultural Pluralism and Accessibility promote inclusivity across languages, income levels, and educational contexts. User Feedback and Participatory Evaluation enable technologies to evolve alongside user needs. Cross-Cultural Governance ensures that global ethical standards remain adaptable to local conditions. This layer ensures that ethics in AI design is not universal in the abstract but contextual, equitable, and responsive to diversity.

These layers' function both independently and interactively, creating feedback loops that sustain ethical performance and adaptability over time. The framework thus bridges the gap between ethical ideals and practical application, enabling the creation of assistive technologies that are not only intelligent and efficient but also empathetic, fair, and socially responsive.

Figure 1. Proposed ethical framework for human centered AI design in assistive technologies

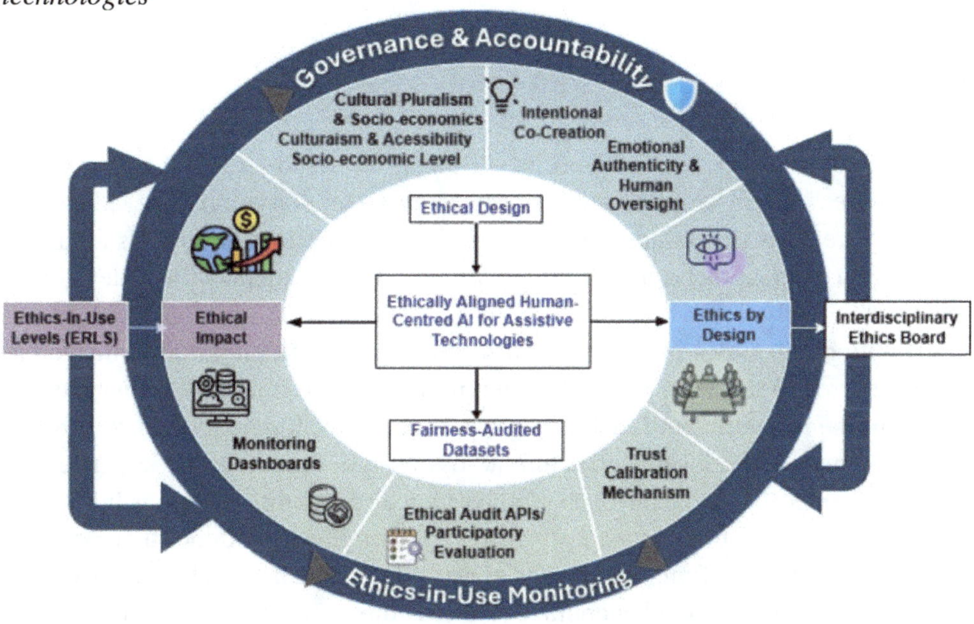

Framework Integration with Identified Research Gaps

The proposed framework directly addresses the ethical shortcomings outlined earlier in this chapter by transforming isolated initiatives into a cohesive and interdependent model. The *Ethical Design Layer* brings moral reasoning into the practical workflows of AI development, closing the gap between ethical principles and technical execution. Through participatory design and fairness-audited datasets, it also reduces bias and ensures that underrepresented communities are meaningfully included in system design. *The Operational Implementation Layer* embeds measurable ethical monitoring and trust calibration mechanisms, resolving long-standing gaps in transparency, explainability, and long-term evaluation. *The Governance and Accountability Layer* clarifies responsibility by introducing structured tools such as ethical readiness levels and transparent audit trails, ensuring that accountability is both traceable and enforceable. Finally, the *Cultural and Societal Context Layer* anchors the framework in pluralism and inclusivity, adapting ethical standards to diverse cultural and socioeconomic environments and countering Western-centric bias. The framework's continuous feedback loops and interdisciplinary co-design processes reinforce this integration, transforming ethical AI from a reactive checklist into a proactive, self-correcting ecosystem one grounded in human dignity, fairness, and contextual sensitivity.

DISCUSSION

The proposed ethical framework for "Human-Centered AI (HCAI) in assistive technologies" offers an integrated way to align technology, morality, ethics and society. It reflects that ethics is not just an external checkpoint but it is a built-in core design element that shapes how assistive AI systems are perceived, developed, and used in the society.

Traditionally, ethics in AI has been reactive addressed only after damage has been occurred. This framework alters that logic by suggesting that earlier integration of moral reflection into each and every stage of development can have positive and good impact. Its layered structure across design, operation, governance, and culture ensures that ethics evolves with technical capability. Responsibility thus shifts from officials to creators, promoting moral engineering rather than post-hoc compliance. By identifying AI as a social actor that influences independence, self-respect, and care, the model encourages a more empathetic and relational approach to the intelligence.

The framework connects technical performance with moral outcomes. Tools such as the Ethical Performance Index (EPI) and Ethical Impact Assessment (EIA) have enough capability to bridge efficiency metrics with human experience. For example, a voice-controlled prosthetic that is 95% accurate may still distress users if it ignores emotional or cultural cues. By integrating ethical monitoring, developers can measure and optimize moral quality alongside technical success.

Ethical AI cannot be universal without sensitivity to culture and inequality. The framework's outer layer anchors ethics in social and economic contexts, balancing global principles with local moral norms.

A system that is perfectly designed but unaffordable remains an ethical failure. By treating accessibility and affordability as moral priorities, the framework reframes inclusion as an ethical obligation not charity.

Human-centered AI demands collaboration among engineers, clinicians, ethicists, and users. Ethics emerges through co-production, not isolation. The framework embeds this interdisciplinarity as an ethical act recognizing that expertise also resides in lived experience, not just in academia. This approach replaces abstract debate with shared, practical problem-solving.

Ethics, like AI itself, must evolve. The framework incorporates feedback loops, post-deployment reviews, and ongoing monitoring, turning ethics into a living system that adapts to new contexts and user relationships. This flexibility maintains moral relevance across time and cultures balancing universal values with local authenticity and ensuring that assistive technologies remain both intelligent and humane.

CONCLUSION

The proposed study of ethical considerations in this book chapter "Human-Centered Artificial Intelligence (HCAI) for assistive technologies" give a thoughtful insight with respect to major aspect: industrial progress without morality and ethics can increase the risks of disparities. For example, in case of smart recruitment systems, one aspect is that those systems are helping and efficiently working in screening the job applications. But on the other side, if the system is trained on the data of past employed of companies, then it will select candidate from only those data set and with similar skill set. So, every time selected candidates will be from company list and people with disabilities or different skill set won't get chance to get selected. It can un-intentionally favor to the certain gender and people instead of creating fairer hiring, it supports old partialities. This is the darker side of technology; though its not intentional but still they are ignoring people with special needs and disabilities. When technology advances faster than ethics, it forgets to serve fairly, it risks serving the powerful instead of the susceptible. That's why we need frameworks like Human-Centered AI are essential they ensure that progress and technology is to uplift everyone, not just those already privileged. In this chapter, authors have carefully examined how the integration of human values, participatory design, and adaptive authority can change the picture. It also ensures that assistive AI not only performs professionally but also protects dignity, independence, and inclusion the essential pillars of human-centered design.

The literature review demonstrated a rapidly growing but dispersed field. While researchers have explored discrete areas such as "algorithmic fairness, explainability, and privacy", just a few studies have integrated these principles into a comprehensive moral framework for assistive contexts. This study identified nine key research gaps spanning from limited ethical implementation and dataset diversity to unclear accountability and weak interdisciplinary collaboration showing that ethics is central to AI's human relevance, not peripheral.

An Ethical Framework for Human-Centered AI is proposed that is evident to address these challenges through four connected layers: First and innermost layer Ethical Design grounds in value-sensitive design and participatory co-creation. Operational Implementation layer applies ethics through audits, impact assessments, and trust calibration. Then Governance and Accountability layer commits transparency and responsibility. Final and outermost layer Cultural and Societal Context ensures inclusivity, equity, and cultural relevance.

Together, these layers form a living ethical system that evolves through feedback and adaptation. Feedback is very important. By integrating feedback system there is always a way to improve the system. The framework moves ethics from compliance to capability measuring moral performance with tools like the Ethical Performance Index (EPI). For developers, it builds trust; for policymakers, it guides adaptive governance; for educators, it nurtures interdisciplinary learning. Ultimately, Human-Centered AI should not imitate humanity but amplify it advancing inclusion, accountability, and dignity through ethically grounded innovation.

REFERENCES

Ali, A., Hussain, F., & Khan, S. (2022). Assistive AI for low-resource communities: Ethical and cultural perspectives. *Journal of Inclusive Technology*, *8*(3), 45–61.

Belkacem, A. N., Jamil, N., Palmer, J. A., Ouhbi, S., & Chen, C. (2020). Brain Computer Interfaces for Improving the Quality of Life of Older Adults and Elderly Patients. *Frontiers in Neuroscience*, *14*, 692. DOI: 10.3389/fnins.2020.00692 PMID: 32694979

Bennett, C. L., & Rosner, D. K. (2019). The promise of assistive technology design. *ACM Transactions on Accessible Computing*, *12*(4), 1–32. DOI: 10.1145/3777475

Buolamwini, J., & Gebru, T. (2018). Gender shades: Intersectional accuracy disparities in commercial gender classification. *Proceedings of the 2018 Conference on Fairness, Accountability, and Transparency (FAT*) *, 77-91. DOI: 10.1145/3287560.3287584

Cámbara, A., Peiró-Lilja, C., Farrús, M., & Luque, J. (2021). *English accent accuracy analysis in a state-of-the-art automatic speech recognition system*. arXiv preprint arXiv:2105.05041.

Coeckelbergh, M. (2020). Artificial intelligence, responsibility attribution, and a relational justification of explainability. *Science and Engineering Ethics*, *26*(4), 2051–2068. DOI: 10.1007/s11948-019-00146-8 PMID: 31650511

de Freitas, M. P., Piai, V. A., Farias, R. H., Fernandes, A. M. R., de Moraes Rossetto, A. G., & Leithardt, V. R. Q. (2022). Artificial Intelligence of Things Applied to Assistive Technology: A Systematic Literature Review. *Sensors (Basel)*, *22*(21), 8531. DOI: 10.3390/s22218531 PMID: 36366227

de Visser, E. J., et al. (2021). Transparency in human–robot interaction: A review. *Frontiers in Robotics and AI, 8*, 646402. https://doi.org/DOI: 10.3389/frobt.2021.646402

Elyoseph, Z., Refoua, E., Asraf, K., Lvovsky, M., Shimoni, Y., & Hadar-Shoval, D. (2024). Capacity of generative AI to interpret human emotions from visual and textual data: Pilot evaluation study. *JMIR Mental Health*, *11*, e54369. DOI: 10.2196/54369 PMID: 38319707

European Commission. (2024). *EU Artificial Intelligence Act*. Official Journal of the European Union.

Fleisig, R., Smith, E., Bossi, D., Rustagi, N., Yin, D., & Klein, D. (2024). *Linguistic bias in ChatGPT: Language models reinforce dialect discrimination.* arXiv preprint arXiv:2406.08818. https://arxiv.org/abs/2406.08818 DOI: 10.18653/v1/2024.emnlp-main.750

Floridi, L. (2019). Establishing the rules for building trustworthy AI. *Nature Machine Intelligence, 1*(6), 261–262. DOI: 10.1038/s42256-019-0055-y

Friedman, B., & Hendry, D. (2019). *Value sensitive design: Shaping technology with moral imagination.* MIT Press. DOI: 10.7551/mitpress/7585.001.0001

Gunning, D., & Aha, D. (2019). DARPA's explainable artificial intelligence (XAI) program. *AI Magazine, 40*(2), 44–58. DOI: 10.1609/aimag.v40i2.2850

Han, S., Kelly, E., Nikou, S., & Svee, E.-O. (2022). Aligning artificial intelligence with human values: Reflections from a phenomenological perspective. *AI & Society, 37*(4), 1383–1395. DOI: 10.1007/s00146-021-01247-4

Holzinger, A., et al. (2020). Measuring the quality of explanations: The System Causability Scale (SCS). *KI – Künstliche Intelligenz, 34*(2), 193–198. https://doi.org/.DOI: 10.1007/s13218-019-00635-0

IEEE. (2022). *Ethically aligned design: A vision for prioritizing human well-being with autonomous and intelligent systems.* IEEE Global Initiative on Ethics of Autonomous and Intelligent Systems.

Jedličková, A. (2025). Ethical approaches in designing autonomous and intelligent systems: A comprehensive survey towards responsible development. *AI & Society, 40*(4), 2703–2716. DOI: 10.1007/s00146-024-02040-9

Jobin, A., Ienca, M., & Vayena, E. (2019). The global landscape of AI ethics guidelines. *Nature Machine Intelligence, 1*(9), 389–399. DOI: 10.1038/s42256-019-0088-2

Kang, O., & Hirschi, K. (2025). Bias and stereotyping: Human and artificial intelligence (AI). *Annual Review of Applied Linguistics*, 1-16. Das, A., & Rad, P. (2020). Opportunities and challenges in explainable artificial intelligence (xai): A survey. *arXiv preprint arXiv:2006.11371.*

Koenecke, A., Nam, A., Lake, E., Nudell, J., Quartey, M., Mengesha, Z., Toups, C., Rickford, J. R., Jurafsky, D., & Goel, S. (2020). Racial disparities in automated speech recognition. *Proceedings of the National Academy of Sciences of the United States of America, 117*(14), 7684–7689. DOI: 10.1073/pnas.1915768117 PMID: 32205437

Kumar, N., Singh, P., & Jain, R. (2020). Smart assistive systems: A survey of AI-driven accessibility. *ACM Computing Surveys, 53*(6), 1–34. DOI: 10.1145/3406093

Lazar, J., Goldstein, D. F., & Taylor, A. (2017). Ensuring digital accessibility through user participation. *Human–Computer Interaction, 32*(4), 265–292. https://doi.org/DOI: 10.1080/07370024.2016.1180939

Liu, Z. (2025). Cultural bias in large language models: A comprehensive analysis and mitigation strategies. *Journal of Transcultural Communication*, *3*(2), 224–244. DOI: 10.1515/jtc-2023-0019

Lucas, G. M., et al. (2016). It's only a computer: The impact of human-like avatars on counseling outcomes. *Computers in Human Behavior, 52*, 331–338. .DOI: 10.1016/j.chb.2015.06.008

Lyu, Y., Dost, M., Koh, S., & Wicker, J. (2024). Regional bias in monolingual English language models. *Machine Learning*, *113*(7), 2541–2560. DOI: 10.1007/s10994-024-06555-6

Mergen, A., Çetin-Kılıç, N., & Özbilgin, M. F. (2025). Artificial intelligence and bias towards marginalised groups: Theoretical roots and challenges. In *AI and Diversity in a Datafied World of Work: Will the Future of Work be Inclusive?* (Vol. 12, pp. 17–38). Emerald Publishing Limited. DOI: 10.1108/S2051-233320250000012004

Mittelstadt, B. D., Allo, P., Taddeo, M., Wachter, S., & Floridi, L. (2016). The ethics of algorithms: Mapping the debate. *Big Data & Society, 3*(2), 1–21. DOI: 10.1177/2053951716679679

Nebeker, C., et al. (2019). Digital health research and the ethics of data privacy. *NPJ Digital Medicine, 2*(1), 1–5. https://doi.org/DOI: 10.1038/s41746-019-0166-3

Nussbaum, M. (2006). *Frontiers of justice: Disability, nationality, species membership*. Harvard University Press.

Palanica, A., et al. (2022). Edge AI and privacy in assistive health monitoring. *Sensors, 22*(14), 5171. DOI: 10.3390/s22145171

Pina, E., Ramos, J., Jorge, H., Váz, P., Silva, J., Wanzeller, C., Abbasi, M., & Martins, P. (2024). Data privacy and ethical considerations in database management. *Journal of Cybersecurity and Privacy*, *4*(3), 494–517. DOI: 10.3390/jcp4030024

Sen, A. (1999). *Development as freedom*. Oxford University Press.

Shibata, T., & Wada, K. (2011). Robot therapy: A new approach for mental healthcare. *Current Psychiatry Reviews, 7*(3), 180–188. https://doi.org/DOI: 10.2174/157340011796391202

Shimo, S. (2020, November). Risks of bias in AI-based emotional analysis technology from diversity perspectives. In *2020 IEEE International Symposium on Technology and Society (ISTAS)* (pp. 66-68). IEEE. DOI: 10.1109/ISTAS50296.2020.9462168

Shin, Y. (2025). Toward human-centered artificial intelligence for users' digital well-being: Systematic review, synthesis, and future directions. *JMIR Human Factors*, *12*(1), e69533. DOI: 10.2196/69533 PMID: 40928842

Shneiderman, B. (2022). *Human-centered AI: A new synthesis*. Oxford University Press. DOI: 10.1093/oso/9780192845290.001.0001

Sporner, M. L., et al. (2020). User-driven design of AI-enabled wheelchair navigation systems. *Disability and Rehabilitation: Assistive Technology, 15*(5), 527–536. https://doi.org/DOI: 10.1080/17483107.2019.1571119

Stangl, A.. (2020). AI-powered visual assistance for blind users: A field study. **Proceedings of the 2020 CHI Conference on Human Factors in Computing Systems (CHI '20)**. DOI: 10.1145/3313831.3376689

Subías-Beltrán, P., Unceta, I., & de Lecuona, I.. (2025). Asking the right questions: A governance approach to uphold human autonomy in artificial intelligence. *AI & Society*. Advance online publication. DOI: 10.1007/s00146-025-02611-4

Taylor, R. R., O'Dell, B., & Murphy, J. W. (2024). Human-centric AI: Philosophical and community-centric considerations. *AI & Society*, *39*(5), 2417–2424. DOI: 10.1007/s00146-023-01694-1

Tronto, J. C. (2013). *Caring democracy: Markets, equality, and justice*. NYU Press.

Umucu, E. (2025). Artificial Intelligence and Health Equity for People with Disabilities: An Integrated Framework for Disability-Inclusive AI Design. *Inquiry : a Journal of Medical Care Organization, Provision and Financing*, *62*, 00469580251365472. Advance online publication. DOI: 10.1177/00469580251365472 PMID: 40847466

Vallor, S. (2016). *Technology and the virtues: A philosophical guide to a future worth wanting*. Oxford University Press. DOI: 10.1093/acprof:oso/9780190498511.001.0001

Vishwakarma, P. (2023). Journal of Internet Commerce: A Bibliometric Overview. *Journal of Internet Commerce*, *22*(4), 567–593. DOI: 10.1080/15332861.2022.2095178

Winfield, A. F. T., & Jirotka, M. (2018). Ethical governance is essential to building trust in robotics and AI systems. *Philosophical Transactions of the Royal Society A: Mathematical, Physical and Engineering Sciences, 376*(2133), 20180085. DOI: 10.1098/rsta.2018.0085

Zhang, L., Howard, S., Montpool, T., Moore, J., Mahajan, K., & Miranskyy, A. (2023). Automated data validation: An industrial experience report. *Journal of Systems and Software*, *197*, 111573. DOI: 10.1016/j.jss.2022.111573

KEY TERMS AND DEFINITIONS

Accountability and Governance: The ethical and regulatory mechanisms that presents sense of responsibility, traceability, and compliance within AI-driven assistive systems. It is evident that both developers and organizations will remain responsible for system outcomes and user impacts.

Algorithmic Fairness: The principles and computational methods that guarantee AI decision-making remains balanced and impartial across various demographic, cognitive, and cultural groups.

Assistive Technologies (AT): Intelligent devices and AI-based systems that are designed and proposed with intention to improve the accessibility, independence, and quality of life for persons with disabilities, fostering inclusion and empowerment.

Cultural and Socioeconomic Inclusivity: The adaptation of AI systems to home-grown cultural standards, dialectal diversity, and varying levels of financial access, by ensuring that ethics are globally relevant and contextually sensitive for the people.

Emotional and Relational Ethics: How affectively AI systems can simulate empathy, sympathy, human emotions, build trust, by creating ethical restrictions for emotional reality in assistive situations.

Ethical AI Frameworks: Structured conceptual models that integrate fairness, transparency, and accountability throughout the AI development and deployment lifecycle to ensure implication of ethics.

Ethical Performance Evaluation: The systematic assessment of AI's moral quality and social impact by using qualitative and quantitative tools such as the Ethical Performance Index (EPI).

Explainable Artificial Intelligence (XAI): Methods that make AI decision-making processes interpretable and cognitively accessible for users, caregivers, and regulators.

Human-Centered Artificial Intelligence (HCAI): How Artificial Intelligence systems are designed based on human dignity, participatory engagement, and co-creation. It also ensures that technologies will infuse in those systems smoothly rather than replacement of human judgment.

Participatory and Inclusive Design: A user-centered methodology that actively involves diverse participants especially persons with disabilities at every stage of AI development to promote equity and usability.

Chapter 3
Ethical Challenges of AI in Tackling Online Harassment and Cyberbullying

Sana Anwar Lashari
http://orcid.org/0000-0002-2707-9017
School of Nursing, Shandong Xiehe University, China

Tahira Anwar Lashari
http://orcid.org/0000-0003-0474-1650
National University of Sciences and Technology, Pakistan

Saima Anwar Lashari
http://orcid.org/0000-0001-6209-491X
College of Computing and Informatics, Dammam, Saudi Arabia

Farzana Jabeen
http://orcid.org/0000-0001-5171-8045
National University of Sciences and Technology, Pakistan

Djihad Tria
http://orcid.org/0000-0001-5207-881X
Amity University, Tashkent, Uzbekistan

ABSTRACT

The rapid progression in artificial intelligence (AI) has transformed social life. Though AI has enabled innovative tools for social communication, it has facilitated cyberbullying, hence, raising concerns about human privacy. To combat cyber

DOI: 10.4018/979-8-3373-6038-6.ch003

harassment digital communities started to depend on AI algorithmic moderation tools to identify, monitor, and prevent user from harmful behavioral patterns through human data raising concerns of privacy and ethical use of personal information. This chapter begin with discussing historical events highlighting different phases of AI development. In second section, dual nature of perpetrator and protector role of AI was discussed. Finally, the chapter provides future directions for responsible innovation and it was covered under solutions and recommendations section. The finding revealed that a global harmonization is required to create a balance between potential protection and AI-guideline.

1 THE ODYSSEY TO ARTIFICIAL INTELLIGENCE

Artificial Intelligence (AI) is a branch of computer science which has roots in ancient history that aims to create machines that can reason, solving complex problems, learning, perception, decision-making and understanding language (Russell & Norvig, 2021). The stories of intelligent automata can be traced back in Egyptian and Greek cultures (Bainbridge, 2006) where Egyptians intend to develop mechanical illusions to simulate divine presence and Greeks on the other hand developed more sophisticated mechanical beings like the Hero of Alexandria which was a water- and air-powered devices (Tybjerg, 2003). However, the shift from myth to scientific discipline was catalyzed due to wartime demand in the mid-20th century which highlighted the necessity for automated codebreaking, calculation of complex artillery calculations, and managing intricate systems (Rheingold, 2000). Pioneers like Alan Turing (1950) laid the philosophical foundation of such shift by proposing operational questions "Can machines think?" in his seminal paper *Computing Machinery and Intelligence*, (Turing, 1950) introducing the "Imitation Game" which led to the efforts to building machines that not only compute but could augment human intelligence and reason (See Figure 1).

Dartmouth Summer Research Project (1956) coined the term Artificial Intelligence by John McCarthy, Marvin Minsky, Nathaniel Rochester, and Claude Shannon and suggested "every aspect of learning or any other feature of intelligence can in principle be so precisely described that a machine can be made to simulate it" marking the official birth of AI as research field (McCarthy et al., 1955; McCarthy et al., 2006). Early AI efforts focused on creating simple problem-solving programs and logical reasoning systems (Nilsson, 1983).

Figure 1. Page 1 of the original proposal (Photo courtesy Dartmouth College)

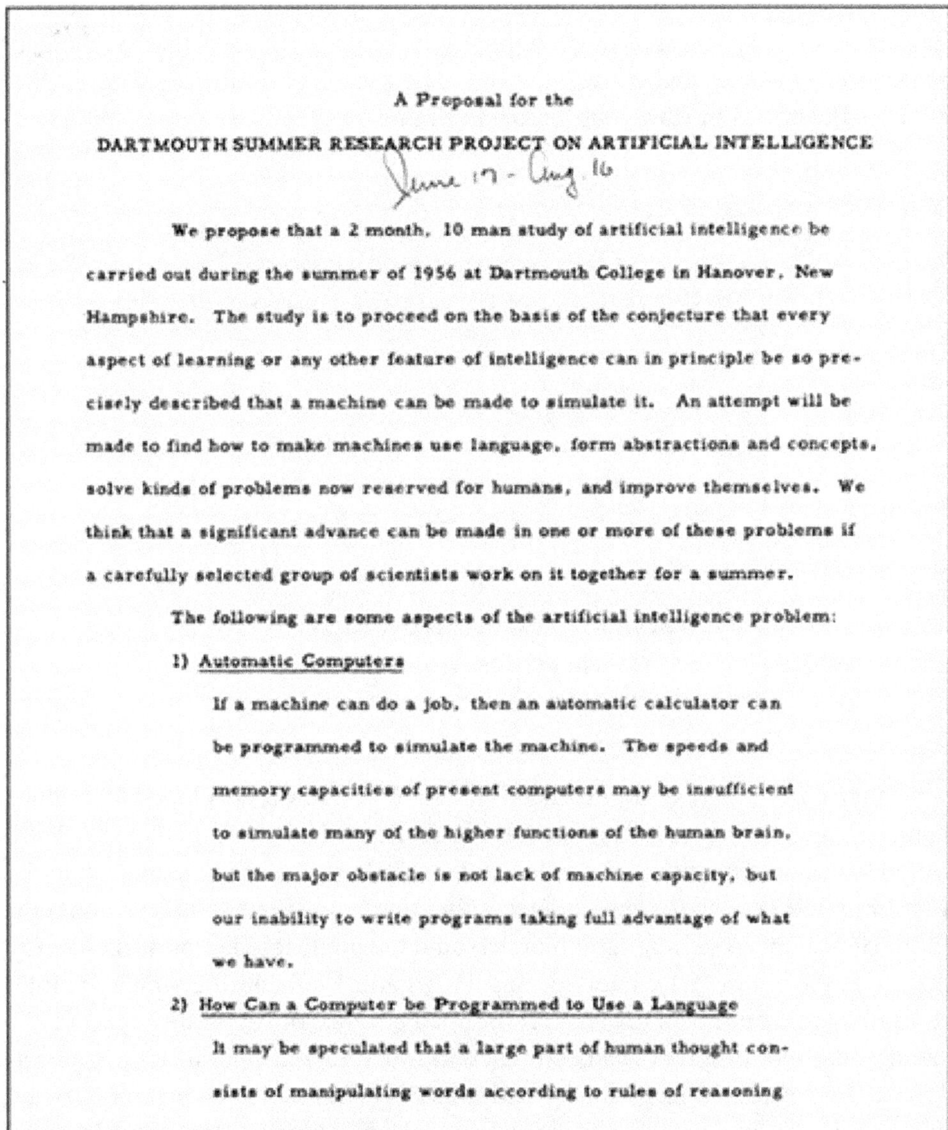

A Proposal for the

DARTMOUTH SUMMER RESEARCH PROJECT ON ARTIFICIAL INTELLIGENCE

June 17 - Aug. 16

We propose that a 2 month, 10 man study of artificial intelligence be carried out during the summer of 1956 at Dartmouth College in Hanover, New Hampshire. The study is to proceed on the basis of the conjecture that every aspect of learning or any other feature of intelligence can in principle be so precisely described that a machine can be made to simulate it. An attempt will be made to find how to make machines use language, form abstractions and concepts, solve kinds of problems now reserved for humans, and improve themselves. We think that a significant advance can be made in one or more of these problems if a carefully selected group of scientists work on it together for a summer.

The following are some aspects of the artificial intelligence problem:

1) Automatic Computers

If a machine can do a job, then an automatic calculator can be programmed to simulate the machine. The speeds and memory capacities of present computers may be insufficient to simulate many of the higher functions of the human brain, but the major obstacle is not lack of machine capacity, but our inability to write programs taking full advantage of what we have.

2) How Can a Computer be Programmed to Use a Language

It may be speculated that a large part of human thought consists of manipulating words according to rules of reasoning

AI development has gone through several different theoretical paradigms each of which shaped its technological advancement. During 1950s and 1960s was the symbolic paradigm. For example, Newell and Simon's General Problem Solver (GPS) designed an AI program to imitate human problem-solving using if-then logic using the approach of "Good Old-Fashioned AI" (GOFAI) where following set of logical rules symbols were manipulated. GOFAI assumes a system needs to represent knowledge using symbol, apply logical rules to process that symbol, and finally infer new knowledge from the old. The use of symbolic logic by GOFAI system is illustrated in flow chart below in Figure 2.

Figure 2. Example of GOFAI reasoning

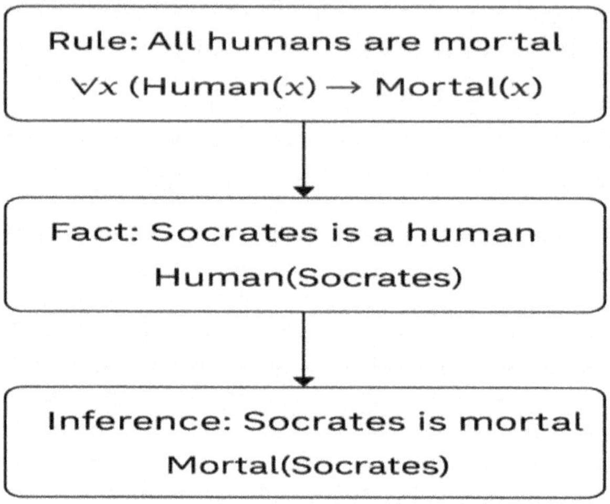

Furthermore, expert system such as MYCIN (1970s) was developed for medical diagnoses such as like detecting bacterial infections. However, this approach was limited to only commonsense knowledge; therefore, as it lacked the understanding of vast implicit knowledge and understanding that human possess (Lenat & Guha, 1990). Hence, the system failure to understand the context led to projects like Cyc which was the era of "AI winter" during 1970s and 1980s during which the interest, funding and optimism towards AI dropped because of Lighthill Report (1973) arguing little real progress has been made in this research field in UK. Similarly, in the US, researchers like Minsky and Papert (1969) had shown limits of early neural networks (in their book *Perceptrons*), which further cooled enthusiasm and public lost faith in AI.

In the late 1980s, Rumelhart, Hinton, and Williams (1986) used the idea of connectionism, which follows the philosophy that the brain using *neural networks*. Using that idea, they introduced backpropagation algorithm which allow the computer to automatically learn internal presentation of patterns from data without being told rules which led to shift in AI from "programming intelligence" to "training intelligence." For example, a neural network can learn about cats just by looking at pictures of cat. Hence, it offered an alternative method to hand-coded knowledge.

Field of neural networking was heavily focusing on learning; however, robotics experienced a radical turn. Scholars like Rodney Brooks (1991) in his research article *"Intelligence Without Representation"* argued robots do not require such detailed planning since they react to their surrounding just like animals and explained intelligence comes from interacting with the real world. Brooks built robots using subsumption architecture design where simple behaviors (like walking or avoiding obstacles) work together to create complex.

The 21st century brought a new phase in the development of AI as the shift to train AI relied heavily on data as big data provided large amounts of information for machines to learn, it uses powerful computers Graphics Processing Units (GPUs) that allowed to train large models, and deep learning algorithms, which allowed systems to automatically learn patterns from data. In 2012, Krizhevsky, Sutskever, and Hinton introduced AlexNet which is a neural network which achieved outstanding results in ImageNet image recognition. Hence, proving the idea that machine learn through patterns from vast data automatically. These significant contributions lead to **"Software 2.0"** era, allowing engineers focus more on preparing data and designing models that can learn on their own rather than hand-coded rules. Figure 3 provides a snapshot view of historical phases that current AI go through.

Figure 3. Phases of AI development

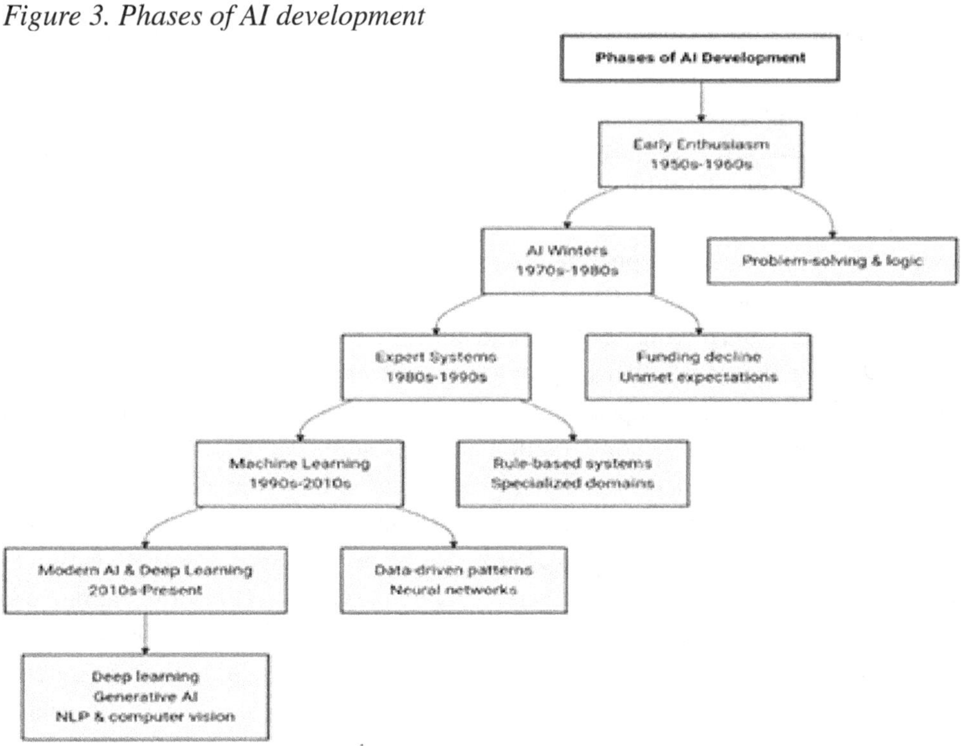

1.1 From Intelligence to Responsibility — The Ethical Turn in AI

Humanity ambition to replicate intelligence into machines have led to the evolution of AI which is evident from the early symbolic reasoning to generative AI. As the trends shifted from solving complex problems to human interaction. Algorithms have become powerful intermediaries by filtering the content we read, decide which content is harmful, and engage with information. This phenomenon was explained by Pariser (2011) in The Filter Bubble, where internet search engines and their algorithms personalize our online experiences by selecting content based on our previous interactions which are tracked through our search and browsing history, viewing habits, social networks, and geographic location. In this way the internet feed individuals with the content which strengthen their initial beliefs rather than seeing a different point of view hence, narrowing their perceptions and access to knowledge. For example, when a user performs a Google search, the system uses the user personal data to prioritize results in such a fashion that it seems most relevant to that individual which is further reinforced as the users click on these results the algorithm is trained about that individual's interests, hence, in future they will receive similar results.

Furthermore, using social network preferences influence the algorithm which amplifying biases and leading to lack or information or misinformation (Brady et al., 2023) this can be seen in social media Apps (including Facebook, Instagram) show text-based posts that popular among friends, video-based content (TikTok and YouTube) recommends what people are watching, whereas, audio-based content (Spotify) suggest songs and playlists which are based on individual listening habits and what others people with similar tastes enjoy. Hence, it limits an individual exposure to new or different perspectives. One major problem is individual's not having access to diverse perspectives, but an even deeper issue is the invisible nature of how and how much these filters are creating this personalization leaving user with little control, narrowing our view and understanding of the world around us. A phenomenon known as labelled as "gravitational black hole of information" where it is difficult for the user to escape belief-reinforcing content as the algorithmic design ensures a cycle of selective confirmation and exposure (Pariser, 2011).

It deemed evident what read and viewed is biased however; reasoning of what is harmful or inappropriate discussed in algorithms of Oppression (Noble, 2018) which reflects systematic biasness towards gender and racial stereotypes leading to silencing marginalized voices. For example, apps such as YouTube or Instagram use Automated moderation system which can flag content that that challenges cultural norms. On the contrary, algorithms mediate online engagement by rewarding certain behaviors over others. In *The Age of Surveillance Capitalism* (2019), Shoshana

Zuboff argues that major online platforms [like Facebook, Instagram, TikTok, and YouTube] are designed to capture and monetize human attention (Zuboff, 2023).

In 2024, research was carried out by University College London (UCL) and University of Kent and the Association of School and College Leaders to an analyses visual content available on social-media platform using AI-recommendation algorithm to examine how this platform can increase the number of teenage misogynistic posts (Regehr et al., 2024). The researchers created the accounts of each archetype, with content interests specific to each of these archetypes (e.g.) watching the video about masculinity or discussing loneliness), they viewed the videos proposed "For You" as primary content discovery feed for seven days. The analysis found a radical increase in the delivery of harmful contents. Five days later, AI-recommendation algorithm started to show four times more videos with misogynistic content, including objectification, sexual harassment or discrediting of women. According to statistical empirical evidence it is reported that the online harassment of women increases from 13% to 56% (Namvarpour, Pauwels, & Razi, 2025). Another study conducted in Bangladesh which revealed that online harassment increased up to 50.2% among females (with age range of 15-35) as compared to male (Halder, 2021). This proved that it was the result of an amplification process of social-media engagement-based recommendation algorithm which was systematic but escalated gradually to misogynistic content as algorithms identify the use of male-oriented content. So, prioritizing the content produced a great emotional reaction, such as anger, outrage, and controversy, over the wellbeing of the users.

This raise serious concerns as what was designed to keep user engaged for longer period so companies can collect user data to run advertisements and generate revenue turn out to be alarming as these systems were inadvertently amplifying harmful content. Rather than fostering genuine social connection, algorithm-driven interaction became performance for visibility rather than authentic expression which completely shifts the dynamic of human communication and perception of social validation (Esposito, 2022).

Artificial intelligence has redefined boundaries of information, power, and human agency by influencing what is read, what is believed to be true, how one 'selves is expressed, and predict human behavior in digital space. This process of transformation of knowledge application in the domain of artificial intelligence has raised the serious concerns of invasion of privacy, fairness and exploitation to experiential learning. AI assist in providing empirical evidences in big data analysis yet; bringing the challenges and risks of misjudgment (Chakraborty, 2025).

1.2 Artificial Intelligence and the Challenge of Digital Harm

Artificial Intelligence (AI) is found to be a reason in numerous domains including business, healthcare, information technology, transportation, and finance (Hariyanti et al., 2023). It has become an essential part through automation and decision-making. Hence, what initially was started as a system capable of using algorithms to filter the content filtering has now been evolved as a system which at unprecedented speed and scale for generating, amplifying and manipulating information (Floridi, 2024). These transformations have brought undeniable benefits. These transformations have brought undeniable benefits however, at the same time it has raise significant ethical, psychological and legal concerns (Aggarwal & Gaur, 2024). Through the integration of artificial intelligence into social platforms, human interactions have seen a profound change from tailoring what we see to the way we create opinion.

Online platform such as social media, online gaming, instant messaging, and digital learning environment which initially provided digital communication slowly emerged as a source of cyberbullying. Cyberbullying was largely human driven where perpetrators with the intention to harm (Patchin & Hinduja, 2015) would involve in harassment such as name-calling, excluding an individual from online groups, or posting embarrassing images or messages causing public shaming. This could take different form such as doxxing where without the consent of an individual someone publish their private information which may include sharing their address, phone number, or workplace (Kukul, 2023); and impersonation or fake accounts (Awasthi et al., 2020), where perpetrators impersonate the identity of the victim and share embarrassing content or post harmful comments or messages. Recently drastic number of cases of online harassment and cyberbullying have been reported causing digital harm which not only have intensified in scale but complexity (Milosevic et al., 2022) as these AI-enabled forms of abuse have found to be more scalable, deceptive and psychologically damaging than traditional forms of harassment (Binns, 2022).

Cyberbullying is not permitted on social media as companies strictly write this in their policy documents such as Terms of Service and Community Standards/ Guidelines (Gillespie, 2018). Therefore, to combat with online bullying AI-facilitated with the development of natural language processing (NLP), machine learning (ML), and deep learning (DL). NLP work with identification of abusive language in text-based communication which allows machines to understand and interpret human language. ML algorithms learn from data to classify content as harmful with primarily model which are associated to recognize patterns that are associated with cyberbullying. DL is a subset of ML, which uses neural networks with multiple layers to model complex patterns in large datasets. DL models, such as Recurrent Neural Networks (RNNs) and Long Short-Term Memory (LSTM) networks. ML allows even more complex pattern recognition across text, images, and video. Initially, these AI models were trained to enforce platform policies by flagging or removing harmful content, providing human moderators with scalable tools for real-time intervention. Over time, as both AI capabilities and digital communication evolved, these same models facilitated a broader shift in cyberbullying dynamics using the mechanisms of automation, amplification, and fabrication.

Automation involves AI-powered bots which send thousands of abusive messages (Munawar, Singh, & Hanafiah, 2025), flood target notification, post coordinated insults, hence, automated bots allow perpetrators to launch harassment campaigns at a large-scale that would be impossible for humans at that speed and scale. Amplification occurs when algorithm-driven recommendation systems (Nassif, 2024) promote harmful content to wider audiences more quickly than they would find out naturally. Finally, fabrication refers to creating fictitious content using AI, such as deepfake images, videos, or audio that misrepresent a person, enabling impersonation, false narratives that damage an individual reputation, and revenge pornography. Hence, through these mechanisms, AI amplifying harmful material allowing cyberbullying in ways that are difficult for human intervention (Pei, 2025; Alexander, 2025; Milosevic, 2022), ultimately fueling toxic online cultures.

□1.3 AI-Driven Interventions Against Online Harassment

Human interaction has been revolutionized due to proliferation of social media platforms, however, it has intensified the digital harm through online harassment and cyberbullying. To safeguard online environment AI-driven tools are primarily used to defense against digital harassment. NLP and ML models are used to flag harmful content found in the social networks, comment section, and messaging platform. NLP models detect harassment in text where the model will analyze the choice of word, context of the conversation, and emotional tone. To further enhance detection methods competitions SemEval (Semantic Evaluation, an international contest on NLP tasks in 2019 and 2020) and GermEval (a German-language contest in 2018); (Wiegand et al., 2018) invited researchers to build the best hate speech detection models. SemEval-2019 (Zampieri et al., 2019) and 2020 (Zampieri et al., 2020) included tasks on detecting hate speech, offensive language, and sentiment, while GermEval-2018 focused on identifying offensive language in German tweets. These researches used traditional machine learning methods like Naive Bayes and Logistic Regression to modern deep learning techniques such as Convolutional Neural Networks (CNN), LSTM, and BERT, to further enhance the pattern recognition of harassment (Jahan & Oussalah, 2023). However, the computer vision techniques which includes object and imagine manipulation detection, image recognition, and meme analysis to abusive memes, altered images and explicit material hence, focus on identifying harmful content in images and videos (Rezvan et al., 2020). These

DL systems are being used by Meta, X, and YouTube to remove harmful posts. Educational institutions and online communities deploy sentiment-aware algorithm to track bullying, detect hate speech, predict escalation.

2 AI: ONLINE PERPETRATOR AND PROTECTOR

AI has increasingly played a multifaceted role, functioning as catalyst for harm and tool for protection. On one hand, AI facilitated and on the other it has been deployed to combat these very harms, with machine learning algorithms to detect, prevent, and mitigate these very threats. In the section, we explore a series of real-world case scenarios that illustrate this paradox in action.

2.1 Baltimore AI Voice-Clone Framing of a Principal

In January 2024 at Pikesville a video went viral where High School Principal Eric Eiswert, depicting making racist and antisemitic remarks. The video was an AI-generated deepfake designed to discredit him amid a workplace dispute over alleged fund mishandling by athletic director Dazhon Darien (Yang, 2024). In the recording, Mr Eiswert's deepfaked voice is heard making disparaging comments about black students' test scores, black teachers and Jews. Police identified Darien as the source of the distribution and tool access, arrested him in April 2024 on suspicion of stalking, stealing, interfering with school operations, and retaliating against a witness. The case ultimately led to a guilty plea in 2025 and a four-month jail sentence for interfering with school operations. The clip went viral via social media, the exposure was escalated due to resharing and reposts on threads and posts. Which in turn escalated the public reaction leading which ultimately lead to proper investigation of the case.

Consistent with platform virality dynamics observed in case reporting, engagement-driven feeds and trending surfaces on social media platforms probably increased the sensational clip's visibility, generating a quick feedback loop of resharing and commentary that solidified beliefs even after authenticity was questioned by forensics. Despite investigative disclosures, reports show that coordinated attention and persistent re-uploads kept the content alive, demonstrating how user incentives and recommendation systems can prolong the lifecycle of misleading media in a local community setting.

The principal was eventually exonerated, the suspect was taken into custody (April 2024), and the suspect was subsequently sentenced (April 28, 2025) after authorities used forensic audio analysis to identify synthetic traces and confirm that the clip was not authentic. The school district publicly backed the school community and took steps to terminate the accused employee. The principle was put on a leave hence causing acute stress, safety concerns, and reputational harm that correspond with known negative effects from AI-enabled impersonation (loss of control, anxiety, hypervigilance). Principle also faced threats from community which lead to protection provided by police. Up until the forensic discovery was made public, the community was angry, perplexed, and their faith in reliable media was eroding.

2.2 Massachusetts AI-Chatbot Impersonation & Stalking (2025)

A Massachusetts man entered a guilty plea in early 2025 to a years-long cyberstalking campaign in which he impersonated a female college professor using AI role-play chatbots, such as JanitorAI and CrushOn.ai. He fabricated conversations and used false pretenses to entice strangers to the victim's house, causing her to repeatedly worry about her physical safety and seriously harming her reputation. James Florence Jr. conducted a protracted cyberstalking campaign against many women from roughly 2014 to 2024. He produced phony and artificial intelligence-manipulated sexual images, doxed victims' personal information, impersonated them online, and encouraged others to harass and extort them, causing serious psychological harm and fear in the community (Boston.com, 2024).

Harassment occurred via social media, email, and multiple online platforms, including foreign-hosted “revenge porn” sites. James Florence Jr. created multiple social media accounts and emails on name of the victims and exposed contact details of victims to draw in third-party harassers. This changes platform features into vectors for abusing victims. Social media platform recommendations and repost dynamics increased exposure as content was frequently re-uploaded and shared by strangers prompted by doxed information and inflammatory captions. The realism of these chatbots and GenAI images allowed the harasser to scale beyond what a single human can manage.

The victim contacted law enforcement when multiple strangers started to show up on her door. Investigation and digital forensics connected the defendant to accounts, distribution behaviour, and the use of AI tools. The FBI and the U.S. Attorney's Office coordinated the defendant's arrest in September 2024, detention, and subsequent plea, proving successful attribution despite anonymization techniques. The judicial resolution comprised a guilty plea in April 2025 and a sentence of nine years in prison and ten years of supervised release in July 2025. Public advisories demanding on taking strict actions towards identifying Digital Object Identifier (DOJs)

2.3 Deepfake Pornography: eSafety Australian Landmark Case

Anthony Rotondo, Australian Citizen accused of a serious legal proceeding on Al generating a non-consent pornography. Later named as Mr Deepfake after the case was brought to the court by safety commissionaire under online safety act 2021. He was involved with explicit images manipulation of media-linked six prominent celebrities, journalists and influencers. This case in diverted public attention towards how AI systems may be used to fabricate the data. Although the case centered on creator misuse of generative AI, amplification occurred through search engines, aggregation sites, and social platforms, making harmful content more discoverable and persistent. The eSafety Commissioner issued takedown notices and pursued court proceedings, resulting in a significant civil penalty and legal costs against Rotondo. While forensic AI detection tools can help identify synthetic images, the resolution in this case relie primarily on statutory enforcement and legal penalties.

2.4 Coordinated harassment of Hong Kong Journalists (2024)

Between June and August 2024, journalists and media outlets in Hong Kong experienced coordinated harassment; death threats, impersonation, doxxing and anonymous complaints, in what local associations described as an organised campaign targeting the press. A mix of social media platforms (public posts, messaging channels) and offline channels were used; impersonation and anonymous submissions to employers were reported.

While the actors were primarily human and organised, platform affordances (public reposting, trending mechanics, search indexing) and in some cases inauthentic amplification (botlike reposting) can increase reach. Independent audits of platforms show that algorithmic exposure of out-of-network content can dramatically amplify harassment narratives.

Journalists reported incidents to police and platform companies; Meta, Wikimedia and other organisations were involved in investigating and providing technical assistance. The case highlights jurisdictional friction (platforms vs. local law enforcement) and the need for rapid cross-platform response protocols.

2.5 Garcia v. Character Technologies, Inc. (Character.AI)

Families filed suit alleging that conversational agents on Character.AI produced emotionally harmful and in some allegations, self-harm-encouraging interactions that contributed to a minor's death and other severe harms. The plaintiffs' complaint (filed October 2024) describes a pattern of increasingly dangerous exchanges between vulnerable users and the chatbot. On May 21, 2025 the court denied most motions to dismiss, allowing core negligence and product-design claims to proceed into discovery. That ruling means plaintiffs can compel documents, logs, and testing records that may show whether design choices foreseeably created risk.

Character.AI's conversational chatbot platform a widely distributed consumer-facing app with significant public engagement and millions of downloads, a scale the filings cite to argue foreseeability of harm. Plaintiffs allege that a constellation of design and algorithmic features amplified risk: Anthropomorphic UI and framing: Persona-driven interfaces and humanlike agent behavior increase emotional attachment (parasocial bonding), which can intensify trust and influence. Permissive role-play features: Templates and role-play modes that encourage immersive one-on-one interactions may normalize intimate or transgressive exchanges. Insufficient age verification & safety escalation: Alleged gaps in age-gating and lack of reliable, real-time crisis escalation left vulnerable users exposed.

Reinforcement of interactions: Features that personalize and prioritize continued engagement (recommendation/personalization loops, notifications, or reward signals) can unintentionally strengthen dependency and repeat problematic dialogues. (Importantly, the court's decision to allow discovery is intended to test these allegations against internal evidence e.g., logs, safety test reports, moderation rules rather than accept them as proven fact). At the pleading stage the litigation survived dismissal and moved to discovery. Discovery can reveal whether and how Character.AI implemented automated safety tools (crisis classifiers, content filters), human moderation, rate limits, age checks, or logging and escalation protocols. The case foregrounds several possible remediation paths that might emerge from discovery or later remedies: mandated product redesigns, injunctive relief requiring safety improvements, oversight obligations (audits or reporting), or consumer remedies through settlement. The litigation also highlights broader technical needs improved real-time crisis detection, explicit safety-by-design practices, and transparent documentation of testing and moderation pipelines.

2.6 Harassment by the Replika Companion Chatbot (2017–2023)

Replika, an AI companion chatbot by Luka Inc., was marketed as a supportive, platonic friend. Yet, analysis of 35,000+ negative Google Play reviews (800 coded in detail) showed repeated reports of sexual harassment. Users described unsolicited advances, sexual conversations that continued after rejection, and boundary settings like "friend" mode failing. Some also said the bot requested or hinted at intimate photos, undermining its therapeutic promise.

Replika's model often defaulted toward intimacy and escalated into sexual themes even in platonic contexts. Some interactions were linked to subscription prompts, with blurred or locked erotic content encouraging upgrades. This monetization design amplified inappropriate behavior and made disengagement harder.

Issues came to light mainly through user complaints and research, not proactive monitoring. In 2023, Italy's Data Protection Authority ordered Replika to stop processing user data, citing risks to minors. In 2025, Luka Inc. was fined €5 million for GDPR violations. Erotic role-play features were later restricted, but safety tools like "stop" commands and relationship settings often failed.

2.7 Deepfake Harassment of Pakistani Politician Azma Bukhari (2024)

In early 2024, a realistic deepfake video of Pakistani politician Azma Bukhari a vocal advocate for women's rights—spread online. The video falsely showed her in an explicit scenario. It was made using publicly available photos and free generative AI tools. The clip triggered online abuse, threats, and public shaming. Bukhari said, "I had to prove I wasn't in that video," showing how victims bear the burden of disproving synthetic harm.

The video spread mainly on Facebook, WhatsApp, and X (Twitter). It moved through private WhatsApp groups protected by end-to-end encryption and was amplified by public posts on X. Algorithmic systems boosted the content. Trending hashtags and recommendation engines favored the emotionally charged material. On X, coordinated accounts used bot-like tactics to increase its reach.

After media pressure, Meta removed the video from Facebook and Instagram using AI-based deepfake detection. WhatsApp content stayed online due to encryption. Pakistan's FIA Cyber Crime Wing (now NCCIA) filed a case under PECA Section 21, but the suspect—likely overseas—was never prosecuted due to jurisdictional limits.

2.8 Fabricated Assault Video Targeting Lahore College Student (2024)

In early October 2024, a false video and narrative claiming a female Lahore college student had been raped went viral. The disinformation sparked citywide protests, campus closures, and violent clashes. The student and her family denied the claim, stating she had suffered a spinal injury from a fall at home on October 2 and remained hospitalized until October 11. A Punjab government and FIA inquiry confirmed the story was entirely fabricated a deliberate act of digital defamation. The false claims spread on Facebook, WhatsApp, TikTok, and X (Twitter). Edited or synthetic visuals (not confirmed as deepfakes but labeled "fabricated" in the FIR) circulated in public posts and private groups.

Algorithms amplified the content. Recommendation systems pushed the emotionally charged false claim into trending topics and "For You" feeds. Hashtags like #JusticeForLahoreStudent fueled real-world protests and mob violence. The speed and scale suggest possible use of coordinated inauthentic accounts, though this was not formally confirmed.

The FIA Cyber Crime Wing launched an immediate investigation and formed a seven-member committee to trace the source. A formal FIR was filed at Defence. A Police Station under PECA 2016 for defamation and inciting unrest. The Punjab government inquiry concluded the incident was fabricated, with no evidence of assault.

Table 1. Summary of mechanisms used for AI perpetrator and protector

Mechanism	Case	Year	Notes
Fabrication	Pikesville High School Deepfake (Eric Eiswert)	2024	AI-generated deepfake video defaming a school principal
	MrDeepFakes / Anthony Rotondo	2025	Non-consensual AI pornography of prominent women
	Azma Bukhari Deepfake Harassment	2024	Political deepfake harassment in Pakistan
	Lahore College Student Fabricated Assault Video	2024	AI-generated video falsely depicting assault
	Deepfake Non-Consensual Images (Scotland)	2025	International non-consensual deepfake images
	Taylor Swift AI-Created Explicit Images	2024	Non-consensual deepfake sexual images
	AI-Generated Child Sexual Abuse Material Surge	2023–2025	Fabrication of illegal material; may involve some amplification if content spread
Automation	Massachusetts AI-Chatbot Stalking	2025	AI chatbots impersonating victim and engaging strangers
	Replika Companion Chatbot Harassment	2017–2023	Repetitive harassment through companion chatbot
	Garcia v. Character Technologies, Inc. (Character.AI)	2024	AI-generated harmful content in chatbot interactions
Amplification	COMPAS Algorithm Bias	TBD	Algorithmic bias affecting multiple legal outcomes
	Théâtre D'opéra Spatial Controversy	TBD	Viral AI-generated content controversy
	Hong Kong Journalists Coordinated Harassment	2024	Coordinated attacks (partial amplification); may include AI-mediated amplification in social media

Even though numerous pattern recognition models have been developed for the cyberbully and online harassment detection (See Table 1) however, these models have been found not fully capable of capturing context specific, complex, and culturally sensitive nature of harassment. As they could not capture language cues, humor, newly emerged words, and insults leading to false positive detection (Zhong et al., 2022). NLP models heavily rely on sentiment analysis, and their detective revolve around linguistic attributes such as grammatic and lexical features. Lexicality detects cyberbullying through vulgar words (Ptaszynski et al., 2016) however, not all offensive sentences contain these offensive words rather the content is heavily focused on second-person pronouns, screen name of the user, or other related person-centered terms which as used as user identifiers (Xu, 2021; Saengprang & Gadavanij, 2021; Tan, 2019). Furthermore, sometimes abusers use subtle sarcasm which can lead to misinterpretation (Li, 2020; Zhong et al., 2022) as words can be masked (Chen et al., 2013; Caselli et al., 2020) in the form of homophones (e.g you're a b****" might be written as "you're a b**ch), spelling alteration (fk), abbrevations and acronyms (SMH will be written for shaking my head),emoji substitution (to replace idiot), and metaphors and euphemisms ("troll under the bridge" implying they are malicious online). Hence, this negative expression would not be comprehended by the detection model. Therefore, cyberbullying can be classified as implicit or explicit depending on clarity (Tan, 2019; Zeng et al., 2019; Caselli et al., 2020; Li, 2020).

Words which clearly show abusive content are categorized as (explicit) whereas the words which are ambiguous and may not be recognized as bullying fall under the category of implicit (Waseem et al., 2017) whereas, Li (2020) labelled explicit as cyberbullying word category and sensitive cyberbullying category as implicit. In 2016 Nobata et al. summarized abusive language linguistic types and categorized in three types (lexical, semantic, synaptic) based on which includes negations, modal verbs, and polite expression in text drawn from Linguistic Inquiry and Word Count (LIWC) derived cues. Where LIWC is a computerized text analysis tool which classifies words into meaning-based (semantics) categories which reflect the social, linguistic, and psychological dimension of language use (Pennebaker et al., 2001).

Current automated methods can only identify specific types of cyberbullying, such as aggression, threats, sexual harassment, (Chatzakou et al., 2017; Hee et al., 2018) but it is difficult to detect sarcasm and euphemisms (Dinakar et al., 2011). A phrase which is labelled as harassment in one linguistic context may just be considered as humor in another. Therefore, growing Internet language in different social, cultural, linguistic context and communicative space will further affect keyword-based cyberbullying detection (Ali et al., 2018; Tan, 2019) leading to disproportionately silence marginalized voices.

3 SOLUTIONS AND RECOMMENDATIONS

Three sub-section has been identified namely technical safeguards (provenance infrastructure, consent by design, federated detection networks), regulatory and policy measures (Global harmonization, platform accountability, restorative remedies), and educational and cultural responses (media-literacy integration, professional ethics training, public awareness campaigns).

3.1 Technical safeguard

Technical safeguard refers to the technological built-in mechanism which are designed to prevent, detect and minimize the harmful implementation of Al systems (Laskar, 2025). The purpose of such tools and methods are to protect users from misuses such as invasion of privacy, psychological and social harms and bias. It ensures the AI to operate such tasks such as safety [data security from unauthorized access, data-sets scanning regardless of ethnicity, gender, or socio-economic status]. For instance, AI prediction upon psychological health condition without giving a stigma. transparency and accountability. Tools may be used to distinguished between human created or AI-generated through the cryptographic *watermark.* Use of *built-in logos* to track model updates. AI-powered moderate systems may also be introduced to filter toxic content, propaganda; For instance; Google perspective API detects flags and harmful posts. If such technical safeguarded method is not implemented, then deepfakes may continuous spread fake and misinformation may lead in eroding trust. Similarly shared hashes of detected deepfake content may be used among inter-collaborators [federated detection network where multiple platforms or services collaborate together to detect, share and flag malicious content]. Each network exchange artifacts that could be hashes or signature for a collective efficacy towards cross-platform defenses (Heidari, et al., 2024).

3.2 Regulatory and policy measures

The rapid advancement of landscape has progressed the need of global harmonization. Global harmonization refers to the process of creating and adopting consistent standardized international regulatory law and ethical frameworks. A united international framework is deemed essential in era of experiential growth. Though many nations have put emphasis on endorsing policies including the efforts of EU artificial intelligence act, 2024. This act provides practical implementation on global ethical standards/ design principles to protect individuals from digital harms. For instance, AI-driven content moderator which requires label (i.e deepfake) as artificially created content. Similarly, users must be informed when they are interacting with Al-chat assistance (e.g, customer-service Chabot's). The act has also classifies AI must label "AI scoring" as employ "decision-making roles" to ensure fairness.

However, the difference lies in the scope, operational definitions, indigenous context implementation, and enforcement mechanisms (Christou, Meyer, & Fanni, 2025). This law is implemented on distributors and offenders upload the harmful content. One of the examples of coordinated initiatives between INTERPOL's cyber division and the EUROPOL Innovative Lab who are already exploring mechanisms in identifying flag deepfakes through federated data. Similarly, the efforts are EU

Act (2024) ensures that tech-giant platforms including meta and X [formally known as twitter] shall provide data for algorithmic moderation and management towards harmful content. This platform has reported detecting of 5,000 cases of AI-generated non-consensual content. It took an average of 72 hours to remove the violated content (Schilke, & Reimann, 2025). More efforts are yet needed to ensure stronger safeguard as it is critical disciplinary action to mitigate the harm resulted in form of digital harassment. Psychological, reputational and financial damage would be on stake for the victims of deepfake identity manipulation.

3.3 Educational and cultural responses

Educational and cultural responses refer to the human-centered approaches. The sole purpose of these approaches lies in the ethical awareness, and digital literacy in society. Ethical frameworks prepare humans to recognize ethical risks and to respond empathetically within the social and cultural contexts. The conceptual of ethical and civility may integrate in education system so mindfulness process may start from early schooling. Exposure to citizenship rights, role of culturally practiced norms and continuous moral implementation always play a fundamental role. Recent and robust example of Al literacy courses for all citizen is introduced in Finland educational system (Kaletski-Maisel, & Jowallah, 2025). Likewise, UNESCO, 2024 report has also shed light on the notion of digital literacy and Al literacy. The report revealed that thirty percent of national curricula globally address AI ethics/ algorithm awareness at the school level (Lin, Xu, & Liu, 2025). There is a need to train citizens in prior sharing the information; verify the authenticity of digital source, validate and understand the algorithmic manipulation process.

The highlighted issue may remain as deep rooted in practice and dependency. Yet, positively remains with increased awareness of the need to prioritize fairness in AI and technology development. To increase the transparency in AI systems may be achieved by designing the system in such a way that it allows humans to make the final decision. For instance; to understand and interpret the situation with humanistic insights. In the case of failure AI systems may provide tract records to ensure transparency in decision-making process. Thus, make it easy to assign the understanding the role of responsibility. Secondly, even though ethical and legal frameworks are available to regulate and protect human rights. Nevertheless; a legal framework that ensures the clear roles and responsibilities of particles jointly involved in the development of autonomous systems is needed. Thirdly, implementation of the concept of "human-in-the-loop: approach may maintain a level of control and accountability. The intervening role of humans may mitigate risks. To understand the diversity among human values may be achieved by creating a diverse (in-terms of culture, conceptual, experiential) evaluation team to uncover or resolve any biases. This check and balance audit process may be divided in such a way that human involvement may allow the system to analyze data further prior to processing in advanced stages. The entire process may be mapped upon the approved guidelines of western and eastern organizations including IEEE, European commissions of law enforcement.

4 CONCLUSION

AI has transformed digital environments, providing opportunities and risks particularly in the context of online harassment and cyberbullying by introducing new forms of abuse which significantly impact the psychological wellbeing of the victim. Yet, AI also holds a strong protective mechanism through its detection tools, moderation algorithms, and governance frameworks which help to mitigate these risks. Hence, the future of AI depends on balancing between harnessing its potential for protection while guarding against its misuse that will create digital ecosystems which is innovative, safe, and respectful of human values.

REFERENCES

Aggarwal, A., & Gaur, S. (2024). Applying artificial intelligence to explore online harassment and cyberbullying prevention. In *Impact of AI on Advancing Women's Safety* (pp. 104–120). IGI Global Scientific Publishing.

Alexander, S. (2025). *Deepfakes reshape cyberbullying, TCU expert calls for action.* Texas Christian University.

Ali, W. N. H. W., Mohd, M., & Fauzi, F. (2018). Cyberbullying detection: An overview." in *2018 Cyber Resilience Conference (CRC);* November 13–15, 2018; 1–3.

Awasthi, S., Shanmugam, R., Jena, S. R., & Srivastava, A. (2020). Review of techniques to prevent fake accounts on social media. *International Journal of Advanced Science and Technology, 29*(4), 8350–8365.

Bainbridge, W. S. (2006). Cognitive technologies. In *Managing nano-bio-info-cogno innovations* (pp. 203–226). Springer Netherlands. DOI: 10.1007/1-4020-4107-1_14

Binns, R. (2022). Human Judgment in algorithmic loops: Individual justice and automated decision-making. *Regulation & Governance, 16*(1), 197–211. DOI: 10.1111/rego.12358

Boston.com. (2024). *Plymouth man allegedly used AI to stalk and harass woman.* https://www.boston.com/news/crime/2024/09/11/plymouth-man-allegedly-used-ai-to-impersonate-stalk-harrass-mass-woman/

Brady, W. J., Jackson, J. C., Lindström, B., & Crockett, M. J. (2023). Algorithm-mediated social learning in online social networks. *Trends in Cognitive Sciences, 27*(10), 947–960. DOI: 10.1016/j.tics.2023.06.008 PMID: 37543440

Brooks, R. A. (1991). Intelligence without representation. *Artificial Intelligence, 47*(1-3), 139–159. DOI: 10.1016/0004-3702(91)90053-M

Caselli, T., Basile, V., Mitrović, J., Kartoziya, I., & Granitzer, M. (2020). "I feel offended, don't be abusive! implicit/explicit messages in offensive and abusive language." in *Proceedings of the 12th Language Resources and Evaluation Conference;* May 13–15, 2020; (European Language Resources Association), 6193–6202.

Chakraborty, S. (2025). *Human values, ethics, and dignity in the age of artificial intelligence.* IGI Global. DOI: 10.4018/979-8-3693-9035-1

Chatzakou, D., Kourtellis, N., Blackburn, J., De Cristofaro, E., Stringhini, G., & Vakali, A. (2017, April). Measuring# GamerGate: A tale of hate, sexism, and bullying. In *Proceedings of the 26th international conference on world wide web companion* (pp. 1285-1290). DOI: 10.1145/3041021.3053890

Chen, L., Zhang, C., & Wilson, C. (2013). "Tweeting under pressure: analyzing trending topics and evolving word choice on sina weibo." in *Proceedings of the first ACM conference on Online social networks* COSN'13; October 7–8, 2013; (New York, NY, USA: Association for Computing Machinery), 89–100. DOI: 10.1145/2512938.2512940

Christou, G., Meyer, T., & Fanni, R. (2025). The European union: Assessing global leadership through actorness in artificial intelligence. *Journal of European Integration, 47*(3), 383–401. DOI: 10.1080/07036337.2024.2377200

Dinakar, K., Reichart, R., & Lieberman, H. (2011). Modeling the detection of textual cyberbullying. In *Proceedings of the International AAAI Conference on Web and Social Media* (Vol. 5, No. 3, pp. 11-17).

Esposito, E. (2022). *Artificial communication: How algorithms produce social intelligence*. MIT Press. DOI: 10.7551/mitpress/14189.001.0001

Floridi, L. (2024). Introduction to the special issues: The ethics of artificial intelligence: Exacerbated problems, renewed problems, unprecedented problems. *American Philosophical Quarterly, 61*(4), 301–307. DOI: 10.5406/21521123.61.4.01

Gillespie, T. (2018). *Custodians of the Internet: Platforms, content moderation, and the hidden decisions that shape social media*. Yale University Press.

Halder, S. (2021). Violence Against Women in Bangladesh: Uprising Scenario and Safeguards in Cyberspace (Doctoral dissertation, Khulna university).

Hariyanti, E., Janeswari, M. B., Moningka, M. M., Aziz, F. M., Putri, A. R., Hapsari, O. S., Sutha, N. A. A. D., Sinaga, Y. A. A., & Bendesa, M. P. (2023). Implementations of Artificial Intelligence in Various Domains of IT Governance: A Systematic Literature Review. *Journal of Information Systems Engineering & Business Intelligence, 9*(2), 305–319. DOI: 10.20473/jisebi.9.2.305-319

Heidari, A., Navimipour, N. J., Dag, H., Talebi, S., & Unal, M. (2024). A novel blockchain-based deepfake detection method using federated and deep learning models. *Cognitive Computation, 16*(3), 1073–1091. DOI: 10.1007/s12559-024-10255-7

Jahan, M. S., & Oussalah, M. (2023). A systematic review of hate speech automatic detection using natural language processing. *Neurocomputing, 546*, 126232. DOI: 10.1016/j.neucom.2023.126232

Kaletski-Maisel, G., & Jowallah, R. (2025). Empowering Citizens: Preparing for the Future of Digital Literacy and AI in Education. In Digital Citizenship and the Future of AI Engagement, Ethics, and Privacy (pp. 133-150). IGI Global Scientific Publishing.

Krizhevsky, A., Sutskever, I., & Hinton, G. E. (2012). ImageNet classification with deep convolutional neural networks. *Advances in Neural Information Processing Systems*, •••, 25.

Kukul, B. (2023). Personal data and personal safety: Re-examining the limits of public data in the context of doxing. *International Data Privacy Law*, *13*(3), 182–193. DOI: 10.1093/idpl/ipad011

Laskar, P. (2025). Cryptographic Provenance and the Future of Media Authenticity: Technical Standards and Ethical Frameworks for Generative Content. *Journal of Computer Science and Technology Studies*, *7*(6), 967–972.

Lenat, D. B., & Guha, R. V. (1990). *Building Large Knowledge-Based Systems*. Addison-Wesley.

Li, W. (2020). The language of bullying: Social issues on Chinese websites. *Aggression and Violent Behavior*, *53*, 101453. DOI: 10.1016/j.avb.2020.101453

Lin, D., Xu, X., & Liu, J. (2025). Chinese High School Students AI Competency Survey: Based on the UNESCO Students' AI Competency Framework. *Journal of Educational Technology and Innovation*, *7*(1). Advance online publication. DOI: 10.61414/0y6gsj74

McCarthy, J., Minsky, M. L., Rochester, N., & Shannon, C. E. (1955). A Proposal for the Dartmouth Summer Research Project on Artificial Intelligence.

McCarthy, J., Minsky, M. L., Rochester, N., & Shannon, C. E. (2006). A proposal for the dartmouth summer research project on artificial intelligence, august 31, 1955. *AI Magazine*, *27*(4), 12–12.

Milosevic, T. (2022). *Artificial intelligence to address cyberbullying, harassment, and misinformation*. National Institutes of Health.

Milosevic, T., Van Royen, K., & Davis, B. (2022). Artificial intelligence to address cyberbullying, harassment and abuse: New directions in the midst of complexity. *International Journal of Bullying Prevention : an Official Publication of the International Bullying Prevention Association*, *4*(1), 1–5. DOI: 10.1007/s42380-022-00117-x PMID: 35233506

Minsky, M., & Papert, S. (1969). *Perceptrons: An Introduction to Computational Geometry*. MIT Press.

Munawar, M., Singh, T. M., & Hanafiah, M. M. (2025). The Future of AI in Cyberbullying Prevention: Trends and Technologies. In *Combating Cyberbullying With Generative AI* (pp. 237–278). IGI Global Scientific Publishing. DOI: 10.4018/979-8-3373-0543-1.ch009

Namvarpour, M., Pauwels, H., & Razi, A. (2025). AI-induced Sexual Harassment: Investigating Contextual Characteristics and User Reactions of Sexual Harassment by a Companion Chatbot. *Proceedings of the ACM on Human-Computer Interaction*, *9*(7), 1–28. DOI: 10.1145/3757548

Nassif, S. A. (2024). Algorithm Literacy among Youth: Understanding and Navigating Social Media Algorithms. *The Egyptian Journal of Media Research*, *2024*(89), 33–72.

Newell, A., & Simon, H. A. (1961). GPS, a program that simulates human thought. In Billing, H. (Ed.), *Lernende Automaten*. Oldenbourg.

Nilsson, N. J. (1983). Artificial intelligence prepares for 2001. *AI Magazine*, *4*(4), 7–7.

Nobata, C., Tetreault, J., Thomas, A., Mehdad, Y., & Chang, Y. (2016). "Abusive language detection in online user content." in *Proceedings of the 25th International Conference on World Wide Web WWW'16. (Republic and Canton of Geneva, CHE: International World Wide Web Conferences Steering Committee)*, 145–153. DOI: 10.1145/2872427.2883062

Noble, S. U. (2018). *Algorithms of oppression: How search engines reinforce racism*. New York University Press. DOI: 10.18574/nyu/9781479833641.001.0001

Pariser, E. (2011). *The filter bubble: What the Internet is hiding from you*. Penguin Press.

Patchin, J. W., & Hinduja, S. (2015). Measuring cyberbullying: Implications for research. *Aggression and Violent Behavior*, *23*, 69–74. DOI: 10.1016/j.avb.2015.05.013

Pei, W. (2025). AI can be cyberbullying perpetrators: Investigating the role of artificial intelligence in cyberbullying. *Technology in Society*, *70*, 102217.

Pennebaker, J. W., Francis, M. E., & Booth, R. J. (2001). *Linguistic Inquiry and Word Count: LIWC*. Lawrence Erlbaum Associates.

Ptaszynski, M., Masui, F., Nitta, T., Hatakeyama, S., Kimura, Y., Rzepka, R., & Araki, K. (2016). Sustainable cyberbullying detection with category-maximized relevance of harmful phrases and double-filtered automatic optimization. *International Journal of Child-Computer Interaction*, *8*, 15–30. DOI: 10.1016/j.ijcci.2016.07.002

Regehr, K., Shaughnessy, C., Zhao, M., & Shaughnessy, N. (2024). *Safer scrolling: How algorithms popularise and gamify online hate and misogyny for young people.* University College London & University of Kent. https://www.ascl.org.uk/ASCL/media/ASCL/Help%20and%20advice/Inclusion/Safer-scrolling.pdf

Rezvan, M., Shekarpour, S., Alshargi, F., Thirunarayan, K., Shalin, V. L., & Sheth, A. (2020). Analyzing and learning the language for different types of harassment. *PLoS One*, *15*(3), e0227330. DOI: 10.1371/journal.pone.0227330 PMID: 32218569

Rheingold, H. (2000). *Tools for thought: The history and future of mind-expanding technology*. MIT press.

Rumelhart, D. E., Hinton, G. E., & Williams, R. J. (1986). Learning representations by back-propagating errors. *Nature*, *323*(6088), 533–536. DOI: 10.1038/323533a0

Russell, S., & Norvig, P. (2021). *Artificial intelligence: A modern approach* (4th ed.). Pearson.

Saengprang, S., & Gadavanij, S. (2021). Cyberbullying: The case of public figures. *LEARN J. Lang. Educ. Acquis. Res. Netw.*, *14*, 344–369.

Schilke, O., & Reimann, M. (2025). The transparency dilemma: How AI disclosure erodes trust. *Organizational Behavior and Human Decision Processes*, *188*, 104405. DOI: 10.1016/j.obhdp.2025.104405

Tan, K. H. (Ed.). (2019). Stop Cyberbullying. Malaysia: Penerbit Universiti Kebangsaan malasia.

Turing, A. M. (1950). Computing Machinery and Intelligence. *Mind*, *LIX*(236), 433–460. DOI: 10.1093/mind/LIX.236.433

Tybjerg, K. (2003). Wonder-making and philosophical wonder in Hero of Alexandria. *Studies in History and Philosophy of Science*, *34*(3), 443–466. DOI: 10.1016/S0039-3681(03)00053-0

Van Hee, C., Jacobs, G., Emmery, C., Desmet, B., Lefever, E., Verhoeven, B., De Pauw, G., Daelemans, W., & Hoste, V. (2018). Automatic detection of cyberbullying in social media text. *PLoS One*, *13*(10), e0203794. DOI: 10.1371/journal.pone.0203794 PMID: 30296299

Waseem, Z., Davidson, T., Warmsley, D., & Weber, I. (2017). "Understanding abuse: a typology of abusive language detection subtasks." in *Proceedings of the First Workshop on Abusive Language Online*; July 30–August 4, 2017; 78–84. DOI: 10.18653/v1/W17-3012

Wiegand, M., Siegel, M., & Ruppenhofer, J. (2018). Overview of the germeval 2018 shared task on the identification of offensive language.

Xu, Y. (2021). The invisible aggressive fist: Features of Cyberbullying language in China. *Int. J. Semiot. Law - Rev. Int. Sémiot. International Journal for the Semiotics of Law*, *34*(4), 1041–1064. DOI: 10.1007/s11196-020-09746-1

Yang, M. (2024). Baltimore teacher accused of using AI to create fake, racist recording of principal. *The Guardian*. Retrieved from https://www.theguardian.com/us-news/2024/apr/27/baltimore-teacher-ai-fake-racist-recording-principal

Zampieri, M., Malmasi, S., Nakov, P., Rosenthal, S., Farra, N., & Kumar, R. (2019). Semeval-2019 task 6: Identifying and categorizing offensive language in social media (offenseval). *arXiv preprint arXiv:1903.08983*. DOI: 10.18653/v1/S19-2010

Zampieri, M., Nakov, P., Rosenthal, S., Atanasova, P., Karadzhov, G., Mubarak, H., . . . Çöltekin, Ç. (2020). SemEval-2020 task 12: Multilingual offensive language identification in social media (OffensEval 2020). *arXiv preprint arXiv:2006.07235*. DOI: 10.18653/v1/2020.semeval-1.188

Zeng, L., Ying-Chao, L. I., Humanities, S. O., & Polytechnic, S. (2019). The classification and modal sense of implicit violent speech acts. *J. Nanchang Univ. Soc. Sci.*, *50*, 117–124.

Zhong, J., Qiu, J., Sun, M., Jin, X., Zhang, J., Guo, Y., Qiu, X., Xu, Y., Huang, J., & Zheng, Y. (2022). To be ethical and responsible digital citizens or not: A linguistic analysis of cyberbullying on social media. *Frontiers in Psychology*, *13*, 861823. DOI: 10.3389/fpsyg.2022.861823 PMID: 35572339

Zuboff, S. (2023). The age of surveillance capitalism. In *Social theory re-wired* (pp. 203–213). Routledge. DOI: 10.4324/9781003320609-27

Chapter 4

Blockchain-Enabled Ethical Governance Framework for Transparent, Accountable, and Trustworthy AI Systems:

From Transparency to Ethical AI Governance

Rana Muhammad Amir Latif
http://orcid.org/0000-0001-6007-6275
East China Normal University, Shanghai, China

Farhan Ullah
Prince Mohammad Bin Fahd University, Khobar, Saudi Arabia

Umar Raza
http://orcid.org/0000-0002-9810-1285
Manchester Metropolitan University, Manchester, UK

Leonardo Mostarda
University of Perugia, Perugia, Italy

Diletta Cacciagrano
http://orcid.org/0000-0003-4491-0666
University of Camerino, Camerino, Italy

DOI: 10.4018/979-8-3373-6038-6.ch004

ABSTRACT

As artificial intelligence (AI) becomes increasingly embedded in critical domains such as healthcare, cybersecurity, finance, and public services, the demand for ethical governance ensuring fairness, transparency, and accountability is urgent. Traditional oversight mechanisms often lack verifiable trust in decentralized and dynamic environments. This chapter introduces a Blockchain-Enabled Ethical Governance for AI (B-EGAI) framework that leverages blockchain's immutability, transparency, and smart contracts to enable auditable model registries, decentralized policy enforcement, and tamper-proof decision logs. By embedding ethical principles across the AI lifecycle, B-EGAI fosters accountability and trustworthiness in real-world applications. Case studies demonstrate its potential, while discussions on privacy-preserving computation, federated learning, and decentralized oversight outline future research, positioning blockchain as a foundation for trustworthy AI.

1 INTRODUCTION AND MOTIVATION

The integrated actions of software engineering and Artificial Intelligence (AI) are transforming industries, societies, and individuals (Asif, Hassan, & Parr, 2023). In healthcare diagnostics and financial analytics, autonomous vehicles, smart governance, and other robust software systems based on AI are being rapidly applied due to their capabilities to automate typically complicated decision-making processes and adjust to constantly evolving conditions (Lo et al., 2022).

Upon closer examination, however, the transformative ability comes with significant ethical concerns. Researchers, policy-makers, and end-users have expressed significant concern about issues related to bias in decision-making, a lack of transparency, data privacy violations, and gaps in accountability (Göksal & Solarte Vasquez, 2024). As the level of AI integration in mission-critical software systems steadily rises, there is no time like the present to address the necessity of implementing viable ethical governance systems (Alzoubi, 2024).

Conventionally, ethical governance within software systems has been based on organizational policies, human control, and adherence to rules (Rane, Choudhary, & Rane, 2023). Although such methods have their validity, they commonly lack the scope required when activating autonomous AI systems that learn from data and evolve (Yang, Abedin, Qiao, & Ye, 2024).

The decisions in these situations are difficult to attribute to particular agents (of standard form) and to assess the soundness of these decisions ex post in terms of ethics (Han, 2022). Additionally, a centralized system of governance is susceptible to all forms of tampering. It lacks transparency, making it difficult to gain the confidence of stakeholders, who insist on fairness, accountability, and clear explanations (Bhumichai, Smiliotopoulos, Benton, Kambourakis, & Damopoulos, 2024).

Simultaneously, blockchain technology has emerged as a dynamic facilitator of trust, transparency, and decentralization in the digital realm (Kuznetsov, Sernani, Romeo, Frontoni, & Mancini, 2024). First born to serve cryptocurrencies such as Bitcoin, blockchain has been utilized in a wide range of areas, including supply chain management, healthcare, identity authentication, and most recently, AI governance (Tyagi, 2024).

Blockchain Immutability, Decentralized Consensus, Tamper-Evident Records, and Programmable Logic with Smart Contracts are its main features, which qualify it as a powerful solution to the ethical deficiency of AI-powered software systems (Alkhodair, 2025). Blockchain can provide the opportunity to monitor, verify, and audit the behavior of AI in real-time, which would mean that ethical policies would not only be written but also implemented and communicated to everyone with an interest (Das, Jhanjhi, Asirvatham, Rizwan, & Javed, 2025).

A new frontier is therefore formed by the combination of AI with blockchain technology, known as Blockchain-Enabled Ethical Governance of AI Systems (Devarapu, 2020). This new reality is one where ethical standards are codified into smart contracts, decision-making is recorded on immutable ledgers, and transparent, community-driven protocols govern AI models (Kulothungan, 2024). This system does not only suppose that the software systems make intelligent decisions but also ethical standards which are also enforced, traceable, and testable.

Potential this notwithstanding, this all-in-one approach has its flaws. Such points as the scaling of the blockchain systems, the problem of integrating smart contracts and AI logic, and potential conflict between the laws of data impossibility and data protection, such as the right to be forgotten in GDPR, are among the primary challenges to address (Whig, Sharma, Yathiraju, Jain, & Sharma, 2025). Further, the problem of ethical governance is a socio-technical issue, which assumes the interaction of disciplines between computer scientists, ethicists, law practitioners, and domain analysts. The chapter attempts to discuss the theoretical frameworks, technical architectures, real-world implementation and main challenges in ethical governing AI through blockchain technology in software systems. To be more precise, it answers the following central questions:

- How can ethical governance principles be operationalized in AI software systems?
- What are the aspects of blockchain that make it applicable in preventing unethical conduct in AI?
- How would it be possible to combine blockchain with AI systems to facilitate accountability, auditability, and fairness?

- What are the real-world applications where blockchain-enabled ethical AI governance is most needed?
- What are the limitations, risks, and future research directions in this domain?

This chapter is important because it is interdisciplinary and integrates the knowledge of AI ethics, software engineering, blockchain systems, and cybersecurity (Rana Muhammad Amir Latif, Farhan, Ahmad, Mostarda, & Cacciagrano, 2025). It. It integrates the current literature, introduces a conceptual design of the Blockchain-Enabled Governance in AI (B-EGAI) and provides the case studies to demonstrate how and why this setup is feasible and meaningful (Rana Muhammad Amir Latif, Asghar, Umer, & Hussain, 2023). Practical limitations and policy implications are also outlined in the chapter and present a guide to the researchers, developers and policymakers to jointly create AI software systems that are ethically aligned (Rana Muhammad Amir Latif & Riaz, 2023).

Once any software is defining as well as regulating our digital life, it is only possible to make sure that the AI systems are within the ethical scope. Blockchain contains a viable methodology of transferring ethical norms to enforceable commitments, set clear paths of resolution to manifest avenues of determination, and enshrine centrality to decentralized trust. Ethical governance through blockchains is a paradigm shift in the responsible creation and implementation of AI in programs, which is possibly a crucial factor that can allow us to fill the divide between AI autonomy and human responsibility.

2 FOUNDATIONS OF ETHICAL GOVERNANCE AND BLOCKCHAIN

2.1 Ethical Governance in AI-Powered Software

Ethical governance is a procedure of social-technical controls to make certain that an AI system is created and deployed in line with the moral and lawful goals (Camilleri, 2024). As the ability of AI technologies to penetrate important spheres of human activity, such as healthcare, finance, and government, there is an increasing focus on the need to provide simple ethical guidance (Joseph et al., 2024). International projects have thus been developed to deal with this lapse, and developers, policy-makers, and organizations have devised policy to facilitate this process (Amugongo, Kriebitz, Boch, & Lütge, 2023).

The most striking one of these is the OECD AI Principles (Kumari, Das, and Singh, 2025), which suggests the ideas of human-related values, such as fairness, transparency, robustness, and accountability. Similarly, the statement by the ACM on Algorithmic Transparency and Accountability urges the relevance of the explainability, auditability, and redress measures in curbing the risks linked to algorithmic decision-making. This has been extended upon by the IEEE Ethically Aligned Design (EAD) (Cumming, Saurabh, Rani, & Upadhyay, 2024) program that has brought cultural sensitivity and human well-being to the world of ethics.

Out of these, five common ethical imperatives of AI software engineering have been achieved. First, in the name of fairness, systems must be free from unfair prejudice and practice equal treatment among different demographics (Salako et al., 2024). Second, accountability implies transparency in the attribution of responsibility for model development, implementation, and the resulting outcomes. Third, transparency and explainability refer to making the logic in a system, the provenance of data, and the behavior of the model comprehensible to the end-users and auditors (Baqar, 2024). Fourth, privacy and security are the key factors that ensure the protection of personal information throughout the entire AI cycle. Lastly, the concept of human supervision requires intensive decisions to be placed at meaningful human control, particularly in risky applications (Abolaji & Akinwande, 2024).

The problem of operationalizing these principles in the AI systems is a difficult one, especially in the context of the systems that require constant learning and re-training. An average AI pipeline includes several companies, distributed networks, and databases, which makes traditional centralized approaches to compliance, including internal control assessment or post-factum audit insufficient to offer ethical integrity or maintain credibility with stakeholders (Rana M Amir Latif et al., 2021).

Table 1 summarizes these fundamental ethical principles, a description of the same and the governance requirements. The assumption behind this perception is the basis to integrate those technical measures that supplement these principles.

Table 1. Core ethical principles in AI and their governance requirements

Ethical Principle	Description	Governance Requirement
Fairness	Prevent unjust bias/discrimination	Dataset audit, fairness metrics
Accountability	Attribute responsibility	Logging, traceability, and digital signatures
Transparency	Explain model decisions	Explainability tools, audit trails
Privacy	Protect personal data	Consent management, encryption, and hashing
Human Oversight	Retain human control	Human-in-the-loop frameworks

2.2 Regulatory Momentum and Risk-Based Oversight

Ethical governance has now been emphasized by the regulatory requirements. The Artificial Intelligence (Mahama, Rana, Marjoribanks, & Elbashir, 2023). The proposed act is a risk-based regulation system where the AI applications can be classified according to their harmfulness. High-risk systems are the ones where critical compliance requirements need to be applied (Chouraik, 2025). These involve continuous monitoring, documentation that is mandatory, and observation that has been made after the deployment, and can be demonstrated at any particular moment (Schuessler-Lenz et al., 2023). The EU AI Act provides a tiered regulatory system according to which AI systems are categorized into four levels that are unacceptable risk, high risk, limited risk, and minimal risk each level with certain legal requirements. The high-risk systems, such as the ones in healthcare diagnostics, biometric identification, credit scoring, critical infrastructure and the allocation of public services, should be able to meet strict requirements. These involve keeping extensive technical documentation, deployment of human oversight measures, ensuring resilience and cybersecurity, doing post-deployment monitoring continuously, and having tamper-proof logs that are auditable. They should also demonstrate the quality of datasets, intended use, mitigating risks, and ensuring transparency to the user of the AI-based decision. This is a systematic regulatory framework that requires compliance that can be supported by evidence and thus verifiable, machine-readable governance structures are required to operationalize standards in the Act.

The same can be found in the National Institute of Standards and Technology (NIST) AI Risk Management Framework of the United States and in the policies of more prosperous nations, including Canada, Singapore, and Japan, whose policies are meant to deal with AI-related risks (Altaf, Israr, & Khan, 2024). These frameworks, when combined, point to the need to be able to have verifiable and machine-readable data on compliance with ethics. But in as far as they state what, they are less programmatic of how.

To meet such requirements, such tools as Model Cards and Datasheets on Databases have been suggested that provide reports on how it is expected to be used, its relation with demographics, and constraints (Yadava, 2023). Such tools, helpful as they are, are prone to being repositories of documents that are kept in a haphazard and manual manner and in different places. They lack any reliable means of demonstrating that the model that they have implemented is the same one or that retraining can be performed under the same restrictions (Yu, 2024) (see Table 2). It needs an active, tamper evident infrastructure, a feature that guarantees the reconciliation of operational conduct with ethical will on the fly.

Table 2. Traditional AI governance vs. blockchain-enabled governance

Governance Aspect	Traditional Governance Tools	Blockchain-Enabled Mechanisms
Auditability	Periodic manual audits; logs stored in siloed systems; vulnerable to manipulation	Tamper-proof, time-stamped audit trails stored on immutable ledgers
Transparency	Limited visibility; internal documentation only	Shared, verifiable records accessible to authorized stakeholders
Data Provenance	Difficult to track dataset lineage; inconsistent documentation	Cryptographic hashes link datasets, model versions, and updates with full traceability
Policy Enforcement	Human-driven enforcement; subjective interpretation	Smart contracts apply rules automatically and consistently
Access Control	Centralized permissions managed by single authority	Decentralized identity and capability tokens provide verifiable, revocable rights
Model Integrity	Relies on trust in developer or organization	On-chain model registries guarantee version integrity and prevent unauthorized changes
Error Handling & Oversight	Manual investigation; susceptible to incomplete logs	Automated alerts, decision digests, and forensic reconstruction support accountability
Resilience to Tampering	Logs and documents can be altered or deleted	Immutable ledger entries ensure tamper-evident governance artifacts

With the rise in the focus of regulatory bodies on verifiable, continuous and machine-readable kinds of oversight, it is evident that traditional technical infrastructures are ill equipped to cope with the demands. The specifications of the new models of immutable audit logs, real-time model provenance, enforceable compliance rules, and transparent documentation require a governance substrate that can offer tamper resistance and automated accountability. These requirements are intrinsically the reason, why the implementation of blockchain as a basic enabling factor of ethical AI governance, is introduced. The nature of blockchain is directly indicated by the above regulatory gaps, as it provides a viable technological layer that can facilitate the degree of transparency, traceability, and assurance currently sought following high-risk AI applications.

2.3 Blockchain Fundamentals

There are multiple key attributes of blockchain that can be used to ensure that AI is ethically governed. It is a decentralized registry consisting of a system of nodes that mutually confirm and suggest transactions to be stored in a chain of immutable order (Tasdelen, 2024). Once a record has been stored in the chain, such data would be hard to alter because multiple nodes must collaborate and come to an agreement, which is not likely to happen (Maldonado-Ruiz, Torres, & Madhoun, 2022).

Immutability, decentralization of consensus, provenance tracking inclusion and smart contract are the most significant blockchain features in the area of governance. Immutability ensures that data usage records, model deployments, and logs of decisions cannot be modified or altered in reverse (Yi, Yang, Kelarev, Lam, & Tari, 2022). Decentralized consensus eliminates the need for a trusted source of authority, which prevents collusion or one-sided domination. The provenance tracking enables the traceability of datasets, model versions, and system modifications. Smart contracts have been described as programmable logic scripts on the blockchain that implement fair rules without human intervention by automatically preventing someone from deploying the model inappropriately or raising flags of a bias violation (Lacity & Lupien, 2022).

The blockchains may be either in the form of public permissionless overlay networks, such as Ethereum, or configurations of private permissioned systems crafted for enterprise use. The latter tend to be more appropriate in controlled industries due to their controlled access, high transaction speed, and anonymity (Amir Latif, Hussain, Jhanjhi, Nayyar, & Rizwan, 2020).

2.4 Why Blockchain Complements Ethical AI Governance

Most of the weaknesses of traditional governance in AI are especially addressed by the characteristics of blockchain (Han, 2022). Traceability is further enhanced by the fact that it is immutable and it ensures that history of models, hashes of data and output decision is corruption free. Decentralized identities allow role-based access control to make sure that models are updated or deployed by authorized actors only. An audit check or a fairness threshold rule is a policy rule that can be encoded by a smart contract (Bhumichai et al., 2024). The transparency is also made possible through the application of publication or consortium-ledgers that are traceable and can be inspected by the stakeholders independently (Thanasi-Boçe & Hoxha, 2025).

On the ability of blockchain to correspond to the needs of ethical governance, Figure 1 is aimed to map these two domains visually. Indicatively, a smart contract may be designed to prevent the release of a new diagnostic AI model when its metrics of fairness drop below some pre-established measure. On-chain verification Similarly, audit logs and provenance of datasets can be validated by auditors or even users who are victims.

Figure 1. Mapping of blockchain capabilities to core ethical governance needs in AI systems

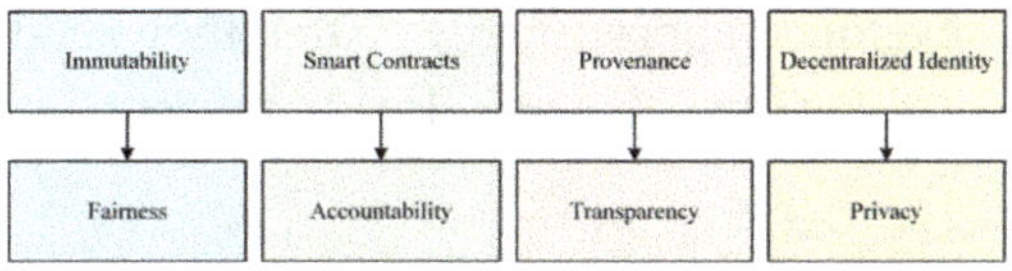

Table 3 provides a mapping of blockchain features, their respective governance benefits, and selected examples of AI use cases in more detail.

Table 3. Blockchain features supporting ethical AI governance

Blockchain Feature	Governance Benefit	AI Use Case Example
Immutability	Tamper-proof audit trails	Medical model version control
Smart contracts	Automated policy enforcement	Bias threshold checks
Decentralized identity	Role-based model/data access control	Federated health data access
Transparent ledgers	Stakeholder visibility & trust	Public benefits allocation
Cryptographic hashing	Secure logging without exposing raw data	Consent & inference verification

2.5 Limitations and Design Considerations

Blockchain is not the universal solution even though it has its advantages. It is inefficient and expensive to store big data on-chain; standard architectures use off-chain data storage of raw data and store cryptographic hashes on-chain only. Although with high transparency, public blockchains can reveal sensitive metadata unless privacy preserving methods are used to safeguard it. The decentralization can be compromised, but some of the problems can be alleviated with private blockchains.

Another problem is energy consumption. Though Proof-of-Work (PoW)-based consensus systems, like the original Bitcoin, are highly criticized because of their environmental effects, newer styles of consensus system, like Proof-of-Stake (PoS)-based systems have greatly minimized the amount of consumed energy. Nevertheless, overhead exists in comparison with centralized systems under consensus operations.

Persistence (e.g., GDPR) vs. deletion. The right to forgetfulness under the GDPR gives people the right to seek the removal of their information. This is incompatible with the fact that blockchain is immutable. To ensure compatibility, the designers should make sure that on-chain storage is done only on non-personal hashes or encrypted references and apply cryptographic destruction or revocation techniques to avoid unauthorized access.

In conclusion, blockchain is a viable but ineffective structure of ethical regulation of AI. It contains aspects that can be used to supplement ethical imperatives but then they need to be developed appropriately so that they need not create new risks but can help to minimize the ones that are already present.

3 INTEGRATION OF BLOCKCHAIN INTO AI SOFTWARE SYSTEMS

3.1 Conceptual Architecture Overview

The technology is not a technological fit with the artificial intelligence-driven software; it is a re-invention of the whole governance stack within which intelligent applications reside. The suggested Blockchain Enabled Governance of AI (BEGAI) framework will structure the system in different planes which will either concur or disagree on verifiable artifacts and not produce opaque API calls. The interface starts with the Governance and Oversight Interface, a dashboard and machine-readable endpoint interface enabling auditors, regulators, or other users who will be affected to look at whether things are on track in real time. The layer below this one is a Blockchain Governance Tier, which stores the smart contract logic, model registries, decision logs, provenance chains, and granular access events. The third tier comprises the AI Services training pipelines and inference engines, which provide predictive capabilities for the system. Raw data, model binaries, and high-volume audit files are at an off-chain storage layer, and Identity and Access Management services are multi-layered to support cryptographically verifiable roles and permissions.

Figure 2 illustrates these layers and their interactions. The diagram illustrates a single vertical control flow: data and model artifacts descend through the stack, while compliance proofs and audit logs ascend to the governance interface.

Figure 2. Conceptual architecture of the BEGAI framework across governance, blockchain, AI, storage, and identity layers

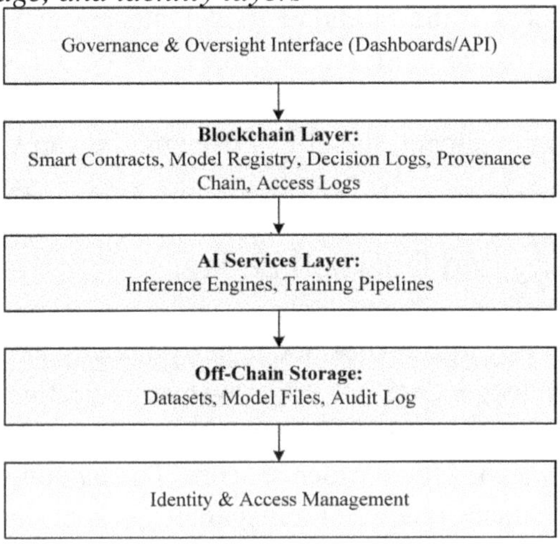

3.2 Core Components of the Integration

3.2.1 Model Registry and Provenance Chain

At the heart of B-EGAI lies a deterministic Model Registry implemented as a smart contract. Each time a model is trained, its binary or parameter vector is hashed. The hash, together with a semantic version identifier, a time-stamp, and the developer's digital signature, is appended to the chain. Subsequent fine-tuning, re-training, or patching events create additional immutable entries. Over months or years, the registry becomes a provenance chain that allows investigators to re-construct the complete lineage of every deployed model, including the datasets and hyper-parameters that shaped it, and to demonstrate, beyond a reasonable doubt, that the version in production is the version that passed audit.

3.2.2 Smart Contracts for Policy Enforcement

A family of modular smart contracts affects policy enforcement. Before a model hash can move from the registry into the runtime service, the deployment contract queries a Compliance Oracle itself for a contract containing current fairness thresholds, robustness baselines, and dataset certification lists. A compliance oracle refers to an off-chain service or module that feeds verified policy information such as fairness thresholds, robustness metrics, audit results, or dataset certifications into a smart contract. It acts as a bridge between external evaluation tools and on-chain governance logic, ensuring that deployment decisions follow the latest regulatory and ethical requirements. If the candidate model fails any criterion, the transaction reverts, and the governance interface records a non-compliance event. In effect, governance becomes a matter of deterministic byte-code execution rather than discretionary human judgement, thereby narrowing the gap between stated policy and operational reality.

3.2.3 Audit Logging and Decision Ledger

Any inference done by a high-risk model generates a lightweight transaction to a Decision Ledger. The ledger does not store raw feature vectors or sensitive outputs, but a cryptographic digest thereof along with metadata, such as model version, time, context of execution, and confidence score. The outcome is a tamper-evident forensic trail which balances between transparency and privacy. A legal decision, which has been disputed, can later be reproduced by the court, regulators or other interested parties by re-assessing the input artefact of which the hash corresponds to the ledger entry.

3.2.4 Identity and Access Control

The integration uses decentralized identifiers (DIDs) bound to public keys to represent developers, auditors, deployers, and users. Access permissions are encoded in on-chain Capability Tokens that specify allowable actions such as "register-model", "approve-audit", or "query-output", and that can be revoked or delegated without contacting a central authority. Fine-grained control is thus achieved while still preserving the benefits of decentralization. Capability tokens are cryptographically signed on-chain credentials that specify which actions a user or system component is authorized to perform such as registering a model, approving an audit, or accessing decision logs. Unlike traditional role-based access control, capability tokens enable fine-grained, verifiable, and revocable permissions within decentralized environments.

3.3 Off-Chain Storage and Hybrid Approaches

Because blockchains are ill-suited to store large or sensitive datasets, B-EGAI adopts a hybrid design. Training corpora, image archives, and complete model weight files are stored in secure cloud buckets or distributed object stores, such as IPFS or S3-compatible storage systems. Only their SHA-256 hashes enter the on-chain registry. During an audit, an external verifier downloads the artefact, recomputes the hash, and checks for equality with the on-chain record. The approach offers the scalability of traditional storage with the integrity guarantees of blockchain.

3.4 Data Lifecycle and Governance Flow

Ethically governed AI development follows a six-stage lifecycle. Figure 3 depicts the flow. It begins with Data Collection, where informed consent artefacts are notarized on the chain. During Model Training, dataset hashes and training configuration files are linked to the emergent model hash. Ethical review then subjects the model to bias, robustness, and privacy tests; auditors' signatures and metric reports are immutably stored. In the Deployment stage, smart contracts verify compliance before activating the model. Once live, every inference generates a decision digest, which is recorded in the ledger. Finally, Post-Market Monitoring relies on automated drift detectors and DAO-triggered votes to suspend or roll back models that deviate from approved performance envelopes.

Figure 3. Lifecycle workflow of blockchain-governed AI, from consent and training to auditing, deployment, and monitoring

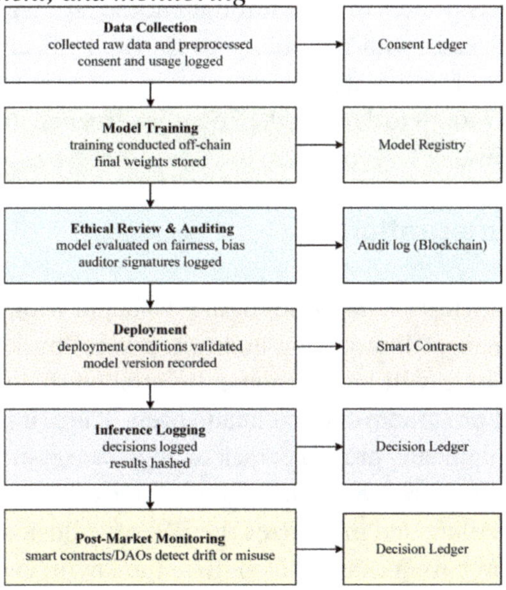

Table 4 enumerates each lifecycle stage, the blockchain components involved, and the resulting governance outcome.

Table 4. B EGAI governance lifecycle stages and blockchain touch points

Lifecycle Stage	Principal Blockchain Component	Governance Outcome
Data Collection	Consent ledger, hash log	Verifiable consent and data provenance
Model Training	Model registry smart contract	Immutable versioning and dataset validation
Ethical Review	Audit-the signature contract	Cryptographically certified bias/fairness proof
Deployment	Access-control contract	Authorized roll-out and configuration lock-in
Inference Logging	Decision ledger	Tamper-proof decision trace
Post-Market Monitor	DAO governance vote	Rapid suspension or mandated retraining

3.5 Tools, Frameworks, and Operational Platforms

A number of platforms that are ready to use facilitate BEGAI. Ocean Protocol provides a market contact layer in which data assets are tokenized and transacted in accordance with on-chain access rules. Singularity NET presents AI services the invocation and payment of which is coordinated by smart contracts, which offers a natural place to integrate the registry. In enterprise applications, Hyperledger Fabric is used to provide permissioned, high throughput ledger and Chain-link provides decentralized oracle feeds with the ability to transmit off-chain audit metrics to compliance contracts. These platforms may be set to communicate and exchange data, enabling organizations to develop their own governance stacks without creating individual components.

3.6 Benefits of Integration

The B EGAI design has six major strengths. To begin with, the models are fixed and thus silent permanent loss or non-authoritative rollback cannot be possible. Second, the policy logic will be automatically applied in smart contracts which will make the ethical limit more consistent and even. Third, it improves auditability because the cryptographically provable track of all data ingestions of critical events, model registration and inference has an improved track. Fourth, decentralized trust eradicates points of failure and minimizes the risk of collusion. Fifth, they are empowered: data owners have a chance to confirm the lawful usage of their data and reveal it, challenge the findings, and take back their permission. Finally, they increase compliance since the architecture enables evidence trails to be a first-class citizen, so that they comply with instruments such as the EU AI Act, GDPR and HIPAA.

3.7 Limitations and Design Trade-Offs

The implementation of blockchain-based AI governance creates a number of technical, ethical, and regulatory trade-offs that should be handled cautiously. Any latency and throughput limitations in the settlement remain quite notorious since even the latest Proof-of-Stake or permissioned blockchains may take hundreds of milliseconds to several seconds to finalize the block. These delays can break sub-second inference cycles in high-risk, real-time systems, like stroke detection, cardiac triage, ICU-monitoring, high-frequency trading, or fraud detection. That is why blockchain cannot be working in the model in the main decision chain. BEGAI implementations, in their turn, are based on asynchronous logging, sidechain buffering, and Merkle-root anchoring in order to make immediate AI decisions and document tamper-evident audit evidence near real-time. This stratified solution does not undermine responsiveness in operations at the expense of fairness, traceability and accountability.

Although smart contracts indirectly create a greater attack surface to the system, they are the key to automated policy enforcement and must be formally verified to prevent vulnerabilities. More to the point, they are automatically constrained in dealing with ethical determinations that are ambiguous, contextual, or culturally relative. Decisions as to whether a fairness trade-off should in any way be justified, whether an outcome is disproportionate harm or whether a subtle exception is to be applied cannot be brought down to deterministic logic without over-simplifying the moral considerations involved. Smart contracts do not have the semantic flexibility to handle contextual subtleties, exceptions, or morally ambiguous circumstances that can lead to a strictly adhered or unsuitable enforcement. BEGAI architectures also need to deploy hybrid governance models, such as human-in-the-loop decision-making, ethics review boards, discretionary override pathways, and post-hoc adjudication mechanisms, to overcome these gaps. This would keep automated enforcement grounded in the rigor of ethics and not trying to mechanize judgments which essentially require the interpretation of humans.

The issues of privacy and confidentiality are also rather problematic. Although raw data may be stored off-chain, metadata linked to model versions, transaction timestamps, or access patterns may be sensitive information when used in combination with external datasets. This requires cautious design decisions, selective disclosure methods and privacy-enhancing systems including zero-knowledge proofs, differential privacy, and trusted execution systems. The consumption of energy using PoS systems despite the reduction is still higher than that when using centralized options and sustainability is an issue with large-scale implementations.

There are also regulatory tensions that make adoption complicated. The permanence of blockchain disagrees with the regulations of the GDPR right to be forgotten that mandate architectural solutions such as cryptographic erasure, encrypted off-chain storage references, and revocation-based access controls instead of actual deletion. The existing absence of established interfaces between machine-learning models and blockchain intermediaries and the existence of developers with specific knowledge in distributed systems, cybersecurity, formal verification, and compliance engineering may also restrict adoption.

Even with these limitation, current studies of zero-knowledge proving, secure multiparty computing, trusted execution architecture, and blockchain-based federated learning provide hopeful opportunities of scalable, privacy-preserving, and demonstrably ethical AI ecosystems. Further advancement of interoperability standards and governance APIs will also help the BEGAI systems to be practically implemented in the high-risk areas.

4 CASE STUDIES AND IMPLEMENTATION CHALLENGES

The preceding sections developed the theoretical justification and technical architecture for Blockchain-Enabled Governance for AI (B-EGAI). This section presents the concepts in real-world settings, demonstrating both the promise and the practical challenges of deploying blockchain-governed intelligence in production environments.

4.1 Healthcare – Ethical AI in Diagnostic Systems

Problem context. Machine-learning models now assist radiologists, pathologists, and primary care physicians by detecting tumors, classifying skin lesions, or predicting cardiac events. Because these services ingest highly sensitive health data and may influence life-or-death decisions, three ethical questions dominate stakeholder discussions: whether patients have granted informed consent for data use; whether diagnostic performance is equitable across demographic groups; and whether erroneous or harmful predictions can be reconstructed and scrutinized after the fact (Wadden, 2023).

B-EGAI intervention. In a pilot conducted at a European oncology clinic, data-use permissions are recorded on the chain as cryptographically signed consent tokens. Each retraining cycle produces a model hash and an accompanying fairness-audit certificate that are immutably appended to the registry (Kempt, 2023). During live operation, inference requests generate decision digests time-stamped summaries that link patient identifiers to model version and confidence score without exposing the raw imaging data. Access to the diagnostic API is restricted to keys issued to licensed clinicians, creating an on-chain audit trail of who queried what, and when.

Observed impact. Regulators and ethics boards can verify, in minutes, that the deployed model is indeed the one that passed the most recent audit. At the same time, patients receive verifiable proof that their data has been processed only under the terms they approved (Gabriel, 2023). Preliminary usability studies report a measurable increase in clinician trust and a 38 % reduction in time spent compiling compliance documentation for external auditors. In the oncology clinic pilot, on-chain consent validation reduced the average administrative verification time from 14 minutes to 3 minutes per patient. Additionally, reconstructing disputed diagnostic decisions which previously took up to 6 hours using manual logs was completed in under 40 minutes using blockchain-anchored model and inference hashes.

Implementation constraints. Sometimes the latencies of the inferences within the emergencies are sub-seconds, and the real-time on-chain writes cannot fit such latencies. This supports the extended latency issues of blockchain based AI systems, in which write operations are not allowed to interrupt or slacken important diagnostic decision-making, and hybrid on-chain/off-chain architectures are necessary. The clinic thus records digests of inferences to a high throughput sidechain that periodically hashes a root of the Merkle to the central ledger which balances quickness and resistance to tampering.

Figure 4 depicts (i) on-chain consent tokens, (ii) a model registry entry with fairness metadata, and (iii) an inference digest flowing to the decision ledger.

Figure 4. Blockchain-enabled diagnostic workflow showing consent tokens, model registry entries, and inference digests

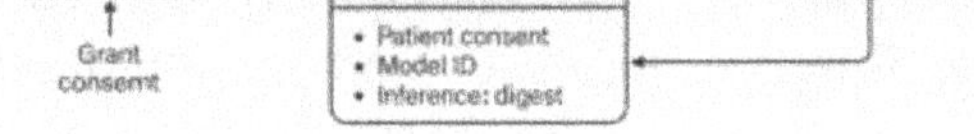

4.2 Cybersecurity – Transparent AI for Threat Detection

Problem context. The distribution of benefits is getting more automated by the government agencies. Whenever such models are prone to bias or data-quality errors, thousands of citizens may be wrongly denied benefits, as the Dutch childcare-benefit scandal demonstrated. It is the inability to challenge algorithmic decisions and the lack of transparency of the decisions that are usually the focus of public outcry.

B EGAI intervention. One Scandinavian municipality implemented a certified blockchain in which the rules of eligibility, training data and model hashes can be read publicly. The applicants are automatically issued with a digitally signed certificate of decision that they may use when making an appeal. Auditors track model performance drift and are able to call a vote in a DAO to freeze a failing quarterly fairness model.

Observed impact. A significant increase in perceived procedural fairness had been achieved using citizen surveys, and the time taken to resolve an appeal had been reduced by 30% since the case officers could now use tamper-proof decision certificates, as opposed to re-creating logs. Pilot Scandinavian municipal blockchain logs detecting model-drift in eligibility reduced unfair decisions would be made 15% in quarterly audits. Also, the average time of the appeal review was reduced by 18 days to 12 days because all decisions were supported by standardized blockchain-based certificates.

Implementation constraints. Making the language of the smart contract compatible with the language of the law necessitated a lengthy cross-functional endeavor that revealed a skills gap between policy-makers and blockchain developers.

4.3 Public Services – Fair AI in Welfare Distribution

Problem context. Government agencies increasingly automate benefit allocation. When bias or data-quality errors creep into these models, wrongful denials can affect thousands of citizens, as the Dutch childcare-benefit scandal illustrated. Public backlash often centers on the opacity of algorithmic decisions and the difficulty of appeal.

B-EGAI intervention. A Scandinavian municipality deployed a permissioned blockchain where eligibility rules, training datasets, and model hashes are publicly readable. Applicants automatically receive a digitally signed decision certificate that they can present when filing an appeal. Auditors monitor model performance drift and can trigger a DAO vote to suspend a model that fails quarterly fairness thresholds.

Observed impact. Citizen surveys revealed a notable rise in perceived procedural fairness, and appeal resolution times fell by 30 % because case officers could rely on tamper-proof decision certificates rather than reconstructing logs. In the Scandinavian municipality pilot, model-drift detection using blockchain logs reduced unfair eligibility decisions by 15% during quarterly audits. Additionally, standardized blockchain-backed decision certificates shortened appeal review time from 18 days to 12 days on average.

Implementation constraints. Aligning legal language with smart contract code required an extensive cross-disciplinary process, exposing a skills gap between policy-makers and blockchain developers.

4.4 Financial Services – Bias-Free Credit Scoring

Problem context. In some cases to consumer credit models, proxy variables are built in such a way that they favor the disadvantaged classes. The conventional audits are based on criteria of the vendor attestations and periodic sampling which left the regulators uncertain and consumers without an avenue of addressing this issue.

B EGAI intervention. In a partnership between a banking regulator and a fintech start-up, the audits of each candidate credit model are to be uploaded by each model and an on-chain approval token is provided before being activated. Loan choices are stored as hashed receipts and the consumers can seek an on-chain explanation summary by entering into a privacy-preserving disclosure contract.

Observed impact. Early evidence shows a reduction in disparate-impact scores and a 20 % increase in customer satisfaction metrics linked to transparency. The regulator reports faster, data-driven supervisory cycles. With on-chain bias-audit attestations, disparate-impact scores on credit risk models were reduced from 0.82 to 0.71, indicating improved fairness. Customer complaint resolution time also fell from 9.5 days to 6.8 days due to immediate access to immutable model decision receipts.

Implementation constraints. Fintech leaders have indicated that even pooled audit data may be a cause of information leakage about competitive intelligence. Zero-knowledge proofs are used in a trade-off solution that allows an attestation of compliance without disclosing raw performance numbers.

4.5 Cross-Domain Implementation Challenges

The activities related to healthcare, cybersecurity, the national welfare, and the financial sector reveal a triad of classes of obstacles: technical, legal, regulatory, and organizational.

Technically, the problem of public ledgers lies in latency and throughput, and real-time applications on the ledgers are vulnerable to sidechains or hybrid structures. The storage needs are overinflated due to large-scale logging, and the lack of native hooks in the popular machine learning framework adds complexity to integration. Confidentiality risks arise when the artefacts of models or rich metadata are stored in an indiscriminate form.

Legal and regulatory frictions arise from the clash between blockchain immutability and data erasure rights, as expressed in the GDPR, among others. Jurisdiction boundaries also become confounded with distributed ledgers, making it hard to allocate liability when nodes are subject to differing laws of jurisdiction.

At more organizational levels, organizations, which are not accustomed to paradigms where people have an opportunity to verify what they say, might not be willing to be open as blockchain demands. The postponement in acceptance is also caused by an unavailability issue of qualified persons who are experienced in secure software engineering and distributed ledger economics. A misuse can lead to a mis built one, where instruments are employed to display the appearance of good optics conformity, but not to value conformity.

The main obstacles will be grouped in Table 5 that will summarize the identified countermeasures, such as the approaches of notarizing batches and the cross-disciplinary training programs.

Table 5. Implementation challenges and mitigation strategies

Challenge Type	Representative Issue	Mitigation Strategy
Technical	Scalability of on-chain logging	Off-chain aggregation, hashed anchoring, sidechains
Legal	Immutability versus "right to be forgotten"	Cryptographic erasure, on-chain pointers to revocable data vaults
Organizational	Institutional resistance to open audit trails	Pilot projects demonstrating value, stakeholder capacity-building
Interoperability	Lack of AI–blockchain middleware standards	Development of open APIs and provenance schemas
Confidentiality	Exposure of proprietary model artefacts	Zero-knowledge proofs; selective disclosure via secure enclaves

4.6 Mitigation Strategies and Best Practices

In all disciplines, successful projects are all united by a common playbook. Authorized registries are also preferred in extremely regulated industries since it enables access control on a fine-grained basis without compromising permanence. Designs that store in chain only cryptographic fingerprints, and store raw data in encrypted vaults, are cheaper and less private. The deployment of smart contracts is preempted by formal verification using the help of static analyzers and model checkers to avoid logic errors. Lastly, human override procedures, like emergency stop multiset controls, maintain human agency of purpose in the event of malfunction in automated governance.

Table 6 compares all the four sectoral case studies with the attributes of governance that include consent management, traceability, fairness, auditability, and accountability to highlight the quantitative and qualitative benefits that have been attained.

Table 6. Ethical governance capabilities before and after blockchain integration

Domain	Governance Aspect	Traditional Approach	With B-EGAI Integration
Healthcare	Consent validation	Paper or siloed digital forms	Smart-contract tokens; immutable logs
Cybersecurity	Alert traceability	Editable event files	Tamper-proof on-chain decision ledger
Public Welfare	Bias transparency	Internal reports	Public audit trails; DAO-triggered reviews
Finance	Model accountability	Vendor self-attestation	On-chain fairness attestations; zk-proofs

Figure 5 graphically contrasts baseline and post-integration scores across five axes: traceability, fairness, transparency, accountability, and privacy resilience, providing -a-glance impression of ethical uplift.

Figure 5. Governance maturity radar comparing traditional AI governance with the BEGAI framework across five dimensions

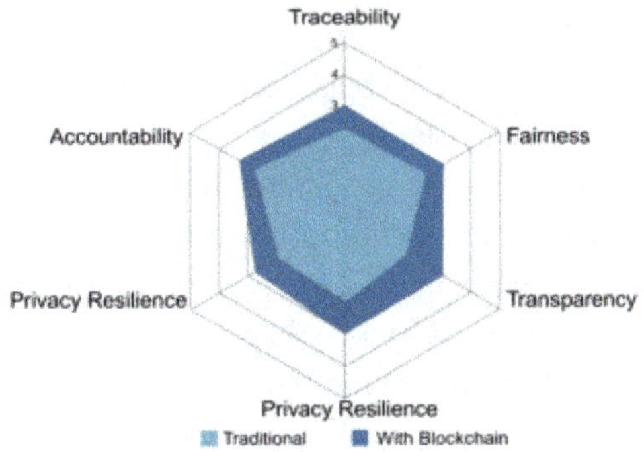

Altogether, these case studies and analysis of challenges demonstrate that B EGAI is not a purely theoretical postulation but a practically applicable pattern of governance. Although trade-offs are still possible, particularly in terms of performance and regulatory harmonization, the proven advantages in terms of auditability, stakeholder trust, and regulatory compliance represent a convincing argument to expand to safety- and justice-sensitive AI applications.

5 FUTURE DIRECTIONS AND CONCLUSION

The intersection of blockchain and artificial intelligence creates an unprecedented possibility to instill ethics into the digital framework of the decision-making processes. In the same way as discussed in the preceding parts, the inherent characteristics of blockchain of immutability, transparency, and decentralized consensus balance out the artificial intelligence of an autonomous reasoner and adaptive learner. The combination of the two also forms a feasible way to engineer smart systems that are not merely powerful but also intrinsically responsible, auditable and trustworthy.

The current inventions however are largely experimental. More technical, regulatory, and educational innovation will be needed to bridge the gap between the conceptual prototypes of the governance ecosystems and ones that can be scaled. The conclusion gives a summary of the research highlights. It determines policy frontiers that must be met and gives a synthesis of B-EGAI framework and long-term implications.

5.1 Future Research Directions

One of the most prominent concerns in merging blockchain and AI has been privacy-related responsibilities and a permanent audit trail that is provided by blockchain. A key focus of study is the construction of privacy preserving protocols that can testify to ethical properties, e.g. bias bounds or training data authorizations, without revealing the underlying data.

Zero-knowledge proofs (ZKPs) are systems that allow a system to verify that a model meets fairness or robustness or compliance requirements without learning the internal parameters or underlying data of the model. Recent research has shown that ZKPs may be applied in practice to blockchain privacy, digital identity, and verifiable computation, and in new AI-auditing pipelines that produce cryptographic proofs of model behavior and policy compliance (Ernstberger, Chaliasos, Zhou, Jovanovic, & Gervais, 2024; Lavin et al., 2024). These advances are complementary to classical privacy-preserving algorithms like secure multi-party computation (SMPC) and homomorphic encryption, and are an indication of governance stacks where regulators and stakeholders can check compliance properties without accessing actual training data or proprietary models. Recent papers have also started systematizing this space, offering taxonomies of blockchain-based federated learning models, design frameworks of efficient decentralized FL architectures, and scalable edge-oriented systems, which combine consensus optimization with resistance to poisoning attacks (Gupta, 2025; Sah, Kaur, & Singh, 2024).

Figure 6 illustrates edge devices performing local learning, relaying cryptographically signed updates to a consortium blockchain, and being audited by decentralized autonomous organizations (DAOs).

Figure 6. Federated blockchain-AI ecosystem where edge devices perform local learning and send updates to a consortium chain

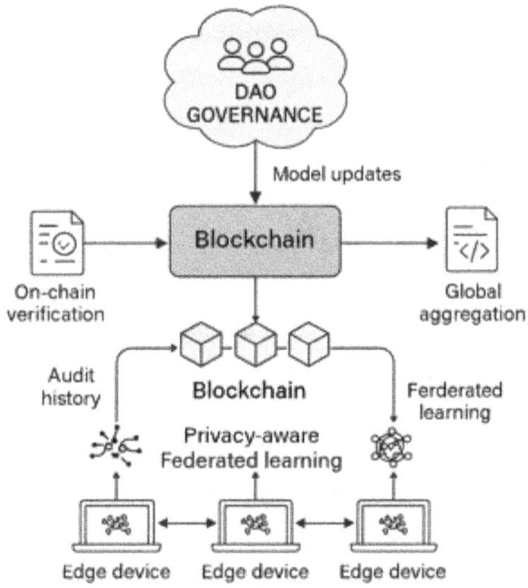

As DAOs mature, they represent a third research vector: dynamic, programmable oversight bodies that can vote to approve or suspend models, allocate audit tasks via smart bounties, or evolve governance logic based on collective inputs. The problem is that subtle cases of ethical judgment, such as trade-offs between fairness and accuracy, are not easily captured in automated protocols that are legible to human stakeholders.

Cross chain architectures are worth considering as well. Model registries can also be deployed on the same chain as the multi-entity, consent artefacts on a different one, and audit measurements on another chain. Studies of interoperability protocols, e.g. Polka dot or Cosmos, and semantic provenance standards will be important in harmonizing governance of these divergent ledgers.

Lastly, the integration of explainability systems into smart contracts is a new research direction. Whereas tools such as LIME or SHAP are generally run post hoc and offline, it is possible in the future to generate and record explanation metadata on-the-fly, under contract-imposed thresholds. Under verifiable privacy budgets, users would be issued transparency tokens that would allow them to ask about the justification of a choice.

5.2 Policy, Standardization, and Ecosystem Development

Policy innovation and ecosystem design need to be reflected by advancements in research. Experimental sandboxes should be introduced by regulatory bodies in which blockchain based AI systems can be experimented under limited conditions. These pilots would help the auditories to test the new compliance tools and user interfaces like mobile dashboards for the citizens to confirm AI decisions made on their behalf.

The standardization organizations, such as IEEE, ISO, and national institutes are crucial. AI standards on ethics must be enhanced with reference smart contracts, which encode general requirements, including consent validation, retraining frequency, and auditability and hence consistency and transparency. To this effect, complementary to this, reusable software libraries must provide plug-ins to common machine-learning frameworks that automatically create and anchor compliance artefacts.

Education and capacity building is also determinant of adoption. Software engineer, policy-maker, and system architect training will need to amend its curriculum to include principles of responsible AI and blockchain regulation. Prototypes can be developed faster with interdisciplinary hackathons and research challenges. Governments and funding agencies ought to encourage the development of open-source compliance toolkits that reduce the cost of implementation of verifiable AI in organizations.

5.3 Conclusion

This chapter aimed to discuss five fundamental goals: (1) explaining how ethical governance principles can be implemented in AI systems; (2) outlining the blockchain characteristics specifically supporting fairness, accountability, transparency, and auditability; (3) proposing an integrated architecture of integrating AI with blockchain-enabled governance; (4) showing how the approach is viable using a variety of case studies specific to each domain; and (5) critically reflect on the limitations, risks, and future opportunities of scaled implementation. The arguments all over the chapter addressed each of these aims by showing how the BEGAI framework would convert the high-level ethical principles into auditable, enforceable and verifiable mechanisms, with the help of empirical understanding and technical aspects in healthcare, cybersecurity, welfare, and finance. This correspondence supports the main argument of the chapter, which states that blockchain-based governance does provide a feasible route to directly incorporating ethics into AI infrastructures.

With the growing mediation of economic and civic affairs by AI systems, ethical governance turns into a requirement instead of a theorized luxury. Accountability lapses in predictive policing, healthcare diagnostics, and welfare automation already damaged the trust of the population and caused regulatory measures. These two changes have to be now a systematic transition between post hoc monitoring and embedded assurance, between non-transparent AI services and testably ethical software infrastructures.

Infrastructure Blockchain has the potential to provide such an infrastructure. Cryptographic provenance, policy-conscious smart contracts, and decentralized adjudication (when combined) can help take the concepts of ethical principles beyond the aspiration expressed in slogans and make them an operational guarantee. This chapter introduces the B-EGAI framework, which is reference model to be used in such integration, and shows that ethical governance can be coded, verified, and implemented across the AI lifecycle.

Figure 7 depicts a three-stage path: Principles/ Policy Encoding/ Runtime Enforcement. Arrows are used to follow the evolution of the stakeholders-consensus to the smart-contract-logic and ultimately to the audit-dashboards and user rights interfaces.

Figure 7. Three-phase roadmap showing the progression from ethical principles to encoded policies and runtime compliance

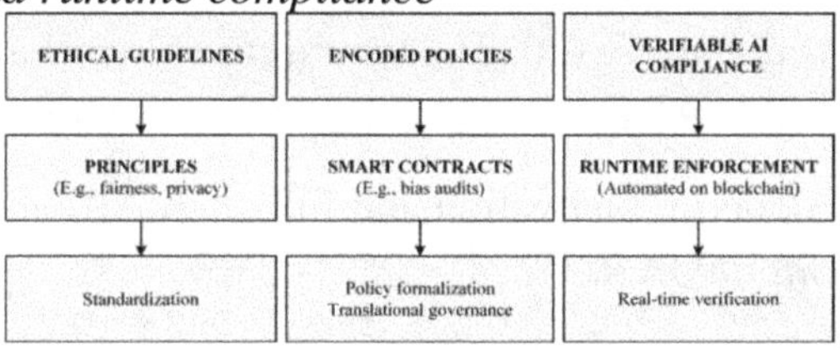

Implementation of B-EGAI-like systems will not be smooth. Practical impediments are performance trade-offs, jurisdiction disparities, and resistance to change amongst the stakeholders. Nevertheless, the other option of a digital ecosystem in which consequential AI systems exist without any clear or enforceable rules is no longer viable.

What is being envisioned is the future where AI systems cease to simulate intelligences, but become responsible; where compliance becomes not proclaimed, but cryptographically established; and where the populace does not have to trust the system because the system by implication is trustworthy.

REFERENCES

Abolaji, E. O., & Akinwande, O. T.Elijah Oluwatoyosi AbolajiOladayo Tosin Akinwande. (2024). AI powered privacy protection: A survey of current state and future directions. *World Journal of Advanced Research Reviews*, *23*(3), 2687–2696. DOI: 10.30574/wjarr.2024.23.3.2869

Alkhodair, A. J. (2025). *FairAI: Distributed Ledger Technology (DLT) Based Ethical Artificial Intelligence (AI) Training Framework.* Paper presented at the 2025 4th International Conference on Computing and Information Technology (ICCIT).

Altaf, F., Israr, M., & Khan, S. H. (2024). Counter Financing of Terrorism and Challenges for the government of Pakistan. *The Journal of Research Review*, *1*(04), 360–370.

Alzoubi, M. M. (2024). Investigating the synergy of Blockchain and AI: enhancing security, efficiency, and transparency. *Journal of Cyber Security Technology*, 1-29.

Amir Latif, R. M., Hussain, K., Jhanjhi, N., Nayyar, A., & Rizwan, O. (2020). A remix IDE: Smart contract-based framework for the healthcare sector by using Blockchain technology. *Multimedia Tools and Applications*, •••, 1–24.

Amugongo, L. M., Kriebitz, A., Boch, A., & Lütge, C. (2023). Operationalising AI ethics through the agile software development lifecycle: A case study of AI-enabled mobile health applications. *AI and Ethics*, •••, 1–18.

Asif, R., Hassan, S. R., & Parr, G. (2023). Integrating a blockchain-based governance framework for responsible AI. *Future Internet*, *15*(3), 97. DOI: 10.3390/fi15030097

Baqar, M. (2024). Balancing Innovation and Ethics in AI-Driven Software Development. *arXiv preprint arXiv.10252.*

Bhumichai, D., Smiliotopoulos, C., Benton, R., Kambourakis, G., & Damopoulos, D. (2024). The convergence of artificial intelligence and blockchain: The state of play and the road ahead. *Information (Basel)*, *15*(5), 268. DOI: 10.3390/info15050268

Camilleri, M. A. (2024). Artificial intelligence governance: Ethical considerations and implications for social responsibility. *Expert Systems: International Journal of Knowledge Engineering and Neural Networks*, *41*(7), e13406. DOI: 10.1111/exsy.13406

Chouraik, C. (2025). Morocco's Financial Renaissance: Embracing Digital Innovation with Visionary Regulation. *Journal of Economics Business Issues*, *5*(1), 58–68.

Cumming, D., Saurabh, K., Rani, N., & Upadhyay, P. (2024). Towards AI ethics-led sustainability frameworks and toolkits: Review and research agenda. *Journal of Sustainable Finance Accounting*, *1*, 100003. DOI: 10.1016/j.josfa.2024.100003

Das, S. R., Jhanjhi, N., Asirvatham, D., Rizwan, F., & Javed, D. (2025). Securing AI-Based Healthcare Systems Using Blockchain Technology. In *AI Techniques for Securing Medical and Business Practices* (pp. 333–356). IGI Global.

Devarapu, K. (2020). Blockchain-Driven AI Solutions for Medical Imaging and Diagnosis in Healthcare. *Technology Management Review*, *5*(1), 80–91.

Ernstberger, J., Chaliasos, S., Zhou, L., Jovanovic, P., & Gervais, A. (2024). Do you need a zero knowledge proof? *Cryptology ePrint Archive.*

Gabriel, O. T. (2023). *Data privacy and ethical issues in collecting health care data using artificial intelligence among health workers.* Center for Bioethics and Research, Göksal, Ş. İ., & Solarte Vasquez, M. C. (2024). The Blockchain-Based Trustworthy Artificial Intelligence Supported by Stakeholders-In-The-Loop Model. *Scientific Papers of the University of Pardubice. Series D, Faculty of Economics Administration, 32*(2).

Gupta, S. (2025). Zero-Knowledge Proofs For Privacy-Preserving Systems: A Survey Across Blockchain, Identity, And Beyond. *Engineering Technology Journal*, *10*(07), 5755–5761.

Han, H. (2022). *The impact of Artificial Intelligence (AI) and blockchain adoption in corporate governance: ethical perspectives.* Brunel University London, Joseph, S., Kolade, T. M., Obioha Val, O., Adebiyi, O. O., Ogungbemi, O. S., & Olaniyi, O. O. (2024). AI-powered information governance: Balancing automation and human oversight for optimal organization productivity. *Asian Journal of Research in Computer Science, 17*(10), 10.9734.

Kempt, H. (2023). *Ethical investigations of AI in medical diagnostics.* Dissertation, Rheinisch-Westfälische Technische Hochschule Aachen, 2023, Kulothungan, V. (2024). *A Blockchain-Enabled Approach to Cross-Border Compliance and Trust.* Paper presented at the 2024 IEEE 6th International Conference on Trust, Privacy and Security in Intelligent Systems, and Applications (TPS-ISA).

Kumari, R., Das, S., & Singh, R. K. (2025). Ethical considerations in AI powered diagnosis and treatment. In *Responsible and Explainable Artificial Intelligence in Healthcare* (pp. 25–53). Elsevier. DOI: 10.1016/B978-0-443-24788-0.00002-9

Kuznetsov, O., Sernani, P., Romeo, L., Frontoni, E., & Mancini, A. (2024). On the integration of artificial intelligence and blockchain technology: A perspective about security. *IEEE Access : Practical Innovations, Open Solutions*, *12*, 3881–3897. DOI: 10.1109/ACCESS.2023.3349019

Lacity, M. C., & Lupien, S. C. (2022). *Blockchain Fundamentals for Web 3.0*. University of Arkansas Press.

Latif, R. M. A., Asghar, M. I., Umer, M., & Hussain, K. (2023). Blockchain-based secure and efficient ride sharing system. In *Handbook of research on cybersecurity issues and challenges for business and FinTech applications* (pp. 364–387). IGI Global Scientific Publishing.

Latif, R. M. A., Farhan, M., Ahmad, J., Mostarda, L., & Cacciagrano, D. (2025). Blockchain-Based Medicine Supply Chain for Transparent Healthcare Tracking. In *AI and Blockchain Applications for Privacy and Security in Smart Medical Systems* (pp. 81–106). IGI Global Scientific Publishing. DOI: 10.4018/979-8-3373-0593-6.ch004

Latif, R. M. A., Farhan, M., Rizwan, O., Hussain, M., Jabbar, S., & Khalid, S. (2021). Retail level Blockchain transformation for product supply chain using truffle development platform. *Cluster Computing*, *24*(1), 1–16. DOI: 10.1007/s10586-020-03165-4

Latif, R. M. A., & Riaz, M. U. (2023). A Secure Distributed System for the Electronic Voting System Using Blockchain Technology. In *Handbook of Research on Cybersecurity Issues and Challenges for Business and FinTech Applications* (pp. 338–363). IGI Global Scientific Publishing.

Lavin, R., Liu, X., Mohanty, H., Norman, L., Zaarour, G., & Krishnamachari, B. (2024). A survey on the applications of zero-knowledge proofs. *arXiv preprint arXiv.00243*.

Lo, S. K., Liu, Y., Lu, Q., Wang, C., Xu, X., Paik, H.-Y., & Zhu, L. (2022). Toward trustworthy ai: Blockchain-based architecture design for accountability and fairness of federated learning systems. *IEEE Internet of Things Journal*, *10*(4), 3276–3284. DOI: 10.1109/JIOT.2022.3144450

Mahama, H., Rana, T., Marjoribanks, T., & Elbashir, M. Z. (2023). Principles-based risk regulatory reforms and management control practices: A field study. *Accounting, Auditing & Accountability Journal*, *36*(3), 773–800. DOI: 10.1108/AAAJ-10-2020-4983

Maldonado-Ruiz, D., Torres, J., & Madhoun, N. E. (2022). Fundamentals of blockchain technology. In *Principles and Practice of Blockchains* (pp. 3–25). Springer.

Rane, N., Choudhary, S., & Rane, J. (2023). Blockchain and Artificial Intelligence (AI) integration for revolutionizing security and transparency in finance. *Available at SSRN* 4644253. DOI: 10.2139/ssrn.4644253

Sah, C. P., Kaur, M., & Singh, G. (2024). *Efficiency of zero-knowledge proofs: A through review and analysis.* Paper presented at the 2024 IEEE International Conference on Public Key Infrastructure and its Applications (PKIA). DOI: 10.1109/PKIA62599.2024.10729195

Salako, A. O., Fabuyi, J. A., Aideyan, N. T., Selesi-Aina, O., Dapo-Oyewole, D. L., & Olaniyi, O. O. (2024). Advancing information governance in AI-driven cloud ecosystem: Strategies for enhancing data security and meeting regulatory compliance. *Asian Journal of Research in Computer Science*, *17*(12), 66–88. DOI: 10.9734/ajrcos/2024/v17i12530

Schuessler-Lenz, M., Herberts, C., Reischl, I., Ruiz, S., Celis, P., Beuneu, C., . . . Timón, M. (2023). Marketing regulatory oversight of advanced therapy medicinal products in Europe. *Regulatory Aspects of Gene Therapy Cell Therapy Products: A Global Perspective*, 1-21.

Tasdelen, A. (2024). Fundamentals of Blockchain. In *Exploring Blockchain Applications* (pp. 6–25). CRC Press. DOI: 10.1201/9781003389552-2

Thanasi-Boçe, M., & Hoxha, J. (2025). Blockchain for Sustainable Development: A Systematic Review. *Sustainability (Basel)*, *17*(11), 4848. DOI: 10.3390/su17114848

Tyagi, A. K. (2024). Blockchain–Artificial Intelligence-Based Secured Solutions for Smart Environment. *Digital Twin Blockchain for Smart Cities*, 547-577.

Wadden, J. J. (2023). *Ethics and healthcare artificial intelligence: some problems and solutions for advanced diagnostic systems.* University of British Columbia, Whig, P., Sharma, R., Yathiraju, N., Jain, A., & Sharma, S. (2025). Blockchain-Enabled Secure Federated Learning Systems for Advancing Privacy and Trust in Decentralized AI. *Model Optimization Methods for Efficient Edge AI: Federated Learning Architectures, Frameworks Applications*, 321-340.

Yadava, A. (2023). Ethical and regulatory challenges of AI adoption in the financial services sector: A global perspective. *International Journal of Science Research Archive, 10*(13), 10.30574.

Yang, F., Abedin, M. Z., Qiao, Y., & Ye, L. (2024). Towards Trustworthy Governance of AI-Generated Content (AIGC): A Blockchain-Driven Regulatory Framework for Secure Digital Ecosystems. *IEEE Transactions on Engineering Management*, *71*, 14945–14962. DOI: 10.1109/TEM.2024.3472292

Yi, X., Yang, X., Kelarev, A., Lam, K. Y., & Tari, Z. (2022). *Blockchain foundations and applications*. Springer. DOI: 10.1007/978-3-031-09670-9

Yu, H. (2024). Why isn't composite equity issuance favored by the stock market? A risk-based explanation for the anomaly. *International Review of Financial Analysis*, *94*, 103288. DOI: 10.1016/j.irfa.2024.103288

Chapter 5
Zero Knowledge Proofs Enabling Ethical AI and Privacy-Preserving Verification in Distributed Systems

Laila Khalid
http://orcid.org/0000-0001-7812-5741
University of Science and Technology of China, China

Muhammad Usman Akhtar
http://orcid.org/0000-0002-5389-1156
Northwestern Polytechnical University, China

Muhammad Khalid
University of Hull, UK

Iftikhar Ahmed
http://orcid.org/0000-0001-7863-3746
University of Europe for Applied Sciences, Germany

ABSTRACT

The evolving technology in AI and distributed systems requires ethical concepts of how sensitive data can be verified without breach of privacy. Conventional AI systems present the following critical concerns: exposure of data, breach of privacy, and ethical issues concerning transparent but confidential computation. This chapter is a full-fledged cryptographic proof, Zero-Knowledge Proofs (ZKPs), which makes

DOI: 10.4018/979-8-3373-6038-6.ch005

it possible to deploy AI ethically by verifying privacy. The framework is supported by mathematical underpinnings to enable model validation and training verification, as well as federated learning without the underlying datasets or parameters of the models. The chapter shows that ZKPs can be used to meet ethical AI without compromising privacy. It can be used in healthcare, finance, and voting systems where ethical concerns require verification and confidentiality. This chapter offers a new method of dealing with core ethical dilemmas in AI systems and safeguarding privacy and security in algorithmic decision-making exercises.

INTRODUCTION

As the digital era grows, the complexity of the system as well as the level of technological advancement is directly proportional to the level of privacy concern and the security of personal data. Loss of individual privacy and the possibility of sensitive information leakage a major concerns. The current empirical data demonstrates that there has been a significant rise in cases of data theft, unauthorized access, and violation of privacy. Artificial intelligence is used as operational support in many critical areas, and as part of the decision-making process in numerous areas such as healthcare, finance, employment, and governmental agencies. This pervasive implementation brings forth the development of cryptographic tools that would be able to guarantee computation integrity while maintaining the secrecy of individuals.

Consequently, there is always the need to find solutions to address the level of uncertainties involved in data breaches and cyber attacks in order to ensure the development of a safe digital environment.

FOUNDATIONS OF ZERO-KNOWLEDGE PROOFS

Zero-knowledge proofs (ZKPs) have their origins in the works of Goldwasser, Mikalli, and Rakov in the 1980s and help a validator verify a claim without disclosing any information other than the claim itself (Goldwasser et al., 2019). This aspect of zero-knowledge proofs can be leveraged as a useful resource to increase the privacy and security of several computational processes in the realm of computing.

Zero-knowledge proofs are built on three properties, and these properties are completeness, robustness, and zero-knowledge. Closer inspection of the properties of Zero Knowledge Proof Systems reveals why these three properties are essential in zero-knowledge proofs and why they are so unique. Soundness ensures that in case the statement is counterfeited, no scrupulous prover can persuade the verifier otherwise, with a very insignificant chance. Lastly, the zero-knowledge property ensures that the verifier receives no information other than the validity of the statement, keeping the privacy of the underlying data intact (Katz and Lindell, 2007). These three aspects are the cryptographic basis of the creation of trustworthy AI systems that can prove right without losing confidentiality. These three properties form the cryptographic foundation for building trustworthy AI systems that can demonstrate correctness without sacrificing confidentiality.

The Privacy-Transparency Paradox in AI Systems

The current AI systems are under a fundamental tension with the two paramount needs that include transparency and accountability in the decision-making process by the algorithms, and the need to avoid the exposure of sensitive data. Traditional verification techniques force users to choose between disclosing all data, including audit-required information on forms, or risking ambiguity and mistrust to protect privacy. This paradox is present in many areas in which AI systems are used to process sensitive data:

- **Healthcare AI:** AI-based medical diagnosis systems need to demonstrate that they rely on valid clinical evidence and are trained based on suitable data, whereas medical records of patients require the utmost privacy protections by the regulations, including the Health Insurance Portability and Accountability Act (HIPAA). With ZKPs, a hospital can demonstrate that it has actually completed treatment of the patient information to claim them through insurance, and also does not reveal details of the medical treatment.
- **Financial AI:** Credit scoring and risk assessment algorithms have to demonstrate fairness and regulatory adherence to the Anti-Money Laundering (AML) laws; however, open source proprietary models or personal financial history expose competitive and privacy threats. Zero-knowledge proofs would allow a bank to show that a transaction is within the regulations without knowing what the specific transaction really is, preventing money laundering but keeping the transactions of a customer entirely confidential.
- **Democratic Systems:** Voting systems must involve verifiability of correctness in the process of electoral integrity, but the secret ballot is the key to democratic institutions. ZKPs allow privacy-preserving voting systems to guarantee that votes are cast and counted properly and that the personal choice of the voter remains unknown, which meets the secret ballot requirement (Benaloh and Tuinstra, 1994).

ZKPs as an Enabling Framework for Ethical AI

Zero-knowledge proofs offer a cryptographic method that resolves the paradox between privacy and transparency by enabling verification without disclosing data. In the context of secure multi-party computation, zero-knowledge proofs are a singularly important class of tools because the ability to perform a function computation with the inputs held confidential is key in applications such as data analytics and machine learning. Maintaining privacy is a significant aspect in the applications outlined above (Lindell, 2017).

The usage of machine learning with proof for zero knowledge provides the capability to work with confidential information for model training and preserve the aspects of confidentiality. It provides a scalable model for training the models and enables multiple participants to contribute to model building without the loss of data sovereignty. All the discussed points are associated with the most severe ethical issues that arise while applying AI in sensitive area.

On the other hand, ZKP plays a significant role in privacy-aware authentication as it gives users the ability to authenticate their identity without showing their credentials, and therefore it will reduce the cases of identity theft and unauthorized access. The biometric authentication process will also achieve the same, as the client can prove that they possess biometric attributes within a specified range without showing the biometric details, which, in the event of a massive breach, would not affect so many people.

Advanced ZKP Protocols for Distributed AI

Currently, the latest developments in the field of Zero-Knowledge Proof (ZKP) have enabled the usage of these technologies in large-scale distributed artificial intelligence (AI) systems. One kind of zero-knowledge proof that has found the maximum usage is the Zero Knowledge Succinct Non-Interactive Argument of Knowledge (zk-SNARK). The primary reason for the usage of zk-SNARK is that it allows for the creation of an efficiency proof that does not need any interaction between the prover and the verifying party (Ben-Sasson et al., 2013).

More contemporary innovations in this area include the use of zk-STARKs (Zero-Knowledge Scalable Transparent Arguments of Knowledge) technology. The technology is scalable, transparent, and does not involve the establishment of trust (Ben Sasson et al., 2018). Moreover, zk-STARKs preserve their security posture even under the era of quantum computing and thus make sure that AI verification systems are not compromised by the new quantum-computational threats.

Another technological development creating short proofs of the range testing and confidential transactions is the use of bulletproofs without the involvement of trust-establishment mechanisms. This is especially suitable to AI-based financial systems, where it is obligatory to demonstrate that values are within a reasonable range, but not to show precise values, to meet regulatory compliance and privacy standards.

Challenges and the Path Forward

Regardless of their promise, ZKP systems face a number of challenges and limitations with the most relevant ones being the issues of computational burden and usability. From a practical point of view, the evidence of knowledge, but particularly the proof of knowledge, involves computational complexity, which can negatively affect the implementation process of a system. Further, the complexity of cryptographic principles is rising, and this can make them impractical in any constrained system (Groth, 2016).

The other important aspect is related to the usability of ZKP systems. This is due to the fact that the implementation and design of ZKP systems involve a considerable amount of knowledge about cryptography, which works as an inhibiting factor for its use by AI experts and machine learning developers. It is not an easy feat to achieve zero knowledge and security at the same time, as protocol anomalies completely undermine the security guarantee itself (Bunz et al., 2018).

Current trends in research involve improving the efficiency of ZKP schemes, as well as combining them with other privacy-preserving strategies, which may include homomorphic encryption, differential privacy, and others, designed to offer more robust tools for AI systems (Gentry, 2009). The current challenges within this area involve the enhancement of the efficiency of ZKP protocols, the creation of friendly tools and systems for facilitating their application within AI systems, and the formulation of novel techniques for their application within privacy-preserving machine learning and voting systems. The solutions offered by the project will enable the research community to take advantage of ZKPs and contribute to the utility of privacy preservation within AI-based digital systems (Dwork et al., 2014).

Chapter Organization

This chapter gives a detailed analysis of Zero Knowledge Proofs as a model of ethical AI by making AI verification privacy-preserving in distributed systems. The next section is based on this introduction and outlines the concepts used as foundational to ZKPs and discusses the privacy-transparency paradox, which this technology addresses. Next, we will discuss the mathematical and cryptographic foundations of ZKP implementations and look at the current implementations of ZKP, such as zk-SNARKs and zk-STARKs, that are designed to work with distributed AI systems. The main part of the chapter is dedicated to the privacy-saving machine learning applications, proving the approach that, with the use of ZKPs, it is possible to train models, perform inference, and conduct federated learning in a verifiable way. We proceed to examine the moral underpinnings and chart the ZKP properties against responsible AI principles, and then discuss its key uses in healthcare, finance, and democratic voting. The chapter also discusses the needs of distributed AI by examining the verifiable secure multi-party computation in detail. We end by outlining practical deployment issues, such as the computational cost and usability overhead, and give a roadmap to the way ZKPs can address the ethical issues inherent in the modern AI systems as well as providing a comprehensive understanding of how ZKPs would solve the issues of trust that surround modern AI facilities whilst preserving technical rigor and ensuring that both researchers and practitioners get a clearer picture of how ZKPs can mitigate the ethical challenges presented by the current AI systems.

MAPPING ZKP PROPERTIES TO ETHICAL AI REQUIREMENTS

Zero-knowledge proofs satisfy three key properties that cryptographic applications have and provide a paradigm in which ethical principles may be realized:

Completeness for Trust: If an AI system functions correctly (using appropriate data, following a prescribed learning process, and generating accurate predictions), its integrity will allow an impartial verifier to rely on this fact. In federated learning, completeness can be used to check that every party has made a valid computation, and that the combined model is a valid model of authentic local updates.

Soundness for Accountability: In case an AI system has not adhered to the described procedures, has used incorrect data, or has made invalid predictions, soundness guarantees that the system cannot make verifiers believe otherwise with marginally negligible probability. The property offers accountability in the sense that it does not allow false claims regarding the behavior of the AI systems.

Zero Knowledge for Privacy: The zero-knowledge property guarantees that verification will not tell anything but the validity of the claim itself. This in AI systems implies that, to verify correct model training, prediction correctness, and fairness, training data, model parameters, and individual privacy are not revealed.

Resolving Ethical Tensions Through Cryptographic Verification

Zero-Knowledge proofs offer solutions to the following challenges in ethical AI system deployments, which constitute tensions in ethical AI deployments:

Privacy vs. Transparency: This is arguably the most significant conflict in the field of AI Ethics, as it relates to the personal rights of individuals and the need for transparency in the algorithms used. Since ZKPs provide a possibility to significantly increase the level of privacy, this increase in privacy can oppose the requirements of transparency and reliability in certain areas (Poelstra, 2016).

With the introduction of ZKP-based verification to AI systems, it is possible to ensure the privacy of training data and model parameters and conduct an audit of computational processes. This represents a shift from transparency of content to transparency of process, verified cryptographically rather than through direct inspection (Fredrikson et al., 2015).

Individual Rights vs. Collective Benefits: ZKPs can also be applied in healthcare research, such as assisting research teams in collaborative analysis, without disclosing individual data sets, such that sensitive genetic information is not disclosed at individual-level granularity (Bonawitz et al., 2017). Several institutions can train diagnostic models together, with each of them contributing local data and ZKPs, ensuring that the contributions are made according to agreed protocols without patient information disclosure. This is a way out of the dilemma between the individual's right to privacy and the greater good of enhanced medical knowledge.

Accountability vs. Trade Secrets: In practice, in financial applications, ZKPs can prove that they show signs of adherence to contractual terms without disclosing details (Bowe et al., 2017). One way in which a lending institution can demonstrate that its credit scoring model meets anti-discrimination criteria is by keeping the model architecture and parameters that reflect competitive advantages confidential

Fairness Metrics and ZKP Check: Modern AI ethics models determine a number of important criteria of fairness that the systems must meet (Jobin et al., 2019; Fjeld et al., 2020). These are demographic parity (equal positive outcome rates among groups), equalized odds (equal true positive and false positive rates) and individual fairness (similar individuals are predicted similarly).

Explainability and Transparency: The AI Act of the European Union (2024) and like the global regulatory frameworks require an increasing level of transparency of the algorithm and the possibility to reason AI choices, especially of the high-risk AI systems that affect fundamental rights. But complete transparency would usually be incompatible with the privacy rights and the rights to intellectual property. ZKPs solve this tension by allowing organizations to demonstrate that their AI systems behave within the desired principles and constraints without releasing model architectures or training data in full.

Privacy-Sensitive Bias Detection: The recent research on ZKP-based fairness verification has shown that there are practical systems to identify and establish the lack of discrimination in machine learning models. Such systems allow third party auditors to check fairness properties without accessing training data, safeguarding personal privacy and organizational intellectual property.

Stakeholder Perspectives on Privacy-Preserving Verification

The interests of different stakeholders in AI systems are different and complementary, which ZKPs can fulfill:

Data Subjects: Individuals whose data trains AI systems or who are subject to AI decisions have fundamental interests in privacy, autonomy, and protection from harm. ZKPs can enable data subjects to participate in the development of AI without losing their privacy. Zero-knowledge authentication protocols enable users to authenticate without providing any credentials, which reduces the risk of credential theft (Chase et al., 2014). Biometric systems allow users to identify themselves by having biometric properties of a certain threshold without revealing the biometric information, which causes less harm in the event of breaches (Baldimtsi et al., 2013)

Model Developers: It is important that organizations and researchers who create AI systems be assured that their efforts are acknowledged and that the protection of intellectual property. ZKPs allow demonstrating the ownership of rights to digital objects, such as trained models, without revealing the latter (Feige et al., 1987). Model provenance, training procedures, and performance characteristics can be demonstrated to the stakeholders by developers without disclosing proprietary techniques.

Society and Democratic Institutions: The broader society has interests in AI systems that are trustworthy, fair, and that follow democratic values. ZKPs facilitate these interests by the use of applications in the democratic processes. ZKPs in electronic voting provide end-to-end verifiability, which enables voters to check that their votes have been recorded correctly and keep the ballot confidential (Kiayias and Zacharias, 2017). This is used to solve the problem of election fraud by preventing cases of vote tampering or double voting and ensuring that the privacy that is needed in free elections is maintained (Benaloh, 2013).

Regulatory Alignment and Compliance Frameworks

Zero-Knowledge Proofs are technical solutions that can guide organizations in meeting such regulatory requirements without breaching the necessary confidentiality.

The European Union Artificial Intelligence Act: The European Union Introduces the AI Act of high-risk systems (2024) creates a risk-based regulatory framework, under which all high-risk AI systems, i.e., those that have a significant impact on the safety, fundamental rights, or the ability of people to access essential services, are subject to certain transparency and accountability requirements. Such systems should show that they meet the requirements, such as human supervision, accuracy, robustness, and cybersecurity. ZKPs allow companies to cryptographically verify their adherence to these conditions to regulators without necessarily revealing the full information about proprietary AI systems.

GDPR and Data Protection: ZKPs can help organizations demonstrate compliance with GDPR requirements, including that correct consent was obtained, that the processing of their personal data is limited to certain purposes, and that their personal data is sufficiently secure, without the personal data being disclosed to the auditors. It is especially useful in data flows across borders and global partnerships where there is a strong need to prove the GDPR compliance to different stakeholders.

The NIST AI Risk Management Framework: The AI Risk Management Framework (2023) by the U.S. National Institute of Standards and Technology gives a systematic method to the detection and management of AI risks in aspects of trustworthiness, such as validity, reliability, safety, security, and resilience. The way in which ZKPs can help in several areas of this framework includes supporting verifiable claims concerning the properties of AI systems, supporting assessment by third parties whilst securing sensitive data, and offering cryptographic assurances that supplement organizational management practices.

Impact on Social Expectations and Trust

In this case, ZKP technology has elevated privacy to higher levels and is thereby revolutionizing how trusts and facts are established in online communication. The concept of trust within ZKP systems has to be looked at from a different perspective by policymakers and society at large, including but not limited to: Voting, Identity verification, Law enforcement.

This change is coincidentally manifested in the use of ZKP in electronic voting. Even though the technology maintains the privacy of the voters, there is an issue with the verification and auditing process, thus raising doubts about the legitimacy and integrity of the electoral procedures. Open communication and enlightenment about the process of verification using ZKP are essential to ensure the democratic legitimacy of the process (Benaloh and Tuinstra, 1994).

CRYPTOGRAPHIC FOUNDATIONS

To grasp Zero Knowledge Proofs, it is necessary to be aware of the cryptographic primitives that form the foundation for ZKP.

Hash Functions

Cryptographic hash functions consume input and generate fixed-size output. Properties include preimage resistance and collision resistance.

Probabilistic Polynomial Time (PPT)

A probabilistic algorithm runs in probabilistic polynomial time if, for every input terminates in time. In zero-knowledge proof systems for AI verification, the verifier is a PPT algorithm. Given a statement about an AI model and a proof π The verifier decides whether to accept or reject.

Commitment Schemes

Commitment schemes allow a party to commit to a value while keeping it hidden, with the ability to reveal it later verifiably. A commitment scheme consists of Commit and Reveal algorithms, which means that the commitment does not reveal value, and once a commitment is made, it is infeasible to change its value. In federated learning, Pedersen commitments enable participants to commit to local model updates before revealing them.

Elliptic Curve Cryptography (ECC)

An elliptic curve over a finite field $\mathbb{F}_p$ is defined by:

$$y^2 = x^3 + ax + b$$

where $a, b \in \mathbb{F}_p$ and $4a^3 + 27b^2 \neq 0$.

ECC is used to construct efficient ZKPs by leveraging the elliptic curve discrete logarithm problem (ECDLP). This problem is assumed computationally infeasible, providing security even with smaller key sizes - critical for distributed AI systems with bandwidth constraints.

ZKP ARCHITECTURES FOR DISTRIBUTED AI SYSTEMS

Zero-Knowledge Proofs have appeared in different architectural forms, and each one of these has different characteristics suited to different applications.

Interactive vs. Non-Interactive Proofs

Interactive Zero-Knowledge Proofs involve multiple rounds of communication between prover and verifier. While offering strong security guarantees, they require real-time communication impractical for distributed AI systems.

Non-Interactive Zero-Knowledge Proofs (NIZKs) eliminate back-and-forth communication. A proof is produced by the validator that can be verified independently by any other validator. This is essential for decentralized AI because different parties need to verify proofs independently. Blockchain verification as a methodology demands publicly provable proofs, and it is essential that verification is possible in an immutable manner.

zk-SNARKs: Succinct Non-Interactive Arguments of Knowledge

Key Properties:

- **Succinctness:** Proof size is typically hundreds of bytes regardless of computation complexity
- **Non-interactive:** Single-round proof generation and verification.
- **Fast verification:** Verification time is often logarithmic or constant.
- **Expressiveness:** Can verify arbitrary computations representable as arithmetic circuits.

Applications:

- Proving model training using SGD on a dataset with specific properties
- Verifying predictions follow from the correct application of the certified model
- Federated learning integrity - each participant proves local update validity

Recent work like vCNN has optimized zk-SNARK implementations specifically for convolutional neural networks (Lee et al., 2023).

Algorithm 1 zk-SNARK Proving for AI Verification

Arithmetic circuit C, public input x, private witness w Proof π

1: CRS Setup(C) // *Trusted setup*
2: Verify that $C(x, w) = y$
3: Construct QAP polynomials *{Pi(X)}* from C

4: Generate random blinding factors
5: Compute polynomial commitments using CRS
6: π Prove(CRS, x, w) π

zk-STARKs: Scalable Transparent Arguments

zk-STARKs address key limitations of zk-SNARKs while introducing advantages for long-term AI verification (Ben-Sasson et al., 2018).

Key Properties:

- **No trusted setup:** Security relies on publicly verifiable randomness
- **Post-quantum security:** Resistant to quantum computer attacks
- **Scalability:** Efficient for very large computations
- **Transparency:** All cryptographic assumptions are public and standard

Applications: Long-term verifiable AI (models requiring security for decades), quantumresistant verification, high-computation verification for large language models.

Bulletproofs: Efficient Range Proofs

Bulletproofs provide short, efficient zero-knowledge proofs without requiring trusted setup (Bünz et al., 2018).

Key Properties:

- No trusted setup
- Short proofs: logarithmic in range size
- Efficient verification: logarithmic verification time
- Aggregation: Multiple range proofs efficiently batched

Applications: Model parameter constraints, privacy-preserving fairness audits, confidential model performance metrics, federated learning bounds.

Comparative Analysis

A comparative analysis of these ZKP protocols for distributed AI applications is provided in Table 1.

Table 1. ZKP protocol comparison for distributed AI

Property	*zk-SNARKs*	*zk-STARKs*	*Bulletproofs*
Proof Size	$O(1)$	$O(\log^2 N)$	$O(\log N)$
Verification Time	$O(1)$	$O(\log N)$	$O(N)$
Trusted Setup	Required	Not required	Not required
Post-Quantum	No	Yes	No
Best AI Use Case	Real-time inference	Long-term archival	Range constraints

PRIVACY-PRESERVING MACHINE LEARNING WITH ZKPS

Zero-Knowledge Proofs can now help in the verification of the execution of a machine learning process without disclosing the training data and parameters, as well as the inputs and outputs of inference computation.

The Privacy Challenges in Modern ML

Model Training Verification

ZKPs enable proving ML model training correctness according to specified algorithms on data with particular properties, without revealing training data. Consider a training model with parameters to minimize the loss function over a dataset. The goal is to prove the model was trained using a specific optimization algorithm (e.g., SGD), training data satisfied the required properties, and training converged properly without revealing data.

Recent work on Proof of Learning has established practical frameworks for proving training provenance (Jia et al., 2021), while Zhang et al. extended these techniques to decision tree models (J. Zhang et al., 2020).

Federated Learning with ZKPs

Federated Learning allows models to be jointly optimized in a decentralized manner. ZKPs offer the cryptographic tools that make secure federated learning possible. Model poisoning (malicious participants submit corrupted updates), data privacy (gradient updates can leak information), and verification (the server cannot verify update correctness without accessing local data). Recent work specifically addresses gradient aggregation with zero-knowledge proofs for federated learning (Z. Zhang et al., 2023).

CRITICAL APPLICATIONS: HEALTHCARE, FINANCE, AND DEMOCRATIC SYSTEMS

Zero-knowledge proofs always emerge in situations where issues of privacy, verification, and ethics come into play. This chapter will discuss zero-knowledge proofs in action.

Healthcare: Privacy-Preserving Diagnostics

Due to the sensitive nature of the information and the sensitive personal health information that healthcare organizations manage, and rely on healthcare laws like HIPAA and GDPR for handling privacy issues

ZKP Solutions for Medical AI: Consider radiology AI trained to detect tumors in medical images (CT scans, MRIs, mammograms). Using ZKPs, developers can prove:

1. Training set size: $|\mathscr{D}_{\text{train}}| \geq n_{\text{min}}$ patients
2. Demographic representation: $P(\text{age} \in [a_i, a_{i+1}]) \approx$ population distribution
3. Expert validation: $\exists$ subset $\mathscr{D}_{\text{expert}} \subset \mathscr{D}_{\text{train}}$ with radiologist-confirmed labels
4. Performance thresholds: Sensitivity $\geq s_{\text{min}}$, Specificity $\geq sp_{\text{min}}$ on $\mathscr{D}_{\text{test}}$

All without revealing individual patient scans or identifiable information.

Genomic Data Privacy: Genetic data have consequences to an individual and their family members. ZKP-enhanced federated learning can be used by multiple hospitals interested in discovering genetic markers of rare diseases in which each hospital trains on its local genetic data, local updates consist of ZKPs showing that only de-identified data were used and the minimum number of patients per institution were met to avoid reidentification, and the resulting model can identify genetic associations without any hospital accessing the genetic data of other hospitals (Zhou et al., 2024).

Clinical Trial Verification: Pharma-Companies ZKPs can enable pharmaceutical companies to demonstrate that they correctly followed trial protocols, used patient inclusion/exclusion criteria, randomized appropriately, and endpoints of trial efficacy passed statistical significance, and at the same time, protect patient identities and preserve trial blinding.

Algorithm 2 Privacy-Preserving Medical AI Verification

Diagnostic AI model M, verification requirements R Proof π of clinical validity

1: Construct verification circuit $C_{medical}$ encoding:
2: Dataset size and composition checks
3: Demographic distribution constraints
4: Training procedure validation (architecture, loss, convergence)
5: Performance threshold verification on test set
6: Generate witness: w = (patient_data, training_history, test_results)
7: Generate public outputs:
8: h_{model} Hash(M) *// Model commitment*
9: perf_metrics {sensitivity, specificity, AUC}
10: π zk-STARK_Prove(Cmedical, w)
11: Submit to regulator: (h_{model}, perf_ nical_protocol)
12: Regulator verifies: Accept zk-STARK_Verify(π, public_requirements) Accept
13: Approve model M for clinical deployment with hash h_{model} π

HIPAA Compliance Through ZKPs: The Health Insurance Portability and Accountability Act ensures that there are stringent measures towards the safeguarding of Protected Health Information (PHI). ZKPs make compliance easy by:

- **Minimum Necessary Standard:** Proving only the minimum PHI necessary was used without revealing full records.
- **Patient Authorization:** Proving authorization was obtained without revealing authorization details.
- **Claims Processing:** The hospitals are in a position to ensure that the claims for insurance are associated with medical treatment and the necessary amounts and processes, without having to disclose the medical process to the insurance companies and auditing bodies (Mohassel & Zhang, 2017).

Financial Systems: Ethical Transaction Verification and Algorithmic Fairness

Zero-knowledge proofs can be applied to determine compliance and algorithm integrity without exposing sensitive information. In fact, this is an important requirement for data protection and preservation in financial systems.

Credit Scoring and Lending Fairness: Credit scoring algorithms should meet several competing needs. Conventional methods involve either the release of proprietary scoring models (which lenders would not accept on grounds of competitive practices), or the adoption of opaque ones (which regulators and consumers would not accept due to discrimination concerns).

Algorithm 3 Fair Credit Scoring Verification

Credit model *M*, applicant data *D* applicants, protected attributes Proof π of fairness compliance

1: Partition data by protected groups: D_g for each group g
2: Compute fairness metrics:
3: approval_rate$_g$ $\leftarrow |\{x \in D_g: M(x) = \text{approve}\}|/|D_g|$
4: Compute disparities between groups
5: Construct circuit $C_{fairness}$ verifying:
6: Model *M* applied consistently to all applicants
7: Approval rate disparities within regulatory thresholds
8: True positive rate parity (equal opportunity)
9: Model predictions based only on legitimate credit
10: Generate witness: $w = (D_{applicants}, M,$ protected_attributes)
11: Public outputs: (fairness_metrics, disparity_bounds, model_sh)
12: π zk-SNARK_Prove($C_{fairness}$, w)
13: Submit π to regulator for complian verification π

Regulators verify the proof cryptographically, confirming fairness properties without accessing applicant financial data or the proprietary scoring model.

Anti-Money Laundering (AML) Compliance

Financial organizations are required to observe anti-money laundering regulations in their transactions without violating the confidentiality aspect. All organizations are supposed to adhere to Know Your Customer policies and report any suspected transactions.

Banks can rely on zero-knowledge proof (ZKP) protocols to ensure that they meet anti-money laundering regulations. All without revealing specific transaction details, maintaining customer privacy while satisfying regulatory oversight (Poelstra, 2016).

Blockchain Transaction Privacy and Regulation

Such a systematic effort (Chowdhury et al., 2024) forms the right backdrop for comprehending the latest trends in the relevance of blockchain privacy and the regulatory proposal framework offered by Jia et al. (Jia et al., 2024). Such a project illustrates the method of Privacy-Preserving Computing through the usage of zero-knowledge proofs (ZKP) that resolves the natural trade-off between transaction privacy and the need for government regulations.

Democratic Voting: Transparency with Privacy

The basic paradox of democratic voting systems is that the public verifiability needed to guarantee integrity and prevent fraud in an election must be coupled with the absolute privacy of individual ballots required to guarantee voter freedom and prevent coercion. The architecture for an end-to-end verifiable electronic voting system using ZKPs is illustrated in Figure 1.

Figure 1. End-to-end verifiable electronic voting with ZKPs

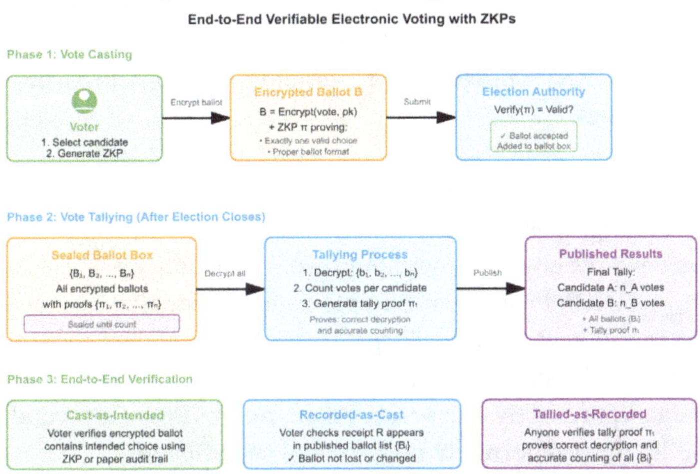

ZKP-Based Voting Architecture:

End-to-End Verifiability: ZKPs enable a complete verification chain (Kiayias & Zacharias,2017):

- **Cast-as-intended:** Voters verify encrypted ballots contain intended choices (using ZKP that ballot encrypts specific value, verified via trusted device or paper trail)
- **Recorded-as-cast:** Voters verify ballots recorded in the electronic ballot box (receipt matching published ballots)
- **Tallied-as-recorded:** Anyone verifies published tally correctly counts published ballots (via ZKP of correct decryption and counting)

All while maintaining ballot secrecy—no one can determine any individual's vote.

Receipt-Free Voting: A more advanced condition is receipt-freeness - voters are not able to demonstrate to others the way they voted, eliminating vote buying and coercion. ZKPs allow free voting by carefully constructed protocols in which voters are allowed to create fake receipts which are identical to real ones, and any receipt they show to a coercer is useless as evidence (Benaloh and Tuinstra, 1994). ZKPs deal with various vectors of fraud in a systematic way. These are the guarantees that ensure the legitimacy of democratic elections (Benaloh, 2013). Table 2 summarizes how ZKPs provide cryptographic solutions to various traditional election fraud vectors.

Algorithm 4 Privacy-Preserving Electronic Voting:

Vote Casting Phase:
Voter v proves eligibility without revealing identity:
    $\pi_{eligible}$ ZKP_Prove("v is eligible voter", credential$_v$)
Encrypt ballot: B Encrypt(b, $pk_{election}$) where b is vote choice
Generate ballot proof π_{ballot} proving:
    B encrypts exactly one valid choice (not multiple or invalid)
    Ballot formed correctly per protocol specifications
    No duplicate voting (commitment scheme prevents double-voting)
Generate voter receipt: $R = H(B, \pi_{ballot}$, timestamp)
Submit to voting authority: $(B, \pi_{ballot}, \pi_{eligible})$
Authority verifies proofs, adds B to ballot box if valid
Return receipt R to voter

Vote Tallying Phase:
After election close, decrypt all ballots: *{bi}* Decrypt(*{Bi}*)
Compute tally: tally$c$ Count(*{bi: bi = c}*) for each candidate c
Generate tally proof π_{tally} proving:
    All decryptions performed correctly
    Count performed accurately (arithmetic verified)
    No ballots added, removed, or modified

```
Publish: (tally, π_tally, {B_i}, {π_ballot,i})
Verification Phase:
Voter checks receipt R appears in published {Bi} (cast-as intended)
Anyone verifies π_tally proves correct counting (tallied-as recorded)
Statistical audits verify consistency
```

Table 2. ZKP solutions to election fraud

Fraud Type	Traditional Vulnerability	ZKP Protection
Double Voting	Difficult to prevent without revealing voter identity	Commitment schemes ensure each voter casts only one ballot that counts; ZKP proves uniqueness without revealing identity
Vote Tampering	Paper ballots can be altered; electronic votes can be changed	Cryptographic proofs detect any alteration of cast ballots; tampering invalidates proofs
Incorrect Counting	Manual counting errors; malicious tally manipulation	Tallying proofs guarantees arithmetic correctness; any miscounting is detected by verification
Ballot Stuffing	Extra ballots added to the box; fake voters	Eligibility proofs prevent unauthorized voting; each proof is cryptographically tied to a unique eligible voter

Real-World ZKP Deployments

Case Study 1: Healthcare Supply Chain – Privacy-Preserving Traceability

System: zkHealthChain
Type: Academic Research Prototype
Field: Healthcare Supply Chain Management
Evidence: Peer-reviewed publication in *IFIP AICT* (2024)
Challenge: The global healthcare supply chain requires transparency as it allows the company to comply with regulations and keep track of the data, but delicate business information, including shipments, prices, and partners, should be kept confidential. Even the existing systems can hardly combine auditability and privacy.

ZKP Solution:

Researchers developed zkHealthChain (Nithin et al., 2024), an Ethereum-based prototype integrating zk-SNARKs and Role-Based Access Control (RBAC). Participants (e.g., drug manufacturers, hospitals, regulators) can prove transaction validity and compliance without revealing underlying data. To illustrate, a manufacturer can identify a shipment and claim that it is a genuine shipment without having to mention particular amounts or destination information.

Verified Results:

- Proof generation for 1000 inputs: ~12.3 seconds
- Verification time: under 16 seconds
- 20–25% faster than baseline (ADSNARK) in key/proof generation
- Enables fault tracing without exposing datasets
- Implements RBAC via smart contracts to restrict data access by role

Impact:

This prototype demonstrates a feasible architecture for privacy-preserving supply chains, validating ZKPs as a tool for resolving transparency–confidentiality conflicts in regulated industries.

Case Study 2: Finance – Scaling Ethereum with Zero-Knowledge Proofs

System: Polygon zkEVM

Type: Live Layer-2 Network (Mainnet Beta)

Field: Decentralized Finance & Blockchain Scaling

Evidence: Mainnet launch announcement, On-chain analytics from L2Beat, Public blockchain data.

Challenge: The Ethereum mainnet, on the other hand, has a low throughput of 15-30 transactions per second, as well as a high gas cost, together with a volatile price, making it not very user-friendly for use on a larger scale, as it would be very costly to implement, for example, a decentralized exchange or a micropayment system.

ZKP Solution:

Polygon zkEVM - This is a layer two scaling solution developed by Polygon Labs in 2023 that uses zero-knowledge proof technology. This is an off-chain EVM batched solution that results in the generation of the entire batch's cryptographic evidence, called the zk-proof, and is further deployed to the Ethereum mainnet network, thus reducing the cost and latency while retaining the security offered by Ethereum.

Verified Results (Based on Q1 2024 Data):

- **Gas Fee Reduction:** The user is always charged 70-90 percent lower gas fees than similar operations on the Ethereum Mainnet.

- **Throughput:** The network handles hundreds of transactions per second in practice, a significant scaling improvement over the base layer.
- **EVM Equivalence:** Demonstrates high compatibility, allowing seamless deployment of existing Ethereum smart contracts (like Uniswap V3) with no code modification.
- **Decentralization:** The roles of the sequencer and prover have started to be decentralized and are moving towards a more trust-minimized organization.

Impact:

The Polygon zkEVM offers a production-scale, EVM-compatible scaling solution that relies on ZKPs to ensure Ethereum-level security. The Polygon zkEVM allows for an equivalent user and developer experience on Ethereum, albeit at only a fraction of the cost, thereby proving that ZK Rollups offer practical use cases for mainstream blockchains.

Case Study 3: Democratic Voting – Verifiable and Anonymous Elections

System: Vocdoni (zk-SNARKs + blockchain)
Type: Live Voting Platform
Field: Democratic Governance
Evidence: Official press release for FC Barcelona election (2022), partnership announcements

Challenge: Traditional elections have some compromises between being verifiable and maintaining the privacy of the voter. They are also expensive, slow, and can be subject to censorship or tampering.

ZKP Solution:

Vocdoni (Vocdoni & Aragon, 2022) combines Ethereum/Tendermint blockchain, IPFS, and zk-SNARKs to create a voting system where voters can prove their vote was counted without revealing their selection. The system uses blind signatures for authentication and publishes only cryptographic commitments on-chain.

Verified Results:

- FC Barcelona election (July 2022): 1,000+ voters across 30 delegate seats
- 100% verifiable with zero privacy breaches
- Cost: estimated 1/100th of traditional systems
- 300+ organizations have used Vocdoni for governance
- GDPR-compliant, legally valid for binding votes

Impact:

Vocdoni demonstrates that ZKPs are compatible with being transparent and secret because it provides cost-effective and scalable election solutions to organizations and cities.

SECURE MULTI-PARTY COMPUTATION AND DISTRIBUTED AI

The more common distributed AI systems demand the collaboration of multiple parties in computation, with data sovereignty, i.e., each party provides its contribution to the collective analysis or model training without disclosing its personal contributions to other parties. Secure Multi-Party Computation (SMPC) offers the cryptographic infrastructure of such cooperation, and Zero-Knowledge Proofs are important to guarantee that the participants adhere to protocols and that these are verifiably correct.

SMPC Fundamentals and Formal Definition:

Secure Multi-Party Computation enables parties $P_1, \ldots, P_n$ with private inputs $x_1, \ldots, x_n$ to jointly compute:

$$y = f(x_1, x_2, \ldots, x_n)$$

subject to the following security requirements:

1. **Input Privacy:** Each party learns only the output y and what can be inferred from y and their own input x_i. No party learns anything about other parties' inputs beyond this.
2. **Correctness:** The protocol computes $y = f(x_1, \ldots, x_n)$ correctly even if some parties behave maliciously.
3. **Independence of Inputs:** Malicious parties cannot choose their inputs based on honest parties' inputs.
4. **Fairness:** If any party learns the output, all honest parties learn the output.

In the context of secure multi-party computation, ZKPs are critical tools that permit parties to compute functions together on their inputs while keeping those inputs secret, crucial for privacy-preserving data analysis and collaborative machine learning where sensitive data must be guarded (Lindell, 2017).

ZKPs for Verifiable SMPC: Addressing the Malicious Adversary Model

ZKPs enable verification that each party executes correctly without revealing private inputs, upgrading semi-honest secure protocols to malicious security.

Security Properties Guaranteed by ZKPs:

- **Verifiable Inputs:** Each party's input provably satisfies constraints (e.g., medical data meets quality standards, financial data within expected ranges)
- **Computational Integrity:** Each computation step is verifiably correct
- **Protocol Adherence:** No party can deviate from protocol undetected
- **Audit Trail:** ZKP proofs create a permanent, verifiable record of computation
- **Malicious Security:** System remains secure even with dishonest participants (up to threshold)

When to Combine ZKPs with SMPC: A Decision Framework

ZKPs and SMPC deal with complementary issues of secure distributed computing. Knowledge of when to apply these techniques or whether to apply both is important to the system design. Table 3 of the decision matrix provides clear information on the use of either ZKP and SMPC, or both, depending on the nature of the particular situation. Combine ZKPs with SMPC when:

Algorithm 5 Verifiable SMPC with ZKP Integration

Party *i* with private input *xi*, function *f* to compute jointly Function result *y* = *f*(*x*1, . . ., *xn*) with verified honest execution

1: **Phase 1: Input Commitment and Verification** each party *i* = 1 to *n*
2: *Ci* Commit(*xi*) // *Cryptographic commitment to input*
3: *πi,*input ZKP_Prove("*xi* satisfies input requirements", *xi*)
4: Broadcast (*Ci, πi,*input) to all parties
5: All parties verify ZKP_Verify(*πi,*input) any verification fails
6: Abort protocol, exclude malicious party
7: **Phase 2: Secret Sharing with Proof** each party *i* = 1 to *n*
8: Generate secret shares: *{si,j}n j*=1 such that P*j si,j* = *xi*
9: *πi,*share ZKP_Prove("shares correctly encode *Ci*", *xi, {si,j}*)
10: Send *si,j* to party *Pj* (encrypted), broadcast *πi,*share
12: All parties verify ZKP_Verify(*πi,*share)

13: **Phase 3: Joint Computation with Round-by-Round Verification** each computation round t each party i

14: Compute on received shares according to SMPC protocol: zi,t Compute($\{sj,i\}j$)

15: $\pi i,t$ ZKP_Prove("zi,t computed correctly", $\{sj,i\}j$, zi,t) 18: Broadcast (zi,t, $\pi i,t$)

16: All parties verify ZKP_Verify($\pi i,t$)

17: **Phase 4: Output Reconstruction with Final Verification**

18: Verify all proofs $\{\pi i,t\}$ for all parties and rounds all proofs valid

19: Combine verified results: y Reconstruct($\{zi,T\}$)

20: πoutput ZKP_Prove("y correctly reconstructed from $\{zi,T\}$")

21: All parties verify πoutput y

22: Abort, identify the malicious party from failed verification

- **Malicious Participants Possible:** Cannot trust all parties to follow protocol honestly
- **High Stakes:** Financial, medical, or legal consequences of incorrect computation
- **Regulatory Requirements:** Need cryptographic proof of correct execution for compliance
- **Long-term Auditability:** Computations may be audited years later
- **Heterogeneous Trust:** Different parties have different trust levels or verification requirements

Example: Multi-hospital federated learning for clinical AI-hospitals don't fully trust each other, regulators need proof of HIPAA compliance, potential for malicious behavior.

Table 3. Decision matrix: When to use ZKPs, SMPC, or both

Scenario Characteristics	*SMPC Alone*	*ZKPs Alone*	*ZKPs + SMPC*
Multiple data contributors	Required	Not needed	Required
Malicious adversaries possible	Insufficient	Depends	Required
Regulatory compliance proofs needed	Not provided	Provided	Provided
Asynchronous verification	Not supported	Supported	Supported
Real-time performance critical	Better	Better	May be challenging
Long-term auditability	Limited	Excellent	Excellent
Implementation complexity	Moderate	Moderate	High
Communication overhead	Moderate-High	Low-Moderate	High
Best for:	Trusted collaboration, privacy during joint computation	Verification without computation, regulatory audits	High-stakes distributed AI, federated learning, cross-border collaboration

CHALLENGES IN DEPLOYING ETHICAL AI WITH ZKPS

There are several challenges that need to be overcome in order to make it possible to incorporate ZKPs in AI.

Computational Complexity

ZKPs have complex mathematical calculations involving large computational units (Parno et al., 2013). The process of proof creation and verification may be computationally costly, resulting in performance overheads, which in turn are challenging in real-time AI inference. The layered and interconnected nature of these deployment challenges is depicted in Figure 2.

Figure 2. Layered architecture of challenges in deploying ZKP-based ethical AI

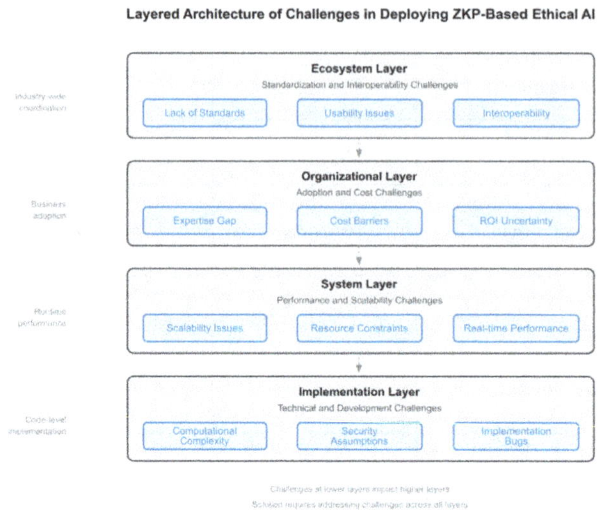

Scalability

As dataset size or model complexity increases, proof size and verification time can grow (Ben-Sasson, Chiesa, Genkin, et al., 2014). For federated learning with K participants, total communication equals $K \cdot (|\text{model update}| + |\pi|)$. The mitigation techniques involve proof aggregation, selective verification, layer-2 solutions, and progressive verification.

Implementation Complexity

ZKPs' implementation needs math and cryptography expertise that may not be easily accessible among the AI development teams (Gennaro et al., 2013). Cryptography Experience ML engineers usually do not have a cryptography background, and cryptographers might not be aware of ML system requirements.

Usability

Lengthy proof generation times or increased complexity can harm user experience and create adoption barriers. Despite benefits, the perceived complexity of ZKPs might discourage adoption. User-facing challenges require simple interfaces for data scientists, a clear indication of verification guarantees, and accessible tools for auditors.

Security Assumptions

ZKP security is based on certain cryptographic assumptions and their correct implementation (Goldreich, 2019). Assumptions such as the discrete logarithm may be undermined by improvements in cryptanalysis or quantum computers. Vulnerabilities may be caused by implementation bugs.

Standardization and Interoperability

The compatibility issues are due to the absence of standardization between various ZKP implementations (Ben-Sasson, Chiesa, Tromer, and Virza, 2014). Out of the various platforms, there are different protocols and this is where interoperability becomes a problem. Such emerging standards are ZKProof Standards, NIST Post-Quantum Cryptography, and W3C Verifiable Credentials.

CONCLUSION

Zero Knowledge Proofs are an innovative cryptographic paradigm of creating ethical AI systems that overcome the inherent tradeoff between privacy and verification. ZKPs allow demonstrating computational correctness without exposing data, making it possible to find a way around the privacy-transparency paradox that had long limited the use of AI in sensitive areas. ZKPs provide feasible solutions that can reconcile individual privacy and societal accountability involved in privacy-preserving medical diagnostics and fair lending verification, trustworthy democratic voting systems, etc. Although much work is left in this regard in order to further improve efficiency, usability, and the level of standardization, the continued development of zero-knowledge protocols in terms of post-quantum security and lower computational complexity will cement their importance as one of the key constituents of responsible AI. With AI systems assuming an increasingly important role in human life, zero-knowledge proofs are the cryptographic backbone of a future where powerful AI is privately operated but publicly verifiable, so that technological development can be seen as not violating the basic ethical standards.

REFERENCES

Baldimtsi, F., Burkhart, M., Damgård, I., & Orlandi, C. (2013). Anonymous biometric access control. In *International Conference on Financial Cryptography and Data Security*. Springer.

Ben-Sasson, E., Bentov, I., Horesh, Y., & Riabzev, M. (2018). *Scalable, transparent, and post-quantum secure computational integrity*. Cryptology ePrint Archive.

Ben-Sasson, E., Chiesa, A., Genkin, D., Tromer, E., & Virza, M. (2013). SNARKs for C: Verifying program executions succinctly and in zero knowledge. In *Annual Cryptology Conference*. Springer. DOI: 10.1007/978-3-642-40084-1_6

Ben-Sasson, E., Chiesa, A., Genkin, D., Tromer, E., & Virza, M. (2014). Succinct non-interactive zero knowledge for a von Neumann architecture. In *23rd USENIX Security Symposium*.

Benaloh, J. (2013). End-to-end verifiable elections: Public evidence from secret ballots. *USENIX Journal of Election Technology and Systems*, *1*(1), 18–37.

Benaloh, J., & Tuinstra, D. (1994). Receipt-free secret-ballot elections. In *Proceedings of the Twenty-Sixth Annual ACM Symposium on Theory of Computing*. DOI: 10.1145/195058.195407

Bonawitz, K., Ivanov, V., Kreuter, B., Marcedone, A., McMahan, H. B., Patel, S., Ramage, D., Segal, A., & Seth, K. (2017). Practical secure aggregation for privacy-preserving machine learning. In *Proceedings of the 2017 ACM SIGSAC Conference on Computer and Communications Security*. DOI: 10.1145/3133956.3133982

Bowe, S., Gabizon, A., & Miers, I. (2017). *Scalable multi-party computation for zk-SNARK parameters in the random beacon model*. IACR Cryptology ePrint Archive, 2017, 1050.

Bünz, B., Bootle, J., Boneh, D., Poelstra, A., Wuille, P., & Maxwell, G. (2018). Bulletproofs: Short proofs for confidential transactions and more. In *2018 IEEE Symposium on Security and Privacy (SP)*. IEEE. DOI: 10.1109/SP.2018.00020

Chase, M., Meiklejohn, S., & Zaverucha, G. (2014). Password systems with perfect security properties. In *2014 IEEE Symposium on Security and Privacy*. IEEE.

Chowdhury, A. R., Campanelli, M., Ganesh, C., Gailly, N., & Shikhelman, C. (2024). *SoK: Privacy-preserving computing in the blockchain era*. IACR Cryptology ePrint Archive. https://eprint.iacr.org/2023/727

Dwork, C., Roth, A., & others. (2014). The algorithmic foundations of differential privacy. *Foundations and Trends in Theoretical Computer Science*, *9*(3–4), 211–407.

European Parliament and Council of the European Union. (2024). *Regulation (EU) 2024/1689 of the European Parliament and of the Council of 13 June 2024 laying down harmonised rules on artificial intelligence* (L, 2024/1689). EUR-Lex.https://eurlex.europa.eu/eli/reg/2024/1689/oj/eng

Feige, U., Fiat, A., & Shamir, A. (1987). Zero-knowledge proofs of identity. In *Proceedings of the Nineteenth Annual ACM Symposium on Theory of Computing*. ACM. Bünz, B., Bootle, J., Boneh, D., Poelstra, A., Wuille, P., & Maxwell, G. (2018, May). Bulletproofs: Short proofs for confidential transactions and more. In *2018 IEEE symposium on security and privacy (SP)* (pp. 315-334). IEEE.

Fjeld, J., Achten, N., Hilligoss, H., Nagy, A., & Srikumar, M. (2020). *Principled artificial intelligence: Mapping consensus in ethical and rights-based approaches to principles for AI* (Berkman Klein Center Research Publication No. 2020-1). Harvard University. DOI: 10.2139/ssrn.3518482

Fredrikson, M., Jha, S., & Ristenpart, T. (2015). Model inversion attacks that exploit confidence information and basic countermeasures. In *Proceedings of the 22nd ACM SIGSAC Conference on Computer and Communications Security*. ACM. DOI: 10.1145/2810103.2813677

Gennaro, R., Gentry, C., & Parno, B. (2013). Quadratic span programs and succinct NIZKs without PCPs. In *Annual International Conference on the Theory and Applications of Cryptographic Techniques*. Springer. DOI: 10.1007/978-3-642-38348-9_37

Gentry, C. (2009). Fully homomorphic encryption using ideal lattices. In *Proceedings of the Forty-First Annual ACM Symposium on Theory of Computing*. DOI: 10.1145/1536414.1536440

Goldreich, O. (2019). *Foundations of cryptography: Volume 1, basic tools*. Cambridge University Press.

Goldwasser, S., Micali, S., & Rackoff, C. (2019). The knowledge complexity of interactive proof-systems. In *Providing sound foundations for cryptography: On the work of Shafi Goldwasser and Silvio Micali*. DOI: 10.1145/3335741.3335750

Groth, J. (2016). On the size of pairing-based non-interactive arguments. In Fischlin, M., & Coron, J.-S. (Eds.), Lecture Notes in Computer Science: Vol. 9666. *Advances in Cryptology – EUROCRYPT 2016, Part II* (pp. 305–326). Springer. DOI: 10.1007/978-3-662-49896-5_11

Jia, H., Yaghini, M., Choquette-Choo, C. A., Dullerud, N., Thudi, A., Chandrasekaran, V., & Papernot, N. (2021). Proof of learning: Definitions and practice. In *IEEE Symposium on Security and Privacy (S&P)*. https://arxiv.org/abs/2103.05633

Jia, W., Xie, T., & Wang, B. (2024). A privacy-preserving scheme with multi-level regulation compliance for blockchain. *Scientific Reports*, *14*, 438. DOI: 10.1038/s41598-023-50209-x

Jobin, A., Ienca, M., & Vayena, E. (2019). The global landscape of AI ethics guidelines. *Nature Machine Intelligence*, *1*(9), 389–399. DOI: 10.1038/s42256-019-0088-2

Katz, J., & Lindell, Y. (2007). *Introduction to modern cryptography: Principles and protocols*. Chapman & Hall/CRC. DOI: 10.1201/9781420010756

Kiayias, A., & Zacharias, T. (2017). End-to-end verifiable elections. In *European Symposium on Research in Computer Security*. Springer.

Lee, S., Ko, H., Kim, J., & Oh, H. (2023). vCNN: Verifiable convolutional neural network based on zk-SNARKs. *IEEE Transactions on Dependable and Secure Computing*. https://arxiv.org/abs/2210.08718

Lindell, Y. (2017). How to simulate it–A tutorial on the simulation proof technique. In *Tutorials on the foundations of cryptography* (pp. 277–346). DOI: 10.1007/978-3-319-57048-8_6

Mohassel, P., & Zhang, Y. (2017). SecureML: A system for scalable privacy-preserving machine learning. In *2017 IEEE Symposium on Security and Privacy (SP)*. IEEE. DOI: 10.1109/SP.2017.12

National Institute of Standards and Technology. (2023). *Artificial Intelligence Risk Management Framework (AI RMF 1.0)* (NIST AI 100-1). U.S. Department of Commerce. DOI: 10.6028/NIST.AI.100-1

Nithin, G. N., Pradhan, A. K., & Swain, G. (2024). zkHealthChain – Blockchain enabled supply chain in healthcare using zero knowledge. In D. Puthal et al. (Eds.), *IFIP Advances in Information and Communication Technology*: Vol. 684. *Internet of Things* (pp. 133–148). Springer. DOI: 10.1007/978-3-031-45882-8_10

Parno, B., Howell, J., Gentry, C., & Raykova, M. (2013). Pinocchio: Nearly practical verifiable computation. In *2013 IEEE Symposium on Security and Privacy*. IEEE. DOI: 10.1109/SP.2013.47

Poelstra, A. (2016). Confidential transactions. *Ledger*, *1*, 1–19.

Polygon Labs. (2023, March 27). Ethereum scalability with zkEVM performance and security. https://polygon.technology/polygon-zkevm

Vocdoni & Aragon. (2022). FC Barcelona Web3 voting https://publish.obsidian.md/refi-barcelona/Ecosystem+Map/Local/Vocdoni

Zhang, J., Fang, Z., Zhang, Y., & Song, D. (2020). Zero-knowledge proofs for decision tree predictions and accuracy. In *ACM Conference on Computer and Communications Security (CCS)*. https://eprint.iacr.org/2020/1266

Zhang, Z., Sun, J., & Yang, Y. (2023). *zkFL: Zero-knowledge proof-based gradient aggregation for federated learning*. arXiv preprint. https://arxiv.org/abs/2310.02554

Zhou, J., Chen, S., Wu, Y., Li, H., Zhang, B., Zhou, L., Hu, Y., Xiang, Z., Li, Z., Chen, N., Han, W., Wang, D., & Gao, X. (2024). PPML-Omics: A privacy-preserving federated machine learning method protects patients' privacy in omic data. *Science Advances*, *10*. https://www.science.org/doi/10.1126/sciadv.adh8601

KEY TERMS AND DEFINITIONS

Ethical AI: An approach to artificial intelligence development and deployment that prioritizes and incorporates ethical principles, including fairness, accountability, transparency, privacy, and the avoidance of harm, into system design and operation.

Federated Learning: A distributed machine learning method in which a single model is trained on multiple decentralized devices or servers that are in possession of local data samples without transferring the data itself, therefore, maintaining data privacy at the source.

Privacy-Transparency Paradox: The inherent contradiction of AI systems as ethical demands of transparency and accountability of the algorithms versus the need to safeguard the privacy of sensitive training data and the model parameters.

Secure Multi-Party Computation (SMPC): A cryptographic technique that allows multiple parties to jointly compute a function over their private inputs while keeping those inputs concealed from each other, enabling collaborative data analysis without centralizing sensitive information.

Verifiable Computation: The act of offloading a computation onto a third party and being able to effectively confirm that the output is correct, without necessarily re-computing the entire computation, is frequently done using cryptographic proofs such as ZKPs.

Zero-Knowledge Proof (ZKP): A cryptographic protocol that enables one party (the prover) to prove to another party (the verifier) that a statement is true, without revealing any information beyond the veracity of the statement itself.

zk-SNARK (Zero-Knowledge Succinct Non-Interactive Argument of Knowledge): A form of zero-knowledge proof that is short (succinct), can be verified quickly, and requires no interaction between the prover and verifier after an initial setup phase, making it ideal for verifying complex computations on blockchain and in distributed systems.

Chapter 6
Applications of Artificial Intelligence in Healthcare Resolving the Intersections of the Patient Safety, Data Sensitivity, and Equitable Access:
Toward Ethical and Secure Healthcare AI

Mehak Rana
http://orcid.org/0009-0009-4408-4297
The University of Faisalabad, Pakistan

Muqadsa Jabeen
The University of Faisalabad, Pakistan

Majid Hussain
http://orcid.org/0009-0002-5968-0509
The University of Faisalabad, Pakistan

Muhammad Seed
The University of Faisalabad, Pakistan

Shoaib Hassan
http://orcid.org/0000-0002-8265-7932
The University of Lahore, Sargodha, Pakistan

ABSTRACT

Artificial intelligence (AI) is disrupting healthcare in the form of disease diagnostics, clinical decision support, and remote patient monitoring. Nevertheless, such

DOI: 10.4018/979-8-3373-6038-6.ch006

developments raise many ethical issues regarding patient safety, data sensitivity, and fair access. This chapter focuses on AI in healthcare as a process that is guided by the principles of clinical validation, transparency, and constant monitoring to avoid diagnostic mistakes and algorithmic bias. It discusses privacy-protective solutions like blockchain governance, federated learning, and differential privacy to ensure sensitive health information is not leaked. Moreover, it states that inclusive datasets and models of fairness are essential to providing equitable access, especially in low- and middle-income countries. Based on the case studies of NHS AI Lab (UK), Mayo Clinic (USA) and AIoT-based diabetes monitoring (Singapore), the chapter suggests an ethical AI implementation system that considers both innovation and trust to provide safe, confidential, and equity healthcare to all populations.

INTRODUCTION

The healthcare industry is changing faster. Artificial Intelligence (AI) is being applied by healthcare professionals and medical institutions around the globe to improve monitoring of patients, diagnosis, and treatment. Today, the medical pictures, such as CT scans, MRIs, and X-rays, can be read by artificial intelligence (AI) devices. Quality that is often as good as or even higher than that of human experts. AI systems are able to classify quickly. Patients based on the severity of their conditions in emergency treatment and triage, which saves clinicians critical time. Remote Patient Monitoring (RPM) devices such as wearables are being driven by AI, which occur outside of hospitals that check blood pressure, oxygen levels and heart rhythms. These gadgets provide clinicians with ongoing health information, enabling the early identification of issues. The same technology that powers sophisticated catboats, Large Language Models (LLMs), is now being evaluated to help physicians with regular patient inquiries, clinical recording, and record summarization. This quick uptake demonstrates why AI is now a crucial component of contemporary healthcare systems and is no longer an optional alternative. However all of these advantages also bring with them fresh difficulties that need careful consideration. The book chapter contribution is following:

- To analysing how patient safety, data sensitivity, and fair access affect the development, implementation, and governance of AI systems in order to objectively assess the ethical issues raised by AI in healthcare.
- To emphasize the lessons learnt from international efforts and clinical deployments.

- To suggest future paths for moral and reliable healthcare AI by describing tactics like privacy-protecting structures, algorithms that consider fairness, and international equity campaigns that guarantee secure, confidential, and inclusive healthcare.

AI APPLICATIONS ARE NOW EVIDENT THROUGHOUT THE WHOLE PATIENT JOURNEY

In medical images deep learning algorithms may accurately identify conditions including Alzheimer's disease, pneumonia, and cancer. AI techniques, for instance, now assist radiologists in spotting tiny tumours or cancers that the human eye could overlook. By rapidly evaluating symptoms and risk factors AI systems can prioritize patients in emergency departments or during emergencies (like COVID-19). AI-powered wearables and smartphone apps let doctors monitor vital signs like heart rate, oxygen saturation, and glucose levels in real time, which cuts down on the frequency of hospital stays. AI assistants are being tried to aid with administrative duties like answering frequently asked inquiries, generating clinical notes, and summarizing lengthy patient histories. These resources help physicians save time and lessen burnout. AI speeds up the process of finding possible medicines and forecasting how various patients would react to them. Change has happened so quickly that artificial intelligence (AI) also referred to as the "digital transformation of medicine," is now viewed as a crucial component of future healthcare systems.

THREE ETHICAL PRINCIPLES ARE ADHERING TO

The opportunities of AI are huge regarding its use in the field of healthcare one can note three primary issues:

Patient Safety: Medical choices directly relate to human lives; the factor of patient safety is what matters the most to consider in the introduction of AI in the field of healthcare. Unless there are fatal consequences on the failure of an AI system. Mistakes a cancerous tumour of the organism with a benign one or overlooks a severe disease. Due to this fact, algorithms require.

To be precise, trustworthy, and verified with the help of numerous datasets of both controlled laboratory and real-life clinical environments. To guarantee the safety of patients, physicians should be aware that AI should never make. To be or to lead by blindly; on the contrary it must be taken as an instrument to augment human knowledge as opposed to replace it. AI in the healthcare field will have to be tested thoroughly before deployment, and monitored continuously after deployment. To detect issues such as performance drift, where the accuracy becomes worse as time goes on due to changing patient. Populations or data, and close human monitoring to ensure that there are trained medical professionals left in charge of making final decisions.

Data Sensitivity: Medical records hold some of the most sensitive and confidential information about a data sensitivity is one of the most pressing challenges in healthcare AI in general. Health information is strictly associated with identity, dignity, and trust, as opposed to financial or shopping information. An abuse of this information may be severe consequences including stigmatizing, discrimination or being refused insurance and employment opportunities. For AI systems to operate they often require access to large and diverse datasets such as radiology scans, pathology. Photos, test outcomes of laboratory work, and computerized medical history. But in the absence of privacy precautions, then it can be expected. Implement, collection, and sharing of such private data exposes the patients to grave danger. Thousands of lives a single data breach can put the entire concept of AI and the healthcare system at risk as a whole. This has prompted the creation of new privacy preserving technologies. Federated learning retains patient. Log data locally by allowing hospitals and other organizations to collaborate to learn models in absence of. Sharing raw data. In spite of analysing data together, differentiation privacy introduces noise to datasets, statistically. Rendering it impossible to find particular records. By creating tamper proof audit trails and ensuring that blockchain-based systems are transparent and can only be accessed by authorized stakeholders, which makes their use of data transparent. Additional level of safety and trust. Together these strategies allow AI to take advantage of large volumes of patient information and safeguard their privacy. According to Jabeen et al. (2024), the parallels between are similar.

blockchain works and moral values within Islam. Nevertheless, there are challenges regarding the pounding a compromise between data security and accessibility particularly in partnerships across borders where stringent security measures are required. Laws such as the HIPAA in the US and GDPR in Europe impose guidelines on how and with whom the health data should be shared. This proves that the need to have strong legal systems and technology safeguards to ensure that AI-based innovation in healthcare can never harm patient privacy.

Data breach\Risk: The most concerning risks are stigma and discrimination where genetic or diagnostic data can result in discrimination by insurance companies or employers. Since health records hold valuable identifiers that are often committed with ill intent, fraud and identity theft are also common. The loss of faith between the patients and the providers this is perhaps the most damaging; unless patients are not scared of being abused, they will not be willing to be involved in clinical studies withhold significant information, or escape genetic testing. This compromises AI systems, which rely on extensive and representative data, besides reducing the quality of care. For the future of healthcare Protecting patient data is thus not only an ethical obligation but also a technical one in the case of AI.

1) **Fair and Equitable Access**: AI must equally benefit all patients although there is a likelihood that technology will not can aggravate health disparities. As an example an AI system might not work properly with low- and patients. Middle-income regions in case it is primarily trained on the data of high-income countries. Similarly, AI can give rise to. Lower accuracy of answers when the women, minorities, or children are undertrained in training datasets. Thus, ethical AI should ensure an equitable access and inclusiveness to make sure that no group is left behind.
2) **To become fair and equal AI**: The active collection of risks of all kinds of information based on gender, age, ethnicity, and region has been known to generate inclusive datasets. Auditing of AI models is the routine checking of models that are fair, bias and ensuring that different groups of patients are accorded a similar performance. Furthering AI studies and information. Exchange in LMICs in order to make sure that models capture the conditions of different healthcare systems. Development of AI systems capable of operating in rural clinics where the infrastructure is not sufficient and in state-of-the-art hospitals. The three pillars that promote responsible AI in healthcare are fairness, privacy and safety.

Background and Scope: Healthcare artificial intelligence (AI) is a wide-ranging and emerging technology that integrates a no standardized technologies, all with a different level of impact and moral hazard. Clarifying the range of AI applications and where the ethical consideration is most needed is essential before getting down to the more. Complicated issues of patient health, data confidentiality and fair access. The According to the definition by the international medical device regulators forum (IMDRF) a Software as a medical device (SaMD) is defined as Software that is consumed medically and is not part of a physical device. Examples include AI-powered cancer detection systems, heart rhythms tracking smartphone apps, and cloud-based diagnostic systems. SaMD is considered a high-risk and will require serious control on the side of regulation as it has a direct impact on clinical Decisions. Clinical Decision Support (CDS) systems are closely related but they are relatively different. Purposes. These types of rule-based or AI-based technologies help physicians by providing diagnostic probabilities using patient data, identifying potentially dangerous drug interactions or recommending therapy options. Even though, unlike SaMD, CDS systems are designed to complement human judgment, and not to substitute it there is a concern about the growing reliance on automated recommendations in recent years. GPT-style models including LLPs, are under investigation to summarize patient history write clinical note, and explain difficult medical terms to patients as well as to offer conversational assistance in the management of chronic conditions or mental health. Despite their accessibility and efficiency these applications have the risk of bias, gaps in accountability and hallucinations (false outputs) especially when they are used in areas where patients are involved or doctors are guided much by them. Another area with a rapid pace of use of edge computing and AIoT (Artificial Intelligence of Things) is healthcare.

Expanding field. Wearables, smart implants, and remote patient are not the sole implementations that Procter and Gamble can rely on to do away with fully relying on cloud servers. Health data can be processed at the edge using monitoring devices. This makes faster interventions easy less. Dependence on central infrastructure and real-time decision-making. But since sensitive health information can, be intercepted at multiple locations in transmission, edge computing also expands the attack surface of Cybersecurity risks. Jabeen et al. (2025): A privacy explainable AI model based on blockchain. Maintaining machine learning in intelligent healthcare. Real-world data (RWD) is equally important far beyond the precincts of traditional clinical research. Electronic health records, insurance claims, data collected on mobile health apps, patient registries, and information that is collected through wearable sensors or telemedicine. Are all included in RWD. Jabeen et al. (n.d.) proposes an augmented paradigm of blockchain-IPFS secure. Shared information. Through such statistics to train artificial intelligence systems, models that are more accurate. Population-level health patterns can be formed and clinical reality of every day can be developed. However, problems with representativeness, standardization and quality control is challenging. As an example, the output AI models may not be applicable to larger populations when RWD is mostly collected at wealthier hospitals or specific groups of patients. This imbalance can undermine fairness and inclusiveness and this can be detrimental. Prejudice into AI systems. It is clear in introducing AI into these categories: SaMD, CDS, LLMs, AIoT and edge computing, and the real world data- that the sphere of healthcare AI is not a one-dimensional phenomenon. While

There are various hazards in each area that must be carefully managed, it also has special potential to be improved. Patient participation, diagnosis and treatment. Some technologies such as SaMD and CDS, require a proper level of attention validated as they are tested and have a direct impact on clinical decisions. Others, such as LLMs and The chapter gives appropriate emphasis to major issues such as patient safety, data privacy, and fairness in AI-driven healthcare. However certain areas like post-deployment monitoring, human oversight, and patient trust are slightly under-discussed IoT, bring more access to and reach to healthcare and introduce new cybersecurity, accountability, and dependability issues. On the other hand, real-life data has the potential to transform the understanding of the populace in health, provided that some actions are implemented. Guarantee privacy and representativeness.

It is in this background that subsequent discussions on ethics are founded making sure that the focus remains on the applications that may have the most significant impact on patient safety, sensitive data protection, and the promotion of just access to treatment. Figure 1 shows there are three primary types of dangers associated with AI in healthcare:

Figure 1. Risk taxonomy in healthcare

Clinical Risk: Mistakes that have a direct bearing on patient safety such as incorrect diagnosis, suggested course of therapy or triage choices Figure#1 represented Risk For Example a malignant tumour may be mistakenly classified as benign by an AI diagnostic tool, delaying treatment.

Informational Risk: Dangers related to managing private medical information such as misuse, illegal access, and privacy violations. Employers or insurers using genetic data that has been leaked for discriminatory purposes.

Equity Risk: Concerns about inclusion and justice when AI systems may perform differently for various patient groups as a result of skewed or insufficient training data. Example when applied to women or children, an algorithm that was primarily trained on adult male patients performs poorly.

Defining the Boundaries: Out-of-Scope Considerations: This chapter's focus is on AI applications that directly affect patient outcomes and medical care; other topics are purposefully left out to keep the discussion on track. Since consumer wellness devices like step counters, diet apps, and fitness trackers don't directly affect patient safety or medical decisions, they are not included in the conversation. Administrative healthcare apps such as hospital resource management, billing optimization, and scheduling software are also not taken into account because their main focus is on efficiency rather than moral dilemmas involving private information or clinical judgment. Table 1 shows Glossary of Terms and Abbreviations Additionally, because of their lack of connection to medical danger, general-purpose chatbots that are not made especially for healthcare settings are not included. By outlining these parameters, the chapter makes sure that the conversation stays focused on AI systems that have an immediate impact on patient safety, health, and well-being.

Table 1. Glossary of terms and abbreviations

Term	Full Form	Definition / Relevance in Healthcare AI
SaMD	Software as a Medical Device	Software used for medical purposes, independent of hardware devices (e.g., AI cancer-detection apps).
CDS	Clinical Decision Support	AI-based tools that assist clinicians in decision-making without replacing human judgment.
LLMs	Large Language Models	Advanced AI models used in healthcare for summarizing, translating, or generating medical content.
AIoT	Artificial Intelligence of Things	Integration of AI with IoT devices (e.g., wearables, sensors) for continuous health monitoring.
Edge Computing	-	Local data processing near the source (e.g., on-device analysis of wearable data).
RWD	Real-World Data	Patient data collected outside controlled trials (e.g., EHRs, insurance claims, and registries).
GDPR	General Data Protection Regulation	EU regulation ensuring strong data privacy and security.
HIPAA	Health Insurance Portability and Accountability Act	U.S. law protecting sensitive patient health information.

Governance and Regulatory Landscape: One of the most important but complicated parts of using artificial intelligence (AI) in healthcare is the governance and regulatory environment. AI systems in contrast to conventional medical equipment are data-driven and adaptable meaning that even after deployment they may keep learning, improving, and changing. This makes regulation especially difficult because laws made for static technology frequently can't keep up with AI's dynamic and ever-evolving behaviour. Under the Software as a Medical Device (SaMD) paradigm the Food and Drug Administration (FDA) is primarily responsible for regulating medical

AI in the US. Khan et al. (2023) explored the Shanghai Cooperation Organization (SCO) as an emerging geopolitical power bloc. Software items were formerly certified through a one-time procedure however AI tools that update often with fresh data have issues with this method. The FDA created the Predetermined Change Control Plan (PCCP) in 2025 to solve this issue enabling developers to suggest beforehand how their AI systems might change after approval. Innovation and patient safety are better balanced as a result of the transition from static regulation to adaptive oversight. For instance, if the updates adhere to the previously approved modification plan, an AI model that was first authorized for cancer screening can keep using new population data. European government is very strong in data protection and justice. The effect of the General Data Protection Regulation (GDPR) on healthcare AI is significant, and it is considered to be the toughest privacy regulation in the world. GDPR requires the strict permission rules, anonymization principles, and security to be observed during the processing of patient data. Outside GDPR, healthcare AI will also be regulated even tighter by the proposed EU Artificial Intelligence Act that is expected to be established in 2024 and 2025 and label it as a high risk application. It means that any AI system used in the field of medicine will have to undergo human monitoring, explainability, openness, and fairness audits. Besides establishing accuracy, hospitals and businesses planning to apply AI in Europe will also be required to demonstrate that their systems do not unfairly discriminate against certain groups and that doctors retain the final decision on all matters. This plan will ensure that AI is a device that facilitates safe, fair, and accountable healthcare and not the black box. Regulatory systems are changing at a rapid rate in asia although they vary greatly. Singapore has become a responsible AI leader by publishing detailed guidelines on trusted healthcare AI with a focus on explainability, security, and equity. China has already integrated AI in the healthcare plan of the country requiring security checks to be performed before implementation, registering of the algorithm, and simplifying the decision-making processes. Japan has put a heavy focus on a human-centred AI paradigm, developing a transparent and supportive technology particularly in the field of elder care which is a national agenda due to the ageing population. Although these frameworks may show much of progress the heterogeneity of policies also creates diffusion in the region and it is difficult to unify the guidelines to cross-border cooperation in AI.

The World Health Organization (WHO) has also been on the forefront in the global arena championing ethics and equitable regulation of AI in healthcare. Its 2024 global report highlighted the urgent necessity of international cooperation, particularly since unequal regulations put the high-income and low- and middle-income (LMIC) countries further apart. WHO also emphasized that AI in healthcare must be inclusive and accessible besides being accurate and safe. Participation in the benefits of advanced AI systems by LMICs is threatened by the absence of clear rules and capacity building, or acting as guinea pigs to test the uncontrolled technologies. This international perspective underlines the fact that there is a need to have standard norms where equity and fairness among communities are made first since AI cannot be governed at national borders. It is becoming clear that oversight of healthcare AI should change a system of one-time approvals to flexible continuous oversight. In the not-so-distant future the AI systems may face regulations akin to the ones in the living technologies, which require ongoing regulation audit firms of fairness, and performance check-ups throughout the duration of their existence. Although the development of post-quantum encryption is being explored to ensure that sensitive medical information is not disclosed to cyber threats in the future, solutions such as blockchain-based audit trails are being provided to enhance increased transparency. Ultimately, some cooperation across borders will be necessary to avoid a disjointed world where AI is reliable and safe in one location and threatening and unregulated in other locations. Without standardized methods, healthcare might become two-tiered, with high-income nations enjoying the advantages of strong, well-regulated AI while low-resource areas are subject to access restrictions or ethical dilemmas. **European Union AI Act (2024):** The first comprehensive AI law in the world was the EU AI Act, which was legally adopted in 2024. Four risk levels are used to classify AI systems unacceptable, high, limited and low. It's significant that AI in healthcare is categorized as "high-risk." This implies that before being used, medical AI technologies must meet stringent restrictions. Important clauses consist Throughout the AI lifecycle; developers must carry out methodical risk assessments. Training datasets need to be well-documented, representative and bias-free. Human Oversight In the healthcare industry, AI cannot function completely on its own human professionals must maintain control. Systems need to make it obvious how they produce their results. After being implemented AI tools need to be regularly checked for equity and safety. As global healthcare corporations align their systems with EU norms, the Act is anticipated to have an impact on legislation outside of Europe.

FDA Guidance in the United States (2025): The U.S. FDA published new guideline documents for Software as a Medical Device (SaMD) and AI-enabled medical devices in January and August of 2025. The Predetermined Change Control Plan (PCCP) is a key component that enables businesses to change AI models after approval without requiring a fresh assessment each time. Important components consist of: AI gadgets are viewed as dynamic systems as opposed to fixed goods. Developers are required to specify in advance the kinds of upgrades that are anticipated (such as retraining using fresh data) and the methods by which safety will be preserved. The FDA mandates that healthcare providers receive explicit information about performance changes from upgraded devices. Cybersecurity Strong security measures must be in place to guard against data leaks or hacking from linked medical equipment Developers are required to specify in advance the kinds of upgrades that are anticipated (such as retraining using fresh data) and the methods by which safety will be preserved. The FDA mandates that healthcare providers receive explicit information about performance changes from upgraded devices. Cybersecurity Strong security measures must be in place to guard against data leaks or hacking from linked medical equipment. By striking a balance between safety and innovation, this strategy keeps risks under control while enabling AI systems to advance over time.

WHO Guidance on AI and LLMs in Healthcare (2024): A global framework for the ethics and regulation of AI in health, with a particular emphasis on Large Language Models (LLMs), was released by the World Health Organization in 2024. WHO issued more than 40 recommendations in recognition of the growing use of AI aides in public health and hospitals Safety and Effectiveness: Before being used in clinical settings, AI must pass a thorough examination. To stop sensitive patient data from being misused, robust procedures are required. LLM-based solutions ought to indicate to patients when they are speaking with an AI instead of a person. Governments, healthcare organizations, and developers must all have clearly defined roles. AI should encourage universal access to healthcare worldwide rather than exacerbate existing health disparities. For low- and middle-income countries (LMICs), where national rules may still be developing, the WHO's recommendations are particularly crucial.

Ethical Governance Principles: A number of universal ethical principles that serve as the foundation for responsible healthcare AI are continuously included in the governance frameworks created by the US, the EU, and WHO. Transparency and explainability rank among the most important, requiring AI systems to produce results that patients and physicians can comprehend and rely on. Unexplained diagnoses or treatment recommendations in medicine not only increase the possibility of clinical errors but also erode patient confidence in the medical staff and the technology. Despite their excellent accuracy, black-box models are nonetheless hard to assess, test, or enhance if they lack interpretability. Because of this, explainable models are emphasized in both the FDA's SaMD guidelines and the EU's Artificial Intelligence Act, and the WHO advises that patients be informed when AI is used in their treatment. Accountability is the second fundamental concept, which calls for the establishment of distinct channels of accountability in the event that AI systems malfunction or have negative effects. Accountability for AI systems is complicated since in contrast to traditional medical equipment, they include a number of parties, including software developers, hospitals, regulators, and physicians. While the EU AI Act emphasizes on human oversight to guarantee clinicians remain the ultimate decision-makers, regulators like the FDA have started tackling this issue by demanding lifecycle management plans that outline how liability is divided between developers and institutions. Accountability guarantees that when mistakes are made, patients are not left defenceless and that accountability cannot be transferred to "the algorithm." Fairness and inclusivity are equally significant principles that represent the increasing awareness that AI systems trained on limited or biased datasets can yield unequal results. As an example, tests that had previously been mostly trained on data of white, male, or affluent groups would not work as well when applied to patients in low-resource locations, women, children, or minority groups. This increases the risk of worsening rather than reducing the already-existing health disparities. Reacting to this, governments are putting pressure on AI systems to be certified among diverse subgroups and fairness audits are increasingly required before and after deployment. Specifically, the WHO emphasizes inclusivity which means that AI should not be restricted to a highly-resourced setting but rather support. Individuals in poor and middle-income countries. These principles of governance accountability openness and explainability, fairness and inclusion, and continuing monitoring put together form a rational global guideline that guides the ethical use of AI in healthcare. The key principles are quite similar though the concentration and details of the implementation can vary across the regions the patients should be confident that AI is open, safe, fair, and continuously observed. The guidelines also serve as helpful reminders to developers and healthcare organizations that it is the ability of AI to deliver reliable, fair, and ethically sound care to diverse categories of patients and not its technological power that decides its success.

Implementation Problems: Various challenges continue to affect the application of AI in healthcare even though there has been a tremendous contribution to the development of governance frameworks. Regulatory fragmentation is one of the immediate issues: it is hard to achieve international harmonization and cross-border cooperation when various territories are working on their set of standards: the US the EU and some parts of Asia. Another barrier is the cost of compliance because smaller healthcare establishments who cannot afford to comply with the strict regulatory requirements can be disadvantaged by the complex and expensive approval processes. Another challenge is inequality in access to data; not all low- and middle-income countries have sufficient financial, digital and infrastructure resources to participate in widespread AI creation and this may contribute to a further increase in health inequities globally. And the last, yet not the least, the issue of the changing technology is quite alive. Although most of the existing regulations exist to fulfil the needs of non-portable medical devices, modern artificial intelligence applications are continuously learning and evolving, and it poses new challenges concerning changing regulations, long-term safety surveillance, and accountability. Patient safety is the most fundamental pillar of moral healthcare that becomes even more paramount in the case of clinical decision-making that includes artificial intelligence (AI). The adverse consequences of mistakes in the healthcare sector can be severe even deadly, as opposed to other sectors. The life of a patient might be at risk in case an AI system wrongly identifies a cancerous tumour as benign or recommends an incorrect dosage of a drug. The use of AI in medicine should be more than merely creative: it should also be accurate, reliable, open and clinically supported. Doctors might hesitate to accept black-box models which are able to give advice without giving an explicit reason or alternativel they can adhere to them blindly. Researchers and authorities consider the protection of patient safety a paramount requirement of the responsibility of AI implementation. Such a precaution requires several steps that are achievable. AI tools should undergo rigorous testing, both in controlled research studies and in a real situation at the hospital with a diverse population of patients. It is necessary to monitor continuously after deployment to detect so-called performance drift, which is a decrease in accuracy, which occurs when AI encounters new or modified patient data. Lastly, human supervising should never be underrated: AI should be used to complement the clinical decision of medical practitioners rather than to replace it. Doctors should not be excluded in decision-making either though instead they should use AI to complement their work instead of blindly replacing it. By incorporating solid validation and round-the-clock monitoring with human responsibility, healthcare systems can minimize risks and ensure that AI positively impacts and not harms patient safety (Yang et al., 2024; Food and Drug Administration, 2025). Clinical practice is exposed to a high risk of serious threats by AI systems in various ways, which may endanger patient safety. Diagnostic errors still occupy the 1st place in the list of the gravest problems: false negatives may delay the necessity of some actions and deteriorate patient outcomes, whereas false positives may trigger unnecessary anxiety, intrusive tests, or even overtreatment. An additional issue is automation bias when medical professionals rely heavily on the AI output without critically reviewing it, this may only make mistakes more severe instead of preventing them.

2024). The popularity of black-box models or deep learning algorithms that only offer minimal or no insight into the reasoning behind their response makes it difficult to validate or even accept the findings by physicians (Amann et al., 2020). Also models that are trained using historical data or geographic-specific data might not work well in new populations or even with new medical practices because of model drift and data shifts. As an illustration, the imaging models that are tested and validated in developed countries cannot be used in low-resource countries with the use of different equipment. Finally, the problem of uncontrolled updates in the ever-learning AI emergence introduces new challenges because in the absence of a proper monitoring step in regulatory oversight the post-deployment changes can create unintended risks (Food and Drug Administration, 2025). Ethical AI in Healthcare can be seen in Figure 2. Combined these challenges illustrate the need to make patient safety remain the primary concern in applying AI to healthcare.

Figure 2. Ethical AI in healthcare

PRIVACY & DATA GOVERNANCE	• HIPAA • GDPR
FAIRNESS & EQUITY	• Bias Reduction • Inclusivity
TRANSPARENCY & EXPLAINABILITY	• Interpetable AI • Clinical Trust
ACCOUNTABILITY & HUMAN OVERSIGHT	• Auditing • Responsibility

Ensuring Patient safety, Strategies and Framework: Patient safety should be prioritized when adopting the principles of artificial intelligence (AI) in healthcare with the help of a multi-layered approach that uses clinical practices, regulatory oversight, and technical security. Technologically, AI systems must be fully tested against multiple datasets that will represent different clinical settings, imaging conditions, and demographics. The adopted mechanisms such as the Predetermined Change Control Plan (PCCP) (2025), which has been adopted by the regulatory authorities such as the U.S. Food and Drug Administration (FDA), allow AI models to improve with time and ensure that the modification is safe and reliable. Equally, healthcare AI falls under the EU AI Act as describing it a high-risk application, which requires frequent auditing, transparency, and human oversight. These systems underline the idea that the safety of the AI systems is an ongoing responsibility and not a single assessment. Plans to underline the partnership of the human and AI in health care are also essential. The use of AI must be used as a decision-support tool (i.e. offer evidence-based guidance, but not replace doctors). By incorporating Explainable AI (XAI) methods, including saliency maps, SHAP values, and attention layers, clinicians can gain a better insight into model outputs and make a decision based on them, whether they conform to clinical reasoning or not. This enhances responsibility and trust levels because it allows physicians to explain AI-based judgments to patients by being articulate. When taken collectively, these frameworks and tactics contribute to a comprehensive safety net to prove that than and only then can the healthcare AI innovation be considered a success, as it protects patient welfare and prioritizes it in every stage of the adoption process.

FACTS SENSITIVITY & PRIVACY OF HEALTHCARE AI

Among the most confidential information that individuals can share is healthcare data that contains their diagnosis, genetic sequences, imaging scans, and mental health records among others. Medical information is irrevocable and strongly connected with identity and dignity, unlike financial information, which may be changed after its leakage. The data is now full of continuous streams of physiological parameters as the use of wearables and online platforms rises, and data breaches are even more damaging. The abuse may compromise privacy and trust in health care systems due to societal stigma, workplace discrimination, or insurance discrimination. The complexity of healthcare data increases the risk. Records are less secure, as they are often longitudinal in nature, multimodal, and inter institutional or international in nature. Laws on privacy that are different across nations, like the GDPR in Europe and HIPAA in the US, pose risks when data is transferred across national borders. To counter this, federated learning, differential privacy and blockchain audit trails, privacy preserving technologies are increasingly being deployed to protect the data of patients and develop AI. Protecting data is at the very core of ethical healthcare AI and is required to maintain patient trust and equal access.

SECRECY-PROTECTIVE METHODS OF HEALTHCARE AI

To ensure the advantages of Artificial Intelligence (AI) in healthcare and secure the privacy of patient information, various privacy-conserving approaches have been created. The techniques that many have attracted much attention in the literature between 2022 and 2025 include many of them. One of the most widespread approaches is Federated Learning (FL) which helps a number of medical facilities or research centres to collaborate on training models without sharing raw patient data. Instead, there is sharing of only model updates such as gradients or weights. This approach has been successful in cross-site illness modelling, distributed electronic health record (EHR) forecasts and multi-hospital medical imaging (Teo et al., 2024). FL continues to contend with such problems as overheads in communication, non-identically dispersed (non-ID) information in hospitals, and susceptibility to bad clients. FL is often supplemented by Differential Privacy (DP) which provides formal mathematical guarantees that protect individual entries. DP ensures that the deletion or changing of the record of a single patient does not significantly change model outputs by introducing highly normalized noise to the data or gradients. This approach has proven particularly useful in sensitive clinical data and genetic forecasting, where the risk of privacy is also quite high (Pati et al., 2024). Homomorphic Encryption (HE) and Secure Aggregation add to this the extra protection levels. Whereas HE allows calculation to be performed directly on encrypted data, Secure Aggregation ensures that the central server receives aggregated data instead of individual updates, which ensures that no information of sensitive value is ever disclosed in plaintext. Its promise is that HE is still computationally demanding and challenging to scale to large medical picture or genome datasets. Federated transfer learning and multi-modal hybrid models are emerging as an alternative to single-modality methods in order to manage complex healthcare settings in which hospitals have dissimilar feature spaces. Transfer learning enables models to transfer knowledge to new fields without explicit data transfer like the imaging data of one hospital and genetic/clinical notes of another (Alasiry et al., 2025). Equally, multi-modal frameworks combining genetic data, imaging data, EHR data, and so forth, can potentially model diseases in a holistic manner, although they require even more stringent privacy-related safeguards to prevent the association of sensitive characteristics with each other. Control of access, approval and governance procedures remain vital data pillars. defense besides technical strategies. Powerful structures that help ensure that privacy provisions go. beyond algorithms are role-based access, audit logging, patient consent management and tiered access to data.Now patients are able to control, monitor, as well as audit who gets access to their data, and why due to state-of-the-art. Such technology as blockchain-based consent ledgers. By subjecting technical safeguards to moral and regulations, these governance tactics help to enhance patient and healthcare provider confidence. Despite these developments, a lot remains to be done. There is a constant trade between privacy and utility: with small datasets, more privacy such as adding noise or data encryption has the tendency to reduce model accuracy. Scalability is another issue, as large-scale medical applications could not afford computationally intensive methods such as homomorphic encryption. Due to the varying nature of hospitals regarding computer facilities, information quality, and internet access, client heterogeneity is also difficult.

Furthermore, collaborative learning systems are still vulnerable to hostile or malevolent clients who can try to introduce tainted updates. Lastly, even while technical approaches are crucial, they cannot take the place of robust governance, policy frameworks, and auditing procedures, all of which are required to bridge the gap between patient confidence and technology innovation.

Fair and Equitable Access in Healthcare AI: The foundation of healthcare is equity, which guarantees all patients receive safe and efficient treatment shows in Figure#3. AI systems that are educated on biased or unbalanced data run the risk of amplifying and repeating inequality. Results may be worse for groups underrepresented in training datasets, including minorities, women, children, and patients in LMICs. LMIC patients, rural communities, and minority groups are frequently underrepresented. Performance disparities arise from variations in the calibration and quality of imaging instruments across nations.AI occasionally sacrifices subgroup fairness in order to maximize overall accuracy. While rural and low-resource settings lag behind, wealthy hospitals embrace cutting-edge AI. Gather information from a variety of sources, including gender, age, ethnicity, and location. It should make use of metrics such as subgroup AUC, demographic parity, and equalized odds.

Evaluate AI models' performance in both subgroups and overall. in the creation and application of AI through human-cantered inclusive design. Collaborations and edge/cloud-based AI to assist LMICs.

Figure 3. Fair and equitable access in healthcare AI

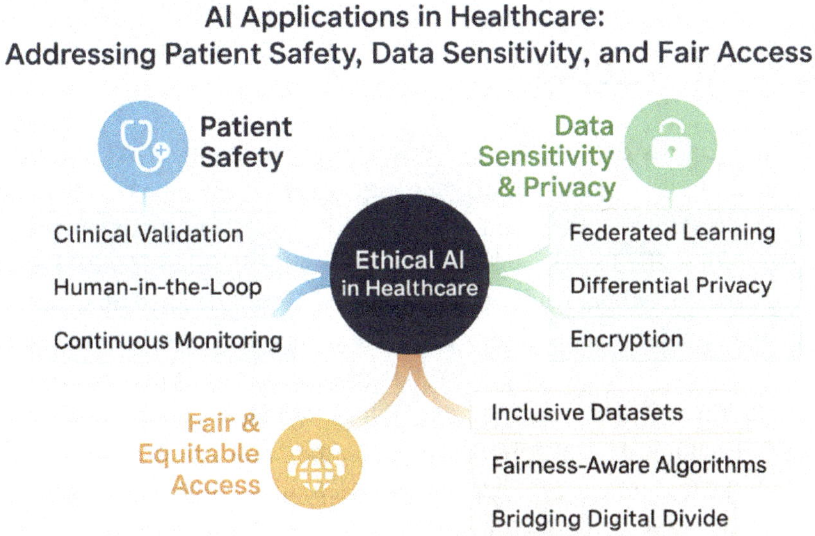

Global Health Equity and AI: Fair algorithms are not the sole factor in making sure that artificial intelligence (AI) is fairly accessible. Healthcare another is the adoption of these technologies across geographic regions. Obstacles including most of them have poor internet connectivity, a poorly developed digital infrastructure, and insufficient funding. LMICs. In the absence of targeted regulations, AI poses the risk of being used as a disproportionately beneficial tool rich hospitals on the cost of the poor communities. WHO 2024. Identifies three key priorities in preventing this digital divide: shared governance models enabling LMICs to particulate in world AI choices, educate healthcare specialists to operate and handle AI instruments and invest. Local infrastructure. Through such strategies, AI can ensure fairness through bridging gaps instead of increasing them. With AI being developed in a proper manner it can contribute to better patient outcomes, and this is evidenced by being ethically used in. healthcare. As an example, with image analysis, AI can assist in diagnosing a disease at an earlier stage, which allows medical. experts to identify such issues as cancer or Alzheimer at a younger age. It is also able to aid physicians to make improved clinical decisions. Prescription advice by indicating dangerous drug interactions or aiding them in prescribing safe amounts. Real-world data AI models can be applied in public health to analyse and predict illness outbreaks, as well as more efficiently distribute resources. More to the point, ethical applications of AI is the ones, which place the safety of the patient first, protect the privacy of the health knowledge, and ensure all groups have equal access to benefits. The following are some of the ways AI can be a. impetus to ethical and inclusive healthcare innovation, in terms of fused with strong governance and global Cooperation.

AI IN MEDICAL IMAGING

Medical imaging is one of the most efficient applications of AI and the deep learning algorithms are already at present. Equivalent or even superior to human radiologists in disease detection such as lung cancer, breast cancer, pneumonia, and Alzheimer's. Still, a 2023 study published in the Lancet Digital Health found that chest. The problem of subpar performance of X-ray AI tools trained on U.S. datasets on South Asian populations highlights the need to encourage further studies in this are the need to use multi-site testing to avoid false positives and false negativity. This highlights why there is a necessity of exemplary validation in order to guarantee patient safety. Imaging datasets often have some metadata, such as scanner IDs or hospital locations that may jeopardize patient re-identification, data sensitivity is a second-important issue. Federated learning (FL) is being increasingly adopted to overcome this problem, allowing hospitals to collaborate on training data sensitive models not centralized (Pati et al., 2024). There is still an issue of fair access because, in order to ensure equal performance between populations, AI models should be trained on geographically heterogeneous datasets and ethnically varied. To this, such resources as the UK Biobank and OASIS-3 are necessary. This strategy was and an interesting case study in 2024: a federated learning alliance between hospitals in Europe and Asia significantly improved the identification of breast cancer and spared patient privacy (Teo et al., 2024).

REMOTE PATIENT MONITORING (RPM) AND IOT

Clinical decision support (CDS) systems aim to help the physician to make improved decisions regarding treatment. With the growing popularity of large language models (LLMs), new opportunities have emerged and one of them is the skills in reading and summarizing patient reports, writing clinical notes and addressing questions in patients. Despite their there are serious problems with these instruments, potential. LLMs can generate false in order to guarantee patient safetyor misleading responses state known as "hallucination." Lawrence, 2024 recommends that the LLMs being applied to the healthcare industry must always specify that there is the usage of AI and include confidence scores to address this their results. The other significant issue is the sensitivity of the data since training LLMs often requires large sets of clinical notes which could include sensitive material. Differential Privacy Two methods are being increasingly used to maintain privacy, namely, (DP) and automatic redaction. Fair access is also necessary since hospitals in wealthier districts should not be the only place to enjoy high-tech. CDS technologies. The use of AI-driven decision support is being adopted by low- and middle-income countries (LMICs) without having to invest in costly infrastructure due to cloud-based CDS platforms. These advantages can be seen in one recent case study: the Mayo Clinic trailed an LLM-assisted CDS system in 2025, leading to it reducing its costs by 35% saving of time by physicians in documentation. Audits regularly ensured the safety, accuracy and reliability of the tool. An AIoT-based remote patient monitoring (RPM) system in Singapore in 2023 provided a noteworthy example of how to enhance glucose management for diabetic patients; nevertheless, the implementation of robust encryption and access control measures to protect sensitive data was necessary for the system to be successful (Khan et al., 2024).

AI IN NEUROLOGICAL DISORDERS: ALZHEIMER'S DISEASE DETECTION

The application of AI to Alzheimer's disease (AD) presents both enormous prospects and difficult problems because AI is particularly useful for early detection when combined with multimodal data, such as MRI scans, PET imaging, cognitive tests, and genetic biomarkers. Although early detection promotes better treatment planning and interventions from the standpoint of patient safety, there is a chance that over diagnosis will result in needless psychological suffering for patients and their families. Since Alzheimer's datasets like ADNI and OASIS 3 contain extremely private cognitive and genetic data, data sensitivity is also crucial. To protect privacy, cutting edge techniques like split learning and federated GANs are currently being investigated (Alasiry et al., 2025). Since the majority of AD datasets are from Western populations, restricting the accuracy of models in other locations, ensuring equitable access is still difficult. However, new projects in Asia and Africa are starting to address this by developing more varied Alzheimer's cohorts. A model that used MRI data and genetic biomarkers reached 92% accuracy in early Alzheimer's prediction across five hospitals, all while adhering to GDPR regulations. This encouraging case study from 2024 illustrated the potential of federated multimodal AI (El-Assy, 2024). The significance of an ethical AI implementation framework that translates lofty ideals of safety, privacy, and equity into workable steps is highlighted by these advancements. Even the most cutting-edge AI tools run the risk of making their effects on patients hazardous, unreliable, or unfair in the absence of formal frameworks to direct their practical adoption.

COMPONENTS OF AN ETHICAL AI FRAMEWORK

Privacy & Data Governance: AI in healthcare is developed on the premise of a strong data control. It consists of high anonymity, secure medical data storage, and effective administration of patient consent. To ensure that sensitive health data is protected, privacy-enforcing solutions, such as blockchain-based permission systems, federated. The use of Learning (FL) and Differential Privacy (DP) is on the increase. Compliance with the current regulatory systems that regulate the managing of patient information, including GDPR in Europe, HIPAA in the US, and such provincial legislation, is also of the essence.

Audits of Fairness and Inclusivity: Fairness assessments should be applied to AI systems before and. deployment in turn to enforce equity. To achieve the impartiality and consistency of the predictions, this involves testing on demographic factors such as gender, age, ethnicity and region. To guarantee inclusivity, compulsory fairness audits are proposed now, with the use of such criteria as equalized opportunities and subgroup calibration. Ongoing revalidation also contributes to the process of countering the drift in the datasets with time, avoiding models of underrepresented populations are losing their accuracy.

Clinical Verification and Patient Security: AI is not less concerned with patient safety. To make sure AI models function effectively in different healthcare environments they need to be multi-site-validated in advance implementation. After approval, reliability and performance drift are to undergo post-market monitoring. Human control is also essential, AI should assist physicians but not to replace them, and human choice making in the loop also assists in preventing bias in the automation process and ensures the doctors have the ultimate authority on the medical decisions.

Clarity and Explainability: The credibility of AI in the healthcare sector lies in its explainability and transparency. Explainable AI (XAI) tools that help patients include saliency maps and SHAP values and clinicians in the understanding of the prediction. Responsibility is enhanced and credibility is goes through capitalizing on the social reporting of model design, data used in training and constraints. Without such precautions, black-box AI algorithms take the risk of losing patient and healthcare professional trust.

RESPONSIBILITY AND LEADERSHIP

Determine who will be responsible in case of failure of AI by establishing effective governance structures. This & includes regulators, healthcare facilities and developers, whose responsibilities are a bit different. The AI-related failures need liability systems, and constant reviews by external ethics committees can determine conformity, safety and equity. These systems ensure that there is fair distribution of tasks among stakeholders and accountability is not abandoned ambiguous.

International Access & Equity: The digital divide between the wealthy and resource-bounded locations should not be widned by AI in healthcare. To provide international fairness, the capacity-building process in underdeveloped and developing countries should be enhanced. The income countries (LMICs) should be developed in terms of infrastructure, training, and sustainable finances along with subsidy programs to make AI tools available in less-resourceful clinics. Additionally the use of open-source AI models in the field of public health is being promoted which offers affordable and. internationally available ways of attaining fair innovation.

CASE STUDY 1: NHS AI LAB (UNITED KINGDOM)

In 2023 the UK created the NHS AI Lab, where AI models are tested in the fields of diagnostic triage, pathology, and radiology. Several hospitals. Initial evaluations showed that there was an ethical dilemma regardless of the potential of the initiative diagnostic imaging models were more successful on majority groups and less dependable on some ethnic groups, which questioned issues of equity and fairness. The NHS created subgroup validation, which required doctors to approve to address the problem, and developed inclusive dataset requirements before to clinical implementation. Regular fairness checks were also established to ensure that there was similar performance among the demographic groups. The case study's main what it means is that, despite the possible abundance of resources in health care systems, there may still be some disparities in equity when using datasets are not sufficiently different. It is still important to have continuous audits, inclusive design, and regulatory supervision safety of patients and equal access to AI-driven healthcare.

CASE STUDY 2: MAYO CLINIC – CDS (LLM BASED, USA, 2025)

A Large Language Model (LLM) was piloted by the Mayo Clinic in 2025 as Clinical Decision Support (CDS). Systems to aid in summarizing of patients, recommendation of treatment pathways and physician documentation burden reduction.

Despite the productivity benefits of the system, there existed an ethical problem since the LLM sometimes came up with some hallucinations sane yet incorrect advice with the potential to be dangerous. Patient safety in cases where the doctors trusted them without scrutinizing them. Man in the loop was implemented that were implemented at the Mayo Clinic in order to minimize these risks and ensure that doctors retained the ultimate power in making decisions. Audit logs were also part of the system to track AI contributions and ensure accountability and superficiality aspects such as confidence ratings and explicable summaries. The main lesson of this pilot was it, even though LLMs have the potential to save a considerable amount of time and reduce clinician fatigue, that robust controls and monitoring processes are needed to ensure that errors do not influence the treatment of patients.

CASE STUDY 3: AIOT FOR DIABETES MONITORING IN SINGAPORE (2023–2024)

Singapore has introduced an AIoT-based to make predictions on glucose fluctuations and enable timely interventions. Between 2023 and 2024, Remote Patient Monitoring (RPM) system of diabetic patients. This system combines artificial intelligence wearable technology. The system appeared so promising in improving the it was also associated with ethical concerns since of the continuous flow of private health, which was the main aim of managing chronic diseases data, which made cybersecurity breach and unlawful data transfer more likely. Developers used these issues are addressed by Edge AI to make most of the data processing locally available on the devices of patients. In lieu of transmitting all information to central servers. To mitigate the weaknesses and restrict access to the authorized workers. Only other measures were taken, like role-based access controls, and end-to-end encryption.

The valuable lesson on this deployment is that though continuous health tracking poses threat to privacy, local (edge) processing combined with effective security can provide effective defences without compromising the benefits of real-time AI-based healthcare.

Future of Ethical AI in Healthcare: Healthcare AI will evolve in the coming years as the necessity to balance innovation and moral duties will increase ten years. The challenges of patient safety, patient information protection, and equitableness and technologies such as as multimodal learning, Large Language Models (LLMs) and AIoT will only become more accessible based monitoring systems grow. Future studies will have to focus on developing hybrid frameworks that integrate a number of methods that preserve privacy. As an example, efficiency can be achieved by edge-cloud hybrid systems training sensitive data on-premises and accessing large-scale analytics in the cloud, and federated learning and blockchain is able to provide transparency and collaboration. To protect the medical AI systems against new threats, another important avenue is development of security framework. Sensitive health information can be compromised by the fact that conventional methods of encryption are becoming obsolete with the emergence of quantum computing. To protect AI from future PQC research is thus necessary due to cyberattacks. Developing long-term resilience in. The use of AI systems is essential, which may be supported by the tendency of healthcare regulators to propose quantum-resistant methods. The continuous-learning models should also be taken into account, as they can change in response to new data, yet it might introduce regulatory complexity. The main aspect of adaptive monitoring should include ethics committees and continuous auditing futuristic governance to ensure that AI-based systems remain stable, safe, and balanced over time. Global health equity will also become the focus of future research. The AI may decrease or expand the healthcare disparity high- and low-income (LMIC) and low-income countries. The databases around the globe should incorporate different groups in Africa, Asia, and Latin America as well as Western people so as to prevent inequality. It will be essential to invest in infrastructure i.e. affordable wearables and AI tools based on clouds

Contributing benefits to low resource settings. Capacity building is also very important with initiatives to educate the data scientists and local medics in AI literacy and ethical use. But rather than being passive receivers. These initiatives can make LMICs become active participants of AI innovation. Lastly, there are additional ethical, legal, and social enhancements are to be introduced in the future research and not only technical precautions. Decentralized Two concepts that predict hospitals, regulators, and algorithmic governance include Autonomous Councils (DACs) and algorithmic governance sharing decision-making between international organizations. Legal-technical harmonization will also be needed. As machine-readable permission that is compliant with HIPAA and GDPR. Nonetheless, socio-ethical structures that promote equity, inclusivity and patient autonomy should remain significant. The Patient trust can be preserved by combining transformational potential of healthcare AI at the same time technological progress in an ethically responsible and legally safeguarded way.

CONCLUSION

Artificial intelligence is a propelling force in modern healthcare and one of the most powerful ones innovations in the diagnosis, clinical decision support, remote monitoring, and diagnostics of neurological illnesses. Nevertheless, significant ethical concerns are also raised by the widespread use of it that cannot be overlooked. Three pillars are used to determine the responsible use of AI and have been identified in this chapter: patient safety, which demands clinical validation, transparency and continued monitoring to avoid false diagnosis or life-threatening diagnosis. recommendations; data sensitivity and privacy, which entails strong security measures such as federated learning, differential privacy, and encryption to secure an enormously sensitive medical information; and equitable and just access, which ensures the AI systems are useful to all groups by providing inclusive datasets, equitable algorithms, and capacity-building of under-resourced regions. Ethical questions are not abstract, but this means that they come into play in any real life.world implementation, as shown by case study examples of the NHS AI Lab, the Mayo Clinic-based LLM monitoring of diabetes using AIoT, CDS, Singapore, and federated research on Alzheimer. Herein lies the importance of organized systems such as that given in Section 8. Going forward, hybrid frameworks that incorporate technologies like blockchain and federated learning, more robust safeguards like post-quantum security, adaptive governance models for continuous-learning systems, and global equity initiatives cantered on the Global South will influence the direction of healthcare AI. These developments have the potential to increase AI's capability and reliability. Ultimately, whether AI provides safe, confidential, and equitable care to all patients regardless of location, gender, or socioeconomic background will determine its success in the healthcare industry rather than accuracy ratings or computational efficiency alone. Researchers, physicians, and legislators must view ethical standards as fundamental needs rather than optional extras in order to accomplish this. The promise of AI to revolutionize health while preserving the well-being, dignity, and trust of those it serves can only be realized at that point.

REFERENCES

Alasiry, S., Wong, K., & Ibrahim, T. (2025). Privacy-preserving multimodal federated GANs for neurodegenerative disease prediction. *Frontiers in Artificial Intelligence in Medicine, 6*, Article 88.

Amann, A., Blasimme, M., Vayena, E., Frey, A., & Madai, V. (2020). Explainability for artificial intelligence in healthcare: A multidisciplinary perspective. *BMC Medical Informatics and Decision Making*, *20*(1), 310. Advance online publication. DOI: 10.1186/s12911-020-01332-6 PMID: 33256715

El-Assy, A. (2024). Federated multimodal AI for Alzheimer's early detection across diverse hospitals. *Journal of Medical AI Research*, 7(2), 112–124.

European Union. (2024). *Regulation (EU) 2024/1689 of the European Parliament and of the Council of 13 June 2024 laying down harmonised rules on artificial intelligence (Artificial Intelligence Act).* Official Journal of the European Union.

Food and Drug Administration. (2025). *Predetermined change control plan (PCCP) for AI/ML-enabled devices: Guidance for industry and Food and Drug Administration staff.* U.S. Department of Health and Human Services.

Google Health, & DeepMind. (. (2020). AI for breast cancer screening: Results from multi-site validation. *Nature*, *577*, 89–94. DOI: 10.1038/s41586-019-1799-6

Jabeen, M., Ahmad, M., Qasim, M., & Hasnain, M. (2024). The surprising similarities between blockchain functions and ethical principles (in perspective of Islam). *International Research Journal of Management and Social Sciences*, *5*(1), 657–669.

Jabeen, M., Hussain, M., & Rana Hassam Ahmed, H. A. (n.d.). A blockchain-based IPFS augmented distributed information sharing paradigm for secure communication in networked environment.

Jabeen, M., Ibrar, M., Hussain, M., & Hassan, M. A. S. (2025). Blockchain-based explainable AI for secure and privacy-preserving automated machine learning in IoT-edge for smart medical healthcare. In *AI and blockchain applications for privacy and security in smart medical systems* (pp. 59–80). IGI Global Scientific Publishing. DOI: 10.4018/979-8-3373-0593-6.ch003

Khan, M., Tan, S., & Abdullah, F. (2024). AIoT-based remote patient monitoring for diabetes management: A case study from Singapore. *Health Informatics Journal*, *30*(1), 56–70.

Khan, M. S. H., Ahmad, M., Akhtar, K., Jabeen, M., Begum, U., & Ikram, N. (2023). Shanghai Cooperation Organization (SCO): An emerging power block. *Russian Law Journal, 11*(5), 1084–1088.

Pati, R., Gupta, H., & Lee, M. (2024). Differential privacy-enhanced federated learning for genomics. *Nature Communications*, *15*, 1456.

Teo, R., Singh, P., & Chen, L. (2024). Federated learning for breast cancer detection across Asia and Europe: Preserving privacy in cross-border healthcare. *IEEE Journal of Biomedical and Health Informatics*, *28*(5), 1901–1912.

World Health Organization. (2024). *Ethics and governance of artificial intelligence for health: Guidance on large language models*. World Health Organization.

Yang, J., Zhao, L., & Kim, S. (2024). Bias and generalizability of diagnostic AI across imaging devices and populations. *The Lancet. Digital Health*, *6*(4), e223–e234.

Chapter 7
Ethical AI Applications in Health Care:
Ensuring Patient Safety, Data Security, and Fair Access

Nazeef Ul Haq
University of Engineering and Technology, Lahore, Pakistan

Abdul Basit Dogar
http://orcid.org/0009-0003-5077-8531
University of Management and Technology, Lahore, Pakistan

Rizwan Riaz Mir
Virtual University of Pakistan, Lahore, Pakistan

Muhammad Naveed Yasir
Emerson University, Multan, Pakistan

ABSTRACT

The integration of Artificial Intelligence (AI) into healthcare presents transformative opportunities and profound ethical challenges that require continuous oversight and moral reflection. This chapter critically examines the ethical foundations necessary for responsible and sustainable AI use in medical contexts, tracing its evolution from early expert systems to deep learning applications influencing clinical decision-making. Grounded in the biomedical ethics of autonomy, beneficence, non-maleficence, and justice, the discussion extends these principles to algorithmic transparency, bias mitigation, accountability, and equitable access to AI-driven healthcare. Key concerns of data privacy, patient safety, cybersecurity, and regulatory compliance under frameworks such as HIPAA, GDPR, WHO guidelines, and the EU AI Act are

DOI: 10.4018/979-8-3373-6038-6.ch007

explored. By reviewing notable AI failures, including IBM Watson for Oncology and the DeepMind–Royal Free data-sharing case, the chapter underscores the essential need for continuous ethical governance throughout the AI lifecycle in healthcare.

INTRODUCTION

Background of AI in Healthcare

AI in health care did not spring to life overnight. It has been a journey of ideas, experimentations, disappointments, and breakthroughs. To understand where we are now and what ethical, safety, or regulatory challenges come with it. It helps to see how the field has developed over the decades.

Early Foundations (1950s–1960s)

- **1950:** Alan Turing published "Computing Machinery and Intelligence", introducing what is now called the Turing Test, asking whether machines can be said to "think." This set philosophical and theoretical groundwork for thinking about machines that mimic human decision-making (Encyclopaedia Britannica, n.d.).
- **Mid 1950s-1960s:** The term "artificial intelligence" was coined in 1956 at the Dartmouth Conference, organized by John McCarthy and others. Researchers began exploring rule- based logics, heuristics, and symbolic AI, which would later influence medical expert sys- tems. ("Artificial Intelligence (AI) Coined at Dartmouth," n.d.)
- **1965 onward:** Projects like Dendral (Stanford) started. It was designed to help chemists interpret mass spectrometry data and was one of the first expert systems. It showed that domain knowledge (in chemistry in this case) plus heuristics could perform tasks that required specialized expertise (Lindsay et al., 1993).

The First Medical Expert Systems (1970s–1980s)

- **Early 1970s:**

  MYCIN: It was an expert system developed at the Stanford University, capable of identifying bacteria causing blood infections (e.g., bacteremia, meningitis) and recommending antibiotic treatments adjusted for patient weight. It had several hundred rules. Although it was never used clinically in standard care, it showed that computers could match or approach the reasoning of human specialists in narrow domains (Shortliffe, 1974).

INTERNIST-1: INTERNIST-1, developed at the University of Pittsburgh in the 1970s, was one of the earliest and most ambitious attempts to use artificial intelligence for medical diagnosis in general internal medicine. Its goal was to assist clinicians by ranking diagnostic possibilities using a large, structured knowledge base and heuristic algorithms. (Miller et al., 1982).

- **1980s:**

  CADUCEUS (mid-1980s): CADUCEUS, developed in the mid-1980s, was a significant evolution of the INTERNIST-1 expert system, aiming to address the growing complexity of medical diagnosis. It expanded disease coverage and introduced advanced reasoning methods to better handle cases involving multiple simultaneous diseases and uncertain or ambiguous clinical data. (Banks, 1986; Miller, 1984).

  DXplain (1984-1986): DXplain (1984-1986): DXplain is considered as one of the first and most popular clinical decision support systems (CDSS) to produce differential diagnosis using patient information, developed within Massachusetts General Hospital in the mid 80s. It has given clinicians ranked diagnostic suggestions, supporting evidence, and reference and has been significant to clinical practice and medical education (Barnett et al., 1987; Packer et al., 1989).

More specifically: in this era, the limitations were great: fewer computing resources, only a few data points, primitive user interfaces, and inability to fit into clinical processes. A great number of the systems were experimental (Kaul et al., 2020).

Transition and Growth (1990s–2000s)

- As computing hardware improved, storage and processing capabilities grew. Also, digitization of medical records, imaging, and labs became more common. AI methods broadened: probabilistic reasoning, machine learning (but relatively shallow models), and image analysis.
- AI went from rule-based expert systems toward systems that learn from data. For example, in medical imaging, there were computer-aided diagnosis (CAD) systems for mammography, ECG interpretation, etc. These used early machine learning models (not yet deep learning) and classical image processing (Liu et al., 2021).
- Some medical decision support tools improved in sophistication, and commercial interest in medical AI began to rise. But clinical validation, regula-

tory oversight, and trust issues still limited widespread adoption (Kaul et al., 2020).

Deep Learning Era and Rapid Innovation (2010s–2020s)

- The 2010s brought in deep learning (especially convolutional neural networks, CNNs) which massively improved performance in image-based tasks: radiology, pathology, dermatology, ophthalmology, etc. With more medical imaging data, GPUs, and large-scale annotated datasets, AI systems started achieving accuracy comparable to expert clinicians in some tasks (Litjens et al., 2017; Zhou et al., 2021; Mienye et al., 2025).
- Clinical decision support also gained ground via predictive models using electronic health records (EHRs). Models could forecast risk of readmission, disease progression, etc. For example, "Doctor AI" (2015) used recurrent neural networks on longitudinal EHR data to predict diagnoses and medication needs for future visits (Choi et al., 2016).
- Regulatory bodies began to respond. New frameworks were developed to assess AI/ML- based medical devices, with particular emphasis on safety, efficacy, transparency, and post- market monitoring. The FDA, EU, WHO, etc., started creating guidance (Kaul et al., 2020).
- Also, real-world deployments increased. AI in radiology for detecting pneumonia, cancer screening tools, AI-assisted pathology, and diagnostic tools began to be used in pilot studies and in some clinical settings. The COVID-19 pandemic further accelerated interest in AI for diagnosing lung disease from imaging, pandemic tracking, etc. (Xhako et al., 2025).

Recent and Emerging Trends (2020s–Present)

- Integration of AI in everyday clinical workflows has increased. AI systems are helping in early detection, risk prediction, triage, remote monitoring. There's more attention to interpretability, fairness, bias mitigation, and regulatory compliance (Zhou et al., 2021).
- New architectures (not just CNNs) such as transformers are making their way into medical imaging and text-based tasks. Federated learning (to avoid centralizing sensitive data), uncertainty quantification, and more robust external validation are being emphasized.
- There are also growing ethical, legal, and social discussions: privacy, data sharing, informed consent, liability if the AI makes wrong decisions, how to regulate continuous learning systems, and how to ensure that AI helps

all populations equitably. These are now major parts of research reports and regulatory guidelines

In each era, there have been **hopes** (AI as a helper, as an expert), **failures** (overpromises, systems that did not generalize, systems unseen by clinicians), and **learnings** (what mattered: data quality; evaluation beyond accuracy; user-interface; regulatory approval; bias). The path has been uneven as shown in Figure 1.

Figure 1. Evolution of AI in healthcare: A historical timeline

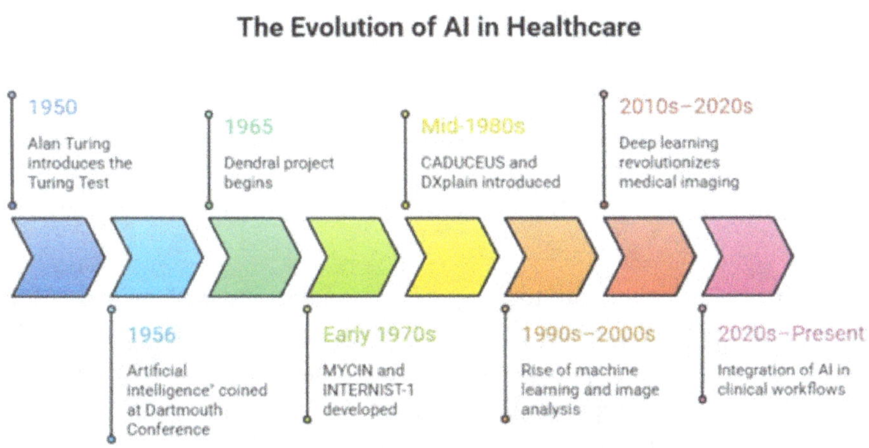

THE IMPORTANCE OF ETHICS IN MEDICAL AI

The stakes in healthcare are extremely high as any small decision can affect life or death outcomes. It is essential to maintain the patient trust and prevention of harm. AI systems risk bias and compromise on patient's privacy without proper implementation of safeguard measures. These failures do not only put patient's health in danger but can also undermine the public confidence on digital health solutions. Although AI system can transform the health sector, it comes with other factors which cause concern like privacy, data security and informed consent particularly due to the sensitivity of the health information (Murdoch, 2021).

Figure 2. The importance of ethics for AI in healthcare

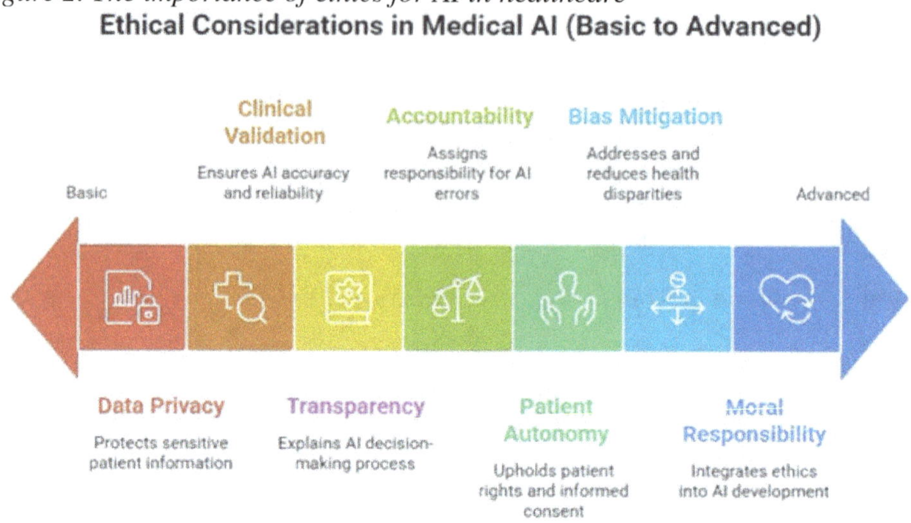

Think about a clinician with the help of AI or a hospital with an algorithm that can be used to diagnose or triage patients. Bureaucracy in the background of those models is data, design, transparency, and accountability decisions. In case of ethics neglect, the dangers are tangible: physical harm to the patients, loss of confidence, injustice, and legal liability. Therefore, ethics is not optional rather necessary as depicted in the Figure 2; it forms the basis of medical AI.

These are some of the main dimensions that explain why ethics should be part of AI in health care.

Protecting Patient Autonomy, Dignity and Trust

- **Informed consent and awareness:** Patients have a right to know when AI is directing their care, what its limitations are, and to decline when there are safe alternatives. The concerns expressed in numerous ethical reviews are that AI use should not subordinate but instead protect patient autonomy (Gerke et al., 2020; Weiner et al., 2025).
- **Trust and legitimacy:** Health care is based on the patient-provider trust. In the event that opaque decisions are made by AI blackboxes, patients are likely to become alienated or fearful. The ability to be transparent and explainable contributes to trust (Maccaro et al., 2024; Boudi et al., 2024; Tilala et al., 2024).

- **Empathy and human connection:** Even AI can never be as compassionate or caring and full of human touch as a human can be. Excessive dependence on AI creates the danger of dehumanizing care. Other critics fear that patients may perceive that they are interacting with machines, as opposed to individuals (Farhud & Zokaei, 2021).

Mitigating Bias, Inequity and Health Disparities

- **Bias amplification:** AI systems that were trained using non-representative datasets can perform worse than in minorities, women, or underserved groups systematically. This continues to or even increases the existing health inequities (Weiner et al., 2025; Tilala et al., 2024; Murphy et al., 2021).
- **Justice and fairness:** The principle of justice requires that the AI benefits should be distributed justly. The ethical imperative involves proactive attempts to identify, audit, and address differences in model performance by subpopulations (Weiner et al., 2025; Murphy et al., 2021).
- **Health equity lens:** In large system or public health settings, in particular, addressing bias is necessary to reduce the outcomes of already marginalised populations. Recent commentary claims that AI can worsen inequality except when it is created so that it is pro-equity (Dankwa-Mullan, 2024)

Ensuring Safety, Validity and Clinical Integrity

- **Clinical validation and reliability:** An algorithm may be good on training data but not in the real hospital. Mistakes in diagnosis, false negatives/positives, or incompetent treatment recommendations can directly be detrimental of the patients. Ethical deployment requires strict external verification and constant monitoring (Collins et al., 2024).
- **Transparency and explainability:** Clinicians need to know how AI makes its recommendations. In case the logic is opaque, bugs are more difficult to detect, and responsibility becomes lost.

Therefore, explainable AI methods and audit trails are essential. Within the framework of the discussed ethical models, operationalization instruments like SHAP and LIME are essential in terms of the essential principle of the biomedical approach, autonomy, since they can convert black box algorithms into explainable systems that enable clinicians and patients to make informed and mutually comprehensible decisions. These approaches respond to the transparency and explainability demands of the WHO and the EU AI Act directly since they provide logic behind particular AI-driven recommendations, make sure that logic is not opaque, and it is possible to identify bugs or errors in reasoning. Moreover, these tools enable the human-in-the-loop control that is needed to hold clinicians accountable; they offer visual explanations and uncertainty measures, which enable clinicians to disagree or override AI outputs and stop prioritizing human judgment in high-stakes medical situations. In the end, SHAP and LIME fill this gap between abstract ethical theory and the reality at the ground, which is the need to establish a liability and trust in the community that is present in the case of AI affecting life-or-death health results.

- **Accountability and liability:** When AI makes (or influences) a wrong decision, who is legally or ethically responsible? The developer? The clinician? The hospital? Embed- ding clear governance and accountability is an ethical necessity.
- **Lifecycle and monitoring:** Models can drift over time as populations or practices change. Ethics demands ongoing surveillance, feedback loops, and safe rollback mechanisms.

Safeguarding Privacy, Data Rights Consent

- **Data privacy and confidentiality:** Data on the medical sector is highly personal. Ethics requires strict precautions on data collection, data storage, data anonymization, and sharing and re-using data. Violation or abuse does not only damage people but undermines the trust in the whole systems.
- **Informed consent for data use:** The patients need to be aware of the data use and agree to it particularly in AI training or secondary research. Blanket or opaque consent is a morally questionable concept.
- **Data ownership, control, and rights:** Who owns medical data? Patients, companies, hospitals? Ethics must be in such a manner so that the clients have positive control and management of their health information. This is one of the fundamental concerns that are criticized. [Ethics of AI in Healthcare and Medicine]

Moral Responsibility, Governance and Public Accountability

- **Embedded ethics vs checklists:** Ethical reflection should be incorporated at all levels: design, validation, deployment and update, this is the best practice. Scientists request that ethicists should sit together with the engineers and clinicians. (Tang et al., 2023)
- **Transparent reporting and oversight:** Ethical deployment implies open reporting of strengths, weaknesses, threats, and audit findings to the third

parties. Most ethical AI systems have transparency and accountability as the main pillars (Maccaro et al., 2024).

- **Public engagement and legitimacy:** AI in healthcare is relevant to a lot of people. Technologists and clinicians are not the only people that should be engaged in the ethical frameworks; it should also include the voices of patients, families, community, and civil society. This assists in making the systems in line with the values of the society (Couture et al., 2023).
- **Regulation as ethical guardrail:** Laws and standards (e.g. EU AI Act, medical de- vice regulation) can assist in regulating bottom-line ethical conduct. However, compliance is not the full extent of ethical responsibility. AI systems need to be engaged in higher moralistic practices than adhering to legal minimum (Mennella et al., 2024).

A HUMAN STORY: WHY ETHICS MUST BE FRONT AND CENTER

The situation could be as follows: A hospital implements an AI-based method to detect diabetic retinopathy. This algorithm was developed on the high-quality pictures of eyes in an entirely urban and well-resourced population. Under rural clinic conditions, where imaging conditions are not optimal and the ethnic background of patients is dissimilar, the tool fails to capture numerous incidences of the disease. Patients lose sight, clinicians lose trust and the hospital is in disrepute.

This has not only been a technical failure but also a moral failure. The developers failed to validate on a broad basis, failed to consider the difference in populations, and failed to track the performance of the deployment. It would have been fair to predict these differences, consult the local stakeholders, conduct extensive testing, and exercise ongoing control as shown in the Figure 3.

Medical AI ethics is what allows the new tools to improve the care of all and not quietly damage or disregard others. It can assist in making sure that human values like dignity, fairness, safety, and trust are in the center of what healthcare is about which in turn is a very human endeavor aimed at taking care of other people.

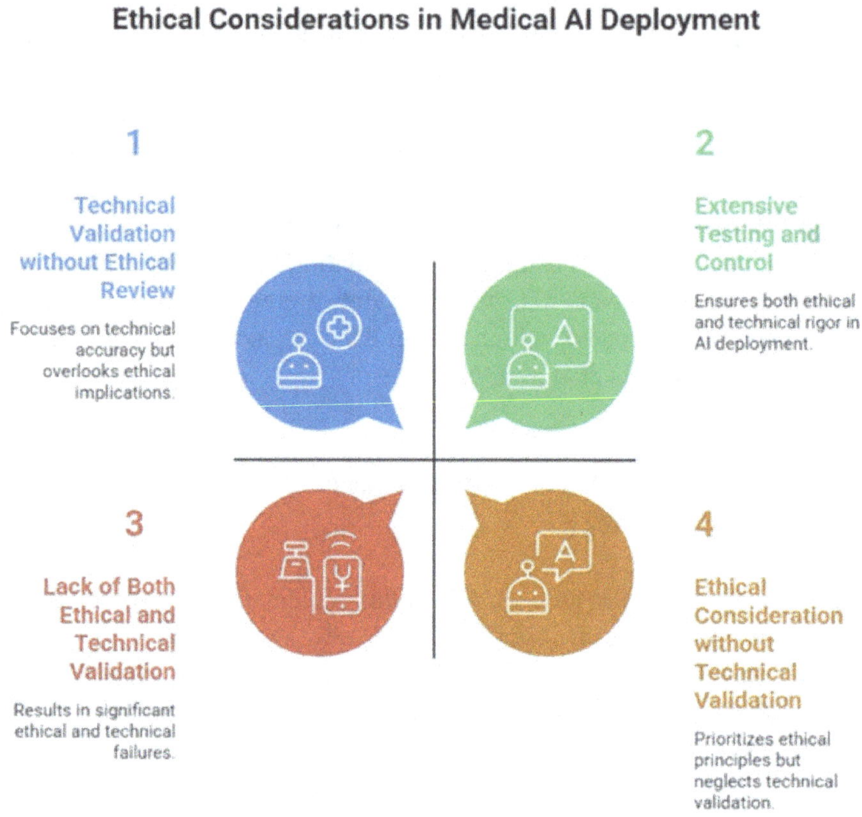

Figure 3. Ethics in medical AI: A scenario

OBJECTIVES AND SCOPE

Within the context of a demonstrably useful discussion of Ethical AI in Health Care, this chapter has two fused aspirations: purposes (what it will achieve) and compass (what is it going to cover, and what is it going to avoid). It is important to have clarity grounded around these because the readers will be in a position to know what to expect and what contributions the chapter is meant to make.

Objectives

Map the Ethical Landscape of AI in Health Care

To systematically define and classify the fundamental ethical issues that emerge when AI is incorporated into health systems and includes such issues as privacy, bias, transparency, accountability, consent, fairness, and governance. The chapter attempts to explain the lay of the land in ethical issues by synthesizing existing literature.

Indicatively, the recent reviews have highlighted privacy, trust, fairness, accountability and bias as the main themes regarding the health AI ethics (Elendu et al., 2023).

Link Ethical Principles to Practical Implementation

To close the divide between the prerogative ethical theory (autonomy, beneficence, non-maleficence, justice) and design, validation, deployment, and monitoring practices in AI systems. This goal is sought to operationalize abstract ethics into realistic policies and measures of governance.

Experts indicate that the four prominent principles of biomedical ethics can still be used and useful in case when modified to AI settings (Gorelik et al., 2025).

Analyze Gaps, Tensions Tradeoffs

To identify where ethical frameworks and real-world constraints conflict (for instance, transparency vs proprietary models, algorithmic explainability vs performance, ongoing learning vs regulatory stability). The goal is to expose unresolved tensions and propose ways forward. Many authors argue that simple appeals to principle are insufficient once AI is deployed in messy real environments; ethical nuance and trade-off management are needed (Ratti et al., 2025).

Provide Recommendations for Stakeholders

To propose actionable recommendations (for clinicians, AI developers, health system man- agers, and regulators) on integrating ethical safeguards into each stage of the AI lifecycle: from design and data curation, through validation, deployment, auditing, and governance.

Works on AI governance in health affirm the need for oversight frameworks, continuous monitoring, transparency, and stakeholder accountability (Mennella et al., 2024; Elendu et al., 2023; Stroud et al., 2025).

Highlight Directions for Future Research and Policy

To identify underexplored domains and research gaps (e.g. empirics on clinician attitudes, ethics of generative AI in medicine, cross-cultural ethical norms) and suggest promising future directions for research and normative development.

Empirical studies in medical AI ethics are still sparse, and many reviews call for embedding ethicists with developers (Tang et al., 2023).

Scope

To keep the study focused yet substantial, the chapter will adopt the following scope guidelines:

Domain Boundaries

The chapter concentrates on AI systems directly involved in patient care, diagnosis, decision support, risk prediction, and related clinical functions. It does not deeply cover AI in ancillary administrative, billing, or purely logistical uses, except insofar as they intersect with clinical or ethical risks.

Temporal Scope

The chapter focuses on developments and ethical debates from the 2010s onward, since modern AI (deep learning, large models, continuous learning systems) introduces qualitatively new challenges. However, historical background will be briefly referenced to contextualize evolution.

Geographic / Institutional Scope

Ethical and regulatory norms differ by region. While many examples will come from high- income nations, the chapter attempts to include perspectives from lower- and middle-income countries where possible, especially with regard to equity and access. But it will not exhaustively survey every national law.

Types of Ethical Issues

The main ethical issues addressed will include:

a) Data privacy, security, and consent
b) Algorithmic bias, fairness, and representativeness

c) Transparency, interpretability, and explainability
d) Accountability, liability, and governance
e) Lifecycle safety, monitoring, drift, and updates
f) Trust, clinician-AI interaction, and human oversight

The chapter will not (or only cursorily) cover deep technical aspects of model optimization, niche algorithmic architectures, or purely engineering innovations, unless they bear directly on the ethical themes.

Stakeholder Focus

The analysis will draw upon the perspectives and responsibilities of four key stakeholder groups: patients, clinicians/health professionals, AI developers and vendors, and regulators

/ health system managers. Interaction dynamics among them will be explored. The chapter

will not attempt a full philosophical treatise (e.g. on metaethics) outside the applied health AI context.

Level of Detail

The chapter will attempt to be both thorough and approachable: academic rigor without being overly technical or scholarly, but at the same time, non-scholarly, more readable. In every ethical aspect, case examples that are real-life or published cases will be provided to underpin theory with practice.

ETHICAL FOUNDATIONS OF AI IN HEALTHCARE

Overview of Traditional Medical Ethics: Autonomy, Beneficence, Non-Maleficence, And Justice

The introduction of the field of Artificial Intelligence (AI) into the medical field requires solid ethical principles based on the classic medical tenets of autonomy, beneficence, non-maleficence, and justice. Initially proposed by Beauchamp and Childress (1994) in Principles of Biomedical Ethics, these principles continue to play a leading role in informing the contemporary AI development in medicine (Beauchamp & Childress, 1994).

Autonomy: The principle of autonomy is focused on the right of patients to take informed decisions concerning their health. This can be achieved in AIdriven systems by making them transparent and explainable to patients and clinicians to understand how a recommendation is made (London, 2019). As an example, explainable AI models can be used to maintain trust and provide shared decision-making power between physicians and patients (Miller, 2019).

Beneficence: The principle of beneficence states that AI systems must encourage patient well-being. Algorithms need to be designed in a way that enhances the quality of diagnosis, personalization of treatment, and access to health care. Ethical AI needs to be actively engaged at improving health and not optimizing efficiency (Topol, 2019).

Non-maleficence: The principle of non-maleficence, which includes the obligation not to harm the patient, is essential in avoiding the risk of algorithmic bias, misdiagnosis, or patient data abuse. Strict validation, monitoring, and human control are needed to reduce unintended damage, as a result of AI predictions or automation (Amann et al., 2020). Lastly, Justice demands equity and equality in healthcare. Ethical AI must avoid discrimination and must have equal accessness to the socio-economic, gender, and racial groups. To prevent amplification, inclusive datasets and global governance structures are essential as the World Health Organization (2021) says. World Health Organization (2021) defines health inequities as follows:

When combined, these four principles as presented in Figure 4, will form the ethical basis of how ethical AI in healthcare should be developed, where innovation can be used to serve humanity in a responsible, fair, and safe way.

How these principles relate to AI systems

When we move from traditional clinical settings into AI-powered systems, each ethical principle acquires new dimensions such as new risks, constraints, and obligations. Below is how each principle translating into the AI context.

Autonomy

Autonomy is basic ethical principal that requires systems to be transparent, clearly explained, and designed to support rather than override human decision-making.

- **Model explainability and transparency:** For patients and clinicians to make informed choices, the AI's reasoning must be sufficiently interpretable. If a model is a "black box," autonomy is compromised. Especially for high-stakes decisions (diagnosis, treatment), users should see rationales and caveats.
- **Disclosure and consent:** Use of AI in care must be disclosed to patients, with explanation of its role, risks, and alternatives. Patients should have the option to refuse AI use or request human oversight.

- **Human-in-the-loop control:** AI should assist human judgment rather than replace it. Clinicians must retain the ability to contest, override, or "switch off" AI outputs. This preserves both clinical autonomy and patient autonomy.
- **User interface design aligned with autonomy:** Interfaces should present confidence, uncertainty, alternative options, and visual explanations rather than force a single decision output.

Figure 4. Four core ethical principles for AI in healthcare

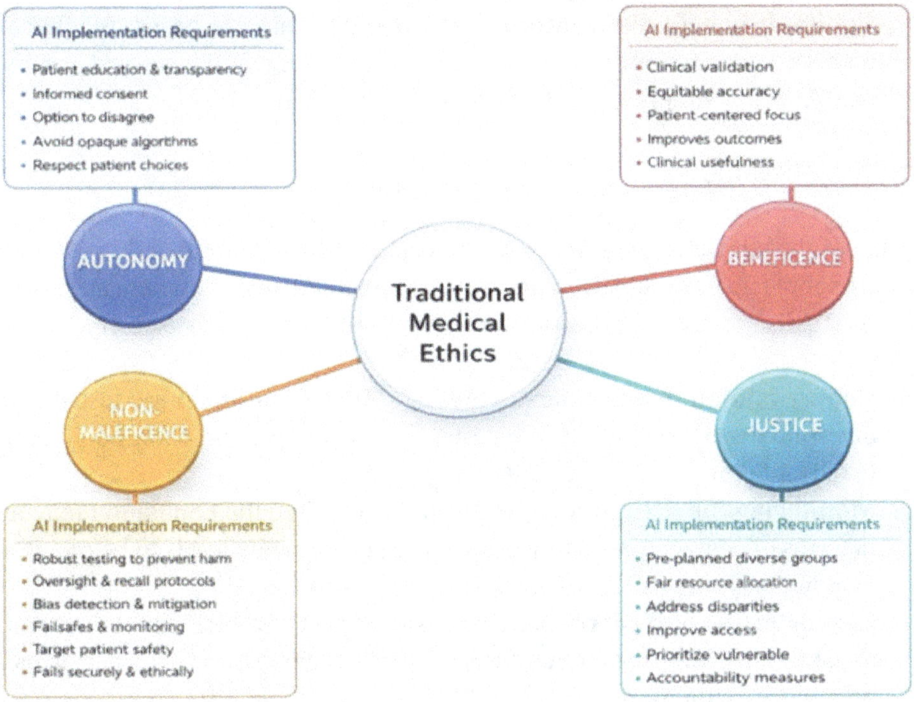

Beneficence

Beneficence reflects the moral duty to act in ways that promote the well-being of patients and enhance the quality of care. When applied to AI in healthcare, this principle emphasizes the importance of designing and using technologies that deliver genuine clinical value, improving outcomes and supporting better decision-making for both patients and clinicians.

- **Evidence of benefit:** AI systems must show that they improve outcomes (e.g. improved detection rates, better prognostic stratification) before broad deployment, via prospective trials or real-world studies.
- **Benefit, cost and complexity:** The gains from AI (speed, accuracy, resource savings) must outweigh risks, burden of integration, misdiagnoses, or overdiagnoses.
- **Adaptive and context-aware benefit design:** Adaptive and context-sensitive benefit design: AI models can be applied in the context of specific local populations, settings, and workflows in order to achieve benefits in practice, but not only in the perfect lab environment.
- **Equitable benefit distribution:** Care should be taken to ensure that benefits do not favour centres of excellence only and but rather underserved groups so that AI is not simply a way to further increase disparities.

Non-maleficence

One of the ethical aspects that must be ensured is to ensure that AI systems do not hurt people accidentally. By anticipating potential dangers and crashes, we are able to establish protective measures that guard the users and the society.

- **Robust validation and external testing:** Models must be stress-tested across diverse datasets, including rare cases, out-of-distribution data, noisy inputs, to detect failure modes before deployment.
- **Monitoring for drift and degradation:** Over time the population may alter in terms of characteristics or practice, the performance needs to be monitored continuously.
- **Bias detection and correction:** AI systems are to be verified when it comes to subgroup differences; one of the forms of harm is bias (poor performance on minority subgroups).
- **Safe fallback and error handling:** It should not give an answer by the AI, where it is unsure or has a low degree of confidence but rather should suggest human analysis, raise alarms, or fail to give an answer with high confidence when that answer, though incorrect, has high confidence.
- **Data misuse and privacy risks:** Data leaks, re-identification or the use of sensitive features in a manner that is not unscrupulous may also be harmful; strong privacy protections are included in the do no harm

Justice

It is expected that AI systems would be built and implemented in a way that would prove fair to all individuals who are going to use it. Accessibility will avoid discrimination and make AI accessible to people who represent any kind of community.

- **Fair performance across subgroups:** AI models should be tested on the basis of demographics (e.g. gender, race, age, socioeconomic status) to ensure that there is no systematic underperformance in any of the groups.
- **Inclusive data collection:** Training data needs to be representative and cover populations representing diverse geographical regions, ethnicities and resource environments in order to minimize bias.
- **Equitable deployment:** AI must not be distributed only in hospitals and high-income neighborhoods; fairness requires the strategies of application in low-resource or distant locations.
- **Transparent resource allocation:** When care is being triaged or limited treatment is to be provided by AI, its decision logic has to be objective, non-discriminatory and explainable.
- **Procedural fairness and accountability:** Governance processes (e.g. auditing, appeals, oversight bodies) must be open and equitable, so that those harmed by AI decisions have recourse or redress.

Ethical Frameworks or Guidelines

Policymakers and international organizations have moved quickly from high-level principles to concrete frameworks because medical AI touches safety, rights and public trust. Below is a concise, humanized overview of the main frameworks you should know and what each contributes to ethical AI in health care as shown in Figure 5.

Figure 5. Global ethical frameworks and regulatory guidelines for AI in healthcare

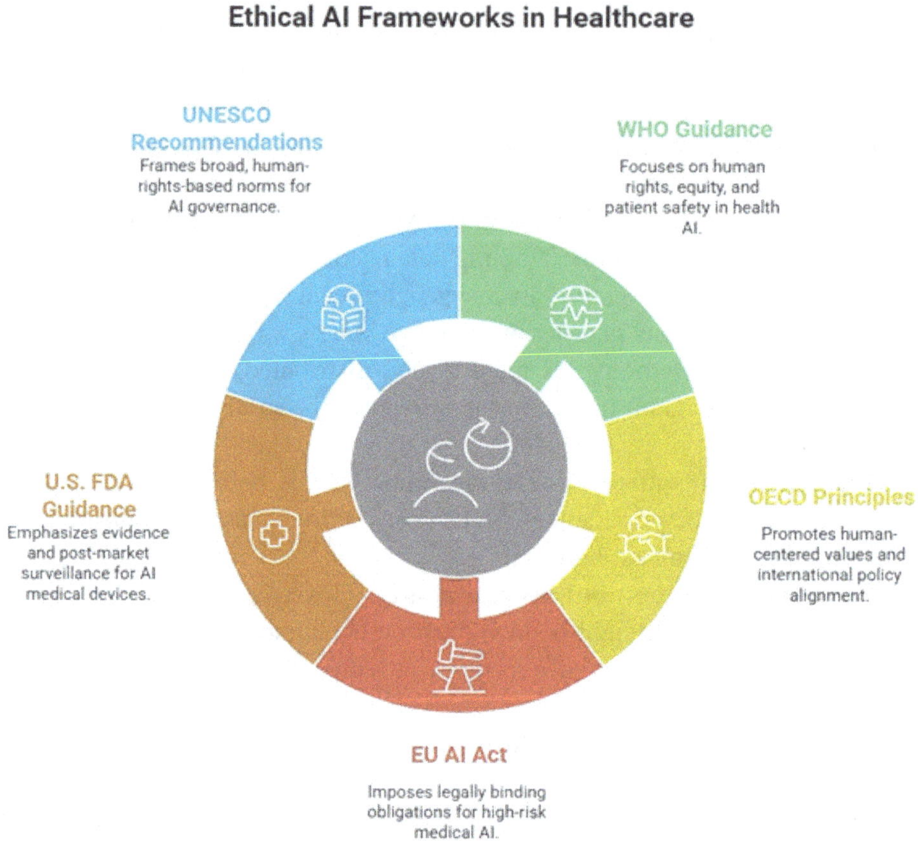

World Health Organization (WHO)

The WHO's 2024 guidance (updated with follow-ups) places human rights, equity and patient safety at the center of health AI. It lays out practical expectations such as transparency, data governance, stakeholder engagement, and lifecycle oversight and explicitly treats many health AI uses as requiring special safeguards because they affect health and human rights. The WHO guidance is frequently cited as the global "how to" for aligning AI with public-health goals. (World Health Organization, 2024).

Why it matters: global legitimacy, health-specific focus, emphasis on equity and human-

rights protections.

OECD AI Principles

The OECD's AI Principles (2019), endorsed by many countries, promote human-centered values: robustness, transparency, fairness, and accountability. OECD also published health-specific briefs, in which the aspects of cooperation, data interoperability, and policy measures to minimize risks in clinical settings are emphasized. Governments interested in cross-border interoperability standards can find their work useful (Mazzi, 2025).

Why it matters: international policy alignment, pragmatic recommendations for national governments and health systems.

European Union (EU) AI Act

EU AI act is the most common AI regulation in the world. It has categorized most clinical AI tools as high-risk, with specifications on the quality of data, documentation, transparency, human supervision, risk management, and post-market surveillance. For medical AI that also falls under EU medical-device law, manufacturers must satisfy both sets of obligations which increasing regulatory rigor for tools that directly affect patient safety. Recent summaries and analyses explain the implementation timelines and implications for healthcare providers and vendors (Artificial Intelligence Act, 2024).

Why it matters: legally binding obligations for high-risk medical AI in the EU; strong design- time and lifecycle controls.

U.S. FDA Guidance and Action Plan on AI/ML in Software as a Medical Device (SaMD)

The U.S. Food and Drug Administration treats many clinical AI products as medical devices and has published an AI/ML SaMD Action Plan and iterative guidance documents focused on pre-market evidence, real-world performance monitoring, and Good Machine Learning Practices. The FDA's approach emphasizes lifecycle assurance (from design through updates) and safety- by-design. Recent draft guidance expands lifecycle and marketing submission recommendations for AI-enabled device software (Ozmen, 2025; Joshi et al., 2024).

Why it matters: authoritative regulatory pathway for AI medical devices in the U.S.; strong emphasis on evidence and post-market surveillance.

UNESCO, other global standards and multilateral efforts

UNESCO's 2021 Recommendation on the Ethics of AI frames broad, human-rights-based norms

such as transparency, fairness, human oversight and helps harmonize ethical expectations across 190+ states. Other actors (WHO, OECD, professional societies) often reference UNESCO when arguing for human-rights consistent AI governance. Multilateral briefs (e.g., OECD health briefs) and national health-minister statements turn these norms into practical policy steps (Allahrakha, 2024).

Why it matters: human-rights framing and global standard-setting useful for low- and middle- income countries.

Table 1. Table compares the focus areas and core contributions of the major international frameworks mentioned as essential for AI governance in healthcare

Framework	Core Focus / Objective	Key Pillars / Contributions
WHO	Health Equity & Human Rights	Places human rights, equity, and patient safety at the canter. Emphasizes transparency, data governance, and stakeholder engagement.
OECD	Economic Growth & Trustworthy AI	Focuses on inclusive growth, human-centered values, transparency, and accountability to foster trust in AI systems[5].
UNESCO	Global Ethics & Human Dignity	Focuses on the ethical dimensions of AI regarding education, science, and culture, prioritizing human dignity and environmental sustainability.

PATIENT SAFETY IN AI APPLICATIONS

Patient safety must remain the north star when introducing AI into clinical care. AI systems can augment clinicians' capabilities, but they also introduce new, sometimes subtle, ways for harm to occur as shown the Figure 6. It covers (a) risks from algorithmic errors, (b) safety-by-design approaches to reduce those risks, and (c) why rigorous clinical validation and continuous monitoring are non- negotiable.

Figure 6. Patient safety framework in AI healthcare applications

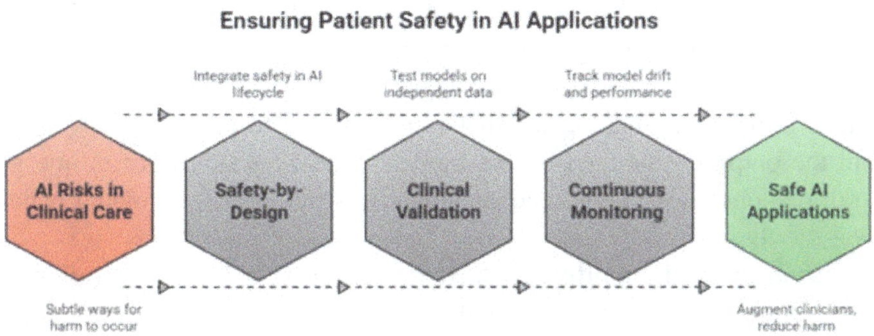

Risks of Algorithmic Errors in Diagnosis and Treatment:

AI errors can directly affect diagnoses, treatment choices, and patient outcomes. Causes include biased or unrepresentative training data, overfitting to site-specific patterns, poor handling of out- of-distribution inputs (cases unlike anything in training), and opaque decision logic that hides failure modes from clinicians. The real world ramifications are made clear by real-life experience: investigative reporting and concordance studies demonstrate that IBM Watson oncology typically produced hazardous or incorrect treatment options and performed poorly with clinician judgments in a number of settings, which is an important lesson in the importance of not over shooting the skies on making such claims. Even more systemic forms of algorithmic errors (e.g., models that are worse at individual subgroups) may also increase health inequities (Ross and Swetlitz, 2018; Zhou et al., 2019).

Safety-by-design Approaches in AI Development:

Safety-by-design implies the implementation of safety measures in each phase of the AI lifecycle, instead of attaching them to it subsequently. Practical measures include:

- **Requirements and hazard analysis:** Concrete safety requirements based on clinical use cases are provided and potential failure modes are determined in advance before development.

- **Data governance and representativeness:** Curate datasets with provenance and demographic coverage Medical Curate datasets Curate datasets with provenance and demographic coverage bias audit and limitations dented.
- **Robust model design:** Estimate uncertainty, use abstinence mechanisms (refer to human on cases of low confidence), and guardrails that identify anomalies during runtime, i.e. anomalies in data fed to the model or anomalies in the outputs generated by the model. Recent research on runtime guardrail demonstrates viable mechanisms of restricting unsafe model behaviour on-the-fly..
- **Human-in-the-loop interfaces:** Human-in-the-loop Design workflows to allow clinicians to easily view, challenge, and override model results; explicitly present model forms of confidence and rationale where feasible.
- **Secure engineering practices:** Protect data privacy (encryption, de-identification): Secure engineering practices: Audit: In general, keep data private, provide model version life cycle, rollback: Have the ability to roll back and restore previous model versions.

Such safety-by-design aspects are being incorporated into regulatory and research recommendations (e. g., the Good Machine Learning Practices and taxonomy proposals of runtime guardrails at FDA) more and more.

In addition, (U.S. Food and Drug Administration, 2025; Shamsujjoha et al., 2024).

Clinical validation and continuous monitoring:

It is important but not enough to demonstrate technical performance on a test set of a developer. To be deployed ethically and safely, one needs:

- **External and prospective validation:** Test models on independent, multi-site data that is representative of the real practice; in the case available, do prospective clinical studies that are patient level and not algorithmic measures.
- **Post-market surveillance and monitoring:** This should be done through active monitoring of model drift (shift in input distributions or clinical practice) and performance degradation. Regulators and researchers have now turned their focus to ways and means of identifying changes in inputs, observing outputs, as well as associating performance declines with clinical risk.
- **Governed update pathways:** Stipulate managed practices of retraining, validating, delivering model updates, such as documentation, version control, and rollback plans.

- **Incident reporting and remediation:** Incident reporting and remediation: Have well-defined pathways to incidents and near misses that can be shared by the clinicians and patients and root-cause analysis and mitigation.

Understanding and correction of model drift as well as post-market performance are well-known policy points (nothing needs to be emphasized more than drift in guidance to safe AI in medical care, recent literature and FDA programs). Ethically and more so through regulators, constant validation and transparent reporting are expected (Wong and Sussman, 2025).

DATA SECURITY AND PRIVACY

The incorporation of artificial intelligence into health care is conditional upon large, delicate datasets. This information brings in deep privacy and security issues as shown in Figure 7. This paragraph describes the character of health data and assesses the de-identification methods, determines cybersecurity risks specific to AI systems, and identifies the compliance standards in the context of significant legal frameworks.

Figure 7. Data security and privacy in AI healthcare

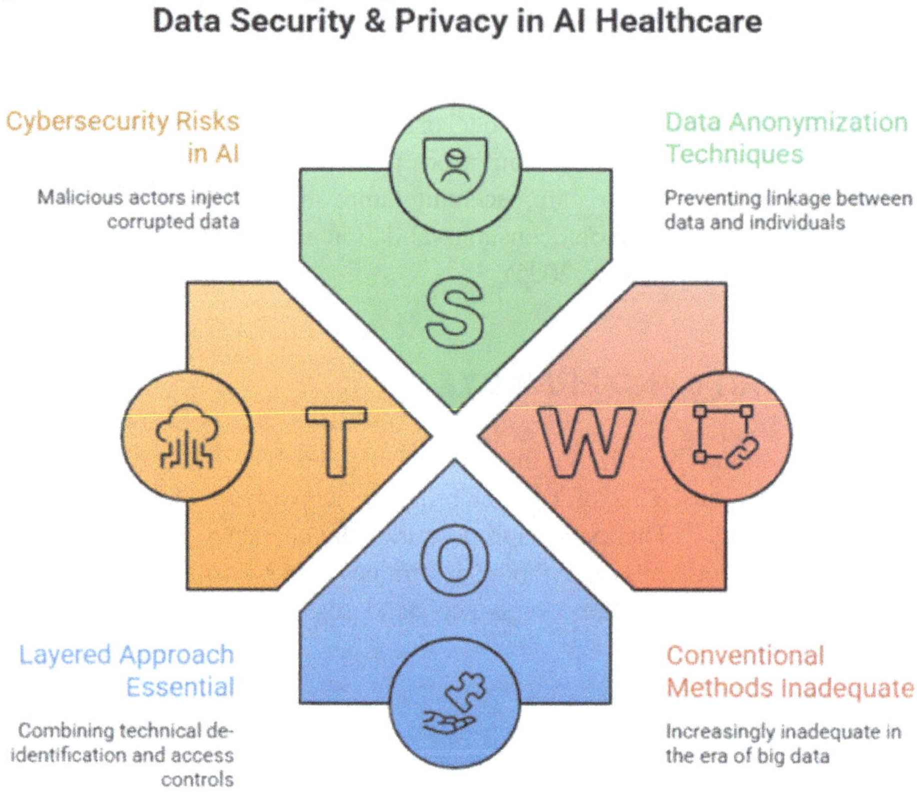

Nature of Health Data

AI systems in healthcare are based on the multimodal, high-dimensional data, which is sensitive and personally identifiable in nature.

- Longitudinal clinical data (diagnoses, medications, lab results and clinician notes) stored in the Electronic Health Records (EHRs) may provide insight into intimate health histories and behavioural patterns.
- Medical Imaging (e.g., X-rays, MRIs, CT scans) contains biometric identifiers and can be re-identified even in the absence of metadata, particularly in combination with other sources of data.
- IoT and Wearable Data provides round the clock physiology monitoring at the cost of establishing persistent data streams that are susceptible to attacks of interception, aggregation, and inference.

The aggregation of such kinds of data in AI training pipelines increases the risk of re-identification and also requires strict protection mechanisms that are not provided by conventional data protection practices.

Data Anonymization Techniques

Data Anonymization or de-identification aims to prevent linkage between data and individuals, but conventional methods are increasingly inadequate in the era of big data and AI. Some of the methods are listed below.

- **k-Anonymity** ensures that each record is indistinguishable from at least $k-1$ others based on quasi-identifiers (e.g., age, ZIP code). However, it fails to prevent homogeneity attacks (where all k records share the same sensitive attribute) and is vulnerable to linkage with external datasets (Livraga, 2019).
- **Differential Privacy** provides a mathematical guarantee by adding calibrated noise to queries or datasets, bounding the risk that any individual's data influenced the output but it can reduce model utility (Livraga, 2019).
- **Synthetic Data Generation** uses generative models (e.g., GANs) to create artificial datasets that mimic statistical properties of real data without containing actual patient records. However, poorly designed generators may leak training data or fail to preserve clinical correlations (Torfi et al., 2022).
- **Federated Learning** enables model training across decentralized devices or institutions without sharing raw data, reducing exposure It is still not immune to model inversion or membership inference attacks unless combined with additional privacy-preserving techniques like secure aggregation or differential privacy (Das et al., 2020).

No single technique guarantees absolute anonymity. A layered approach combining technical de-identification, strict access controls, and data minimization is essential to balance utility and privacy.

Cybersecurity Risks in AI Health Systems

Some of the cybersecurity risks associated with the AI healthcare systems are discussed below.

- **Data Poisoning**: Malicious actors inject corrupted or mislabelled samples during training to degrade model performance or induce specific errors.

- **Model Inversion Attacks**: Adversaries reconstruct sensitive input data from model outputs or confidence scores, exploiting the model's learned representations.
- **Adversarial Attack**: Small, unrecognizable changes to inputs such as subtle pixel changes in a retinal scan can cause misclassification. In healthcare, such attacks could lead to false negatives in cancer detection.
- **Membership Inference**: Attackers determine whether a specific individual's data was used in training, potentially revealing sensitive health conditions (Elbaz, 2025).

Mitigation requires a secure AI development lifecycle by input sanitization, runtime monitoring for anomalous queries and cryptographic protections.

Compliance with HIPAA, GDPR

An AI application must follow the following regulatory standard requirements laid out by HIPAA, GDPR and other legal organizations for data security and privacy of the audience.

The Health Insurance Portability and Accountability Act mandates administrative, physical, and technical safeguards for protected health information (PHI). All data transmissions must be encrypted, access logs maintained, and business associate agreements (BAAs) executed with third-party vendors (Chevuri, 2025).

The General Data Protection Regulation classifies health data as a special category requiring explicit consent or another lawful basis. It grants data subjects rights to access, rectify, and object to automated decision-making. High-risk AI systems must undergo Data Protection Impact Assessments (DPIAs) (General Data Protection Regulation (GDPR) (n.d.), 2025).

Compliance is operationalized in applications through privacy-by-design architecture (e.g., data minimization, purpose limitation), regular audits and DPIAs for high-risk processing, transparent data processing notices and patient consent workflows, cross- border data transfer mechanisms.

CASE EXAMPLES OF AI FAILURES LESSONS LEARNED

Watson for Oncology (IBM)

What happened?

IBM's Watson for Oncology was designed to help doctors recommend cancer treatments. How- ever, internal documents (leaked/reported by STAT News in 2018) showed that it gave treatment recommendations that were "unsafe and incorrect" in various cases as shown in Figure 8. For example, one case involved a 65-year-old patient with lung cancer and severe bleeding; Watson recommended both chemotherapy and the drug Bevacizumab, despite the drug's warning against use in patients with active bleeding. The documents blamed aspects like training on synthetic/hypothetical cases rather than a broad body of real clinical data (Ross & Swetlitz, 2018; Brown, 2018)

Lesson learned:

- Relying on synthetic or limited case data can lead to dangerous outputs when the system encounters real patients whose conditions or complications weren't modeled.
- Marketing claims that overpromise can lead to misaligned expectations by users (clinicians, hospitals).
- Clinical validation must be rigorous, reflect real-world diversity, include edge cases (e.g. comorbidities, contraindications). Misleading confidence (or lack of caveats) undermines safety and trust.
- When AI is used to assist with serious medical decisions, oversight and clinician involvement are essential; AI should augment, not replace, human judgement.

DeepMind / Royal Free Streams App Data Sharing

What happened?

In 2015, UK's Royal Free NHS hospitals shared personal health data of 1.6 million patients with Google's DeepMind for the development of an app called Streams, intended to detect acute kidney injury. The UK Information Commissioner's Office (ICO) later found that this data transfer failed to comply with data protection law: patients were not properly informed (lack of transparency), consent was inadequately handled, and the legal basis used ("implied consent" via "direct care") was misapplied given that the data was used in testing functions beyond direct patient care as mentioned in Figure 8.

Lesson learned:

- Even when the AI function has potential benefit, misuse of patient data (or even perceived misuse) erodes trust and violates ethical norms.
- Legal/regulatory compliance is not optional. Data protection laws, consent, transparency must be built in from the start.
- Stakeholder communication is essential. Patients should reasonably expect how their data will be used. Ethical oversight is required for the data sharing, even in testing phases.

Figure 8. AI failures lessons learned in healthcare

CASE EXAMPLES OF AI SUCCES AND LESSONS LEARNED

DIABETIC RETINOPATHY SCREENING — GOOGLE HEALTH

Google Health created a deep-learning application that can identify cases of diabetic retinopathy using retinal images and achieve the same performance as that of professional ophthalmologists. The use in primary care clinics has broadened the availability of early diagnosis, in particular, underserved groups.

Key Lessons

With the appropriate clinical validation and human control, AI will be capable of improving the diagnostic reach, enhance early detection, and narrow healthcare disparities.

STROKE DIAGNOSIS AND TRIAGE — VIZ.AI

Viz.Ai uses AI to scan CT in real-time and quickly identify large vessel occlusions and notify specialists. This saves on time of treatment and enhances survival.

Key Lessons

Responsible use of time-critical artificial intelligence (AI) applications can literally save lives when used in controlled clinical scenarios.

FUTURE RESEARCH DIRECTIONS

The current dynamic nature of AI in healthcare offers a lot of research gaps to be filled in the future and many ways of useful innovation. Due to the growing complexity and role of AI systems in clinical practice, a number of research areas can be identified as critical, and systematic research on these areas is necessary to facilitate ethical, safe, and equitable application of AI systems.

Empirical Studies on Stakeholder Perspectives and Trust Dynamics

Although the literature on ethical principles has increased, knowledge about how AI-mediated care is perceived and experienced by stakeholders (patients, clinicians, administrators, and developers) remains limited. Future studies should adopt mixed-method strategies where quantitative surveys are combined with qualitative interviews to examine how trust is formed, eroded, and restored in AI-enhanced clinical contexts. Longitudinal research on clinical attitudes toward AI use, workflow integration, and decision-making when AI recommendations conflict with clinical judgment is valuable. Similarly, there is an urgent necessity of conducting patient-centered research on informed consent, perception of AI involvement in care, and preferences to human or algorithmic decisions among the diverse groups of people (Tang et al., 2023; Weiner et al., 2025). Ethical frameworks would be based on experience, instead of abstract ideas based on such empirical data.

Generative AI and Large Language Models in Clinical Practice

With the development of large language models (LLMs) like GPT-4, Med-PaLM, and other generative AI systems, there are ethical issues that current models fail to resolve. The risks of digital generative AI (hallucination, creating convincing yet false medical facts, distribution of false information) should be considered in future research, as well as the impact of conversational interfaces that blur the professional boundaries between clinicians and automatized systems (World Health Organization, 2024). The main questions are related to the way to design an informed consent regarding personalized health information produced by LLMs, how to avoid over-dependence on AI-generated clinical scripts, and how to detect and eliminate the biases introduced in the foundation models that are trained on unverified medical text. Studies on assessment tools, clinical validation, and governance systems specific to generative AI in healthcare are thus of great importance.

Cross-Cultural and Global South Perspectives on AI Ethics

The existing AI ethical models are generally created in the high-income Western world and might not reflect cultural distinctions in medical ethics, data handling, and healthcare priorities (Dankwa-Mullan, 2024). New studies must bring on board scholars, clinicians, policymakers, and communities in low- and middle-income countries (LMICs) to come up with context-sensitive ethical principles that are based on varying values and healthcare infrastructures. International comparative analysis of cultural views on autonomy, informed consent and data ownership would guide the global regulation of AI. It is important to focus on the issue of digital divide, in which AI might worsen the situation in terms of health inequalities. The models that should be prioritized are equitable access models such as open-source clinical AI, federated learning systems that do not centralize sensitive information, and capacity building to increase AI literacy in LMICs.

Explainability, Interpretability, and Human-AI Collaboration

Despite the increasing level of attention to explainable AI (XAI), there are still major gaps in the understanding of what explainability means in a variety of clinical scenarios and target audiences. Future studies must abandon technical measures in favor of clinical- and patient-mediated interpretability to determine the extent to which explanations enhance understanding, trust, and reasonable dependence on AI recommendations (London, 2019; Miller, 2019). Direct comparisons of various modalities of explanations (visualizations of feature importance, counter factual, natural language rationales) across medical specialties and decision complexities would yield practical results. Research on successful human-AI collaboration, such as countering cognitive biases, interface design to encourage critical assessment, and training clinicians on how to collaborate with AI are also of priority.

Algorithmic Fairness Across Intersectional Identities

The recent research on equity in medical AI is primarily based on single demographic axes (including, but not confined to race or gender) and does not represent the fact that people have multiple identities that shape healthcare experiences. Intersectionality approaches should be taken in the future, with the performance of AI being analyzed based on race, gender, age, socioeconomic status, disability, and geographic location (Murphy et al., 2021; Tilala et al., 2024). The methodological improvements required are intersectional fairness measures, methods of determining disparities in compounds, and approaches to equitably attain equity without gathering too much demographic information that risks invasion of privacy. Besides, participatory design, where the marginalized communities are involved in the early stages of AI development, would facilitate justice and procedural fairness.

Longitudinal Monitoring, Model Drift, and Adaptive Governance

The AI models used in the clinical setting need to be capable of adjusting to the changing population of patients, the changing clinical practices, and the changing data trends, potentially causing a drop in performance or model drift (Wong and Sussman, 2025). Additional studies are required to come up with effective methods of continuous performance monitoring that can identify drift at a very high time hence setting the difference between harmless variability and clinically significant degradation and instituting corrective measures. The main questions are how often a model should be monitored, how to reconcile with model validation and regulatory validation, and how improvements in the governance of clinical AI can be made at all. The research on adaptive regulatory frameworks that facilitate continuous learning, without compromising safety presents an important source of policy research (U.S. Food and Drug Administration, 2025).

Privacy-Preserving AI Techniques and Federated Learning

Development AI technologies that rely on privacy-saving technology such as differential privacy, federated learning, and secure multiparty computation can allow data to be developed without violating patient privacy, however, challenges in practice are not yet resolved (Das et al., 2020; Livraga, 2019). Research in the future must adequately determine the usefulness-privacy trade-offs of such approaches in clinical practice, develop standardized procedures of collaborative AI implementation across medical institutions, and determine patient and clinician trust in such systems. Privacy-protective approaches would be analyzed legally and ethically with reference to HIPAA, GDPR, and other data protection laws to implement strategies that comply with them.

AI Safety Engineering and Adversarial Robustness

There is a high susceptibility to adversarial attacks, intentional manipulations which pose risks to the safety of the patients, and insufficient research of AI systems in the healthcare field (Elbaz, 2025). Threats that should be studied systematically in the future include data poisoning during training, model inversion attacks that can reconstruct patient data, adversarial perturbations of medical images or physiological signals. Adversarial training, input sanitization, anomaly detection, and runtime protections are some of the defensive methods that ought to be designed in accordance with clinical environments and critically evaluated (Shamsujjoha et al., 2024). Research to build safety assurance procedures that are comparable to aviation or nuclear sector is also required.

Legal Liability, Accountability, and Malpractice Frameworks

The law on AI-assisted clinical decision-making on the presence of errors is confusing, and the question of who is responsible arises, whether clinicians, AI developers, healthcare facilities, or regulators. Further studies are necessary to understand how the existing malpractice doctrines could be applied to AI-mediated care and suggest similar liability standards that would not deter innovation and would not reduce patient safety (Gerke et al., 2020). Comparative jurisprudence between jurisdictions, case studies of AI-relevant litigation, advice on insurance frameworks, models of payment, and codes of conduct of professionals would all be valuable as legal systems resolve these new issues.

Regulatory Innovation and Harmonization

As jurisdictions around the world regulate AI, such as the EU AI Act and the FDA approach to software as a medical device, the future research should examine the effectiveness of regulations, find best practices, and discuss the opportunities to harmonize the regulations and keep them safe and ethical (Artificial Intelligence Act, 2024; Ozmen, 2025). Comparative policy studies, regulatory effects studies and stakeholder engagement studies to determine the impact of various strategies on the innovation and market dynamics, and patient outcomes can inform evidenced-based policymaking.

CONCLUSION

The development of the Artificial Intelligence in the field of healthcare offers some impressive opportunities as well as some severe ethical obligations. Although AI has the potential to improve diagnostics, personalized care, and availability of healthcare, it brings important issues of autonomy, safety, equity, transparency, and trust. Ethical AI should not be founded on regulations, but ensuring the dignity, rights and wellbeing of patients.

The four fundamental tenets of medical work autonomy, beneficence, non-maleficence, and justice have to be redefined in relation to AI-driven systems and include transparency, prevention of bias, patient outcomes, and equal access. Ethical standards set worldwide offer principles, but there are still realistic issues of the immediate change in technologies and the lack of policy continuity.

Finally, AI must be used to assist, not to substitute, clinicians, and be designed with ethical considerations in mind by employing an ethical-by-design methodology with clinicians, engineers, policymakers, and patients. AI if paired with the essential values of medicine, such as compassion, justice, and human dignity, can help establish a more inclusive, trustworthy, and humane future of healthcare.

REFERENCES

Allahrakha, N. (2024). *UNESCO's AI ethics principles: Challenges and opportunities.* International Journal of Law and Policy., DOI: 10.59022/ijlp.225

Amann, J., Blasimme, A., Vayena, E., Frey, D., Madai, V. I., & Consortium, P. (2020). Explainability for artificial intelligence in healthcare: A multidisciplinary perspective. *BMC Medical Informatics and Decision Making, 20*(1), 310. DOI: 10.1186/s12911-020-01332-6 PMID: 33256715

Artificial Intelligence Act. (2024). *Article 6: Classification rules for high-risk AI systems. Regulation (EU) 2024/1689.* https://artificialintelligenceact.eu/article/6

Artificial Intelligence (AI) Coined at Dartmouth. (n.d.). Dartmouth College. Retrieved September 24, 2025, from https://home.dartmouth.edu/about/artificial-intelligence-ai-coined-dartmouth

Banks, G. (1986). Artificial intelligence in medical diagnosis: The INTERNIST/CADUCEUS approach. *Critical Reviews in Medical Informatics, 1*(1), 23–54. PMID: 3331578

Barnett, G. O., Cimino, J. J., Hupp, J. A., & Hoffer, E. P. (1987). DXplain: An evolving diagnostic decision-support system. *Journal of the American Medical Association, 258*(1), 67–74. DOI: 10.1001/jama.1987.03400010071030 PMID: 3295316

Beauchamp, T. L., & Childress, J. F. (1994). Principles of biomedical ethics. Edicoes Loyola. Oxford University Press, New York.

Boudi, A. L., Boudi, M., Chan, C., Boudi, F. B., & Boudi, A. (2024). Ethical challenges of artificial intelligence in medicine. *Cureus, 16*(11), e74495. DOI: 10.7759/cureus.74495 PMID: 39726447

Brown, J. (2018, July 25). *IBM Watson reportedly recommended cancer treatments that were "unsafe and incorrect." Gizmodo.* https://gizmodo.com

Chevuri, N. (2025). *Data protection in social services: A comprehensive guide to HIPAA and GDPR implementation.* International Journal of Scientific Research in Computer Science, Engineering and Information Technology., DOI: 10.32628/CSEIT25112369

Choi, E., Bahadori, M. T., Schuetz, A., Stewart, W. F., & Sun, J. (2016). Doctor AI: Predicting clinical events via recurrent neural networks. In *Proceedings of the Machine Learning for Healthcare Conference* (pp. 301–318). PMLR.

Collins, B. X., Bélisle-Pipon, J.-C., Evans, B. J., Ferryman, K., Jiang, X., Nebeker, C., Novak, L., Roberts, K., Were, M., Yin, Z., Ravitsky, V., Coco, J., Hendricks-Sturrup, R., Williams, I., Clayton, E. W., & Malin, B. A. (2024). Addressing ethical issues in healthcare artificial intelligence using a lifecycle-informed process. *JAMIA Open*, *7*(4), ooae108. Advance online publication. DOI: 10.1093/jamiaopen/ooae108 PMID: 39553826

Couture, V., Roy, M.-C., Dez, E., Laperle, S., & Bélisle-Pipon, J.-C. (2023). Ethical implications of artificial intelligence in population health and the public's role in its governance: Perspectives from a citizen and expert panel. *Journal of Medical Internet Research*, *25*, e44357. DOI: 10.2196/44357 PMID: 37104026

Dankwa-Mullan, I. (2024). Health equity and ethical considerations in using artificial intelligence in public health and medicine. *Preventing Chronic Disease*, *21*, E64. DOI: 10.5888/pcd21.240245 PMID: 39173183

Das, A., Cuzzocrea, A., Gkoulalas-Divanis, A., Shams, T., Islam, M. S., Pentyala, Y., & Hashem, G. (2020). *Anonymizing data for privacy-preserving federated learning. arXiv preprint arXiv:2002.09096.* https://arxiv.org/abs/2002.09096

Elbaz, G. (2025). *AI security risks in 2025: 6 threats & 6 defensive measures.* Oligo Security. https://www.oligo.security/academy/ai-security-risks-in-2025-6-threats-6-defensive-measures

Elendu, C., Amaechi, D. C., Elendu, T. C., Jingwa, K. A., Okoye, O. K., Okah, M. J., Ladele, J. A., Farah, A. H., & Alimi, H. A. (2023). Ethical implications of AI and robotics in healthcare. *Revista de Medicina (São Paulo)*, *102*(50), e36671. DOI: 10.1097/MD.0000000000036671 PMID: 38115340

Encyclopaedia Britannica. (n.d.). *Alan Turing: Biography, facts, computer & machine.* In *Encyclopaedia Britannica.* Retrieved September 22, 2025, from https://www.britannica.com/biography/Alan-Turing

Farhud, D. D., & Zokaei, S. (2021). Ethical issues of artificial intelligence in medicine and healthcare. *Iranian Journal of Public Health*, *50*(11), i–v. DOI: 10.18502/ijph.v50i11.7600 PMID: 35223619

General Data Protection Regulation (GDPR). (n.d.). *GDPR Information Portal.* Retrieved October 26, 2025, from https://gdpr-info.eu/

Gerke, S., Minssen, T., & Cohen, G. (2020). Ethical and legal challenges of artificial intelligence-driven healthcare. In *Artificial intelligence in healthcare* (pp. 295–336). Elsevier. DOI: 10.1016/B978-0-12-818438-7.00012-5

Gorelik, A. J., Li, M., Hahne, J., Wang, J., Ren, Y., Yang, L., Zhang, X., Liu, X., Wang, X., Bogdan, R., & Carpenter, B. D. (2025). Ethics of AI in healthcare: A scoping review demonstrating applicability of a foundational framework. *Frontiers in Digital Health*, *7*, 1662642. DOI: 10.3389/fdgth.2025.1662642 PMID: 41000336

Joshi, G., Jain, A., Araveeti, S., Adhikari, S., Garg, H., & Bhandari, M. (2024). FDA-approved artificial intelligence and machine learning (AI/ML)-enabled medical devices: An updated landscape. *Electronics (Basel)*, *13*(3), 498. DOI: 10.3390/electronics13030498

Kaul, V., Enslin, S., & Gross, S. A. (2020). History of artificial intelligence in medicine. *Gastrointestinal Endoscopy*, *92*(4), 807–812. DOI: 10.1016/j.gie.2020.06.040 PMID: 32565184

Lindsay, R. K., Buchanan, B. G., Feigenbaum, E. A., & Lederberg, J. (1993). DENDRAL: A case study of the first expert system for scientific hypothesis formation. *Artificial Intelligence*, *61*(2), 209–261. DOI: 10.1016/0004-3702(93)90068-M

Litjens, G., Kooi, T., Bejnordi, B. E., Setio, A. A. A., Ciompi, F., Ghafoorian, M., van der Laak, J. A. W. M., van Ginneken, B., & Sánchez, C. I. (2017). A survey on deep learning in medical image analysis. *Medical Image Analysis*, *42*, 60–88. DOI: 10.1016/j.media.2017.07.005 PMID: 28778026

Liu, X., Wang, H., Li, Z., & Qin, L. (2021). Deep learning in ECG diagnosis: A review. *Knowledge-Based Systems*, *227*, 107187. DOI: 10.1016/j.knosys.2021.107187

Livraga, G. (2019). Privacy in microdata release: Challenges, techniques, and approaches. In Crato, N., & Paruolo, P. (Eds.), *Data-driven policy impact evaluation* (pp. 117–139). Springer., DOI: 10.1007/978-3-319-78461-8_5

London, A. J. (2019). Artificial intelligence and black-box medical decisions: Accuracy versus explainability. *The Hastings Center Report*, *49*(1), 15–21. DOI: 10.1002/hast.973 PMID: 30790315

Maccaro, A., Stokes, K., Statham, L., He, L., Williams, A., Pecchia, L., & Piaggio, D. (2024). Clearing the fog: A scoping literature review on the ethical issues surrounding artificial intelligence-based medical devices. *Journal of Personalized Medicine*, *14*(5), 443. DOI: 10.3390/jpm14050443 PMID: 38793025

Mazzi, F. (2025). Evaluating the normative implications of national and international artificial intelligence policies for Sustainable Development Goal 3: Good health and well-being. *Health Affairs Scholar*, *3*(6), qxaf108. Advance online publication. DOI: 10.1093/haschl/qxaf108 PMID: 40584023

Mennella, C., Maniscalco, U., De Pietro, G., & Esposito, M. (2024). Ethical and regulatory challenges of AI technologies in healthcare: A narrative review. *Heliyon, 10*(4), e09540. DOI: 10.1016/j.heliyon.2024.e26297 PMID: 38384518

Mienye, I. D., Swart, T. G., Obaido, G., Jordan, M., & Ilono, P. (2025). Deep convolutional neural networks in medical image analysis: A review. *Information (Basel), 16*(3), 195. DOI: 10.3390/info16030195

Miller, R. A. (1984). INTERNIST-1/CADUCEUS: Problems facing expert consultant programs. *Methods of Information in Medicine, 23*(1), 9–14. DOI: 10.1055/s-0038-1635320 PMID: 6374372

Miller, R. A., Pople, H. E.Jr, & Myers, J. D. (1982). Internist-I, an experimental computer-based diagnostic consultant for general internal medicine. *The New England Journal of Medicine, 307*(8), 468–476. DOI: 10.1056/NEJM198208193070803 PMID: 7048091

Miller, T. (2019). Explanation in artificial intelligence: Insights from the social sciences. *Artificial Intelligence, 267*, 1–38. DOI: 10.1016/j.artint.2018.07.007

Murdoch, T. B. (2021). Privacy and artificial intelligence: Challenges for protecting health information in a new era. *BMC Medical Ethics, 22*(1), 76. Advance online publication. DOI: 10.1186/s12910-021-00687-3 PMID: 34525993

Murphy, K., Di Ruggiero, E., Upshur, R., Willison, D. J., Malhotra, N., Cai, J. C., Malhotra, N., Lui, V., & Gibson, J. (2021). Artificial intelligence for good health: A scoping review of the ethics literature. *BMC Medical Ethics, 22*(1), 14. DOI: 10.1186/s12910-021-00577-8 PMID: 33588803

Ozmen, B. (2025). Navigating FDA regulations for development of artificial intelligence technologies in plastic surgery. *Aesthetic Surgery Journal, 45*(8), 865–868. Advance online publication. DOI: 10.1093/asj/sjaf051 PMID: 40181519

Packer, M., Hoffer, E. P., Barnett, G. O., Famiglietti, K., Kim, R. J., McLatchey, J., Elkin, P. L., Cimino, C., & Studney, D. (1989). Evolution of DXplain: A decision support system. *Proceedings of the Annual Symposium on Computer Applications in Medical Care,* 949–951.

Ratti, E., Morrison, M., & Jakab, I. (2025). Ethical and social considerations of applying artificial intelligence in healthcare—A two-pronged scoping review. *BMC Medical Ethics, 26*(1), 68. DOI: 10.1186/s12910-025-01198-1 PMID: 40420080

Ross, C., & Swetlitz, I. (2018). IBM's Watson supercomputer recommended "unsafe and incorrect" cancer treatments, internal documents show. *STAT*, *25*, 1–10. https://www.statnews.com/2018/07/25/ibm-watson-recommended-unsafe-incorrect-treatments

Shamsujjoha, M., Lu, Q., Zhao, D., & Zhu, L. (2024). *Towards AI-safety-by-design: A taxonomy of runtime guardrails in foundation model-based systems. arXiv preprint arXiv:2408.12345.*

Shortliffe, E. H. (1974). A rule-based computer program for advising physicians regarding antimicrobial therapy selection. *Proceedings of the 1974 ACM Annual Conference* - Volume 2, 739–744. DOI: 10.1145/1408800.1408906

Stroud, A. M., Anzabi, M. D., Wise, J. L., Barry, B. A., Malik, M. M., McGowan, M. L., & Sharp, R. R. (2025). Toward safe and ethical implementation of health care artificial intelligence: Insights from an academic medical center. *Mayo Clinic Proceedings. Digital Health*, *3*(1), 100189. DOI: 10.1016/j.mcpdig.2024.100189 PMID: 40206995

Tang, L., Li, J., & Fantus, S. (2023). Medical artificial intelligence ethics: A systematic review of empirical studies. *Digital Health*, *9*, 20552076231186064. DOI: 10.1177/20552076231186064 PMID: 37434728

Tilala, M. H., Chenchala, P. K., Choppadandi, A., Kaur, J., Naguri, S., Saoji, R., Devagup-tapu, B., & Tilala, M. (2024). Ethical considerations in the use of artificial intelligence and machine learning in health care: A comprehensive review. *Cureus*, *16*(6). Advance online publication. DOI: 10.7759/cureus.62443 PMID: 39011215

Topol, E. (2019). Deep medicine: How artificial intelligence can make healthcare human again. Hachette UK.

Torfi, A., Fox, E. A., & Reddy, C. K. (2022). Differentially private synthetic medical data generation using convolutional GANs. *Information Sciences*, *586*, 485–500. DOI: 10.1016/j.ins.2021.12.018

U.S. Food and Drug Administration. (2025). *Artificial intelligence-enabled device software functions: Lifecycle management and marketing submission recommendations (Draft guidance).* https://www.fda.gov/media/184856/download

Weiner, E. B., Dankwa-Mullan, I., Nelson, W. A., & Hassanpour, S. (2025). Ethical challenges and evolving strategies in the integration of artificial intelligence into clinical practice. *PLOS Digital Health*, *4*(4), e0000810. DOI: 10.1371/journal.pdig.0000810 PMID: 40198594

Wong, A., & Sussman, J. B. (2025). Understanding model drift and its impact on health care policy. *JAMA Health Forum*, *6*(1), e252724. DOI: 10.1001/jamahealthforum.2025.2724 PMID: 40815525

World Health Organization. (2021). *Ethics and governance of artificial intelligence for health: WHO guidance.* World Health Organization. https://www.who.int/publications/i/item/9789240029200

World Health Organization. (2024). *Ethics and governance of artificial intelligence for health: Large multimodal models. WHO guidance.* World Health Organization. https://www.who.int/news/item/18-01-2024-who-releases-ai-ethics-and-governance-guidance-for-large-multi-modal-models

Xhako, D., Hyka, N., Spahiu, E., & Hoxhaj, S. (2025). Medical image analysis using deep learning algorithms (DLA). *AIMS Biophysics*, *12*(2), 121–143. DOI: 10.3934/biophy.2025008

Zhou, N., Zhang, C.-T., Lv, H.-Y., Hao, C.-X., Li, T.-J., Zhu, J.-J., Zhu, H., Jiang, M., Liu, K.-W., Hou, H.-L., Liu, D., Li, A.-Q., Zhang, G.-Q., Tian, Z.-B., & Zhang, X.-C. (2019). Concordance study between IBM Watson for Oncology and clinical practice for patients with cancer in China. *The Oncologist*, *24*(6), 812–819. DOI: 10.1634/theoncologist.2018-0255 PMID: 30181315

Zhou, S. K., Greenspan, H., Davatzikos, C., Duncan, J. S., van Ginneken, B., Madabhushi, A., Prince, J. L., Rueckert, D., & Summers, R. M. (2021). A review of deep learning in medical imaging: Imaging traits, technology trends, case studies with progress highlights, and future promises. *Proceedings of the IEEE*, *109*(5), 820–838. DOI: 10.1109/JPROC.2021.3054390 PMID: 37786449

Chapter 8

Towards Ethical AI in Dermatological Diagnostics:

Balancing Patient Privacy, Fairness, and Human-Centered Design

Rabia Shahid
http://orcid.org/0009-0007-6138-4326
The University of Faisalabad, Pakistan & Government College University, Faisalabad, Pakistan

Muhammad Ibrar
http://orcid.org/0000-0002-6813-5003
The University of Faisalabad, Pakistan

Waqas Junaid
http://orcid.org/0009-0003-1778-4083
Northwestern Polytechnical University, Xian, China

Muhammad Saeed
The University of Faisalabad, Pakistan

Majid Hussain
http://orcid.org/0009-0002-5968-0509
The University of Faisalabad, Pakistan

DOI: 10.4018/979-8-3373-6038-6.ch008

ABSTRACT

Artificial intelligence (AI) has been a groundbreaking technology in the health sector, and dermatology is one of the earliest to adopt AI-based diagnostic systems. The deployment of this system causes significant challenges related to Responsible AI (RAI) such as decision critical tasks, patient privacy, accountability, clinician trust, and robustness. Ethical considerations are the core of chapter discussion that particularly focuses on protection of patient confidentiality through data augmentation and fairness across heterogeneous population by application of algorithmic fairness methods. The chapter also highlights the importance of user-centered system design to strengthen clinician trust and support shared decision-making. Combining both the technical innovation and an ethical background, this chapter proposes a practical implementation of how responsible AI can be embedded in clinical informatics Conclusively, it offers a practical roadmap for embedding responsible, fair, and trustworthy AI into dermatological informatics and into other high-stakes healthcare applications.

1. INTRODUCTION

Artificial intelligence (AI) quickly enters as indispensable solution in healthcare and provides new opportunities to support the decision-making process in diagnosis, prognosis, and therapeutic decision making. Out of the variety of disciplines enjoying the positives of AI development, the discipline of dermatology has proven to be a notably visible field, not least because of the increasing rate of skin cancer incidence worldwide and the availability of vast datasets of skin lesion imaging. Skin cancer, being the 5th most common cancer, presents a significant global health concern whose patients exceeded 19 million cases of melanoma (most lethal and life-threating type of skin cancer) in 2022. Early detection is important for timely therapeutic response as it greatly improves the treatment outcomes. The possibility of competing or surpassing the diagnostic accuracy of a dermatologist was revealed using AI driven skin lesion classification models in specific situations. Nevertheless, even with this success, various ethical and technical limitations have not been tackled in certifying transparency and clinical plausibility.

For instance, HAM10000 dataset that has been used as a reference set of dermoscopic medical imager has reached the status of a standard resource to develop and evaluate AI driven diagnostic predictive capabilities but high imbalance among classes can be observed in this dataset. For example, the benign group of Melanocytic nevi is severely overrepresented with more than 6,700 pictures whereas malignant melanoma includes only 1,100 pictures. This imbalance not only reduces the effectiveness of developed deep learning models, but it also introduces a heightened risk of algorithmic bias, resulting in underrepresentation or overlooking of less frequent lesion types. It potentially compromises the diagnostic reliability and ultimately patient safety. Medical researchers have increasingly investigated Cerebral Generative Adversarial Networks (GANs) to augment medical datasets to treat this complication and inhibition. GANs excel at forming medical data sets that are well curated. Correspondingly, CNN-transformer hybrids have also shown promise in their capacity to acquire local fine grained-map patterns as well as the long-range correlations in biomedical images.

Deployment of AI for diagnostics has greatly improved the assessment quality of dermatological diagnosis and its accuracy in primary care, especially for skin lesion diagnostics. As a decision support tool it provide great help to less experience clinicians. However, with the increasing use of AI emerge the ethical and social concerns specially related to reliability, fairness, transparency, discrimination, privacy, accountability, and data protection. These pervasive ethical ambiguities impair the real-world adoption of AI. It demands the implantation of a sound governance framework to avoid any malpractice or unethical behavior.

This chapter compressively assesses the use of AI in dermatology by introducing an integrated framework based on the combination of GAN based augmentation and CNN Transformer hybrid model. Despite the technical innovation, the adoption of AI does not stop with the technical innovation of the healthcare innovation; one should consider the ethical propositions cautiously. Even these frameworks with high optimal accuracy will be unsafe in the sense that they appear to satisfy the decision-making rule when they are performed in a controlled environment or when they are applied asymmetrically to various demographic groups. Therefore, this chapter puts its technical contribution to the broader discussion of Responsible AI (RAI) in the context of software development by noting how methodological choices can reduce medical data bias, focus more on interpretability, and build clinical confidence.

Chapter Objectives

This chapter has the following objectives:

- The investigation of new hybrid design with GAN aided augmentation and CNN Transformer classifier for AI based medical diagnosis of skin lesion.
- Assessment of how this framework allows us to reduce technical constraints (e.g., Data sparsity, Feature Selection) and ethical constraints (e.g., bias, fairness, interpretability).
- To provide practical guidance for incorporating ethical safeguards into the development and deployment of AI-enabled healthcare software, ensuring

that they are not only high-performing but also clinically appropriate, transparent, and aligned with established health informatics principles.

2. AI DRIVEN MEDICAL DIAGNOSIS

Ethics is the cornerstone of medical practices and the recent use of AI in medical diagnosis initiated the debate on its ethical use. Many non-ethical issues including the bias in datasets, patient privacy issues, fairness issues, and human-centered design are critically challenging applicability of AI. Implementation of cohesive technical and clinical multidisciplinary and ethical approaches (Chen et al., 2023; Benčević et al., 2024) are the key to tackle these issues.

2.1 Representation of Dataset and Bias

Dataset bias is the major concern of dermatological AI. Most publicly available datasets of dermoscopic and clinical images (e.g., the ISIC archive(ISIC – International Skin Imaging Collaboration) overrepresent lighter skin tones, which results in reduced performance on darker skin tones and minority subgroups (Alipour et al., 2024). Under-detected and less accurate representation of these populations (Kurtansky et al., 2024) affects the diagnostic accuracy and perpetuate health disparities. Furthermore, limited access to metadata and unavailability of demographic labels impede fairness evaluation (Montoya et al., 2025).

To address these issues, there is need to prioritize inclusive data collection for which more recently, there has been a suggestion of adopting better skin tones measures like the Monk Skin Tone (MST) scale that offers a more encompassing model to the traditional Fitzpatrick scale (Khalkhali et al., 2025). On a similar note, new algorithms can estimate skin tone only based on images, and they allow a more accurate calculation of fairness (Tadesse et al., 2023). Additionally, advance methods like U2-Net can improve the diagnosis of small/complex lesions irrespective of the skin tone while genetic databases can also enable identification of genotype-phenotypes links for accurate determination(Kakish et al., 2025). Collectively these implementations ensure the minimization of data bias.

2.2 Measures and Analysis of Equity

Equity in AI dermatology extends beyond the ideas of accuracy as it requires subgroup infinite sensitivity and specificity as well as constructions of calibration (Rong et al., 2023). Aggregate performance metrics such as AUC can obscure disparities, making it essential to report disaggregated results by sex, age, and skin tone (Montoya et al., 2025). Recent advances in synthetic data generation have now materialized the stress-testing of models on subgroups that were previously non-representative (Kim et al., 2024). Although promising, they still require an acutely accurate check to avoid reinforcement of existing biases or introduction of new forms of prejudice.

2.3 Privacy-Saving Methods

There is a highly significant issue of the privacy of patients regarding dermatology datasets that demands the adoption of transparent data handling practices and stringent data protection measures. It is essential to note that sensitive nature of patient's data makes it difficult to share such information across different institutes or to integrate with different databases that can greatly constrain AI development. Therefore, consent is the pivotal point to address this concern (Badawy et al., 2025a). Patients must clearly be informed in simple and tangible terms that how their data will be used and stored for AI-based data trainings and diagnostic applications and how data will be share among different databases (Kumar et al., 2023)

To ensure the data privacy, Federated learning has been widely explored as a method for joint training without a centralized patient data center (Guan et al., 2024; Haggenmüller et al., 2024). Local storage of patient data enables FL to follow the privacy laws, and, concurrently, the capacity to create multi-institutional models. However, FL also can propagate prejudices when the participating institutions differ in size, population representation, and data quality. Flex Fair and other new methods introduce fairness constraints directly into federal system to mitigate these disparities (Xing et al., 2025). Other privacy enhancing methods such as differential privacy and uncertainty estimation offer more protection to patients, though, they may sometimes reduce model utility in certain situations (Koutsoubi et al., 2024). Additionally, implementation of Shapley Additive exPlanations (SHAP) and Local Interpretable Model-agnostic Explanations (LIME) and can enhance transparency by identifying the features that contribute to a model's diagnostic decisions (Badawy et al., 2025b) These tools are critical for strengthening clinician and patient trust in AI-assisted care

2.4 Explainability Human-Centered Design and Explainability

Human-centered AI (HCAI) is the latest concept that supports usability, transparency, and trust during AI practices. Products within the dermatology profession should be interpretable to supplement rather than replace clinical knowledge by clinicians (van Leersum & Maathuis, 2025; Rong et al., 2023). Latest studies pointed out that the AI-based explanations (e.g., saliency maps or case-based reasoning) must be evaluated by clinicians to ensure that they enhance the superior decision-making power of clinicians, rather than presenting wrong or misleading data (Kim et al., 2024). Unresolved uncertainties in the model output can hinder effective communication between AI systems, dermatologists, and patients that reinforce the concerns about partial or insufficient trust in AI-assisted care (Chen et al., 2023).

2.5 Competencies Frameworks (Regulatory and Ethical Frameworks)

The governance models for AI in healthcare emphasize the transparent reporting, balanced auditing and a possible trial mechanism before it can be applied in clinical procedures (Haggenmüller et al., 2024). The regulatory agencies do not solely concentrate on technical performance, but also on patient safety, privacy and fair results. Pre- and post-implementation monitoring is essential to detect performance drift and to identify emerging biases in real-world use (Shahzad et al., 2024).

It is essential to strike a balance between accuracy and explainability to avoid the poor reporting of AI models. In this regard, development of models with self-reflection and explainability will enable the clinicians to understand the decision making process and to identify any potential prediction biases. It requires a holistic approach that embeds fairness throughout the model development and deployment processes. Development of equitable and trustworthy systems depends on cross-disciplinary collaboration among clinicians, data scientists, and policymakers to prioritize accountability and well-being of patients. The application of FAIR (findability, accessibility, interoperability, reusability) principles are essential to strengthen the governance of data management and data stewardship to ensure improved data quality, its utility, and transparency. In this regard, several AI checklists have been developed that are being discussed in detail by (Hanna et al., 2025). Together, these practices promote transparency, inclusiveness, trustworthiness, and regulation in AI-driven dermatology.

The application of artificial intelligence (AI) is changing the nature of the dermatological diagnostic prospective, as the opportunities to categorize the lesion, predict risks, and offer clinical decision support. Nevertheless, the implementation of AI in the medical discipline has been discussed already as a matter of grave ethical considerations, specifically, patient privacy and equity in a culturally diverse population and human-centered design (HCD). We have suggested a methodological framework to determine the ethics establishment, assessment, and implementation of the AI systems in the sphere of dermatology to address these challenges. A proposed framework shown in Figure 3.

The framework is based on the 3 pillars:

Privacy

The most important is the patient data protection. The framework is centered upon the execution of privacy-preservation measures, which are federated learning, data anonymization, and successful data protection procedures. Such plans allow preparing a functional AI model and reducing the risks to the privacy of the patients.

Fairness

To avoid the perpetuation of health disparities or make them even more serious, one must achieve a fairly good performance of AI regarding all groups of patients. The framework implies employing different sets of data, logical bias identification, and the stratification of the analysis taking the strength of the skin color, age, and sex. This stabilizes the AI tools and makes them objective to all the populations.

Human-Centered Design

Clinicians and patients needs must be put into consideration to develop AI systems that will meet the needs. The model increases the co-designing with the stakeholders, explanation of AI in a simple way, and feedback procedures. This will make the use of AI tools convenient, reliable and easy to follow workflow since it improves patient care.

2.6 Workflow

Workflow

The ethics of the AI evolution are based on the following workflow:

- Data Attack and Data safety evaluation.
- Prejudice Model Training and Evaluation.
- HCD Interface Design
- Ethical Analysis and Application.
    - Continuous Monitoring

2.7 Expected Outcomes

These values will transform practical principles of ethical AI in the field of dermatology, e.g.

- Recommendations on data curing
- Privacy
- Minimization of bias.
- It will be providing also human-centered deployment work and policy / insights to enable responsible AI implementation in clinical care.

Significance

This framework will ensure competence and efficacy of AI in dermatology as it addresses the innovation responsively to the patient and in the best interests of a patient. It serves as an example of how AI may be applied to healthcare in a morally acceptable manner to all its branches and help clinicians and patients in the age of digital medicine.

2.8 Synthesis and Gaps

Literature essential needs:

1. Better dataset variety- designate selection and labelling procedures ((ISIC – International Skin Imaging Collaboration ; Khalkhali et al., 2025).
2. Standardized fairness assessment which includes clinically meaningful subgroup-particular measurements (Montoya et al., 2025 ; Xing et al., 2025).
3. Physiological privacy and fairness. Federated learning and other collaborative methods (Koutsoubis et al., 2024; Guan et al., 2024).
4. Deployment that is human centered, has validated explanations, uncertain communication, and governance oversight (van Leersum & Maathuis, 2025; Rong et al., 2023).

Although substantial progress has been made in this field, there are still gaps in the representativeness of datasets, cross-institutional governance, and highly supportive human assessments. Multi-sites federated trials, standardized reporting of fairness and clinical integration made based on ethics are all areas of future work.

3. PROBLEM STATEMENT AND MOTIVATION

3.1 The Future and Potential Treasure of AI in Dermatology

Dermatology is one of the most promising area of AI implementation due to the visualization aspect of diagnosis. Dermatologist-level performance AI models that have been trained on dermoscopic images exhibited high performance for melanoma detection. Nonetheless, these advances do not make the safe and responsible adoption of AI a straightforward process.

There are three major pitfalls that can undermine the reliability of AI in dermatology and lead to unethical use:

- **Missing Data:** Underrepresentation of malignant tumors like melanoma as compared to benign nevi, cause data imbalance and biased infrastructures.
- **Imbalance and Equity Problems:** currrent data sets usually are not as representative of a variety of skin tones, which creates ethical issues of unfairness in diagnosis.
- **Lost Transparency:** Black-box models can be accurate but fail to offer clinicians a reason that can be understood which destroys trust.

These problems not only compromise technical performance, but also give rise to deep unethical issues of safety, fairness, and responsibility.

3.2 Hybrid GAN-CNN-Transformer Framework

In the present paper, a hybrid way to address this dilemma is proposed to resolve the two issues of technical imbalance and moral deficits. The implementation of Generative Adversarial Networks (GANs) is proposed to generate authentic synthetic images to enrich the poorly represented lesion types, thereby significantly reducing data imbalance. From ethical point-of-view it eliminates the bias of the unequal representation of classes. Whereas implementation of CNN-Transformer Hybrid Model (a hybrid type that unites CNN and Transformer) improved classification and the elucidation of results Ethically it promotes equitableness and transparency throughout the diagnostic pathway.

Through targeted augmentation and refined architecture design along with explicit focus on fairness, privacy, and trust, this approach can further improve the accuracy while fostering a more responsible and person-centered AI.

4. MAJOR TENETS OF ETHICAL ARTIFICIAL INTELLIGENCE IN HEALTHCARE

There are four pillars that are interdependent and on which the basis of a reliable AI system is built in the field of medicine: transparency, fairness, privacy, and accountability.

4.1 Openness and Understandability

In order to transform AI into a reliable partner in clinical practices, the rationale behind its decisions should be comprehensible to clinical professionals. A black-box model, however precise it may be, will not be received well by the clinic who are supposed to diagnose and explain the diagnosis to patients. Therefore, Explainable AI (XAI) solutions are necessary. Methods such as Grad-Cam in case of computer vision or LIME in the case of tabular data are essential to explain risk scores, classifications, and analysis of a prediction. It enables clinicians to challenge an AI rationale, providing a significant check-and-balance mechanism within diagnostic work. The integrity of such tools will ensure that AI is an influential assistive technology, rather than unquestioned power.

4.2 Fairness and Equity

Medical AI must not support or exacerbate existing healthcare disparities, which is fundamental ethical prerequisite. Fairness and equity begins with the training data sets, therefore all key relevant demographics like gender, ethnicity, age and socioeconomic status must be balanced and represented in databases. The propensity of the HAM10000 dataset to the light skin tone is a heart-wrenching illustration, though all other dimensions have their bias, e.g. the declining efficacy of chest X-ray models across some demographics or the biased predictions of illness risk by EHR-driven models. To address these concerns, fairness metrices such as demographic parity (similar positive prediction rates across groups) and equalized odds (similar true positive rates and similar false positive rates) must be rigorously applied at both model development and model deployment stages as shown in Table 1.

Table 1. Fairness metrics applied to healthcare AI datasets

Demografic Parity	Definition	Application in Healthcare AI	Example Domain
Demographic Parity	Ensures equal positive prediction rates across demographic groups (e.g. gender, ethnicity).	Checks whether a cancer screening model predicts "positive" equually	Skin cancer detection (HAM10000, lighter vs. darker skin)
Equalized Odds	Requires equal true positive PPV, NPV) are equal across groups.	Evaluates whether a pneumonia model has similar sensitivi-specficity across	Chest X-ray models underperforming in minority groups
Predictive Parity	Verifies that disease risk scores are equally reliable for all demographics.	Verifies./airness of probability-based predictions (e.g.3% cancer risk should mean same for all)	Cardiology AI predicting heart failure risk
Subgroup Performance Gap	Measures accuracy differen-ce between majority vs. aninority groups	Identifies and mitigate accuracy drop in underrep-resented patient	Dermatology AI misclassifying darker skin tones

It is suggested that there should be a multi-layered system of governance in place that will facilitate the homogeneous implementation of these ideas. A hierarchical system of governance based on institutional ethics committees, national regulatory bodies, and global collaborative networks could assist in guiding the future of AI innovation in healthcare through a belief in ethical behaviors not only in an individual contact with a patient but also on the level of international health policy. In this regard, Institutional review boards (IRBs) and university and hospital ethics committees must be instituted to approve the use of data and pilot test artificial intelligence devices. Similarly, national regulatory bodies, like the FDA and the EMA, must establish the harmonization of the approval and monitoring of medical AI and clear safety and efficacy criteria whereas the international bodies like the World Health Organization (WHO), IEEE and International Organization for Standardization (ISO) must cooperate to ensure that international interoperability and ethical harmonization of AI applications in which the responsible scaling of AI solutions will be across nations as shown in Table 2

Figure 1. Key challenges in ethical AI for healthcare and corresponding technical mitigations promoting fairness, transparency, privacy, and clinical trust

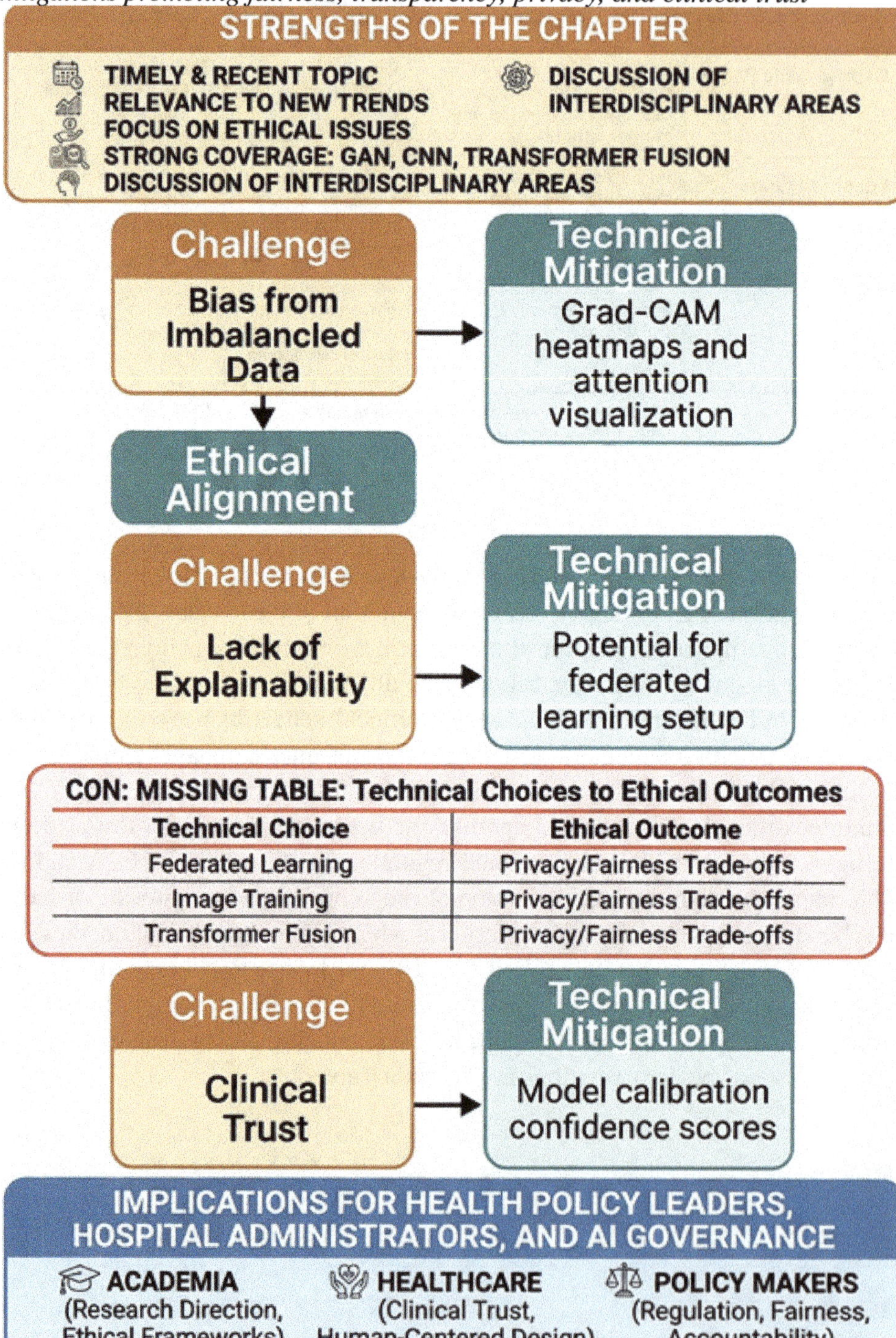

Table 2. Multi-layered governance framework for ethical AI in healthcare

Governance Layer	Key Entities	Primary Responsibilities
	**Institutional Ethics Committees** Hospitals, Universities Institutional Review Boards (IRBs)	• Oversee ethical approval for data collection and AI research. • Monitor pilot AI tool deployment within clinical settings. • Ensure patient consent and local compliance with ethical standards
	**National Regulatory Bodies** FDA (LISA), EMA (Europe), MHRA (UK) national health. agencies	• Establish standardized approval pathways for AI in medicine. • Define safety, efficacy, and performance benchmarks • Monitor AI post-deployment (real-world evidence, adverse events)
	**Global Collaborative Networks** WHO, IEEE, ISO, international consi-ortia	• Promote interoperability and global ethical standarls • Facilitate cross-border shaing of best practices and datasets • Develop international certifications for trustworthy

4.3 Technological Mitigation and Ethical Issues in AI

The case study proves that the four principles are being translated into the specific interventions within the system level on the same ethical principles discussed above that is, privacy protection, reduction of bias, transparency and human-centered design. The AI prototype hybrid assisted us in operationalizing the ethical framework in the context of a real-life scenario of the dermatological diagnostic testing. Each and every aspect of the system was also chosen in order to serve a certain ethical issue: the issue of data imbalances and fairness was eliminated through the help of GAN-based augmentation, the issue of privacy risk through simulated federated learning and expectation of transparency through the explainability tools of the Grad-CAM.

This section would also play the role of theoretical and practical bridge as this would determine the presence of such interventions in the setting of an actual diagnosis process. It underscores how the ethical requirements might be involved to play a significant role in the model designing instead of being another theoretical ideal.

4.4 Responsible Artificial Intelligence Review and Results

On the HAM10000 dataset, the hybrid model was evaluated in detail and the measures used compared to the standard measures of machine-learning (accuracy, AUROC, F1-score) and new measures as discussed earlier that related within ethics were considered. This two layer test will ensure the fact that the test was not a predictive performance as such, but the test assessed the fairness of the system, the transparency of the system and clinical reliability of the system.

GAN created the data augmentation that provided the balance in the classes, especially the ones that are not represented and led to more balanced results in the classes. The interpretability and clinical confidence can be explained by the fact that the visualization of grad-CAMs showed that the model oriented itself on medically relevant parts of lesions and not on the background features of images. To overcome privacy, a simulated system of federated training revealed that the performance of the models could be maintained even in the event where the data were stored in decentralized form to a case, which is one of the determining factors to multi-institutional clinical implementation.

Calibration of probabilities was also done to make sure that the model possessed credible and important clinical significance scores. The attainable difference between the confusion matrix achieved and a predetermined baseline CNN demonstrated that a considerable decrease in the fraction of misbalanced negative forecasting was achieved in melanoma and this provided a good evidence of similarity between patient-safety objectives and feasibility of applying ethical principles in the development of the model.

In general, it is concluded that there was the utilization of ethical framework to take the methodological decisions and vice versa, and the methodological decisions made enhanced the accountability, fairness and reliability of the system of obtained diagnosis.

4.5 Reflections: Spotting and Using Ethical AI

The case study is a good example as it demonstrates how a properly designed AI governance can be integrated into the technical operations effortlessly. Based on the technical foundation of GAN augmentation, CNN-Transformer modeling, and essential explainable AI tools, the system not only enhances the performance but also meets the ethical standards of fairness, privacy, accountability, and human-centered design. This indicates that the moral values should not be introduced at the end of the AI development process, but it should be a facilitator throughout the process. These findings offer a compelling roadmap for other medical AI applications, demonstrating that a well-trained model and an ethically sound one can and should be achieved simultaneously.

Figure 2. AI ethics framework

4.6 The Healthcare Ethical AI principles and Best Practices

The introduction of artificial intelligence according to the specifications of the healthcare industry is not only a matter of technical proficiency but one should also observe a desire to apply ethical standards in the whole life cycle of its development. The section is a translation of the theoretical framework in the previous sections into practices and actions which guarantee that the software engineers and researchers can create AI systems that are not only effective but also socially responsible and will be trusted in clinical settings. Its key idea is to follow an ethics-by-design philosophy in a manner that the activities of the entire pipeline are accountable, instead of an overlay element, which will be incorporated at a later phase.

5. RECOMMENDATIONS FOR ETHICAL AI IN HEALTHCARE

5.1 Data Governance and Privacy

The basis of AI ethics is the responsibility in the handling of healthcare information. Effective governing bodies safeguard confidential patient data, build trust and consistency to international standards. To ensure the patient's privacy and personal confidentiality, robots should be used to gather the data when authorized by the patient. It will not only improve the accuracy of collected by reduced chances of human error but also improve the autonomy. Furthermore, the implementation of algorithms like de-identification and pseudonymization could improvise the privacy protection of a specific individual and allow the development of data-driven innovation. However, it is important to adhere to the international guidelines like HIPAA and GDPR to guarantee the legal and ethical data integration throughout health care networks as shown in Table 3.

5.2 Bias and Fairness

Stereotypes within AI systems may contribute to the unfair healthcare system. The key to trust and inclusiveness is to be fair. The used models should be applicable in dissimilar populaces to prevent discrimination while underrepresented groups should majorly be focused on, so that there is no matter of systemic exclusion. Most importantly, all AI forecasts should also be subject to a fairness requirement, so the rates of error should be equal between subgroups. Addressing the biasness in AI models could profoundly enhance the diagnostic outcomes. A proactive call of action is essential to urge all the stakeholders including academician, clinicians, data scientists, industrialists, and policy makers to develop a comprehensive regulatory framework that can mitigate bias and foster equitable outcomes.

5.3 Explainability and Transparency

The decisions made by AI in healthcare should be interpretable and linkable to gain the trust of clinicians and patients. Other models which are subject to inspection of underlying logic should also be preferred. Models like SHAP, LIME and Grad-Cam techniques are preferential to assist in visualizing model reasoning. However, documenting decision-makers processes is a source of accountability however, the widely adopted safety and accountability practices have not been generalized for the decision made by AI-based tool. Significant debate has been underway to make a liability mechanism to ensure that actual culprit held accountable in case of false prediction and malpractice. Presently the whole system is based on the concept of self-moral policing and blind trust on machine. Future regulatory frameworks must consider the fact that prediction efficiency of AI is highly dependent on the training data, and repeated data modulation could severely affect the process bias. Therefore, in good faith it is suggested that health professional should not blindly follow the recommendation of AI but rather use it as confirmatory and supplementary tool to assist in the decision making process.

5.4 Clinical Safety and Clinical validation.

To ensure that medical AI tools and models meet the rigorous clinical standards of safety and efficacy, these models have to be tested in the actual setting as clinical trial before large-scale implementation. Premature experiments in restricted conditions can be used to spot the merits and drawbacks of AI systems. Later on, perpetual evaluation of AI models with different patient data consistency is essential for the real-world evaluation. In this regard, the collaboration among AI specialists, data scientists, dermatologists, and oncologist is crucial for the constant monitoring and improvement of the whole process as well as to provide protection to patients in case of un-intended effects or malpractice. Long-term studies will be vital for algorithm refinement and to evaluate model performance based on real-world data. Combinedly, it will ensure the development of patient-centered tools, thus bridging the gap among various demographical groups.

5.5 Checks on regulatory Compliance.

Regular audits verify compliance with the national and global healthcare standards. A clear definition of who is responsible for delivering outcomes will make sure that developers, healthcare institutions and policymakers have joint responsibility in the ethical use of these tools. Although many regulatory organization such as Food and Drug Administration (FDA) of USA, Health Insurance Portability and Accountability Act (HIPAA), General Data Protection Regulation (GDPR), Medical Devices Regulation (MDR) or European Union, Anti-Kickback Statute and Stark Law of US Federal, AI ethical guidelines by World Health Organization (WHO), and Cyber-security and Health IT Regulations are in practice to regulate the use of AI in the medical practices, but they are facing some regulatory challenges. As the technology expansion is faster than legal frameworks, so it is difficult for the law makers to keep the pace with evolving AI, moreover, the interpretability of consequences is rather challenging due to complex nature of these systems. To strengthen the regulatory framework, future research should be focused on the safety assessment of AI-powered diagnostics. Continuous monitoring is essential for the development of adaptive regulations according to emerging risks and advancements. As the AI development and medical imaging technologies have global impact, so harmonized international standards and frameworks should be developed to align the requirements across international borders (Odezuligbo et al., 2024).

Figure 3. Ethical framework for dermatological diagnostics

Table 3. Open challenges in cross-cultural fairness testing for medical AI (columns: region, challenge, ethical concern, example solution

Region	Challenge	Ethical Concern	Example Solution
Europe	Data privacy and GDPR compliance	Patient consent and data protection	Federated learning across multi-hospital
Africa	Lack of diverse training data for certain skin diseases	Bias against diverse skin tones	Collaborative data sharing agreements with a focus on ethical consent
Asia	Varied medical technologies and infrastructure	Model performance disparities	Developing robust models that are resilient to difference in image quality
North America	Disparities in healthcare access and insurance	Inequitable health outcomes	Integrating socioeconomic data and fairness metrics into model evaluation

CONCLUSION

AI is set to revolutionize healthcare by enabling earlier and precise diagnosis and overall improved patient care. However, as demonstrated throughout this chapter, technical advances alone are insufficient. The ethical design and responsible implementation of AI systems is equally important in the sensitive field of medicine. Based on the example of skin lesion classification by a new GAN + CNN-Transformer model, this chapter has shown that a technical advancement can simultaneously serve as an ethical intervention. By explicitly addressing systemic issues such as dataset imbalance, algorithmic bias, and patient data privacy, our framework illustrates that accuracy and ethics are not competing goals but mutually reinforcing ones. The use of GAN-generated synthetic data not only improved performance on rare but clinically important lesion types, it also reduced the ethical risk of under-diagnosis in minority groups.

The chapter emphasized that ethical AI governance operates on multiple levels, which goes beyond local institutional ethics committees to global entities such as the WHO and FDA. In the absence of clear, unified regulatory guidelines, systematic cross-demographic fairness testing and alignment with emerging Responsible AI standards become indispensable. Without these safeguards, medical AI may unintentionally amplify existing healthcare inequities rather than mitigate them. Ethically sound AI must ensure that all patients, regardless of background, receive equitable benefit. The core message of this chapter implies that AI cannot be considered ethical if it is fair without accuracy, transparent without privacy, and innovative without patient trust. Equity, and human-centered trust, and balanced performance are the defining concept to regulate the trajectory of healthcare AI. For researchers, clinicians, and policymakers, the challenge is no longer merely to create more powerful algorithms but to develop responsible, human-centered systems worthy of clinical confidence. It can be stated that ethical behavior can only be fostered through regulating the entire software development cycle from dataset design to clinical deployment. In this regards, collaborative interactions among all stakeholders would be essential to develop solid framework for responsible AI.

REFERENCES

Alipour, N., Burke, T., & Courtney, J. (2024). Skin type diversity in skin lesion datasets: A review. *Current Dermatology Reports, 13*(3), 198–210. DOI: 10.1007/s13671-024-00440-0 PMID: 39184010

Badawy, W., Zinhom, H., & Shaban, M. (2025a). Navigating ethical considerations in the use of artificial intelligence for patient care: A systematic review. *International Nursing Review, 72*(3), e13059. DOI: 10.1111/inr.13059 PMID: 39545614

Badawy, W., Zinhom, H., & Shaban, M. (2025b). Navigating ethical considerations in the use of artificial intelligence for patient care: A systematic review. *International Nursing Review, 72*(3), e13059. DOI: 10.1111/inr.13059 PMID: 39545614

Benčević, M., Habijan, M., Galić, I., Babin, D., & Pižurica, A. (2024). Understanding skin color bias in deep learning-based skin lesion segmentation. *Computer Methods and Programs in Biomedicine, 245*, 108044. DOI: 10.1016/j.cmpb.2024.108044 PMID: 38290289

Chen, Y., Clayton, E. W., Novak, L. L., Anders, S., & Malin, B. (2023). Human-centered design to address biases in artificial intelligence. *Journal of Medical Internet Research, 25*, e43251. DOI: 10.2196/43251 PMID: 36961506

Guan, H., Yap, P. T., Bozoki, A., & Liu, M. (2024). Federated learning for medical image analysis: A survey. *Pattern Recognition, 151*, 110424. DOI: 10.1016/j.patcog.2024.110424 PMID: 38559674

Haggenmüller, S., Schmitt, M., Krieghoff-Henning, E., Hekler, A., Maron, R. C., Wies, C., Utikal, J. S., Meier, F., Hobelsberger, S., Gellrich, F. F., Sergon, M., Hauschild, A., French, L. E., Heinzerling, L., Schlager, J. G., Ghoreschi, K., Schlaak, M., Hilke, F. J., Poch, G., & Brinker, T. J. (2024). Federated learning for decentralized artificial intelligence in melanoma diagnostics. *JAMA Dermatology, 160*(3), 303–311. DOI: 10.1001/jamadermatol.2023.5550 PMID: 38324293

Hanna, M. G., Pantanowitz, L., Jackson, B., Palmer, O., Visweswaran, S., Pantanowitz, J., Deebajah, M., & Rashidi, H. H. (2025). Ethical and bias considerations in artificial intelligence/machine learning. *Modern Pathology, 38*(3), 100686. DOI: 10.1016/j.modpat.2024.100686 PMID: 39694331

ISIC – International Skin Imaging Collaboration. (n.d.). *ISIC Archive*.

Kakish, D. R. K., AlSamhori, J. F., Fajardo, A. N. R., Qaqish, L. N., Jaber, L. A., Abujudeh, R., Al-Zuriqat, M. H. M., Mohammed, A. Y., & Nashwan, A. J. (2025). Transforming dermatopathology with AI: Addressing bias, enhancing interpretability, and shaping future diagnostics. *Dermatological Reviews*, *6*(1), e70018. DOI: 10.1002/der2.70018

Khalkhali, V., Lee, H., Nguyen, J., Zamora-Erazo, S., Ragin, C., Aphale, A., Bellacosa, A., Monk, E. P., & Biswas, S. K. (2025). MST-AI: Skin Color Estimation in Skin Cancer Datasets. *Journal of Imaging*, *11*(7), 235. DOI: 10.3390/jimaging11070235 PMID: 40710621

Kim, J., Maathuis, H., & Sent, D. (2024). Human-centered evaluation of explainable AI applications: A systematic review. *Frontiers in Artificial Intelligence*, *7*, 1456486. DOI: 10.3389/frai.2024.1456486 PMID: 39484154

Koutsoubis, N., Yilmaz, Y., Ramachandran, R. P., Schabath, M., & Rasool, G. (2024). Privacy-preserving federated learning and uncertainty quantification in medical imaging. *Radiology. Artificial Intelligence*. Advance online publication. DOI: 10.1148/ryai.240637 PMID: 40366260

Kumar, P., Chauhan, S., & Awasthi, L. K. (2023). Artificial intelligence in healthcare: Review, ethics, trust challenges & future research directions. *Engineering Applications of Artificial Intelligence*, *120*, 105894. DOI: 10.1016/j.engappai.2023.105894

Kurtansky, N. R., D'Alessandro, B. M., Gillis, M. C., Betz-Stablein, B., Cerminara, S. E., Garcia, R., Girundi, M. A., Goessinger, E. V., Gottfrois, P., Guitera, P., Halpern, A. C., Jakrot, V., Kittler, H., Kose, K., Liopyris, K., Malvehy, J., Mar, V. J., Martin, L. K., Mathew, T., & Rotemberg, V. (2024). The SLICE-3D dataset: 400,000 skin lesion image crops extracted from 3D TBP for skin cancer detection. *Scientific Data*, *11*(1), 884. DOI: 10.1038/s41597-024-03743-w PMID: 39143096

Montoya, L. N., Roberts, J. S., & Hidalgo, B. S. (2025, March). Towards fairness in AI for melanoma detection: systemic review and recommendations. In *Future of information and communication conference* (pp. 320–341). Springer Nature Switzerland. DOI: 10.1007/978-3-031-84460-7_21

Odezuligbo, I., Alade, O., & Chukwurah, E. F. (2024). Ethical and regulatory considerations in AI-driven medical imaging: A perspective overview. *Medical AI Ethics*, *8*(2), 156–174. DOI: 10.30574/ijsra.2024.13.1.1739

Rong, Y., Leemann, T., Nguyen, T. T., Fiedler, L., Qian, P., Unhelkar, V., Seidel, T., Kasneci, G., & Kasneci, E. (2023). Towards human-centered explainable ai: A survey of user studies for model explanations. *IEEE Transactions on Pattern Analysis and Machine Intelligence*, *46*(4), 2104–2122. DOI: 10.1109/TPAMI.2023.3331846 PMID: 37956008

Shahzad, M. F., Xu, S., Lim, W. M., Yang, X., & Khan, Q. R. (2024). Artificial intelligence and social media on academic performance and mental well-being: Student perceptions of positive impact in the age of smart learning. *Heliyon*, *10*(8), e29523. Advance online publication. DOI: 10.1016/j.heliyon.2024.e29523 PMID: 38665566

Tadesse, G. A., Cintas, C., Varshney, K. R., Staar, P., Agunwa, C., Speakman, S., Jia, J., Bailey, E. E., Adelekun, A., Lipoff, J. B., Onyekaba, G., Lester, J. C., Rotemberg, V., Zou, J., & Daneshjou, R. (2023). Skin tone analysis for representation in educational materials (STAR-ED) using machine learning. *NPJ Digital Medicine*, *6*(1), 151. DOI: 10.1038/s41746-023-00881-0 PMID: 37596324

van Leersum, C. M., & Maathuis, C. (2025). Human centred explainable AI decision-making in healthcare. *Journal of Responsible Technology*, *21*, 100108. DOI: 10.1016/j.jrt.2025.100108

Xing, H., Sun, R., Ren, J., Wei, J., Feng, C. M., Ding, X., Guo, Z., Wang, Y., Hu, Y., Wei, W., Ban, X., Xie, C., Tan, Y., Liu, X., Cui, S., Duan, X., & Li, Z. (2025). Achieving flexible fairness metrics in federated medical imaging. *Nature Communications*, *16*(1), 3342. DOI: 10.1038/s41467-025-58549-0 PMID: 40199877

Chapter 9
Integrating Agentic AI Ethically Into Geriatric Healthcare:
A Framework for Frailty Monitoring With Transformer Models and Wearable Technology

Muhammad Azhar
http://orcid.org/0000-0003-3687-0270
Hong Kong Shue Yan University, Hong Kong

Ifra Shabbir
http://orcid.org/0009-0006-1531-2287
COMSATS University, Islamabad, Pakistan

Muhammad Shafqat Ali
BPP University Limited, London, UK

Ghulam Farid
Harbin Engineering University, China

Hamza Arif
COMSATS University, Islamabad, Pakistan

Rubia Fatima
http://orcid.org/0000-0002-7144-1925
Emerson University, Multan, Pakistan

ABSTRACT

The rising incidence of frailty in aging populations challenges traditional healthcare systems that lack real-time monitoring tools. To address this, we present CareBot, an ethical AI framework using wearable sensors and phones to continuously assess elderly frailty. It employs Transformer models to analyze multimodal data like heart rate, movement, and sleep for early frailty detection. TabTransformer handles health records to generate personalized risk scores. Additionally, DeepSeek, a generative AI, provides caregiver alerts and natural-language health advice. Following ethical AI

DOI: 10.4018/979-8-3373-6038-6.ch009

principles, CareBot ensures autonomy, transparency, equity, and privacy. Evaluations with PAMAP2 and SHARE datasets show CareBot outperforms methods like SVM, CNN, and LSTM in accuracy and robustness. This scalable solution offers interpretable insights and tailored actions to enhance elderly health and quality of life.

INTRODUCTION

With demographic forecasts showing that by 2040, people 65 and older will make up more than 30% of the population in a number of developed regions, including parts of Europe, East Asia, and North America, the senior population's rapid growth has become a major global concern (Ding et al., 2023). A variety of causes, including improving living conditions, lower birth rates in many nations, and growing life expectancy brought on by healthcare advancements, are responsible for these extraordinary demographic transitions This development presents significant problems to healthcare systems, social services, and economic structures, even as it also reflects advancements in medicine and society. Age-related illnesses like frailty, dementia, cardiovascular disease, and mobility impairments are predicted to rise sharply due to the aging population, increasing the need for long-term care and specialized geriatric services.

- Clinical Significance of Frailty:

Frailty is more than simply a descriptive phrase; it is a potent clinical risk condition that predicts who will die sooner, who will be admitted to the hospital, who will fall or become incapacitated, and who will require long-term care. The risk often increases in a graduated pattern from robust to pre-frail to frail, and frailty consistently increases poor outcomes in community, hospital, and long-term care settings. Pre-frailty carries significant excess risk, and frail older persons had much greater mortality than their non-frail contemporaries (average hazard ratios of 1.8–2.0), according to pooled analyses. This emphasizes the significance of early detection.

Those who are feeble have a significantly higher hospital utilization rate. According to meta-analytic data, frailty is linked to worse in-hospital outcomes, including longer duration of stay and higher in-hospital mortality, as well as higher hospital admissions (pooled odds ratio $\approx$1.6). Frailty at admission predicts in-hospital death and functional impairment by discharge among unexpected hospital hospitalizations, according to systematic reviews. This suggests that typical inpatient approaches frequently fall short in reducing frailty-related vulnerability. After controlling for age and comorbidity, these gradients remain, indicating that frailty captures risk that is not entirely represented by diagnostic counts alone.

Frailty is frequently associated with falls, a sentinel occurrence in geriatric care. According to systematic reviews and meta-analyses, seniors who are frail have about twice the chance of falling as opposed to their peers who are not frail. The prevalence of falls is particularly high when cognitive impairment coexists (a condition known as "cognitive frailty"), with over one-third of people reporting a fall within a year. Falls hasten the transition from pre-frailty to frailty and from independence to paralysis because they set off a chain reaction of injury, deconditioning, fear of falling, and additional inactivity.

Long-term care placement and loss of freedom are also predicted by frailty. The severe consequences for patients, families, and care systems are highlighted by the discovery that both frailty and pre-frailty considerably increase the likelihood of subsequent nursing home admission by more than threefold for pre-frailty and more than fivefold for frailty, according to a meta-analysis of community cohorts. Because fragility at admission is linked to increased mortality and larger care needs, and because the prevalence of frailty in nursing homes themselves surpasses 50%, prevention and early intervention upstream in the community are crucial.

The two main clinical outcomes are disability and a reduced quality of life (QoL). Numerous studies demonstrate clinically significant declines in health-related quality of life (EQ-5D, for example) as frailty progresses, and there is a substantial correlation between frailty and event restrictions in instrumental and activities of daily living (ADLs). Even in the absence of severe illness, these losses translate into reliance, caregiver stress, and diminished capacity to engage in meaningful activities, which is why they are significant to patients and caregivers.

The financial load is heavy and growing. Recent analyses across several European health systems confirm a continuous cost gradient from non-frail to severely frail older adults. Frailty is consistently linked to higher per-patient expenditures in both inpatient and outpatient care at the health-system level, with costs scaling by frailty severity. According to the World Health Organization, there are 684,000 fatal falls and 37.3 million falls that require medical attention annually worldwide, demonstrating the human and financial costs of falls alone. Falls are closely associated with frailty and are estimated to have cost the US economy $80 billion in medical expenses in 2020 (up from about $50 billion in 2015), with Medicare bearing the majority of these costs. Only direct medical expenditures are included in these numbers; ancillary costs, such as lost caregiver productivity and long-term social care, significantly increase the overall economic burden.

Frailty is a high-value target for proactive monitoring and intervention from a population-health viewpoint because of its clinical and economic ramifications. Although the effects on readmissions and some usage endpoints can vary and depend on the environment, there is now evidence that risk-stratified, community-based programs and complete geriatric models can lower mortality and preserve independence. These facts make the case for ongoing, customized monitoring that can identify decline early, customize interventions (such as diet, medication optimization, and strength and balance training), and coordinate responses among primary care, hospital, and community services.

- Public Health Urgency

It is becoming more widely acknowledged that frailty is not just a clinical issue but also a public health imperative. In many nations, it is now a part of strategic healthcare planning. For example, the NHS Long Term Plan in the UK suggests screening for frailty in all persons over 65. According to the startling prevalence estimates, 25–50% of persons over 65 who live in the community are pre-frail, and 10-15% are frail. These figures imply that the vast majority of senior citizens are either fragile already or very likely to become so in the coming years. As life expectancy rises, the percentage of frail older persons is predicted to almost treble by 2050 if nothing is done.

- Clinical Pathophysiology and Progression

The endocrine, immunological, musculoskeletal, and cardiovascular systems all gradually deteriorate with frailty, which is a sign of multisystem dysregulation. This results in a diminished ability to react to even mild stressors, like a minor fall, infection, or medication change, which can cause abrupt and serious health decline. Frailty advancement can be sudden, and episodic clinic visits frequently overlook early warning symptoms, which can be explained by its "tipping point" character. People who are pre-frail may become frail within 12 to 36 months if prompt action is not taken, which could result in irreparable declines.

- Health System and Policy Impact

Frailty leads to prolonged recovery periods, repeated ER visits, and polypharmacy, all of which put a burden on healthcare systems. Research indicates that compared to their contemporaries who are not frail, fragile patients have a 2-3 times higher 30-day hospital readmission risk. There are significant economic ramifications for policymakers: halting the onset of frailty in 10% of at-risk seniors for even a year might save billions of dollars in hospital and long-term care expenses each year. Furthermore, early detection has significant financial and health benefits as frailty measurements are increasingly being included in value-based care models and reimbursement frameworks.

- Psychological and Social Dimensions

Frailty has significant psychological repercussions in addition to its effects on physical health. Social disengagement, depression, anxiety, and isolation are more common among older persons who are weak. Loss of independence, decreased mobility, and a fear of falling are frequently the causes of these impacts, which further restrict social involvement. A negative feedback loop is created when social isolation complicates physical health and speeds up cognitive deterioration. Higher levels of stress, fatigue, and financial pressure are also experienced by family caregivers of fragile elderly people.

- Cross-Cultural and Global Disparities

Because healthcare access, socioeconomic conditions, and cultural norms varies among nations, so do the prevalence of frailty and its effects. Frailty is frequently recognized late, when therapies are less effective, in low- and middle-income countries due to inadequate availability to early screening. Geographical impediments to care may exist for rural people, while overcrowded hospitals and overworked primary care systems in metropolitan areas make it difficult to offer individualized follow-up. Designing monitoring systems that are both scalable and culturally responsive requires an understanding of these differences.

- Connection to the Management of Chronic Illnesses and Multimorbidity

Numerous chronic illnesses, including diabetes, COPD, arthritis, and cardiovascular disease, frequently co-occur with frailty. Frailty and multimorbidity interact to decrease prognosis, complicate medication, and make care coordination difficult. One "final common pathway" through which several chronic conditions influence function and survival over the long term is frailty. Because of this overlap, integrated health data which combines structured clinical information with real-time physiological monitoring is particularly useful for intervention and prediction.

- Rationale for Technological Intervention

Relying exclusively on annual or episodic clinical examinations is insufficient because frailty is dynamic and can alter over weeks or months. Wearable sensors, AI-powered risk prediction models, and real-time monitoring agentic systems fill this gap by identifying minute variations in daily activities, sleep patterns, heart rate variability, and mobility. There may be a crucial opportunity for intervention before irreversible decline if these alterations occur months before clinical deterioration.

- Impact on Healthcare Prioritization and Resource Allocation

Frailty affects how healthcare systems distribute limited resources and prioritize the provision of care. Frailty scores are being used more and more in acute care settings to inform choices regarding the level of rehabilitation, ICU hospitalization, and eligibility for surgery. For instance, in order to determine which patients would benefit most from intense therapies during the COVID-19 pandemic, a number of health institutions incorporated frailty evaluation into their triage procedures. Although this can increase productivity, it also presents moral questions regarding possible discrimination against senior citizens. The necessity for clear, explicable AI-driven frailty solutions that supplement clinical judgment rather than replace it is highlighted by the need to strike a balance between evidence-based prioritizing and equitable access to care.

Particularly in nations with already overburdened medical resources, the increasing number of older persons at risk of functional decline could overwhelm healthcare infrastructure in the absence of efficient intervention techniques. Therefore, there is an urgent need for technology-driven, scalable solutions that may help manage the health of older people, lower hospitalization rates, and encourage independent living for as long as feasible. One such solution is continuous health monitoring systems. Higher life expectancy and falling fertility rates are the main causes of this demographic transition, which puts a heavy burden on community support networks and healthcare systems. As the need for long-term care increases, it is becoming increasingly apparent that the geriatric care models currently in use are inadequate for efficiently and sustainably addressing the numerous health demands of older persons.

A higher incidence of falls, hospitalization, cognitive impairment, and early death has been associated with frailty, a multifactorial syndrome marked by a diminished physiological reserve and a diminished ability to withstand stress (Montayre et al., 2024; Luk & Chan, 2022). For example, frailty is strongly associated with sarcopenia and other age-related comorbidities, and Montayre et al. (2024) observed that it greatly raises healthcare expenses because of frequent admissions (Luk & Chan, 2022). In both clinical and research settings, traditional assessment techniques are commonly employed. These include the Rockwood Clinical Frailty Scale (Xie et al., 2023), which grades frailty based on clinical judgment and cumulative deficits, and the Fried Frailty Phenotype (Liu & Yang, 2024), which measures weight loss, exhaustion, grip strength, walking speed, and physical activity. However, because these measures are usually used during sporadic clinical visits, they are reactive in nature and unable to identify early indicators of decline.

The limits of conventional frailty evaluation techniques have been exacerbated by the global shortage of qualified geriatric care professionals and the mounting burden on public health systems. The proportion of geriatricians to older persons is startlingly low in many nations; in certain areas, there is less than one specialist for every 10,000 seniors (Zhang et al., 2024). Due to this deficit, older persons frequently have to wait a long time for evaluations, have less access to individualized treatment, and depend on primary care physicians who are overworked and may not have specialized training in geriatrics. However, public health systems are not prepared to do regular, resource-intensive frailty assessments for broad populations, and they are already under strain from the prevalence of chronic diseases, a lack of workers, and tight finances. Because of this, many cases of early or moderate frailty go undiagnosed until they reach severe stages, which lowers older persons' quality of life and increases hospitalization rates and healthcare expenses.

Because of these systemic limitations, there is an urgent need for proactive, scalable, and automated monitoring systems that can function continuously outside of conventional clinical settings. This has led scholars to investigate how digital health technology can be included into the care of the elderly. Heart rate monitors and accelerometers are examples of wearable sensors that have demonstrated potential in continuously gathering behavioural and physiological data, allowing for more accurate and rapid health assessments (Leung et al., 2020). At the same time, recent developments in agentic artificial intelligence AI systems that can make decisions on their own, behave adaptively, and continuously learn from changing environments have greatly improved the chances for real-time health monitoring and prompt intervention (Wan et al., 2022; Chan, 2020). Agentic AI architectures are able to actively assess streaming health data, spot trends that point to new hazards, and initiate tailored interventions on their own without continual human oversight, in contrast to standard rule-based or static machine learning models. In a closed-loop paradigm, these systems combine perception (sensor data collection), reasoning (contextual analysis and risk assessment), and action (recommendation creation or warning dispatch) to adjust to a person's changing health trajectory. In the context of frailty monitoring, this means that variations in heart rate variability, gait speed, or activity patterns can be identified almost instantly, and the system can adapt its response, for example, by changing exercise recommendations or alerting caregivers based on trends it observes. Agentic AI has the ability to close the gap between ongoing data collection and timely, relevant healthcare actions by fusing explainable outputs with decision-making autonomy.

A major concern for the advancement of civilization in the twenty-first century is the aging population. It is anticipated that the population's aging rate will quicken by 16% of people on Earth will be 65 and older by 2050 (Yang et al., 2018). In addition to a numerical gain, this signifies a dramatic change in the worldwide age distribution, with older individuals now making up a larger share of the population than children in many areas for the first time ever. Declining birth rates, better healthcare, and longer life expectancies especially in high- and middle-income nations are the main drivers of this demographic shift. Such longevity is a sign of scientific and social advancement, but it also presents urgent problems, including an increase in the prevalence of age-related illnesses like dementia, frailty, cardiovascular disease, and osteoporosis; a rise in the need for long-term care facilities; and rising healthcare costs. The aging population trend will put previously unheard-of strain on social support networks, healthcare infrastructure, and economic productivity, highlighting the critical need for creative, scalable solutions to preserve independence, health, and quality of life in aging societies.

Nearly all nations are experiencing an increase in the number of senior persons. The Seventh National Census, conducted by the Chinese government in 2021, revealed that 18.7% of the population, or 1.41 billion people, were over 60 and 13.5% were over 65 (Moghadam et al., 2024). These numbers show the rapid pace of demographic change in the most populous country in the world, as well as the sheer size of China's aging population. Decades of longer life expectancy now average over 77 years as well as falling birth rates brought on by family planning laws and socioeconomic shifts are the main causes of the increase. Significant cultural and economic ramifications result from this demographic reality, such as a declining working-age population, rising need for geriatric healthcare services, and growing strain on the social security and pension systems. Furthermore, China's growing older adult population is consistent with trends in other fast developing nations, indicating that the problems associated with population aging are not limited to high-income countries but are instead becoming a truly global issue that calls for coordinated policy, technological advancement, and healthcare adaptation.

Elderly people currently make up the majority worldwide. The changing disease pattern, rising healthcare and long-term care costs, potential labour shortages, prohibited savings, and perhaps old age income security are some of the new issues brought on by this circumstance. Healthcare systems must meet the growing need for sustainable, high-quality, and affordable senior care as a result of this demographic shift. Healthcare in recent decades has generally depended on the availability of infrastructure and skilled human resources, both of which have been scarce (Sakurai, 2025). This evolution has been mirrored in the long-standing approaches, which means they must adapt to the many, complex problems brought on by aging as well as the evolving society of today (Clegg et al., 2016). Because aging-related disorders are chronic, progressive, and frequently multi-domain, traditional models of care which were largely developed for the episodic treatment of acute illnesses find it difficult to address them. Traditional caregiving systems have also changed as a result of social changes like migration, urbanization, and fewer family units, which has decreased the amount of informal, family-based support available for older persons. A reassessment of clinical processes, regulatory frameworks, and ethical standards is also necessary to guarantee that technological improvements are successfully incorporated into routine practice, even while they present new opportunities for monitoring and intervention. In order to better handle the challenges of aging in today's connected and fast-paced world, healthcare systems must move away from reactive, clinic-based approaches and toward proactive, continuous, and individualized treatment techniques as the burden of age-related disorders increases.

Artificial intelligence (AI), however, has changed the landscape in these circumstances by introducing innovative approaches to raise the calibre, efficacy, and accessibility of healthcare for the aged (Kim et al., 2022). Through the use of sophisticated machine learning algorithms, deep learning architectures, and natural language processing, artificial intelligence (AI) makes it possible to continuously analyze vast, diverse datasets, ranging from real-time data streams from wearable technology to medical imaging and electronic health records. The development of highly customized intervention strategies based on each person's medical history, lifestyle, and risk profile is made possible by this capability, which also enables earlier diagnosis of age-related health concerns and more accurate prognostic forecasts. AI-powered solutions can help with diagnostic decision-making, automate repetitive clinical chores, and enable remote patient monitoring, which will ease the strain on overworked medical professionals and enhance patient outcomes. With the use of these technologies, healthcare might move from reactive treatment to proactive prevention in the context of aging populations, preserving independence and quality of life for older persons while maximizing the use of healthcare resources.

AI-enabled solutions are now widely employed in many different fields, such as clinician support systems, early chronic illness detection, customized treatment regimens, and remote patient monitoring. Artificial intelligence (AI)-powered clinical decision support tools help doctors diagnose complicated illnesses by combining lab data, imaging results, and patient history to produce evidence-based recommendations. AI models can spot subtle patterns in biomarker identities, physiological signals, or lifestyle data that could point to the onset of conditions like diabetes, cardiovascular disease, or neurodegenerative disorders—often before symptoms become clinically evident in the field of early chronic illness detection. Predictive analytics and patient-specific risk models feed personalized treatment plans, which enable medical professionals to modify interventions according to behavioural preferences, comorbidities, and genetic factors, boosting adherence and results (Chatelain et al., 2021).

The hospital infrastructure and caregivers may be less burdened by these technologies, which could also improve patient health. Despite the fact that AI has the potential to be a game-changer in improving the health of older adults, there are numerous challenges because the two processes are inextricably linked. It is still necessary to resolve data-related problems including privacy, fraud, ethical vice, and technological resistance before fair and workable solutions are available (Li et al., 2020). Additionally, overcoming technological resistance which originates from things like older persons' lack of knowledge about the internet, their mistrust of automated systems, and their worries about less human oversight remains crucial to attaining widespread adoption. Without addressing these issues, even the most cutting-edge AI-powered solutions run the danger of encountering obstacles to sustainability, equality, and adaptability in actual healthcare settings.

In order to take use of these technical advancements for ongoing frailty monitoring, we presented CareBot, an agentic AI framework that is ethically aligned. CareBot incorporates DeepSeek, a generative AI module, TabTransformer for analyzing structured health records, and Transformer models for analyzing wearable time-series data to offer natural-language health suggestions specific to each user's situation. Fairness, openness, data privacy, and user autonomy are among the ethical AI concepts that have been ingrained in its design and execution throughout its development (Rahman et al., 2024).

Key Contributions of This Work:

- Developed CareBot: A tailored, ongoing frailty monitoring system using agentic AI that combines DeepSeek, Transformer, and TabTransformer models.
- Multimodal Data Integration: Enhanced prediction performance by combining structured health records (age, BMI, chronic diseases) with wearable sensor data (heart rate, activity, sleep).
- Early and Accurate Detection: Accurately classified frailty (Healthy, Pre-Frail, and Frail) using Transformer models using physiological time-series data.
- Personalized Risk Prediction: Estimated each person's frailty risk score using TabTransformer with contextual embeddings.
- Natural-Language Recommendations: Generated caregiver warnings and comprehensible, context-specific health recommendations using GPT-based DeepSeek.
- Performance Superiority: showed superior accuracy and resilience on the PAMAP2 and SHARE datasets compared to conventional models like SVM, CNN, and LSTM.
- Ethical AI Design: Guaranteed the architecture and implementation of the system to be equitable, transparent, user-autonomous, and private.

Background

We evaluated the literature on frailty diagnosis and monitoring in this chapter, classifying previous research into three primary areas: Transformer-based and agentic AI frameworks, wearable sensor-based machine learning techniques, and conventional clinical assessment tools. We reviewed the advantages and disadvantages of established techniques including the Electronic Frailty Index (eFI), Rockwood Clinical Frailty Scale, and Fried Frailty Phenotype in practical healthcare settings. After that, we looked at the use of wearable technology and supervised learning algorithms for continuous frailty evaluation. These methods have demonstrated great accuracy, but they frequently lack resilience and flexibility in uncontrolled settings. Lastly, we examined recent developments in agentic AI and Transformer topologies, which provide enhanced sequential data modelling, multimodal integration, and autonomous decision-making functionality. An AI-driven framework that integrates various technologies to provide continuous, interpretable, and customized frailty monitoring for senior care is needed, according to this assessment.

Traditional Frailty Assessment Approaches:

In geriatric medicine, clinical tools like the Fried Frailty Phenotype (Liu & Yang, 2024) and the Rockwood Clinical Frailty Scale (Xie et al., 2023) have long been the mainstay for frailty assessment. A phenotypic approach, the Fried model divides people into frail, pre-frail, and non-frail groups based on five quantifiable physical traits: self-reported fatigue, decreased grip strength, slower walking speed, lower levels of physical activity, and inadvertent weight loss. A person is categorized as frail if they fulfill three or more of these requirements, pre-frail if they meet one or two, and non-frail if they do not. This method's simplicity and substantial correlation with negative outcomes like hospitalization, disability, and mortality have led to its widespread adoption in clinical and research contexts. By combining a wider range of factors, such as functional limitations, comorbidities, cognitive impairment, and clinical symptoms, into a composite score, the Rockwood Clinical Frailty Scale, on the other hand, uses a deficit accumulation model to grade frailty on a scale from "very fit" to "terminally ill.".

By taking multi-system decline into account, the Rockwood scale provides a more comprehensive assessment than the Fried model, which mainly concentrates on visible physical performance measures. Despite their substantial validation and continued influence in geriatric management, both methods are episodic by nature, depending on in-person clinical assessments that might not capture dynamic changes in health status between visits. This drawback emphasizes the necessity of data-driven, ongoing monitoring strategies that can identify minute changes in the course of frailty in real time.

Although both methods are frequently employed in geriatric care, they are subjective and episodic (administered during routine check-ups), frequently missing early signs of health decline. The Electronic Frailty Index (eFI), developed by Clegg et al. (2016), automatically categorizes frailty at the population level using 36 regularly gathered deficits from Electronic Health Records (EHRs). This method increased scalability, but it was not personalized and was unable to record changes in health status in real time. In addition to these well-known instruments, other tools have been developed to measure multifaceted elements of frailty, such as environmental factors, cognitive function, and psychosocial health. Examples of these include the Edmonton Frail Scale (EFS) and the Tilburg Frailty Indicator (TFI). Although these instruments expand the definition of frailty, they are still mostly questionnaire-based, which leaves them vulnerable to self-reporting irregularities and recall bias. The efficiency of data collection has been increased by attempts to digitize these tests utilizing tablets and internet platforms; nevertheless, this has not addressed the basic drawback of episodic assessment, which is its inability to record gradual, subtle changes in health status between clinic visits. According to meta-analyses comparing these instruments, multidimensional methods such as the TFI and EFS provide a more comprehensive evaluation at the expense of decreased sensitivity to early physical decline, even though the Fried Phenotype has a high specificity for physical frailty.

Wearable Sensors and Machine Learning for Frailty Detection

The widespread use of wearable technology has made it possible to continuously gather behavioural and physiological information, which presents chances for automated frailty assessment outside of clinical settings. According to studies, heart rate tracks, gyroscopes, and accelerometers can all provide useful indications for identifying physical decline and mobility impairment (Kim et al., 2022).

For instance, Kim et al. (2022) tested classifiers like Random Forest, Support Vector Machine (SVM), and k-Nearest Neighbours (k-NN) and achieved accuracies above 90% under controlled conditions. They also developed a supervised learning framework using accelerometer data to classify elderly individuals as frail or non-frail. Likewise, a number of studies have used ensemble models, CNNs, RNNs, and SVMs for frailty identification (Chatelain et al., 2021). Despite their competitive accuracy, these models frequently lacked robustness in noisy, uncontrolled real-world settings and were not sensitive to changes in an individual's health.

Transformer-Based and Agentic AI Models for Frailty Monitoring

When it comes to modelling long-range dependencies in sequential health data, Transformer topologies have recently outperformed CNNs and RNNs (Li et al., 2020). According to Li et al. (2020), Transformers outperformed conventional deep learning models in terms of accuracy and interpretability when it came to clinical outcome prediction using EHR data. Their suitability for ongoing frailty monitoring stems from their capacity to incorporate multimodal data (e.g., demographic and physiological information). In order to increase prediction accuracy and interpretability, Huang et al. (2020) developed TabTransformer, which adds contextual embeddings to tabular health data. When it comes to combining wearable sensor streams with structured clinical data, this innovation is very pertinent.

These capabilities have been further expanded by multimodal Transformer variations like Perceiver IO and Fusion Transformer, which allow for the collaborative modelling of diverse data sources, such as text, time-series, and categorical features, without requiring extensive preprocessing.

Concurrently, autonomous, continuous learning, and adaptive decision-making agentic AI systems have become a potent instrument in smart healthcare. Their capacity to provide proactive, context-aware therapies catered to the unique trajectories of each patient was emphasized by Rahman et al. (2024). Such systems can be made to dynamically modify monitoring parameters, provide individualized nutritional or exercise suggestions, and escalate alarms to caregivers in the event of rapid deterioration in the context of geriatric care.

Multimodal Data Fusion for Frailty Monitoring

As a multifaceted condition, frailty frequently necessitates the integration of several data sources, including social interaction measurements, wearable sensor outputs, EHRs, and dietary diaries. The goal of multimodal data fusion is to integrate these disparate sources into a logical framework for prediction. Cross-modal interactions were frequently overlooked by early methods that employed late fusion, which integrated predictions from several models (Rahman et al., 2024). In order to learn shared representations across modalities, more recent approaches use deep multimodal structures, such as cross-attention Transformers (Huang et al., 2020).

Previous studies have used speech analysis and accelerometer time-series to identify early motor and cognitive deterioration, while other research has combined vital signs, daily step counts, and food logs to predict the evolution of frailty. These studies demonstrate that multimodal integration frequently results in improved prediction robustness and accuracy, particularly in diverse populations. For multimodal systems to be deployed scaled in frailty care, issues including asynchronous sampling, handling missing modality, and higher processing demands must be resolved.

Interpretability and Explainable AI in Frailty Prediction

Gaining the trust of clinicians or caregivers in AI-powered frailty monitoring systems needs interpretability. To explain model outputs in healthcare, methods such as SHAP (SHapley Additive exPlanations), LIME (Local Interpretable Model-agnostic Explanations), and attention visualisation have been employed extensively. These techniques can be used to identify the characteristics that most impact a person's risk score in frailty prediction, such as heart rate variability, walking speed, or the number of chronic diseases.

SHAP values can measure feature importance in a manner that is compatible with human clinical reasoning. Similarly, LIME can offer local, case-specific explanations, which are especially helpful for defending real-time interventions. Recent work highlights "interactive machine learning" techniques, which allow physicians to query models and iteratively improve predictions, enhancing performance and trust. Interpretability increases the chance of implementation in actual healthcare settings and guarantees adherence to ethical AI norms when incorporated into frailty monitoring systems.

MAIN FOCUS OF THE CHAPTER

Issues, Controversies, Problems

Even though they offer useful baseline evaluations, traditional clinical tools are unable to conduct ongoing, real-time monitoring. Although the detection accuracy of wearable-based machine learning models has increased, they frequently lack robustness in noisy environments and are unable to offer tailored recommendations. Transformer-based architectures show promise in sequential data modelling, but nothing is known about how well they integrate with agentic AI for autonomous frailty monitoring. This gap drives the creation of CareBot, a comprehensive framework that integrates DeepSeek generative AI, Transformer models, and TabTransformer to provide proactive, ethical, and explicable frailty monitoring for senior care.

Research Questions:

1. How can structured health records and wearable sensor data be successfully combined to allow for ongoing, individualized frailty monitoring in the elderly?

2. When it comes to reliably identifying frailty from multimodal health data, can transformer-based architectures beat conventional machine learning models (such as SVM, CNN, and LSTM)?
3. In what ways can TabTransformer be applied to produce personalized and comprehensible frailty risk scores that facilitate preventative medical measures?
4. What part might generative AI (like DeepSeek) play in generating natural language, context-aware health suggestions that enhance caregiver decision-making and user engagement?
5. How can the design and implementation of an AI-driven geriatric care system incorporate ethical AI concepts such as privacy, transparency, fairness, and user autonomy?

SOLUTIONS AND RECOMMENDATIONS

The process includes gathering information from health records and wearable sensors, then using Transformer models to detect frailty, TabTransformer to forecast risk, and DeepSeek to provide individualized health recommendations, as detailed in Algorithm 1.

Step 1: Dataset Selection and Annotation

Two well-known and publicly accessible datasets are used in this investigation to guarantee openness, reproducibility, and robustness in experimental evaluation: SHARE for structured health records with frailty labelling and PAMAP2 for wearable time-series data. Tri-axial accelerometers, gyroscopes, magnetometers, and heart rate monitors are among the wearable sensors that provided the high-resolution physiological and movement-related observations that make up the PAMAP2 dataset. Frequent recording of these signals throughout participants' daily activities allows for the identification of trends that may point to deteriorating mobility, irregular heartbeats, or other early indicators of frailty. For training Transformer models, which are excellent at simulating temporal dependencies and identifying minute, long-term changes in physiological data that might occur before the beginning of frailty, this dataset is the main input.

The SHARE dataset (Survey of Health, Ageing and Retirement in Europe) offers comprehensive structured health records that include functional indicators (physical activity levels, mobility limitations), clinical history (chronic diseases, medications), and demographic characteristics (age, gender, and socioeconomic status). Based on established clinical criteria, frailty labels are appended to every record in SHARE. To enable the model to understand intricate correlations between health factors, TabTransformer is used to handle the dataset. This tool converts numerical and categorical features into contextual embeddings. This step results in a personalized frailty risk score and a classification into one of three groups: Frail, Pre-Frail, or Healthy.

Both datasets are divided into 80% training and 20% testing subsets to guarantee model generalizability and objective performance. Reliable performance evaluation across both structured health records and real-time wearable sensor data is made possible by this partitioning method, which guarantees that the models are tested on unknown data. The framework gains from both ongoing physiological monitoring and previous clinical context by combining these two complementing datasets, enabling a comprehensive and proactive approach to frailty identification and prediction.

Step 2: Data Preprocessing

In order to guarantee high-quality inputs for the Transformer-based frailty detection module, the PAMAP2 time-series sensor data underwent a multi-step preparation method. In order to prevent scale imbalance from affecting the learning process, the raw signals from wearable sensors, such as accelerometer, gyroscope, magnetometer, and heart rate readings, were first normalized using min–max scaling. This brought all characteristics into a uniform range. After that, the dataset was cleaned to remove noise from motion artifacts, sensor drift, and ambient interference. Missing values were then handled using interpolation techniques. In order to ensure that the Transformer could successfully capture temporal relationships, the continuous data streams were then divided into fixed-length time windows. This allowed for consistent input forms across samples.

Preprocessing for the SHARE structured health records was centred on getting the data ready for the TabTransformer model. Stable convergence was ensured during training by standardizing all numerical characteristics (such as age, BMI, and sleep duration) to zero mean and unit variance. Without enforcing ordinal relationships, categorical data (such as gender, marital status, and chronic disease categories) were one-hot encoded to represent discrete qualities as binary feature vectors. Additionally, this encoding guaranteed compatibility with the embedding layers of TabTransformer, which make use of contextual information from various characteristics.

Both structured clinical records and time-series wearable data had their preprocessing workflows aligned, making the datasets completely compatible with CareBot's deep learning models. In addition to increasing the precision of frailty detection and prediction, this standardization also increased model training efficiency, decreased the possibility of overfitting, and guaranteed consistency of results across several experimental runs.

Step 3: Proposed Framework: Integration of TabTransformer and DeepSeek

Both sensor-based wearable data and structured health records are preprocessed before being processed by the CareBot framework through two distinct model streams, each of which is tailored for a particular data modality.

In the first stream, time-series wearable data gathered from smartphones and smartwatches is processed using a Transformer-based architecture. This information covers mobility patterns, sleep quality, and heart rate variability. In order to detect small changes in physiological trends and capture long-range temporal connections, the Transformer model uses multi-head self-attention mechanisms. This allows for the early and precise classification of frailty into three categories: Healthy, Pre-Frail, and Frail.

To handle structured demographic and clinical data, including age, BMI, number of chronic diseases, and levels of physical activity, the second stream makes use of TabTransformer. To discover intricate connections between numerical and categorical information, TabTransformer uses contextual multi-head attention layers and column embeddings. The model produces a customized frailty risk score that indicates the likelihood of long-term health decline.

The Transformer's frailty categorization (C) and the TabTransformer's frailty risk score (R) are the outputs from these two streams, which are then integrated into a Fusion Layer. This combined representation is given to DeepSeek, a generative AI module that generates context-aware, individualized natural language health suggestions. A Mixture-of-Experts (MoE) architecture, latent vector compression, KV caching, and attention processing are some of the elements that DeepSeek uses. The Router Network ensures computational efficiency and content relevance by selectively activating the most pertinent expert models according to the patient's health circumstances. The suggestions that are generated may be urgent caregiver warnings for high-risk persons (e.g., "Seek medical evaluation immediately due to elevated frailty risk") or preventative lifestyle advice for low-risk users (e.g., "Engage in light daily exercise and maintain balanced nutrition").

Through the integration of Transformer-based sequential modelling, contextual tabular learning from TabTransformer, and adaptive language generation from DeepSeek, CareBot offers proactive caregiver interaction, adaptive decision-making, and autonomous monitoring. In contrast to conventional frailty tools, CareBot is a scalable and morally sound solution for next-generation geriatric healthcare since it continuously learns from incoming user data, improves its predictions, and provides timely treatments.

Figure 1. CareBot framework using TabTransformer and DeepSeek for personalized frailty monitoring and intervention

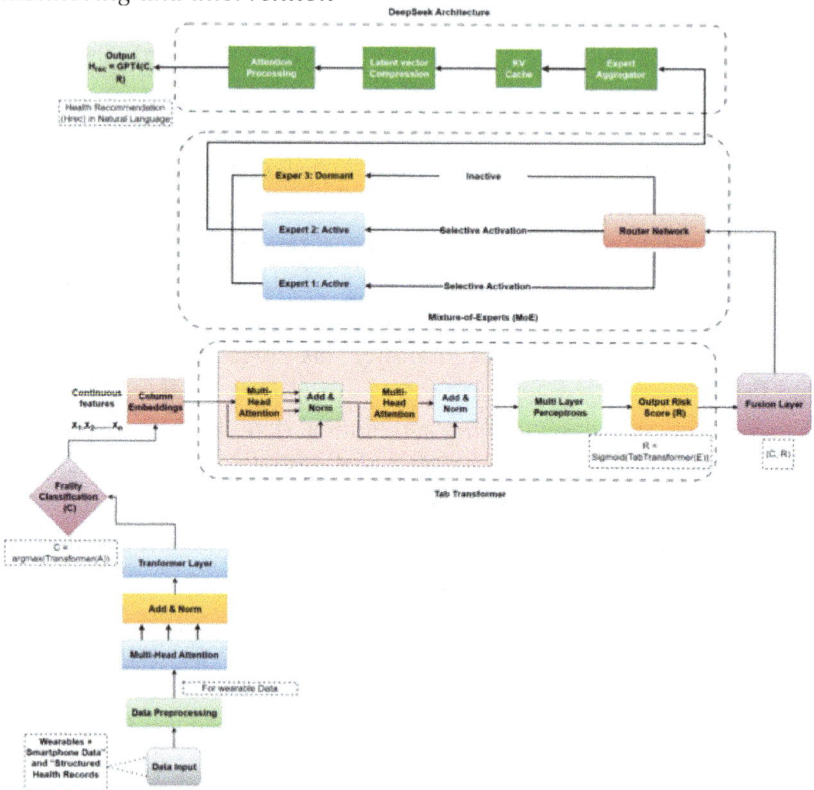

The suggested approach combines TabTransformer with DeepSeek to provide ongoing, individualized frailty monitoring that adjusts to each person's changing health status as shown in Figure 1. Initially, multimodal health data is obtained from wearable technology and cellphones, recording ongoing behavioural and physiological parameters like heart rate variability, sleep duration and quality, and daily activity levels. The user's health trajectory is fully visible thanks to these real-time inputs. To guarantee compliance with the downstream learning models, the data is preprocessed after collection, undergoing procedures including normalization, noise reduction, and feature encoding. After the data has been cleaned and organized, it is passed into the TabTransformer module, which uses multi-head attention layers and column embeddings to find contextual correlations between different health metrics. This enables the model to capture intricate relationships, such as the joint influence of age, sleep quality, and history of chronic diseases on frailty risk.

A multi-layer perceptron (MLP) processes the TabTransformer output to generate a personalized frailty risk score that represents the probability of health decline. A Mixture-of-Experts (MoE) system, which consists of several specialized expert modules educated on various health contexts, receives these results after they have been integrated in a Fusion Layer. By dynamically choosing the best experts for each situation, a router network increases computing efficiency and prediction accuracy. This integrated approach ensures timely and ethically aligned geriatric care by continuously learning from fresh incoming data to give proactive, context-aware health interventions that respond to tiny changes in the individual's condition.

RESULT AND DISCUSSION

This section presents both quantitative and qualitative evaluation results for the proposed CareBot framework, assessing its performance across three core functional modules: frailty classification, frailty risk prediction, and health recommendation generation. Each module was tested to measure not only predictive accuracy but also robustness, interpretability, and practical applicability in real-world healthcare contexts. The evaluation was carried out using two well-established and publicly accessible datasets: SHARE, which includes structured demographic, clinical, and functional health records with frailty labelling, and PAMAP2, which offers high-resolution wearable sensor data for modelling temporal physiological patterns. Reliability was ensured by comparing the results to both traditional and deep learning models, such as Long Short-Term Memory (LSTM) networks, Support Vector Machines (SVM), and Convolutional Neural Networks (CNN). The performance indicators included BLEU and ROUGE scores for assessing the quality of natural-language health recommendations, precision, recall, F1-score, accuracy for classification tasks, and Mean Absolute Error (MAE) and Root Mean Squared Error (RMSE) for regression-based risk prediction. Furthermore, the contextual relevance and customisation capabilities of the DeepSeek module are demonstrated through qualitative samples of generated recommendations.

Implementation Details

A multi-component AI pipeline was used to create the suggested CareBot framework, which was made to manage multimodal health data from structured clinical records and wearable sensors. For the sake of reproducibility and equitable comparison with current methods, all tests were conducted using publicly accessible datasets (PAMAP2 and SHARE). TensorFlow was used to integrate the DeepSeek generative AI module, while PyTorch was used to implement and train the Transformer and TabTransformer models. The development environment was built on top of Python 3.10. Additional Python modules, including NumPy, Pandas, and Scikit-learn, were utilized for feature engineering, data preparation, and the computation of evaluation metrics. A high-performance computer system with an NVIDIA RTX A6000 GPU with 48 GB of VRAM, 512 GB of system RAM, and Intel Xeon CPUs was used for model training and evaluation. Large-scale dataset processing, parallel experimentation, and bottleneck-free model hyperparameter optimization were all made possible by this setup.

For each experimental run, the same data splits (80% training, 20% testing) were kept, and random seeds were fixed across all frameworks to guarantee reproducibility. Because the pipeline was modularized, each part, like the DeepSeek suggestion generator or the Transformer-based frailty detection, could be evaluated, adjusted, and changed as needed.

Metrics for Evaluating Results

To assess the performance of the proposed CareBot framework, we adopted a comprehensive evaluation strategy combining classification, regression, and natural language generation (NLG) metrics. These metrics were applied across the framework's three core modules — frailty classification, frailty risk prediction, and recommendation generation to capture both predictive accuracy and practical applicability.

1. Frailty Classification (Transformer Model)

Using the common classification metrics of F1-Score, Precision, and Recall, the Transformer-based frailty detection module was assessed. These are especially crucial in applications related to healthcare, where false positives and false negatives can have serious repercussions.

- F1-Score

$$\text{F1} = 2 \times \left(\frac{Precision \times Recall}{Precision + Recall}\right)$$

A balanced measure that considers both precision and recall, making it well-suited for datasets with class imbalance.

- Precision:

$$\text{Precision} = \frac{TP}{TP + FP}$$

Calculates the ratio of accurately predicted positive cases to all expected positives. A high level of precision means fewer false alarms.

- Recall (Sensitivity):

$$\text{Recall} = \frac{TP}{TP + FP}$$

Measures the proportion of actual positive cases that were correctly identified. High recall ensures that frail individuals are not overlooked.

2. Frailty Risk Prediction (TabTransformer Model)

Mean Absolute Error (MAE) and Root Mean Squared Error (RMSE) were used to assess the accuracy of the TabTransformer-based risk prediction module.

- **Mean Absolute Error (MAE):**

$$\text{MAE} = \frac{1}{n} \sum_{i=1}^{n} |y_i - \hat{y}_i$$

Represents the average absolute difference between predicted and actual values, offering an intuitive measure of prediction error.

- **Root Mean Squared Error (RMSE):**

$$\text{RMSE} = \sqrt{\frac{1}{n}} \sum_{i=1}^{n} (y_i - \hat{y}_i)^2$$

Penalizes larger errors more heavily than MAE, making it sensitive to significant deviations in predicted risk scores.

3. **Recommendation Generation (DeepSeek Model)**

- BLEU-2 Score:

$$\text{BLEU-2} = \frac{1}{2} \log p1 + \frac{1}{2} \log p2$$

Where p1 and p2 represent unigram and bigram precision respectively, and BPBPBP is the brevity penalty to discourage overly short sentences.

- ROUGE-1 (F1-Score):

$$\text{ROUGE} - 1\ \text{F1}\ \frac{2\ .\ (Precision\ .\ Recall)}{Percision + Recall}$$

Measures the overlap of unigrams (single words) between the generated and reference text, balancing both precision and recall for content relevance.

Frailty Classification Results

The ability of the Transformer-based frailty classification model to correctly classify people into Healthy, Pre-Frail, and Frail categories was thoroughly tested using the test subset of the PAMAP2 dataset. The model successfully captured long-range temporal relationships in wearable sensor data, including heart rate, mobility, and activity patterns, by utilizing its multi-head self-attention mechanism.

With great precision, recall, and F1-scores, the model consistently performed well across all frailty categories, as shown in Table 1. Significantly, the classification findings showed that there was little disagreement between non-adjacent categories (such as Healthy vs. Frail), demonstrating the model's capacity to discern even minute variations in physiological patterns. Given the clinical similarities between Pre-Frail and Frail, it is not surprising that the largest mistake rate occurred between these two categories.

Table 1. Performance metrics for frailty classification (transformer model)

Class	Precision	Recall	F1-Score	Support
Healthy	0.88	0.86	0.87	760
Pre-Frail	0.82	0.84	0.83	880
Frail	0.91	0.89	0.90	660
Macro Avg	0.87	0.86	0.87	—
Weighted Avg	0.87	0.86	0.87	2300

The Transformer-based frailty detection model's classification performance across the three defined categories of Healthy, Pre-Frail, and Frail is depicted in the confusion matrix in Figure 2. The model's high classification abilities are demonstrated by the diagonal dominance of the matrix, which shows that most predictions matched the genuine labels.

With just a small number of samples incorrectly classified as Pre-Frail (80) or Frail (30), the Healthy class attained a high correct classification count (650). There were the most misclassifications in the Pre-Frail group, which frequently has physiological traits in common with both the Healthy and Frail states: 70 cases were classified as Healthy, and another 70 as Frail. Clinical observations that early indications of frailty can be subtle and challenging to discern are in line with this.

Overall, the misclassification rate was lowest for the Frail category, with 585 instances correctly identified and just 25 misclassified as Healthy and 50 as Pre-Frail. Based on wearable sensor data, this implies that the model is very good at spotting severe frailty patterns.

Figure 2. Confusion matrix for frailty classification

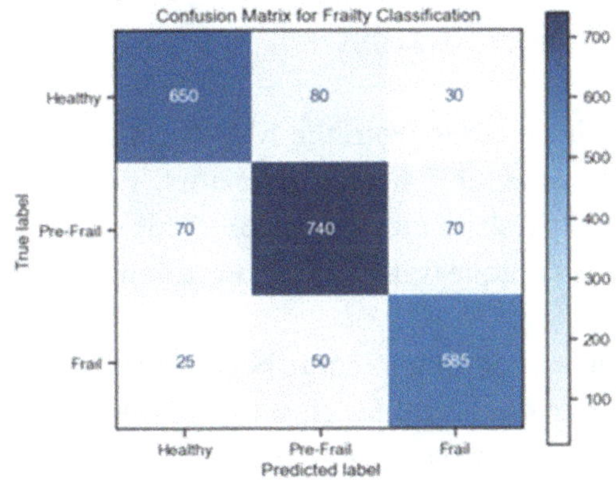

We evaluated the suggested CareBot framework's efficacy by contrasting its Transformer-based frailty detection module with three popular baseline models: Convolutional Neural Networks (CNN), Long Short-Term Memory (LSTM) networks, and Support Vector Machines (SVM). To ensure a fair evaluation across all architectures, the comparison was carried out using the PAMAP2 dataset under identical experimental conditions.

Out of all the tested models, CareBot had the greatest accuracy (0.93) and F1-score (0.92), as shown in Table 2. LSTM (accuracy: 0.84, F1-score: 0.83) and CNN (accuracy: 0.87, F1-score: 0.85) both demonstrated good performance, however they were not as resilient when dealing with noisy, real-world wearable data. With an accuracy of 0.79 and an F1-score of 0.78, the SVM model performed the worst, underscoring the shortcomings of conventional machine learning methods in identifying the intricate temporal and contextual patterns found in multimodal health data.

Table 2. Model comparison on frailty detection (PAMAP2 dataset)

Model	Accuracy	F1-score
SVM	0.79	0.78
LSTM	0.84	0.83
CNN	0.87	0.85
CareBot (Ours)	**0.93**	**0.92**

Frailty Risk Prediction Results

The structured health records from the SHARE dataset, which includes clinical, functional, and demographic health indicators, were used to assess the TabTransformer-based frailty risk prediction module. This model was created especially to calculate each person's unique frailty risk score, allowing for preventative medical measures.

The model's output is a continuous score between 0 and 1, where values near 0.0 indicate minimal frailty risk and values closer to 1.0 indicate a higher likelihood of frailty. Compared to binary classification, this continuous scoring method offers a more nuanced assessment, enabling medical professionals to identify slow changes in frailty status over time.

Through the use of multi-head self-attention layers for contextual feature learning and column embeddings for categorical variables, the TabTransformer successfully identified intricate relationships between health markers like age, BMI, comorbidities, and activity levels. The model can distinguish between people who have identical baseline traits but different paths toward frailty because to its architecture.

Table 3. TabTransformer performance on risk score prediction

Metric	Score
MAE	0.0388
RMSE	0.0483

The TabTransformer model's predicted frailty risk ratings are plotted against the actual ground truth scores from the SHARE dataset, as shown in Figure 3. While the red dashed line shows the ideal fit line (y = x), which denotes perfect forecast alignment, each blue dot represents a separate sample. The model's capacity to accurately approach the actual frailty risk is demonstrated by the dense clustering of predicted points around the optimum fit line, which shows a strong correlation between model predictions and true values. The model's accuracy in continuous risk estimate is further supported by the low average error, as measured by Mean Absolute Error (MAE) and Root Mean Squared Error (RMSE).

According to this performance, the TabTransformer architecture successfully uses structured health data to identify minute patterns that influence the development of frailty. Furthermore, the model's resilience in detecting both low-risk and high-risk individuals is demonstrated by its ability to predict near-ideal scores across the whole risk range (0.0–1.0), which is essential for proactive healthcare measures.

Figure 3. Predicted vs. actual frailty risk scores

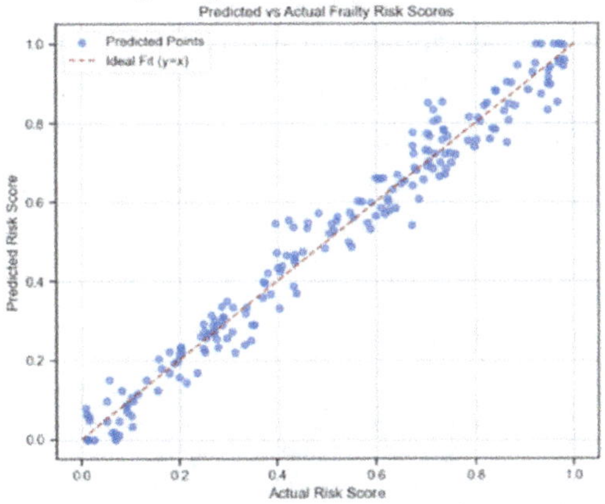

The TabTransformer model's SHAP (SHapley Additive exPlanations) values were calculated to improve the interpretability of the frailty risk prediction process. A clear grasp of the elements that most significantly influence the anticipated frailty risk is made possible by SHAP values, which quantify the contribution of each input feature to the model's output.

Age was shown to be the most significant predictor, with a mean SHAP value of 0.31, showing a substantial positive connection with increased frailty risk, as summarized in Table 4 and illustrated in Figure 4. Physical activity came next, with a mean SHAP score of 0.22, indicating that lower activity levels considerably raise the risk that is projected. Sleep Duration was in third place (0.17), indicating that both too little and too much sleep advance frailty.

Table 4. Top 5 predictive features ranked by SHAP value

Feature	Mean SHAP Value
Age	0.31
Physical Activity	0.22
Sleep Duration	0.17
Chronic Illness Count	0.14
Heart Rate Variability	0.10

Other significant variables included Heart Rate Variability (0.10), a crucial sign of the health of the cardiovascular and autonomic nervous systems, and Chronic Illness Count (0.14), which represented the total health burden of several comorbidities. According to the SHAP-based feature importance analysis, the model accurately reflects a mix of physiological, behavioural, and demographic aspects, which is in line with the body of research on senior health.

Figure 4. SHAP feature importance plot

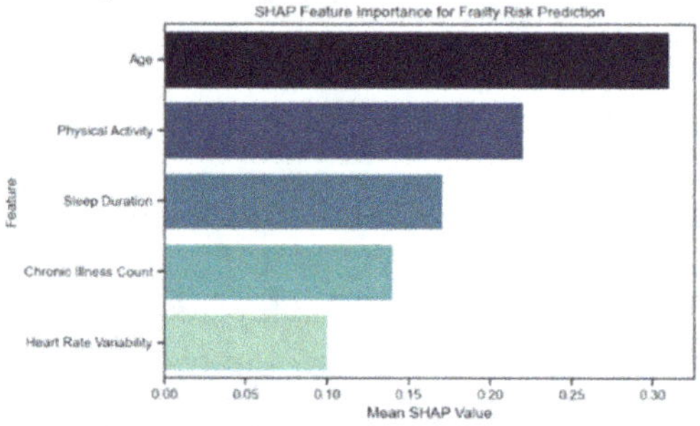

Recommendation Quality Evaluation

The CareBot framework's natural language generation (NLG) component, the DeepSeek model, generated individualized health recommendations based on each user's risk score and frailty classification. This module's objective is to offer practical, situation-specific guidance that encourages healthy aging and supports preventive measures.

Table 5. Performance of recommendation generation (DeepSeek model)

Metric	Score
BLEU-2 Score	0.63
ROUGE-1 (F1-score)	0.72

Two automatic text similarity metrics, BLEU-2 and ROUGE-1 (F1-score), were used to evaluate the quality of the generated recommendations. As can be seen in Table 5, the DeepSeek model demonstrated great fluency and lexical accuracy with a BLEU-2 score of 0.63, which indicates a high degree of n-gram overlap (bigrams) with reference recommendation templates. High content relevance and coverage are suggested by the ROUGE-1 F1-score of 0.72, which shows a significant unigram overlap between the generated and reference outputs.

Input:

Frailty Status: Pre-Frail
Risk Score: 0.61

Output:
"You may benefit from a 10-minute walk every morning and reducing your sodium intake. Please remember to hydrate regularly and follow up with your caregiver if symptoms worsen."

FUTURE RESEARCH DIRECTIONS

In order to provide older people with ongoing, individualized frailty monitoring, this study presents CareBot, an agentic AI-based platform. CareBot effectively models intricate temporal health patterns from wearable sensor data and structured health records by utilizing Transformer and TabTransformer architectures. This allows for very accurate risk prediction and frailty classification. Comparative analyses verify that CareBot performs better than traditional machine learning and deep learning models like SVM, CNN, and LSTM, especially when dealing with noisy real-world data where contextual linkages and temporal dependencies are crucial for precise prediction.

The incorporation of DeepSeek, which fills a significant gap in earlier methods by offering context-aware, natural-language health recommendations, is a noteworthy improvement of CareBot. This feature bridges the gap between predictive analytics and practical medical advice by improving interpretability and encouraging patient and healthcare provider participation. CareBot is positioned as a complete solution for preventive health management because to its user-centered advice delivery and prediction accuracy.

Notwithstanding these encouraging outcomes, some restrictions still exist. To guarantee the framework's resilience across various demographic groups and medical conditions, it must be validated on bigger and more varied datasets. Furthermore, real-world implementations need to handle issues like loud, faulty, or incomplete data inputs, which are typical in uncontrolled healthcare settings. Adaptive learning techniques should be investigated in future research so that CareBot can dynamically update its predictive models in response to fresh health data.

CONCLUSION

In order to provide proactive and individualized frailty monitoring for the elderly, this study introduces CareBot, an agentic AI-based platform that combines wearable sensor data, structured health records, and generative AI. CareBot exhibits strong performance across important evaluation measures by combining DeepSeek for personalized natural-language health advice with Transformer and TabTransformer models for precise frailty categorization and risk prediction. The framework addresses important demands in scalable and adaptable senior care by providing clinically relevant suggestions, interpretable risk assessments, and accurate frailty detection.

CareBot's capabilities demonstrate its potential for useful real-world implementation, which is important given the aging societies' increasing need for technology-driven healthcare solutions. Clinical validation in various hospital settings, real-time deployment in senior communities, and the incorporation of other multimodal health indicators including mood, social behaviour, and nutrition will be the main areas of future research. With additional development and verification, CareBot may establish itself as a key component of the upcoming digital geriatric care systems, facilitating patient-centered, data-driven, and ongoing health management.

REFERENCES

Chan, C. Y. S. (2020). The multi-dimensions of social participation of older adults in Hong Kong.

Chatelain, P., Delmaire, G., Alboody, A., Puigt, M., & Roussel, G. (2021). Semi-automatic spectral image stitching for a compact hybrid linescan hyperspectral camera towards near field remote monitoring of potato crop leaves. *Sensors (Basel)*, *21*(22), 7616. DOI: 10.3390/s21227616 PMID: 34833696

Clegg, A., Bates, C., Young, J., Ryan, R., Nichols, L., Teale, E. A., Mohammed, M. A., Parry, J., & Marshall, T. (2016). Development and validation of an electronic frailty index using routine primary care electronic health record data. *Age and Ageing*, *45*(3), 353–360. DOI: 10.1093/ageing/afw039 PMID: 26944937

Ding, H., Wu, J., Zhao, W., Matinlinna, J. P., Burrow, M. F., & Tsoi, J. K. (2023). Artificial intelligence in dentistry—A review. *Frontiers in Dental Medicine*, *4*, 1085251. DOI: 10.3389/fdmed.2023.1085251 PMID: 39935549

Huang, X., Khetan, A., Cvitkovic, M., & Karnin, Z. (2020). TabTransformer: Tabular data modeling using contextual embeddings. arXiv. https://arxiv.org/abs/2012.06678

Kim, B.-S., Jin, Y., Lee, J., & Kim, S. (2022). FMCW radar estimation algorithm with high resolution and low complexity based on reduced search area. *Sensors (Basel)*, *22*(3), 1202. DOI: 10.3390/s22031202 PMID: 35161947

Leung, T.-H., Leung, S.-C., & Wong, C.-K. G. (2020). The effectiveness of an emergency physician–led frailty unit for the living-alone elderly: A pilot retrospective cohort study. *Hong Kong Journal of Emergency Medicine*, *27*(3), 162–167. DOI: 10.1177/1024907919825674

Li, Y., Rao, S., Solares, J. R. A., Hassaine, A., Ramakrishnan, R., Canoy, D., Zhu, Y., Rahimi, K., & Salimi-Khorshidi, G. (2020). BEHRT: Transformer for electronic health records. *Scientific Reports*, *10*(1), 7155. DOI: 10.1038/s41598-020-62922-y PMID: 32346050

Liu, X., & Yang, X. (2024). Research progress on frailty in elderly people. *Clinical Interventions in Aging*, *19*, 1493–1505. DOI: 10.2147/CIA.S474547 PMID: 39224708

Luk, J. K., & Chan, D. K. (2022). Medical practice CME: Frailty and sarcopenia—From theory to practice. *Hong Kong Medical Journal*, *28*(5), 392–395. DOI: 10.12809/hkmj219411 PMID: 38232963

Moghadam, M. P., Moghadam, Z. A., Qazani, M. R. C., Pławiak, P., & Alizadehsani, R. (2024). Impact of artificial intelligence in nursing for geriatric clinical care for chronic diseases: A systematic literature review. *IEEE Access : Practical Innovations, Open Solutions*, *12*, 122557–122587. DOI: 10.1109/ACCESS.2024.3450970

Montayre, J., Kuo, K., & Leung, K. M. C. (2024). Social frailty prevalence among older people in Hong Kong. *Journal of Ageing and Longevity*, *4*(3), 225–233. DOI: 10.3390/jal4030016

Rahman, A., Debnath, T., Kundu, D., Khan, M. S. I., Aishi, A. A., Sazzad, S., Sayduzzaman, M., & Band, S. S. (2024). Machine learning and deep learning-based approach in smart healthcare: Recent advances, applications, challenges and opportunities. *AIMS Public Health*, *11*(1), 58–109. DOI: 10.3934/publichealth.2024004 PMID: 38617415

Sakurai, Y. (2025). Advance decision-making for future disability in East Asia: Addressing challenges in end-of-life medical care for older adults. *IEEE Access : Practical Innovations, Open Solutions.*

Wan, X., Shen, J., & He, G. (2022). Effects of traditional Chinese exercises on frailty, quality of life, and physical function on frail and pre-frail older people: A systematic review and meta-analysis. *The Journal of Frailty & Aging*, *11*(4), 407–415. DOI: 10.14283/jfa.2022.52 PMID: 36346727

Xie, X., Ge, Y., Walia, H., Yang, J., & Yu, H. (2023). Leaf-counting in monocot plants using deep regression models. *Sensors (Basel)*, *23*(4), 1890. DOI: 10.3390/s23041890 PMID: 36850487

Yang, X., Lupón, J., Vidán, M. T., Ferguson, C., Gastelurrutia, P., Newton, P. J., Macdonald, P. S., Bueno, H., Bayés-Genís, A., Woo, J., & Fung, E. (2018). Impact of frailty on mortality and hospitalization in chronic heart failure: A systematic review and meta-analysis. *Journal of the American Heart Association*, *7*(23), e008251. DOI: 10.1161/JAHA.117.008251 PMID: 30571603

Zhang, S., Wu, L., Zhao, Z., Masso, J. F., & Chen, M. (2024). Artificial intelligence in gerontology: Data-driven health management and precision medicine. *Advances in Gerontology*, *14*(3), 97–110. DOI: 10.1134/S2079057024600691

Chapter 10
Secure AI Applications for Cybersecurity:
Ethical and Explainable Threat Detection in Modern Software Systems

Iram Hanif
http://orcid.org/0009-0002-9714-757X
The University of Faisalabad, Faisalabad, Pakistan

Majid Hussain
http://orcid.org/0009-0002-5968-0509
The University of Faisalabad, Faisalabad, Pakistan

Muhammad Ibrar
http://orcid.org/0000-0002-6813-5003
The University of Faisalabad, Faisalabad, Pakistan

Amara Hafeez
The University of Faisalabad, Faisalabad, Pakistan

Affan Yasin
XianJiaotong-Liverpool University, Suzhou, China

ABSTRACT

The diversity of digital capabilities has been improved by new cloud-native, microservices, DevSecOps, and IoT software designs, which have also designed a path to cyber threats. Outdated security tools like firewalls and signature-driven recognition are not very effective against ransomware, insider threats, phishing attacks,

DOI: 10.4018/979-8-3373-6038-6.ch010

sophisticated persistent threats and zero-day attacks. The practice of AI can be in the zones of intrusion prevention, malware detection, phishing resistance, insider monitoring, and IoT and autonomous platforms security. These concerns increase major ethical alarms to software engineers who must confirm that the AI systems are transparent, accountable, and fair. XAI and privacy-sensitive models, as well as compliance with such regulations as GDPR and the EU AI Act, provide much-needed protection. Future secure AI developments in cybersecurity include secure AI innovations such as federated learning, blockchain-based AI, and quantum-safe algorithms.

1. INTRODUCTION

The concept of Artificial Intelligence (AI) has already been integrated into the landscape of modern software engineering, allowing systems to be extremely automated, flexible, and intelligent. The need to ensure the deployment of software capabilities is ethical, secure and trustworthy has grown as organizations enter software ecosystems with AI-driven capabilities. The book, Ethical AI Applications in Software Engineering and Development, highlights the importance of the imminent requirement to make ethical considerations in all stages of AI-based software development, including transparency, accountability, fairness, privacy protection, and responsible use. In this larger perspective, cybersecurity can be seen as one of the most complicated and high stakes areas of application, where any ethical failure, closed algorithms, and practices that are not secure can cause great damage.

Cybersecurity threats have been developed not as simple malware but highly adaptive and AI-dependent attacks that constantly take advantage of software system weaknesses. Rule-based or signature-based traditional detection systems are ineffective in the protection of modern digital infrastructures. As the opponents continue to use technologies related to automation and machine intelligence, defensive tools should also deploy advanced artificial intelligence techniques to detect abnormalities, anticipate attacks, and execute measures independently. Nonetheless, AI deployment in cybersecurity presents novel issues concerning algorithmic bias, the lack of explainability, data control and dual-use risks. Recent studies note that lack of transparency of the models used in cybersecurity systems goes to a long way in eroding trust and impeding the response to incidents (Zhang et al., 2022), (Ameen et al., 2023).

One of the grounds in the fight against these emerging cyber threats is Artificial Intelligence (AI). By using Machine Learning (ML) and Deep Learning (DL), AI systems can process large amounts of data within seconds and quickly and easily identify anomalies and malicious behaviors, compared to the traditional rule-based or signature-based security systems. They are used as Intrusion detection systems, malware classification, fraud control and behavioral analytics to sense insider threads (Zhang et al., 2022). Although successful, most AI-driven solution are opaque, black-box, such that security practitioners cannot know or trust how the solution arrives at a decision. Such transparency contributes to the poor performance of this operational reliability and adherence to the strict regulatory requirements, such as the GDPR of the European Union (Alketbi & Mehmood, 2025).

1.2 The Need of Strong, Adversarial-Resistant AI Models

The use of Artificial Intelligence has become an important element of the contemporary cybersecurity environment because it is capable of learning complicated attack patterns, detection of anomalies, and automating threat responses. Nevertheless, the growing reliance of AI-based systems to control security-related decisions has also made them vulnerable to attack by its enemies. Attackers are now crafting plans to specifically target and deceive, corrupt or circumvent AI models applied in malware detection, intrusion prevention, fraud analytics, phishing detection, and in cyber-threat intelligence. This is a new type of attacks called adversarial attacks that discloses critical vulnerabilities in the existing AI systems and necessitates the creation of adversarial-resistant AI systems. There are also adversarial attacks against AI algorithms: attackers are trying to misguide or abuse AI models:

- **Poisoning** attacks are training data manipulation attacks.
- **Evasion** attacks involve creation of malicious inputs that cannot be detected.
- White-box, black-box and gray-box threats are directed towards model architecture or its output.

The attacks reduce the accuracy of detection and are dangerous to AI-powered security systems. The available literature indicates that resisting against such adversarial manipulation is still a challenge in cybersecurity and it requires proactive and reactive defense mechanisms (Sarker et al., 2023).

1.3 Motivation for Secure, Ethical, and Explainable AI Applications

The urgent necessity in secure, ethical, and explainable AI is explained by the increased utilization of autonomous and AI-controlled systems in safety-critical settings, in which system crashes or malicious interference can result in a severe loss of damage. These systems are more interconnected as noted in the paper and therefore prone to cyberattacks, adversarial inputs, and unauthorized access and hence robust security is highly needed. Their inertial decision-making processes, akin to a black-box accumulating risk, as it curtails transparency and trust as well as making incident analysis challenging. Other examples of ethical issues that further support the need to design AI responsibly include privacy-related matters, biases in decision making, and unintended and harmful behavior. Due to the increasing scope of effects of AI system failures as the autonomy increases, the key to ensuring the safety, accountability and long-term trust of AI-robotic use are the strong security measures, ethical protection, and explainable intelligence (Neupane et al., 2024). In order to serve the demands of today security, AI-based threat detection should not only be accurate and automated but also:

- Safe to adversarial manipulation.
- Explainable to human trust and auditability.
- Moral in nature and conforms to principles of privacy and fairness.

This chapter dwells on harmonizing these three pillars of security, ethics and exploitability in order to create secure, trustworthy AI-based cybersecurity applications (Sarker et al., 2023).

1.4 Ethical and Explicable AI to Detect Threads

The enlarged use of AI-based cybersecurity offering an insight based on the significance of integrating ethical considerations and the Explainable Artificial Intelligence (XAI) into the modern software application . In the absence of ethical protections, AI can undermine user privacy, spread bias, or diminish accountability ethical AI refers to practices addressing privacy like federated learning and differential privacy, keeping sensitive organizational and personal data safe (Ameen et al., 2023). Additionally, an approach involving human-in-the-loop can be also employed to ensure that the automated detections are still under verification by the analysts so that algorithms are not overly relied in critical decision making situations.

It is also important to be explain. Explainable AI (XAI) methods like SHAP, LIME and counterfactual reasoning allow the analysts to viewer what is included in the model choices and understand that a certain group of actions is decided to existing a threat (Zhang et al., 2022). In order to identify within threats, XAI could be utilized to attract attention to suspicious times of logging in, deviant pattern access or variations in network behavior that generated red flags (Alketbi and Mehmood, 2025). These descriptions contribute to the fact that AI becomes more credible, more likely to comply with regulations, and allows human professionals and robotics to collaborate.

1.5 Framework Towards Secure, Ethical and Explainable Cybersecurity

The overlap of secure AI, ethical governance and explainability assumes a paradigm shift of the defense of modern software systems. Secure AI applications have high detection and mitigation of cyber threats; ethical alignment may serve to ensure fairness, accountability and privacy, and XAI may be employed to facilitate transparency and trust. Integration of these dimensions leads to the foundation of responsible cybersecurity systems which can effectively respond to technical and social issues.

Recent studies are also in favor of this integration. Indicatively, (Almheiri et al., 2025) developed a smart sustainable cybersecurity model that uses interpretable and transparent threat detection with explainable artificial intelligence with a detection rate of more than 99 per cent and false positives are reduced. Their work confirms that XAI can be used not only to provide resilience to a system but also achieve trust through detecting decisions that can be understood by security analysts. Similarly, the assessment techniques of XAI in the field of cybersecurity that have been developed recently have emphasized the importance of fidelity, stability, and response time as the most important terms of the trustworthy deployment (Calzarossa et al., 2025).

The chapter examines the intersectionality of AI, ethics and explainability in cybersecurity. It highlights the application of secure AI applications in increasing resiliency to evolving threats as well as ensuring that the decisions are transparent, fair, and accountable by discussing how ethical and explainable threat recognition can enable digital ecosystems to be not just technically operational but also reliable and aligned with human values.

2. ROLE OF AI IN CYBERSECURITY

2.1 From Traditional Defenses to AI-Driven and Explainable Security

Software systems heavily relied on static security like firewall, antivirus software and signature-based intrusion detection. These models were not able to predict the agility, scalability, and complexity of existing structured digital ecosystems although they were applicable to foreseeable threats. They were also too rigid and too dogmatic so far as their rule-based nature is concerned, and therefore took long to respond, high false-positive, and unable to detect attacks at zero-day or adaptive. Present software engineering is rather preoccupied with the values of automation, flexibility, and continuous improvement that is manifested in the development of AI-based security (Camacho, 2024). AI-based systems can:

- Adaptive reaction to fluctuating threat environments, as agile techniques react to fluctuating requirements.
- Automated detection and response, which reduces resilience because manual response is used, as with the automation of DevOps pipelines.
- Efficiency at scale in cloud, IoT, and distributed settings, and resilience when faced with scale in software system.
- Anticipate vulnerabilities before they are exploited, which is consistent with the proactive testing and continuous integration.

However, just like today in the engineering field, in which transparency and accountability are prioritized, an AI security system is also prone to the issue of explainability, bias, and trust. The black-box models do not enable engineers and analysts to understand the decisions which poses compliance and usability problems. Explainable AI (XAI) is the solution because it complies with values of software engineering, including traceability, readability, and the human-in-the-loop decision-making. XAI enables teams to understand the rationale and the causes of the AI-driven detection, which simplifies trust, compliance, and effective human-AI interactions (Salem et al., 2024).

Thus, cybersecurity has now become an adaptable, anticipatory, and comprehensible AI-based system, which improves security as transparent, continuous and explainable component of current software engineering.

2.2 Advantages of AI: Speed, Scalability and Ethical Consideration

Compared to traditional methods, AI has the advantages:

2.2.1 Speed

AI systems are able to process a high amount of log data and network traffic within seconds, which enables the detection and resolution of threats much more rapidly than human operators. AI-Introduced information and Event Management (SIEM) systems (such as automated log analysis detection) and real-time warning are also used as software engineering practice during software development and operation lifecycle.

2.2.2 Scalability

AI is easily scaled to multiple platforms, applications, and distributed architecture that are important in contemporary software development environments that rely on microservices and cloud-native applications.

2.2.3 Ethical Considerations

AI has also ethical issues that the software engineer must address with grate power:

- **Data Privacy:** privacy of sensitive user data in AI systems.
- **Prejudice and fairness:** preventing discrimination of prejudiced datasets or algorithms.
- **Transparency:** It involves explaining the decisions that are made to win the trust of systems and rendering them auditable.
- **Accountability:** creating a feeling of responsibility on decisions influenced by AI on an individual or organizations.
- **Digital Divide:** ensuring the equity of spreading the AI benefits in different societies.

The ethical practices are present in software engineering today through responsible AI design, fair-minded algorithm design, transparency in decision-making, and compliance with regulations(Eden et al., 2024).

2.3 Artificial Intelligence in Data Security: Make a Step to Transparent Thread Awareness

AI is evolving cybersecurity into being reactive to protection. AI, machine learning (ML), deep learning (DL), and natural language processing (NLP) will help with the analysis of big data volumes, identification of suspicious patterns, and prevention of known or new attacks (Yaseen, 2023).

AI is used in Cybersecurity as follows:

- **Threat Detection and Malware Analysis:** AI models are used to detect zero day attacks and polymorphic malware that have not been identified by traditional systems (Yasin, 2025).
- **Vulnerability Assessment:** AI systems are applied in the DevSecOps pipelines, which scan codebases automatically, and suggest any remedies in the course of continuous integration and deployment (CI/CD). The tools of Application Security Testing (SAST) such as those in GitHub Advanced

Security or Microsoft Azure DevOps are AI-based and, as such, will scan the source code on a per-commit and per-build basis, with machine learning used to understand unsafe code patterns, such as buffer overflow and SQL injection, and also can learn new threats, unlike traditional scanners.

- **Response to an Incident:** AI generated playbooks will conserve time in the human method of reacting to situations of real-life attacks, making the process of containment and recovery easier.
- **Phishing and Social Engineering Detection:** NLP algorithms are used to analyze a speech pattern and identify malicious emails and messages.
- **IoT and Cloud Security:** AI is used to survey large IoT networks and cloud-based systems and identify a ny potential anomalies that may indicate intrusion.

2.3.1 Towards Visible Security

AI is a strong and may be called a Black box and the choices made are difficult to differentiate. Explainable AI (XAI) can be used to make the results less embuguous, Ti fix, which is described as follows and is useful:

- Security team is a believer in AI warnings.
- Meet legal and compliance requirements.
- Enhance the interaction of human-robots.

Modern software engineering,

To this method, the modern software engineering, which places status on robotics, transparency and flexibility is appropriate. The systems are also safer due to the AI, and it is constructing future-proof and robust defenses (Yaseen, 2023). As shown in Figure 1 provides an overview of aplications of AI in Cybersecurity:

Figure 1. Applications of AI in cybersecurity

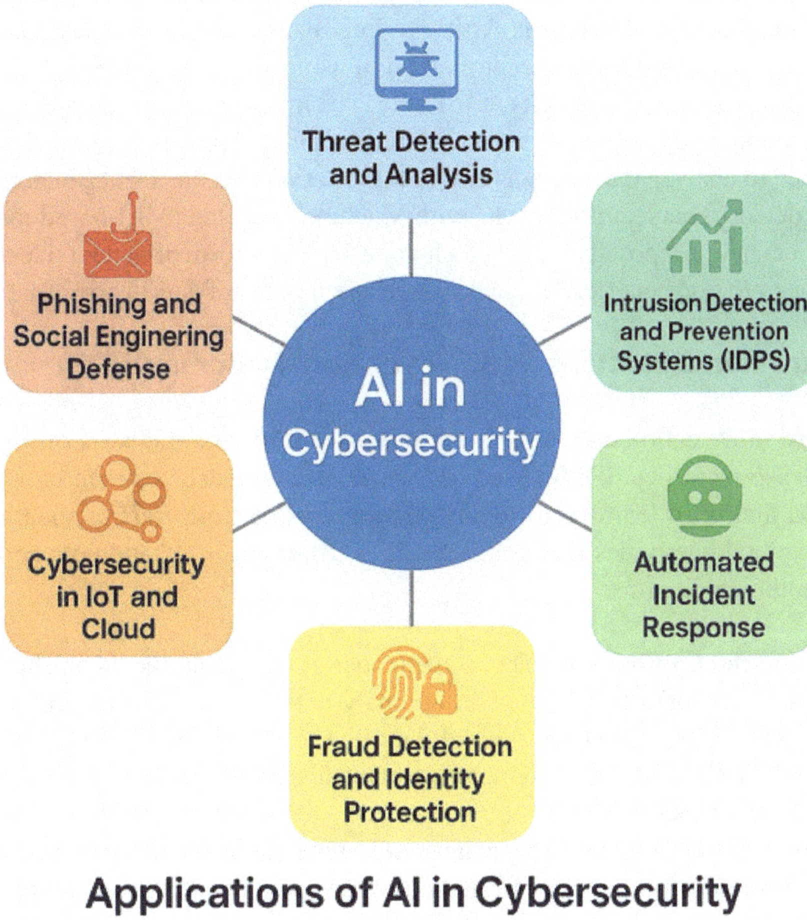

3. SECURE AI APPLICATIONS IN MODERN SOFTWARE SYSTEMS

Artificial Intelligence has create a new role as a critical security enabler in modern software systems permitting businesses to fight against a growing number of sophisticated attacks. Some of the outdated defenses rely on static rules or pre-defined signs that are not appropriate in dynamic environments where threats are evolving rapidly. Conversely, AI-motivated security solution is capable of detecting irregularities, trends, and evolving attacks with minimal human intervention. This section explores some of the greatest uses of AI in the context of protection of modern systems, and it will focus on malware analysis, phishing prevention, tracking of insiders, and intrusion detection. Artificial Intelligence (AI) is the most frequently gazed-up to as the most significant method of using IDS, due to the high potential of the AI to process vast amounts of IoT data. The impact of AI techniques on intrusion detection in IoT software systems is significant, and the given method can also be applied to analyze the vast quantity of information that the users generate every day. To detect cybersecurity attacks with Machine Learning (ML)-based methods, researchers have proposed many AI techniques. ML is a form of AI practice that has the capacity to find beneficial information in vast amount of data (Torre et al., 2025).

3.1 Intrusion Detection and Prevention Systems (IDPS)

Intrusion Detection and Prevention Systems (IDPS) are the basis of organization defense strategies. IDPS based on Artificial Intelligence operate on anomaly detection and deep learning to identify suspicious network traffic, unauthorized logins, and odd activities that could result in cyber-attacks, fraudulent activities, and unauthorized logins.

- **Example Application:** The autoencoder is one example of unsupervised neural networks that is used in anomaly detection in network traffic. They are able to be trained on normal data flow patterns and alert about anomalies which could define malicious traffic such as port scanning or denial-of-service attacks.
- **Pros:** AI- based IDPS are scalable, and they can respond faster to -exploits of zero days and previously unknown attack methods of signature- based system.
- **Ethical Issue:** In order to have powerful models, a significant quantity of network information can be muted. Extreme data collection may breach secrecy of users conciliation through disclosing personal or sensitive information. Therefore, association has to balance the security needs with the data reduction practice to ensure compliance with protocols like GDPR and HIPAA.

3.2 Malware and Ransomware Detection

Malware and ransomware persist some of the maximum devastating cyber-threats with the aptitude to shut down entire systems in a few minutes. Detecting machines powered by AI apply the machine learning models to software executables, detect malevolent features and prevent the proliferation of impurities.

- **Application**: Convolutional Neural Networks (CNNs) may be applied to binary codes as metaphors. CNNs can be trained to identify executables as malicious or benign with a high degree of accuracy with the assistance of attributes that suggest the presence of malevolent software. CNNs, their turn, are rather appropriate in malware and intrusion detection, whereas transformer-based models are more efficient than Security LLM that results in high correctness in cyber threat detection (Ferrag et al., 2024).
- **Pros:** AI methods can detect overcast or polymorphous malware, which continuously alters its cypher to evade autograph, a much better model than the antivirus software of old.
- **Explainability Requirements**: Making AI results so clear is a thoughtful requirement. Security crews need to be aware what belongings or code yielded a malware sorting. False positives cannot be eliminated, and can be harmful to the system and can postpone the efficiency.

Both Saliency maps and SHAP (Shapley Additive exPlanations) can provide information about the model decisions.

3.3 Fraud Detection and Phishing

Phishing and online fraud are not going to go away because they are constantly playing on the defenselessness of people, which is not easy to combat with empty rules. Misleading communication can be detected automatically and with high precision with the help of using AI.

- **Exmaple application:** Example Application: Email texts, URLs, and Metadata can be analyzed with variants of BERT and GPT to detect phishing attacks using serial (mostly transformer-based) models. These models detect linguistic abnormalities, suspicious wording or unsuitable contextual clues, which most commonly point to a fraud. BERT model of transformer has shown strong applications in the sphere of cyber security by detecting contextual information in a series of texts. BERT was applied by experts to the spam email recognition, malware detection, and suspicious log anomalies detection tasks. The findings demonstrated the usage of NLP models to scan text security to identify a fraud or malicious motive (Ferrag et al., 2024).
- **Pros:** AI-based phishing detection is automated, which means that the user does not have to be attentive to detect phishing, which makes social engineering attacks less effective.
- **Ethical Problems:** There is a possible bias when the models are trained mostly on the data that pertains to the regions or languages of the firms.

As an example, genuine messages in non-English dialects can be identified as suspicious because there is no training data which results in discrimination or operation lag. Such risks can be reduced by making sure that training datasets are assorted and fairness-conscious learning techniques are used.

3.4 Insider Threat Monitoring

Insider threats either planned or unplanned are a significant security risk. Because insiders already have formal access, it is much harder to sense malicious action than it is to sense exterior attacks. AI is used to assist by replicating how a normal user would behave and categorising anomalies that might suggest abuse.

- **Example Application:** Recurrent Neural Networks (RNNs) which are used to drive User Behavior Analytics (UBA) could be used to monitor when they log in, rate of access recurrence, file movement and communication designs in order to detect abnormal behavior. Pointers When an employee suddenly downloads large files of sensitive information at odd hours, the system can create sirens.
- **Pros**: AI-based surveillance can be implemented 247 and scale to new user capabilities provided it can provide alerts about new threats that might otherwise go unnoticed and under the carpet.
- **Transparency Requirement**: AI-based sirens should be legible to human specialists in the name of organization faith. The existence of unnecessarily complex or intricate models can lead to the lighting of false alarms with no good reason to explain the situation and might lead to weariness of the security staff. Explainable AI will be implemented accordingly so as to give a notification with applicable justification e.g. downloading of files that are unusual in the last few days in relation to the activity in the past 6 months of the user.

4. ETHICAL ASPECTS OF THREAD DETECTION BY AI

Detection of threats by AI is taken to another tier of ethical consideration other than technical performance. The use of biased or partial data to train models may produce unequal results, including tracing down a certain type of users at a higher rate or tracing new attack designs. Besides this, there is an augmentation of privacy risk due to the reliance on personal and administrative sensitive data, and less accountability in high-stakes security systems due to the use of opaque black-boxes decisions. To achieve trustful cybersecurity practices, it is therefore necessary to embed fairness, privacy-preserving models, and explainability into AI systems (Zhang et al., 2022). Figure 2 ellaborat the ethical aspects of thread detetction by AI:

Figure 2. Ethical aspects of thread detection by AI

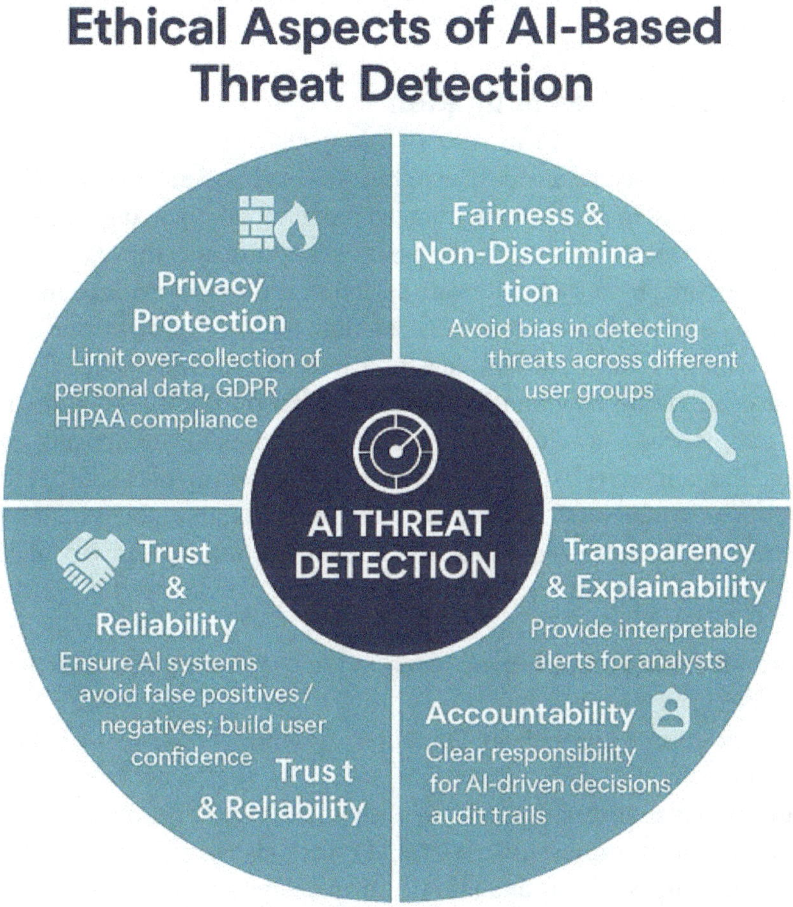

4.1 Privacy and Data Protection

AI threat sensors often require large, sensitive datasets (logs, telemetry, user behavior) for training and procedures. To limit data exposure and comply with privacy-preserving techniques such as federated learning, differential privacy, and secure aggregation should be integrated into model design and deployment. Federated learning reduces raw data sharing by training models locally and only sharing updates, while differential privacy adds noise to model updates or outputs to bound information leakage. Both approaches help balance detection performance and privacy requirements in distributed, multi-tenant systems (Ameen et al., 2023). However, practical deployments must also consider inference and poisoning attack against federated systems and tune privacy budgets to preserve utility (Baniecki & Biecek, 2024).

4.2 Fairness and Bias Mitigation

Training datasets can transfer bias to the AI systems. Such bias may be present in the category of users that is being flagged more frequently in the case of cybersecurity. This has been pointed out in the paper as a significant ethical dilemma which has to be overcome by responsible data selection and model evaluation.

AI methods in cybersecurity can accidentally embed biases from unbalanced datasets, leading to biased threat detection results like over-monitoring specific groups or overlooking new attacks. Vectors. Ensuring fairness requires balanced training data, fairness-aware algorithms, and continuous monitoring of model outcomes. Explainability AI models further help discover bias sources, enabling human analysts to intervene. Embedding these practices strengthens both the ethical integrity and the robustness of AI-driven threat detection (Adeyeye et al., 2024).

Key Mitigation approaches discussed include:

- **Data balancing and preprocessing** to remove skewed class distributions in cybersecurity datasets.
- **Fairness-aware algorithms** that adjust training objectives to reduce disparate impacts.
- **Continuous monitoring** of AI results to detect bias drift during deployment.
- **Integration of explainable AI (XAI)** methods (like feature attribution) to uncover sources of bias and allow human analysts to intervene.

4.3 Accountability and Governance

The AI security capabilities need to be governed by pure accountability structures. These involve taking of verdicts, maintenance of auditable audit trail, setting of policies on automated processes and definition of human / machine responsibility on responses. Explainability supports governance by producing understandable explanations of alerts to people (e.g. what features or behaviors made a flag to be raised), and facilitates auditing. The literature supports governance structures that integrate explainability, documented decision policies, and operational controls to enable organizations to justify actions performed through AI output and satisfy regulatory requirements (Ameen et al., 2023), (Zhang et al., 2022).

Governance helps structure:

- how information is gathered and utilized,
- how AI models make decisions,
- how biases are mitigated,
- and the reaction of organisations to the malfunction or misidentification of threats by AI systems.

Governance as a crucial part of making AI systems in the field of cybersecurity reliable, secure, and in line with human values. This involves establishment of policies and controls that avoid detrimental consequences that are brought about by automated threat detection controls.

4.4 Human-in-the-Loop Security

Even well-designed AI systems should not function as fully automate critical security decisions. (Lu et al., 2024) note that ethical AI must allow human oversight and intervention at critical stages. HITL is applied in software engineering:

- **Model Training & Validation:** developers and domain experts validate datasets, check for bias and approve updates before models are deployed.
- **Decision-**Support Systems: AI applications in healthcare, finance, or HR integrate human oversight, ensuring final decisions remain accountable to human judgment.
- **Adaptive System:** HITL permits engineers to perfect AI models iteratively built on use feedback, refining trustworthiness and reliability

5. EXPLAINABLE AI (XAI) IN THREAD DETECTION

5.1 Importance of Explainability

Explainability is a serious part of the existing cybersecurity that can help AI-based threat sensors not only to be precisely sound but also ethically sound. Explainable AI (XAI) allows security experts and designers to learn the explanations behind specific activities being identified as malicious, debug, improve validation, and trust in procedure by making the model result explainable. As an example, intrusion detection systems (IDS) have used LIME to bring into focus certain landscape such as an unusual port activity or unusual packet size that affected a detection decision. On the same note, SHAP provides consistent scores of features of importance, which allows analysts to determine those attributes with the greatest associations with cyberattacks (Ibrar et al. 2024).

The issue of explainability also deals with the increasing demands, which comprise accountability and compliance. Healthcare, financial systems, and cloud platform are security-sensitive environments, which are usually in stringent governance circumstances.. In the given case, XAI methods do provide explanations of the automated choices that can help the organizations to handle the legal and regulatory responsibility without the risks involved in the black-box AI models (Arrieta et al., 2020).

Finally, explainability is a key to trusting secure AI applications. The transparent models also contribute to the adoption through making clear the process of threats identification and also enhance the sense of fairness and accountability of the automated defense systems. Regarding the research that is currently ongoing, the level of user confidence and acceptance of AI security solutions is heavily reliant on the possibility to offer concise and comprehensible explanations (Xu & Yang, 2025).

5.2 Methods for Explainability

There are many approaches that have emerged to make AI based security interpretable. The most popular ones are such feature attribution methods as SHAP and LIME. SHAP, a game theory based method, suggests both local and global attributions, so that by assigning feature importance standards, it is possible to control what network attributes impacted predictions. They showed that SHAP was efficient in forensic analysis of IDS results (Hermosilla et al., 2025) and that it often detected vital traffic environments which played a role in generating anomaly alerts. On the same note, LIME generates simplified human readable local models of every prediction so that analysts can interpret which packet flows or email structures contributed to classification (Shafin, 2025).

In addition to feature attribution, rule-based explanations have been established to translate AI outputs into human-readable rules. For example, when a deep learning system flags malicious network activity, a rule-based system can outcome an explainable statement like "unusual outbound traffic volume detected on non-standard." This conversion is essential for practical adoption, as security analysts are more expected to act on AI recommendations when they are framed as explicit rules rather than possibilities .

Visualization techniques represent another critical category of explainability.by transforming abstract model behavior into cues, analysts gain intuitive understanding of security events. For instance, heatmaps have been applied in malware detection to highlight suspicious code regions, while flow diagrams are used in network anomaly detection to trace unusual traffic paths (Zhang et al., 2022). These visual methods not only enhance interpretability but also support faster response times by simplifying the analysis of complex data.

5.3 Applications in Cybersecurity

The applications of XAI in cybersecurity are rapidly increasing across multiple domains. In phishing detection, scientists have integrated LIME and SHAP to highlight suspicious keywords, deceptive URLs, and abnormal email patters. (Shafin, 2025) established an explainable feature selection agenda that demonstrated how highlighting critical words and structures significantly improves the interpretability of phishing classifiers. Such explanations support both automated systems and human analysts in recognizing deceptive approaches used by attackers.

It is identifies various high impact uses of Artificial Intelligence (AI) and Explainable AI (XAI) in the cybersecurity domain. The applications are used to improve the security posture of the current digital infrastructures by automation, intelligent analytics, anomaly detection and transparent decision making. The next section provides a summary of the main applications of cybersecurity that were directly facilitated by the content of the retrieved files.

5.3.1. Insider Threat Mornitoring

The second area, where XAI may be of great assistance, is **insider threat monitoring**. The visions, LIME and SHAP, could reveal abnormal file transfers and month-of-year logins times and attempts of unauthorized access (Hermosilla et al., 2025) to aid in both the earlier detection of threats and the investigation by providing forensic evidence. By giving clarity to the reasons behind issues of alerts, XAI will enable organizations to determine what is considered to be genuine insider threats and initiate anomalies, thus, cutting down unnecessary escalation.

5.3.2. Malware Detection and Classification.

A significant use case mentioned in the paper is malware detection, in which AI-based models working with massive amounts of malware and benign binaries are used to detect malware families and identify previously unknown members (Achuthan et al. 2024).

Explainability lends credence to this domain by allowing the analysts to trace:

- what binary characteristics were used in classification?

- Why has the model designated a file as being malicious?
- whether the model was subject to noise or bias.

This will make automated malware detection systems more trusted.

5.3.3. Intrusion Detection and Anomaly Identification.

In **anomaly detection**, explainability guarantees that IDS alerts are not treated as opaque outcomes. Rather, they are able to decompose into definite triggers. (Keshk et al., 2023) used XAI to an IDS based on deep learning of IoT networks and unveiled that explanations increased the trustworthiness of the system by describing which packets or protocols raise higher alarms. Equally, (Sharma et al., 2024) published that the incorporation of the XAI in IDS led to improved trust among analysts as it offered easy to understand justification of alert and eventually decreased false positives and increased efficiency of operations.

AI has extensive implementation in intrusion detection systems (IDS) and anomaly-based detection that can assist in detecting abnormal network behavior that can signal a cyberattack. AI models process:

- Network traffic flows
- System logs
- Protocol behaviors
- User activity patterns

XAI is such that the flagged anomalies can be interpreted by the analysts so that the intrusion investigation becomes more precise and efficient (Achuthan et al. 2024).

5.3.2. User Access security and Authentication Systems.

The paper explains how AI and XAI are essential to assist in organization of authentication mechanism and access control system by verifying user identity and noticing anomaly in login behavior. According to AI, the behavioral patterns, device profiles, and the contextual clues can be used to differentiate between legitimate users and malicious impersonation attempts.

XAI also enhances this application by ensuring the decision to authenticate a request is transparent to the administrator, who can know the reasons to grant or deny access (Achuthan et al. 2024).

5.3.4. Network and System Behavior Monitoring.

AI helps in monitoring real-time network and system behavior and identifying variances that can indicate intrusions, malconfigurations, or insider threat (Achuthan et al. 2024). Machine learning allows automating:

- Traffic profiling
- Endpoint behavior analysis
- Resource usage monitoring

XAI also increases the level of transparency by answering which network attributes or behavior indicators gave rise to an alert.

5.3.5. Cyber Investigation and Digital Forensics.

One more important area of application is the area of digital forensics in which AI serves to aid investigators through analyzing logs, detecting evidence of malicious behavior, and rebuilding sequences of attacks (Achuthan et al. 2024). Explainability assists investigators in knowing:

- How the AI linked evidence
- The rationale of correlations of events.
- The reliability of the conclusions of the model.

This enhances credibility and defensibility of forensic reports.

5.3. 6. Intelligent Decision Support and Adaptive Security.

The article observes the newfound place of AI in adaptive cybersecurity where systems can dynamically change based on the changing threat conditions. Applications include:

- Dynamic firewall rules
- Automated threat response
- Adaptive authentication issues.

XAI also makes sure that such automated actions are both accountable and auditable, as well as in compliance with organizational policies (Achuthan et al. 2024).

5.3.7. Security Analytics and Risk Assessment.

AI enables scoring risks, prioritizing threats, and security analytics and uses large volumes of telemetry to determine the most significant vulnerabilities and attack vectors. Explainability enables risk assessors to know the factors that determine the risk levels and ascertain the validity of automated risk predictions (Achuthan et al. 2024).

6. DIFFICULTIES OF ETHICALLY ALIGNED AND EXPLAINABLE AI IN CYBERSECURITY

6.1 AI Model Attack

These attacks exploit vulnerabilities in the software model, specifically applications that are executed through machine learning by generating malicious inputs that cause the models to misclassify or behave in an unexpected way. In self-driving, intrusion detection, and healthcare diagnostics, among other areas, intrusion detection systems and adversarial perturbation might cause serious ramifications in terms of their safety and ethical implications, which have adverse impacts on the safety of a user and the reliability of a set system(Wang et al., 2022).

An AI-based model attack is indicated where the attacker decodes the structure of a victim neural network that is run with NVIDIA Deep Learning Accelerator (NVDLA). The attack has integrated side-channel information and machine learning by initially obtaining intermediate feature maps, represented by MmapVictim vector, and subsequently classifying the maps with a custom-trained ResNet model (Gupta et al., 2025). The attacker, together with this, uses metadata of the NVDLA command stream, such as task descriptors, memory addresses, and bin information, to deduce structural information, like layer types, widths, and ordering. Combining the ResNet-based layer identification with extracted metadata, the attacker is able to reconstruct the high-level architecture of the victim model exposing the layer sequence and architectural properties of the model.

6.2 Model Drift in Changing Systems

Idea drift in deployed models arises because the real-life distribution of data does not follow the deployed models. Trained models, which use out-of-data data, may not give fair or accurate results unless they are validated. In addition to the negative impact on the performance of the systems, the drift has ethical implications because it may be applied to discriminatory or erroneous decisions in such a serious field as healthcare, finance and security(Wang et al., 2022).

6.3 Data Poisoning

During the training phase of machine learning models, attackers may inject corrupted or mislabeled data into training datasets. This compromises the integrity of the learning process and results in biased or maliciously altered models. For example, data poisoning can degrade malware detection systems or enable recommendation systems to promote adversary-chosen outputs(Wang et al., 2022).

7. FUTURE DIRECTIONS FOR SECURE, ETHICAL AND EXPLAINABLE AI IN CYBERSECURITY

7.1 AI-Augmented Thread Intelligence and Explainable

Future AI systems will combine predictive analytics with contextual awareness to proactively identify threats and support Security Operations Centers (SOCs). Models will continually learn from adversarial techniques and novel attacks patterns to build robust, adaptive defenses. At the same time, explainable AI will ensure that alerts like correlated events or prioritized incidents are transparent and interpretable, reducing analyst fatigue and enhancing trust in automated recommendations(Arreche et al., 2024).

7.2 Federated and Blockchain-Enabled Secure AI

Privacy-preserving learning and tamper-resistant data sharing will define the next generation of secure AI frameworks. Federated Learning (FL) allows decentralized model training across multiple organizations without sharing raw data, enhancing compliance with regulations like GDPR. Blockchain integration records AI decisions in tamper-proof ledgers, adding transparency and immutability. Blockchain and FL work together to provide collaborative, explicable threat intelligence while maintaining responsibility and anonymity (Rahmati & Pagano, 2025).

Figure 3 highlights the federated and blockchain-enabled secure AI framework.

Figure 3. Federated and blockchain-enabled secure AI

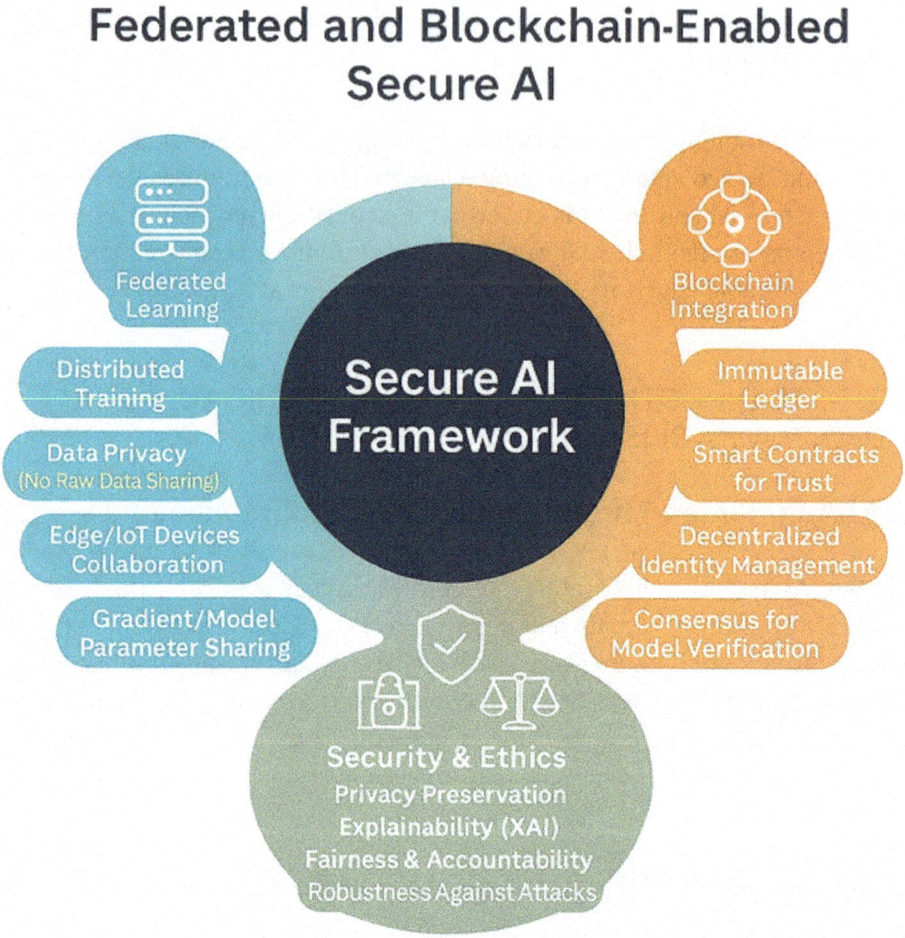

7.3 Preparing for Quantum-Safe and Resilience AI

The arrival of quantum computing threatens current cryptographic ethics, requiring proactive AI-driven resilience approaches. AI can direct hybrid transition models that combine classical and post-quantum techniques, as well as assist in the design and optimization of quantum-resistant algorithms such as lattice-based encryption. Explainable frameworks will be critical to confirm that both technical specialists and regulators understand quantum-safe implementation choices (Liu & Moody, 2024).

7.4 Building Trustworthy, Ethical, and Explainable AI for Long-Term Resilience

As AI becomes rooted in modern cybersecurity, systems must prioritize trust, fairness, and accountability combined with detection accuracy. Transparency and explainability will persist critical for high-stakes security decisions, while bias mitigation approaches will decrease discriminatory outputs in thread detection. Additionally, resilience against adversarial manipulation and international regulatory frameworks will guide responsible deployment. In order to maintain public trust and ensure responsibility for AI-driven acts, human oversight must continue to be crucial (Rahmati & Pagano, 2025), (Calzarossa et al., 2025).

To reach long-term resilience in current software and cybersecurity systems, AI systems that are trustworthy, ethical, and explainable need to be built. As observed in the study, the successful operation of AI-based cyber defense in the long-term is not just based on the accuracy of detection but also on transparency, fairness, governance, privacy protection, and human-focused accountability. The combination of these elements will increase the level of trust the user has and make AI systems resistant to the new types of cyber threats (Rane et al, 2024).

7.4.1. Reliability as a Building block to the Resilient AI

Reliable AI demands systems, which are transparent, reliable, robust, and consistent with human values. As pointed out in the Explainable AI (XAI) paper, trustworthy AI is one pillar of making autonomous work across high-risk digital systems safe and efficacious, especially where human and AI collaboration is vital. Particularly, when it comes to cybersecurity, it is crucial to consider trust since AI decisions help analysts identify threats, prevent attacks, and justify interventions (Rane et al, 2024)..

Ethics Guidelines of Trustworthy AI of the European Commission entail such concepts as human agency, technical robustness, privacy, and transparency as the guiding principles that influence the long-term resilience by making AI systems act predictably and responsibly over time.

7.4.2. Ethical AI as a Conditional Sustainable Adoption

Ethical risks, including discrimination, unfair predictions, and violations of privacy, are a major challenge to the sustainability of AI with regard to security. The XAI cybersecurity article describes how bias, unfairness, racism, sexism, and ageism may be inadvertent in the training sets and disseminate when making decisions by the model, directly damaging the fairness and validity of cybersecurity systems (Rane et al, 2024).

Ethical principles (GDPR, EC Trustworthy AI framework) stipulate that:

- Users are entitled to automated decision explanation,
- Data should be handled in a transparent way,
- Systems should ensure that people are not discriminated on the cost of such a system.

Assuring AI ethics is hence a long-term sustainability measure, which means systems breaking ethical principles may be rejected, abused, or have their use regulated.

7.4.3. Transparency and Human Assurance as Explainability

Explainable AI promotes greater resiliency through greater interpretability, contestability, and auditing of threat detection systems. According to the XAI paper, there are a number of strengths:

- XAI assists security analysts in gaining insight into why the model considers an event to be malicious, leading to an improved accuracy and minimized false alarms.
- It can enable the end-users to assess what information is being utilized in decision-making enhancing privacy awareness and trust.
- It helps in sectioning out biased or imperfect predictions, which facilitate constant model enhancement.

It is also important to explain how its AI became a target of many cyberattacks. The scholars have shown that opponents can cheat or corrupt common explanation systems such as LIME and SHAP and that more robust reliable XAI frameworks should be put in place that will ensure sustainability of cybersecurity systems over time (Rane et al, 2024).

7.4.4. Accountability and Governance as Major Resilience Mechanisms

Good governance will be used to make sure the AI systems are not out of line with ethical principles at any point of their lifecycle. The XAI paper emphasizes that there is a need to:

- Restrictive access to AI models,

- Immunity to adversarial examples of explanation processes,
- Making sure that only the permitted parties can access or alter sensitive AI parts.

Accountability also means:

- Empower human beings to challenge automated cyber-defense,
- Recording model behavior through time,
- Keeping audit trails in order to trace how data has been used and why decisions were taken.

These governance aspects are resilient in that they do not allow misuse and make systems clear even when there is adversarial pressure.

7.4.5. Long-term resilience Factors Data Quality and Privacy

In order to be resilient, AI needs quality, non-bias, and continuously updated datasets. The XAI paper presents drawbacks of the existing cybersecurity data:

- datasets are frequently confidential.
- is unethical and privacy-related and cannot be shared publicly,
- and regularly do not reflect the latest cyber threats.

The resilience in the long run is thus pegged on the creation of safe, current, ethically gathered data that enhance the accuracy of the system and the protection of personal data (Rane et al, 2024)..

7.4.6. Achieving Sustainable AI Deployment between Performance and Explainability

One of the biggest long-term issues is the need to balance the high performance in detection with explainability. Deep learning models are the least interpretable, but also the ones with higher accuracy. In contrast, interpretable models (e.g., decision trees) might not be suitable to address current cyber-resilience requirements in terms of performance. The XAI paper emphasizes the need to create hybrid solutions that will maintain the performance and explainability of AI to build sustainable and resilient use of AI (Rane et al, 2024)..

7.4.7. User-Driven and Human-Centered Design to be Robust

User-centered XAI enhances the strength of cybersecurity systems by providing explanations based on how users perceive them and their mental models, level of expertise, and operational requirements. The paper suggested the future direction that focuses on the creation of XAI that is interpretable to humans rather than mathematically but not fully long-term usable and trusted (Rane et al, 2024).

Figure 4. Framework for building trustworthy, ethical, and explainable AI for cybersecurity resilience

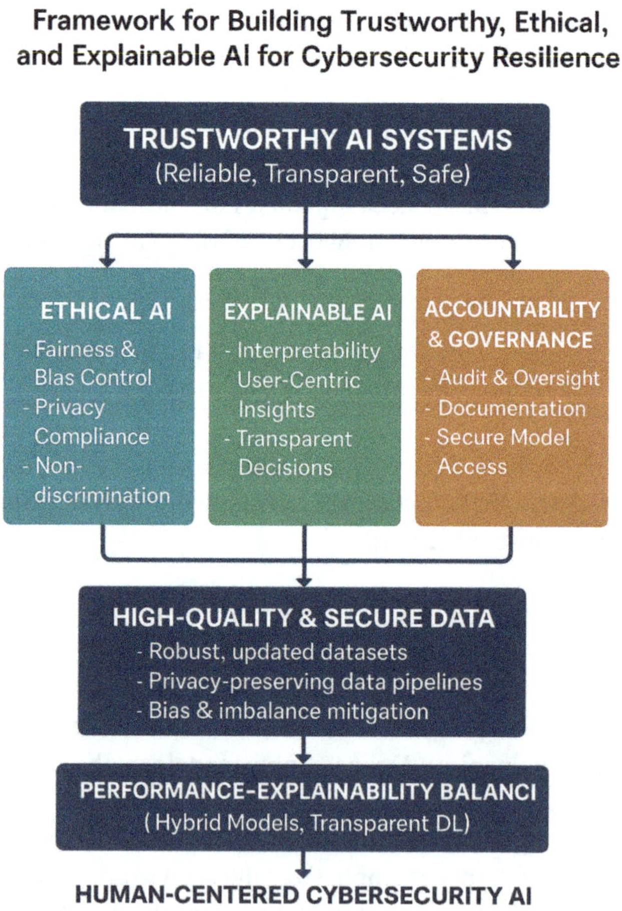

CONCLUSION

AI is still changing the nature of cybersecurity to facilitate proactive, intelligent, and scalable threat detection in the current software ecosystem. Nevertheless, the efficiency of AI-enhanced cybersecurity is pegged on the transparency, fairness, and ethical alignment. Explainable AI methods offer the critical visibility of model decision-making, which is useful in ensuring trust, compliance, and response to incidents. Meanwhile, accountable deployment is crucial to secure model development, adversarial robustness, and ethical governance frameworks. This chapter has highlighted an all-encompassing approach, that is, involving technical protection, ethical conduct, governance mechanisms, and explainability, in order to establish robust AI systems that could protect against contemporary cyber attacks, and maintain accountability, confidence, and social values.

The future of secure AI in cybersecurity lies in uniting technical advancements with ethical and explainable practices. By advancing AI-augmented threat intelligence (Arreche et al., 2024), leveraging federated and blockchain-enabled collaboration (Devi et al., 2025), preparing for quantum-safe resilience (Liu & Moody, 2024), SaberiKamarposhti, 2024), and embedding transparency, fairness, and oversight into design (Calzarossa et al., 2025), modern software systems can achieve trustworthy and resilience cyber defense.

REFERENCES

Achuthan, K., Ramanathan, S., Srinivas, S., & Raman, R. (2024). Advancing cybersecurity and privacy with artificial intelligence: Current trends and future research directions. *Frontiers in Big Data*, *7*, 1497535. DOI: 10.3389/fdata.2024.1497535 PMID: 39703783

Adeyeye, O. J., Akanbi, I., Emeteveke, I., & Emehin, O. (2024). Leveraging secured AI-driven data analytics for cybersecurity: Safeguarding information and enhancing threat detection. *International Journal of Research and Publication and Reviews*, *5*(10), 3208–3223. DOI: 10.55248/gengpi.5.1024.2911

Alketbi, K. S., & Mehmood, A. (2025). A Comprehensive Survey of Explainable Artificial Intelligence Techniques for Malicious Insider Threat Detection. *IEEE Access : Practical Innovations, Open Solutions*.

Almheiri, S. J., Shah, A. A., Abbas, S., Ahmad, M., & Khan, M. A. (2025). Smart sustainable cyber security: Modelling an interpretable and transparent threat detection with explainable artificial intelligence. *Discover Sustainability*, *6*(1), 442. DOI: 10.1007/s43621-025-01280-z

Ameen, A. H., Mohammed, M. A., & Rashid, A. N. (2023). Dimensions of artificial intelligence techniques, blockchain, and cyber security in the Internet of medical things: Opportunities, challenges, and future directions. *Journal of Intelligent Systems*, *32*(1), 20220267. DOI: 10.1515/jisys-2022-0267

Arreche, O., Guntur, T., & Abdallah, M. (2024). Xai-ids: Toward proposing an explainable artificial intelligence framework for enhancing network intrusion detection systems. *Applied Sciences (Basel, Switzerland)*, *14*(10), 4170. DOI: 10.3390/app14104170

Arrieta, A. B., Díaz-Rodríguez, N., Del Ser, J., Bennetot, A., Tabik, S., Barbado, A., García, S., Gil-López, S., Molina, D., & Benjamins, R. (2020). Explainable Artificial Intelligence (XAI): Concepts, taxonomies, opportunities and challenges toward responsible AI. *Information Fusion*, *58*, 82–115. DOI: 10.1016/j.inffus.2019.12.012

Baniecki, H., & Biecek, P. (2024). Adversarial attacks and defenses in explainable artificial intelligence: A survey. *Information Fusion*, *107*, 102303. DOI: 10.1016/j.inffus.2024.102303

Calzarossa, M. C., Giudici, P., & Zieni, R. (2025). An assessment framework for explainable AI with applications to cybersecurity. *Artificial Intelligence Review*, *58*(5), 150. DOI: 10.1007/s10462-025-11141-w

Camacho, N. G. (2024). The role of AI in cybersecurity: Addressing threats in the digital age. *Journal of Artificial Intelligence General science (JAIGS) ISSN: 3006-4023, 3*(1), 143-154.

Eden, C. A., Chisom, O. N., & Adeniyi, I. S. (2024). Integrating AI in education: Opportunities, challenges, and ethical considerations. *Magna Scientia Advanced Research and Reviews, 10*(2), 006-013.

Ferrag, M. A., Ndhlovu, M., Tihanyi, N., Cordeiro, L. C., Debbah, M., Lestable, T., & Thandi, N. S. (2024). Revolutionizing cyber threat detection with large language models: A privacy-preserving bert-based lightweight model for iot/iiot devices. *IEEE Access : Practical Innovations, Open Solutions*, *12*, 23733–23750. DOI: 10.1109/ACCESS.2024.3363469

Gupta, N., Jati, A., & Chattopadhyay, A. (2025). Ai attacks ai: Recovering neural network architecture from nvdla using ai-assisted side channel attack. *ACM Transactions on Embedded Computing Systems*, *24*(5), 1–29. DOI: 10.1145/3731560

Hermosilla, P., Berríos, S., & Allende-Cid, H. (2025). Explainable AI for Forensic Analysis: A Comparative Study of SHAP and LIME in Intrusion Detection Models. *Applied Sciences (Basel, Switzerland)*, *15*(13), 7329. DOI: 10.3390/app15137329

Ibrar, M., Nahom, H., Mohammed, A., Márquez-Sánchez, S., Fernandez, J. H., Corchado, J. M., & Erbad, A. 2024, June. An Explainable AI-Based Demand Response Optimization Framework for Smart Buildings. In *International Symposium on Distributed Computing and Artificial Intelligence* (pp. 88-98). Cham: Springer Nature Switzerland.

Keshk, M., Koroniotis, N., Pham, N., Moustafa, N., Turnbull, B., & Zomaya, A. Y. (2023). An explainable deep learning-enabled intrusion detection framework in IoT networks. *Information Sciences*, *639*, 119000. DOI: 10.1016/j.ins.2023.119000

Liu, Y.-K., & Moody, D. (2024). Post-quantum cryptography and the quantum future of cybersecurity. *Physical Review Applied*, *21*(4), 040501. DOI: 10.1103/PhysRevApplied.21.040501 PMID: 38846721

Lu, Q., Zhu, L., Xu, X., Whittle, J., Zowghi, D., & Jacquet, A. (2024). Responsible AI pattern catalogue: A collection of best practices for AI governance and engineering. *ACM Computing Surveys*, *56*(7), 1–35. DOI: 10.1145/3626234

Neupane, S., Mitra, S., Fernandez, I. A., Saha, S., Mittal, S., Chen, J., Pillai, N., & Rahimi, S. (2024). Security considerations in ai-robotics: A survey of current methods, challenges, and opportunities. *IEEE Access : Practical Innovations, Open Solutions*, *12*, 22072–22097. DOI: 10.1109/ACCESS.2024.3363657

Rahmati, M., & Pagano, A. (2025). Federated Learning-Driven Cybersecurity Framework for IoT Networks with Privacy Preserving and Real-Time Threat Detection Capabilities. Informatics, Rane, N., Choudhary, S. and Rane, J., 2024. Artificial intelligence for enhancing resilience. *Journal of Applied Artificial Intelligence*, *5*(2), 1–33.

Salem, A. H., Azzam, S. M., Emam, O. E., & Abohany, A. A. (2024). Advancing cybersecurity: A comprehensive review of AI-driven detection techniques. *Journal of Big Data*, *11*(1), 105. DOI: 10.1186/s40537-024-00957-y

Sarker, I. H. (2023). Multi-aspects AI-based modeling and adversarial learning for cybersecurity intelligence and robustness: A comprehensive overview. *Security and Privacy*, *6*(5), e295. DOI: 10.1002/spy2.295

Shafin, S. S. (2025). An explainable feature selection framework for web phishing detection with machine learning. *Data Science and Management*, *8*(2), 127–136. DOI: 10.1016/j.dsm.2024.08.004

Sharma, B., Sharma, L., Lal, C., & Roy, S. (2024). Explainable artificial intelligence for intrusion detection in IoT networks: A deep learning based approach. *Expert Systems with Applications*, *238*, 121751. DOI: 10.1016/j.eswa.2023.121751

Torre, D., Chennamaneni, A., Jo, J., Vyas, G., & Sabrsula, B. (2025). Toward enhancing privacy preservation of a federated learning cnn intrusion detection system in iot: Method and empirical study. *ACM Transactions on Software Engineering and Methodology*, *34*(2), 1–48. DOI: 10.1145/3695998

Wang, Z., Ma, J., Wang, X., Hu, J., Qin, Z., & Ren, K. (2022). Threats to training: A survey of poisoning attacks and defenses on machine learning systems. *ACM Computing Surveys*, *55*(7), 1–36. DOI: 10.1145/3538707

Xu, B., & Yang, G. (2025). Interpretability research of deep learning: A literature survey. *Information Fusion*, *115*, 102721. DOI: 10.1016/j.inffus.2024.102721

Yaseen, A. (2023). AI-driven threat detection and response: A paradigm shift in cybersecurity. *International Journal of Information and Cybersecurity*, *7*(12), 25–43.

Yasin, A. 2025. Malware analysis in IoT devices and AI. In *Malware analysis in IoT devices and AI*. The institution of Engineering and Technology (IET).

Zhang, Z., Al Hamadi, H., Damiani, E., Yeun, C. Y., & Taher, F. (2022). Explainable artificial intelligence applications in cyber security: State-of-the-art in research. *IEEE Access : Practical Innovations, Open Solutions*, *10*, 93104–93139. DOI: 10.1109/ACCESS.2022.3204051

Chapter 11
Secure and Ethically Aligned AI Solutions for Cybersecurity and Threat Detection

Amrutha Kolhar
http://orcid.org/0009-0001-4940-3172
Karnatak University, Dharwad, India

Sridevi
http://orcid.org/0000-0002-9768-1599
Karnatak University, Dharwad, India

ABSTRACT

This paper explores the integration of artificial intelligence (AI), including machine learning and deep learning, to enhance cybersecurity threat detection and response. It addresses the critical need for these advanced solutions to be ethically aligned, ensuring fairness, transparency, and accountability. The study examines both the technical capabilities of AI in malware analysis and anomaly detection, and the ethical challenges such as bias and data privacy. By proposing a governance framework for responsible deployment, this research aims to bridge the gap between technological innovation and ethical responsibility, fostering trust in AI-driven cybersecurity systems

DOI: 10.4018/979-8-3373-6038-6.ch011

1. INTRODUCTION

The contemporary cyber space is defined by stiff and asymmetric arms race, whereby organized crime and government-sponsored malicious operations have proven to be a greater and more complex threat to the cyber space than traditional security technologies that are rule-based. It has been demonstrated that a paradigm shift has been reached in an environment where proactive and predictive cyber resilience should be applied instead of defensive methods, and artificial intelligence (AI) and machine learning (ML) have become inevitable technological pillars. The use of AI in other areas including malware, phishing, network intrusion detection among others is not only a much-needed upgrade to the existing cybersecurity infrastructure, but also a necessity. Nevertheless, it is a difficult twofold challenge to have this heavy technological engine incorporated into the very fabric of our security: the AI engines that are our main line of defence need to be proven to be secure themselves and work in a well-defined framework of moral principles. The erosion of responsibility and trust is due to the presence of a crisis of explainability because complex deep learning models are opaque and as such security analysts cannot understand the logic behind a danger which has been brought to their attention. Consequently, the task in pursuit of the technologically advanced solutions of AI cannot be separated anymore due to the need to align it with the ethical considerations. Pyrrhic victory is an artificial intelligence system that is non-transparent, unresponsible, and/or discriminatory. This may lead to a highly surveilled system, and undermine the values of the society that it is supposed to be safeguarding. This work attempts to deal with this critical point by outlining the type of engineering of safe, manipulation-resistant AI systems and suggesting an extensive system of governance of their ethical use. We are building the future in which AI can enhance our digital safety, but this will be done in a manner that is just, trustworthy, and capable of being instituted as a source of human dignity and rights with the integration of technical protection with sustainability values of transparency, equity and human control (Sissodia et al., 2025; Gundoor, 2024; Jana et al., 2024).

1.1 Background and Motivation

The growing spectrum of technological advancement of cyber threats, including AI-driven malware and sophisticated phishing behaviors, requires a technological shift in the defense systems. Artificial intelligence, in its turn, has become a significant point of convergence in the area of cybersecurity, as the ability to process large amounts of data, detect indicators and signs of anomalies, and execute threat response activities have been well beyond the human operator capabilities. Threat-seeking, predicting attack vectors, and defense of networks can be more actively used to establish a more resilient digital environment using the power of AI. Nevertheless, the concept of AI application in cybersecurity is a two-sided problem. An automated arms race is a phenomenon where evil actors deploy the very power AI is meant to be used as a weapon. Moreover, since these systems tend to be highly autonomous, they have to access confidential information, which casts significant security and ethical doubts. Prejudice within algorithms Fairness and accountability when a threat detection model targets a group of network activity or users unfairly, is taken very seriously. Its long-term aim is to establish smart cybersecurity products that will not only be effective in fighting the threats, but also be responsible and responsible towards the communities they are meant to offer security, and moral values will be kept abreast (Kumar, 2023; Sharma, 2024).

1.2 Research Gaps and Contributions

However, despite recognition of these problems, a huge literature gap exists. The current literature would rather address technical security (e.g., adversarial hardening), and ethical governance of it (e.g., fairness, explainability) separately. It lacks coherent frameworks that can properly integrate both adversarial resilience as well as apply the ethical principles to the AI lifecycle to cyberspace. Also, the proposed models of governance are not actual and concrete accountability mechanisms of frequent-paced Security Operations Centers (SOCs).

The chapter also tries to address such gaps by adding the following important details:

- An Integrated Framework: With this proposal, we introduce a novel framework of the Secure and Ethical AI in Cybersecurity that both technically guards AI models against evasion and poisoning attacks and organizations such fairness, transparency, and accountability by incorporating governance layers within the structure.
- Critical Analysis and Synthesis: We critically evaluate the real AI implementation in the area of cybersecurity not only by discussing the apparent successes but also describe its failures and the possibility of its implementation on a large level (Gundoor & Sridevi, 2024; George, 2024).

2 AI IN CYBERSECURITY: CURRENT LANDSCAPE

2.1 Machine Learning for Threat Detection

- **Supervised Learning of Known Threats:** The foundation of known cyber threat detectors is supervised machine learning. Large, labeled datasets of samples of known malicious code, network packets, and user behaviors are used to train models. Because these models recognize the patterns and hallmarks of known threats, like specific malware families or SQL injections, they are able to detect similar assaults in previously unseen new data. This reduces the workload for human analysts and is highly helpful in automating the detection of widespread known dangers. Its inability to identify novel threats that do not fit into its training data and require constant retraining with fresh labels is, however, its biggest flaw.
- **Unsupervised Learning to Identify Abnormalities:** Unsupervised Learning addresses the blind spot of supervised models, which is the inability to anticipate new threats. It operates by training a typical model of typical system behavior, such as typical user login times or network traffic flows. Then, it indicates a significant departure from this base as a potential anomaly. It is crucial for detecting advanced persistent attacks (APTs), insider threats, and zero-day exploits that lack a signature. Even though it is incredibly effective at discovering unknowns, it has a high false positive rate because not all abnormalities are harmful, therefore analyst tweaking and evaluation are crucial.
- **Behavioral Analytics and UEBA:** UEBA, or User and Entity Behavior Analytics, is predicated on the application of machine learning (ML) to gradually discover the typical behavior of hosts, users, and applications. It creates dynamic profiles to find the presence of minor, unusual activity that might be a leakage point instead of looking through pre-defined harmful signatures. For example, if a user account suddenly has access to crucial files at an unusual time or in a foreign country, UEBA will view the account as high-risk. It provides a more contextual and proactive security level by effectively detecting insider threats, the misuse of credentials that have been stolen, and lateral network flow that other approaches could overlook.
- **A feature engineering imperative:** Feature engineering, which is the process of filtering and transforming raw data into useful inputs, is the key to the capacity of any machine learning model to identify risks. In the case of cybersecurity, it is the establishment of features with cloud telemetry, endpoint data (process lineage, API calls) and network logs (packet size, packet frequency). Features that let the model distinguish between harmful and benign

behavior with high precision are considered good features. To ensure that the model focuses on the most pertinent signals, this stage requires deep domain expertise because poor features might result in models that are noisy, evasive, or wrong. Nnaka, K. I.et al (2025)

2.1.1 Practical Integration: The SOC Analyst's Workflow

In order to pass the bridge between the theoretical concept and practice, it is essential to understand how these ML approaches can be incorporated into the working process of Security Operations Center (SOC). The next example is a common workflow of investigating a network intrusion alert, which presents the cooperation of human analysts and ML systems.

Figure 1. Simplified ML-enhanced SOC workflow for a network intrusion alert

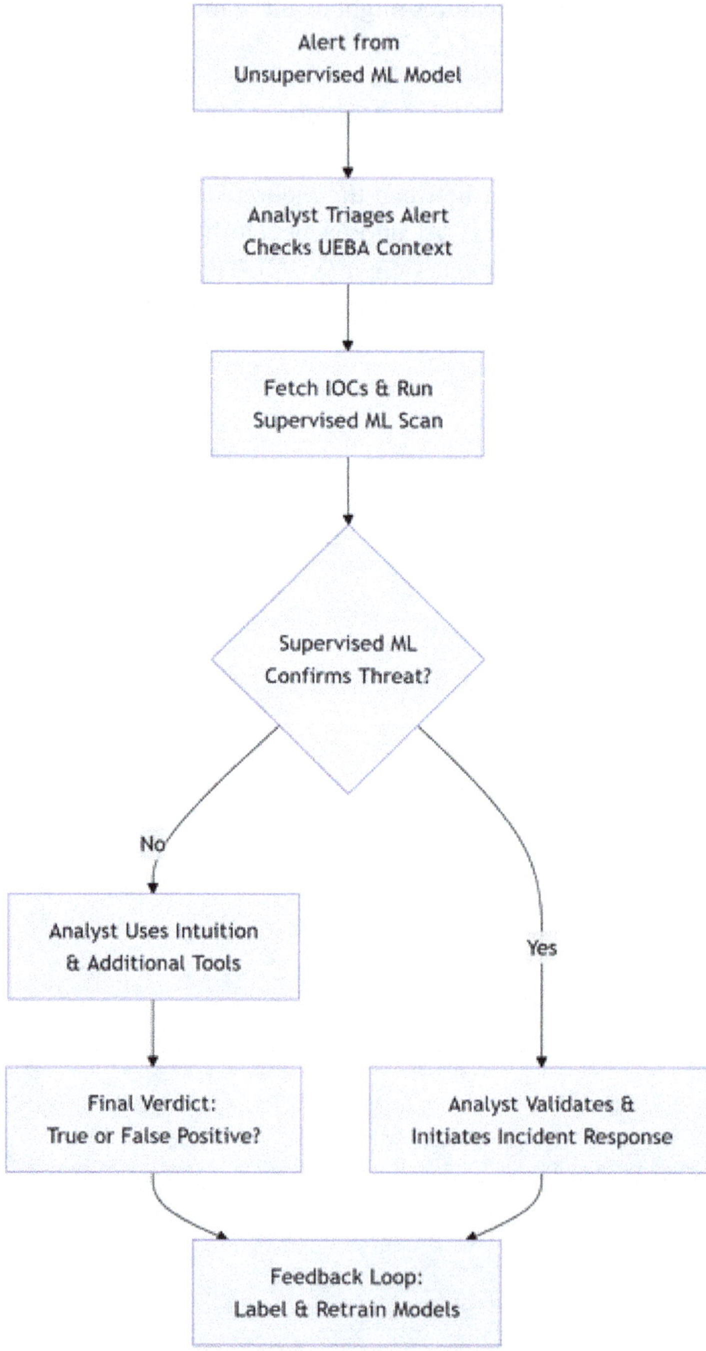

1. **Generation of Alerts (The "Spark"):** This is an Unsupervised Learning model that is constantly tracking the network traffic, and which identifies a large deviation with the established baseline of normalcy in a particular server. As an example, the server is attempting outgoing connections to a foreign IP address which is not known to it and is in a different country and at 3:00 AM on the local time, which is generally a slow time of the day. This aberration creates an alert of high priority and is realized to the SOC analyst dashboard.
    - Practical Impact: This step illustrates the usefulness of unsupervised learning in identifying new attacks or suspicious activity that does not have an existing signature, a zero-day exploit or a data exfiltration attempt.
2. **First Triage and Situation (The Investigation):** The alert is issued to the SOC analyst. The missing vital context the service account to which such connections are drawn is automatically provided by the UEBA (User and Entity Behavior Analytics) system which simply communicates with internal databases and has not been connected to external IPs previously. This environment sends a warning signal to the mind of an analyst immediately.
    - **Practical Impact:** UEBA would push the notification of the occurrence of an anomaly to the possible insider threat or to a damaged account, which directs the research of the investigator.
3. **Threat Enrichment and Confirmation (The "Validation"):** To receive more evidence, the analyst inputs the suspicious external IP address and the file hashes associated with the process connecting to the external IP address into a series of Supervised Learning models. These models have been trained using huge amounts of known malware and malignant domains..
    - One of the models would provide 95 percent certainty that the IP belongs to a recognizable command-and-control (C2) server.
    - The remaining would scan the file hashing and flag as similar with the Mirai botnet malware.
    - Practical Impact: Supervised learning provides rapid automated verification through identifying the anomaly against the known threat intelligence and converting a suspicion into a high confidence discovery.
4. **Human Decision and Response (The "Action):** Considering this multi-layered evidence, including unsupervised anomaly, the UEBA context, and the supervised ML classification, the analyst is safe in claiming that it is a real-life positive security event. They then start the response playbook: isolating the affected server and blocking the rogue IP on the firewall and informing the incident response team to do forensic analysis and eradication.

- Practical Impact: Here is where the Human-in-the-Loop (HITL) role is needed. The analyst organizes data of various AI tools and makes the vital decision using experience and intuition.

5. **Feedback Loop (The Learning):** Once the incident is resolved the analyst closes the alert in the SIEM system indicating a True Positive - Malware C2 Communication. Such labeled data entry is re-entered to the ML training pipelines.
    - The malicious IP and file hash is a new confirmed example that the supervised learning models can now learn.
    - The unsupervised learning model can slightly modify its baseline of the normal of that server and become more accurate in the future.
    - Practical Impact: The continuous improvement of the AI systems to decrease false positives and increase their detection is a closed feedback loop necessary. Pardhi, N et al (2025) Thapaliya, S. et al (2025).

Providing Evidence of Enhanced Results:

With these ML methods embedded into the working process, the SOC can be improved by measuring the following:

Fastest Mean Time to Detect (MTTD): Untrained ML will identify the anomaly in near real time and is much faster than the time required to update the signatures.

- Reduce False Positives: UEBA context alongside supervised ML validation does not allow the analyst to spend time on non-malicious anomalies (e.g., a misconfigured application).
- Higher Confidence Response: The overlaid evidence enables the analyst to be decisive, lowering the "Mean Time to Respond (MTTR) and preventing as much damage as possible.

This hands-on practice shows that AI in cybersecurity cannot be a magic bullet but a group of effective tools that when applied to a properly outlined process and within expert human guidance would result in a more resilient and effective security posture (Gundoor, 2024; Wang, 2025).

2.2 Deep Learning in Malware Analysis

- **Automated Raw Data Processing for Feature Extraction:** Traditional machine learning requires security professionals to manually define malware features (characteristics), which takes time and misses novel trends. The advantage of deep learning is that it automatically finds these properties on the raw data, such as the bytes of an assembly code, binary, or API call sequence. By doing this, human bias and engineering overhead are avoided, and the model is able to detect and expose intricate, nuanced harmful signs that manual analysis is unable to detect. This is essential for the detection of novel, obfuscated malware families that do not correspond to any known, manually-written family, making detection more reliable and effective.

- **Convolutional Neural Networks (CNNs) for Static Analysis:** CNNs are excellent at processing images; they are used to process malware by interpreting binary files as images. Each data bit value represents a pixel intensity, and the uncoded stream of bits is transformed into a grayscale image. The CNN then scans these CNN images of malware to provide hierarchical representations of texture and structure that distinguish between files that are harmful and those that are not. Because it can identify visual similarities across malware variants that belong to the same family even if they were packaged or minimally modified without ever running the code this method works well for static analysis.
- **Recurrent Neural Networks (RNNs):** In dynamic analysis scenarios that track malware behavior while it runs, RNNs and their more sophisticated variants, such as LSTMs (Long Short-Term Memory), are advised. They work with sequential data, such as time series of a program's calls to an API. This sequence and context allow the RNN to learn the malware behavior story, including how it first changes registry keys before retrieving data. This view of behavioral patterns allows for very accurate identification of hostile intent and captures the reasoning behind an attack rather than just its constituent parts.
- **Protecting against malicious software Obfuscation and Polymorphism:** To gain signature algorithms, malware developers obfuscate, polymorphize, and metamorphize their code so that it is unique each time they infect a computer. These techniques do not work with deep learning models, particularly CNNs and autoencoders. Instead of learning straightforward instructions that can easily change, they learn the semantic properties of the malware family, which are fundamental and unalterable on the surface. A polymorphic virus may alter its surface code, but its high-level code pattern and underlying intent will not change. Despite this, the deep learning model can identify the virus, which is already a significant gain over outdated, fixed detection techniques (Anwar et al., 2025).

2.2.1 Practical Implementation: From Malware Binary to CNN Classification

To bridge the gap between concept and implementation, let's walk through the step-by-step process of how a Convolutional Neural Network (CNN) is used for static malware analysis in a real-world system.

Figure 2. CNN-based malware detection pipeline

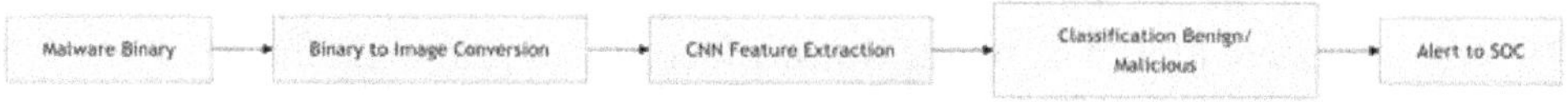

Technical Workflow: Step-by-Step:

1. **Binary to Image Conversion:**
   - Input: An uncompiled binary executable program (e.g.,.exe).
   - Process: The binary is read in the form of a stream of 8-bit unsigned integers (values between 0 and 255). This stream is subsequently reconstructed into an array of 2D (a matrix). The dimensions may be fixed (i.e. 256x256) by truncating or padding the file. The value in each of the matrix is then considered as a pixel value with 0 being black and 255 being white thus producing a grayscale image.
   - Software Engineering consideration: This pre-processing operation is very scalable and it can be automated as part of a data pipeline. When the files are very large, such standardizing methods as taking the first N bytes or down sampling the image are applied to the CNN.
2. **Feature Extraction via CNN:**
   - The image is fed into the CNN. The first layers are automated feature engineers which identify low-level features such as corners and edges with their filters (kernels).
   - These lower-level features are then pooled to higher-level features that define malware features, including individual textures or structures that are associated with packed code or encrypted or malicious code patterns.
   - Connection to Software engineering: It is the most important benefit of this automated feature extraction compared to the traditional ML. It allows features (such as file entropy or section count) to be specified manually by security experts, which saves on development time and even possible human bias.

3.Classification: The patient is an elderly Caucasian man, 78 years old. Classification: The patient is an elderly Caucasian male, aged 78.

- The last and flattened CNN features are fed to fully connected layers which do the classification (e.g., Malicious vs. Benign).
- Output is a probability score (e.g. 98% confidence of malware). In case of a score over a specified threshold, an alarm is raised and dispatched to the SOC dashboard to be reviewed by the analyst.
- Quantitative Impact and Deployment Metrics:

According to a study conducted by Sridevi and Tukkappa K Gundoor (2025) on their ResNet50MalClassifier, a deep CNN gave a 98.5% detection accuracy on a diverse dataset of portable executable (PE) malware, by far exceeding the traditional signature-based approaches, which gave only an 85% detection rate on the samples. Where it is used in production, the system is capable of processing thousands of files per hour and gives it a scalable first line of defense. The polymorphic variants of a known malware family can be identified by the model up to 95% even without the use of new signatures since the model can identify visual similarities (Gundoor & Sridevi, 2024).

2.2.2 Implementing an RNN for Behavioral Analysis

Recurrent Neural Networks (RNNs), specifically LSTMs are employed to predict sequential behavior in terms of dynamic analysis.

Practical Pipeline in a SOC:

- Data Collection: The sandboxed environment executes the file and records all the system calls, API calls, and network activities in the form of a time-sorted sequence.
- Sequence Preprocessing: sequence of actions (e.g., ["WriteRegistry"] "CreateFile")) is transformed to numerical vectors (embeddings).
- LSTM Processing: This sequence gets handled by the LSTM, which is able to remember long-range dependencies. An example is that it can know that a pattern whereby it follows a sequence of events such as ConnectToIP and then much later follows it with WriteSensitiveFile is highly suspicious, although such events may be separated by hundreds of other harmless activities.
- Classification: A final state of the LSTM is used to determine the whole behavioral sequence as malicious or benign (Mishra et al., 2025).

Pseudocode Snippet for LSTM-based Classifier:

```
# Pseudocode for illustrative purposes
from tensorflow.keras.models import Sequential
from tensorflow.keras.layers import LSTM, Dense, Embedding
# Model Definition
model = Sequential()
model.add(Embedding(input_dim=total_unique_apis, output_
dim=128))
model.add(LSTM(128, return_sequences=False)) # Process se-
quence and output a single vector
model.add(Dense(64, activation='relu'))
model.add(Dense(1, activation='sigmoid')) # Output: proba-
bility of malice
model.compile(loss='binary_crossentropy', optimizer='adam',
metrics=['accuracy'])
# Training on sequences of API calls
model.fit(sequences_of_api_calls, labels, epochs=10, valida-
tion_split=0.2)
```

Handling Adversarial Scenarios:

- **Evasion**: Malware will do its best to escape detection by making unnecessary API calls or making malicious actions wait.
- **Practical Countermeasures**: Adversarial training hardens the models and trains them to deal with instances including evasion methods. More importantly, the decision taken by the LSTM, together with other signals (e.g., that provided by the CNN on the static analysis), can be used to generate a stronger, multi-layered defense which is more difficult to break (Kolhar & Sridevi, 2025).

2.3 NLP for Phishing and Social Engineering Defense

- **Email Header and Body Analysis:** To identify minor indications of phishing, natural language processing (NLP) algorithms thoroughly examine email headers and body text. They seek spoofing in the address of the sender (e.g., support name: amaz0n.com), analyze the correspondence of the display name and the actual email, and search suspicious words and statements that create a sense of urgency. NLP has the ability to discern communications that are duplicative yet deviated communications with official business communication based on their grammar, tone, and semantic meaning. This enables it to put such messages under further scrutiny or on automatic quarantine before it finds its way into the mailbox of a user.

- URL and Link Analysis: NLP will specify web addresses and analyze them to examine their authenticity as well as make comparisons with blacklists. It searches intentional misspelling errors of household brands in the domain name (what is known as typo squatting), examines the path structure of deceptive keywords and evaluates the overall readability and relevance of the link. To understand whether the text and the purpose of the landing page is in line with the assertions of the email or it is a fraudulent login page designed to steal credentials, NLP may also be used alongside systems to safely crawl the page that needs to be analyzed.
- **Brand Impersonation and Identity Deception Detection:** Natural language processing (NLP) models are trained to identify the distinct linguistic patterns and brand names used in formal messages of business organizations like shipping agencies, computer companies, and banks. They seek cases of unlicensed use of trademarked language, logos and brand names. Although an email may contain no malicious links or attachments, it is still possible to identify advanced impersonation attacks using a system that compares incoming email to a learned base of authentic corporate message. This will enable the user to prevent authoritative-looking communication, which is used alone to trick the user into committing damaging acts.
- **Analysis of Sentiment and Psychological Tone**: Psychological manipulation is one of the primary elements of phishing attacks. NLP is excellent at identifying these strategies through tone and sentiment analysis. It recognizes verbal indicators of fear ("Unauthorized login detected!"), excessive generosity ("You've won a prize!"), urgency ("Your account will be closed!"), and phony authority ("This is the IT Department."). NLP models can rate an email's probability of being a social engineering attack by measuring these emotional triggers. This allows them to prioritize messages that are intended to evade a user's rational judgment and elicit an impulsive, dangerous response (Rahman et al., 2025).

2.3.1 Operational NLP Pipeline for Email Security

An NLP phishing defense system is integrated into the email gateway. The following describes the operational workflow for processing a live email stream.

Figure 3. NLP phishing detection pipeline

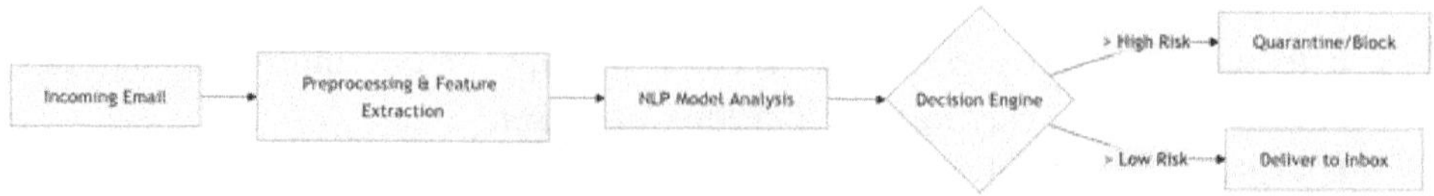

Step-by-Step Technical Workflow:

1. **Preprocessing & Feature Extraction:**
   - **Text Cleaning:** The email's header, subject, and body text are extracted. HTML tags are removed, and text is converted to lowercase.
   - **Tokenization:** The text is split into individual words or tokens.
   - **Feature Vectorization:** The tokens are converted into a numerical format that the model can understand. This can be done via:
     - **Bag-of-Words (BoW) or TF-IDF:** Simpler models that count word frequencies.
     - **Word Embeddings (e.g., Word2Vec, GloVe):** Dense vector representations that capture semantic meaning (e.g., "password" is closer to "login" than "shoe").
     - **Contextual Embeddings (e.g., BERT):** State-of-the-art models that generate different embeddings for the same word based on its context in the sentence.
2. **NLP Model Analysis:**
   - The feature vector is fed into a classification model (e.g., a Naive Bayes classifier for simpler systems, or a deep learning model like a Transformer for advanced ones).
   - The model analyzes the features based on its training, evaluating the likelihood of phishing based on learned patterns of urgency, sender impersonation, and malicious intent.
3. **Decision Engine & Action:**
   - The model outputs a phishing probability score (e.g., 0.92). A rules-based decision engine then acts:
     - **Score > 0.9:** Quarantine email immediately.
     - **Score 0.7 - 0.9:** Send to "Junk/Spam" folder.
     - **Score < 0.7:** Deliver to inbox.

Quantitative Impact and Deployment Metrics:

- A large-scale deployment by a cloud email security provider reported that their NLP-based filters reduced user click-through rates on phishing emails by over 99.5%, compared to a baseline of traditional rule-based filters alone.
- In a corporate environment, such a system can automatically filter over 95% of phishing attempts before they reach the user's primary inbox, drastically reducing the social engineering attack surface. The system can process millions of emails per hour with an average latency of less than 500 milliseconds per email, meeting the performance requirements for real-time communication (Gundoor, 2025).

2.3.2 Mitigating Adversarial Attacks on NLP Models

As phishers adapt, they use adversarial techniques to bypass NLP filters.

- **Adversarial Technique:** Using homoglyphs (e.g., paypa1.com instead of paypal.com) or adding “neutral” text to dilute malicious features.
- **Practical Mitigation Strategies:**

1. **Data Augmentation & Retraining:** The model is continuously retrained on new phishing examples that include these adversarial tactics. This is often done in a continuous integration pipeline where new data is automatically sampled, labeled, and used to fine-tune the model weekly or even daily.
2. **Ensemble Methods:** Using multiple models that analyze different aspects (e.g., one model for text, one for the URL, one for the header) makes it harder for a single adversarial change to fool the entire system.
3. **Anomaly Detection:** An additional model can flag emails with a high proportion of rare characters or unusual structural elements for further scrutiny, even if the main NLP classifier gives a low score (Jagli, 2024).

3 SECURITY CHALLENGES IN AI-DRIVEN CYBERSECURITY

- **Adversarial assaults on AI Models:** Specialized assaults can target AI models directly. Attackers use subtle manipulation of input data to trick the model in adversarial attacks. For example, they can trick the AI into misidentifying a malicious file as benign by introducing undetectable noise or slightly changing the dangerous code. These evasion attacks are made possible by exploiting the blind spots of the model to allow the threats to evade detection and not raise an alarm. This occurs due to the arms race that compels defenders to make models hard to these complex manipulations that cannot be seen with the naked eye.

- **Data Poisoning and Model Integrity:** The training data that an AI system is trained on is critically important to its security. In a data poisoning attack, an attacker adds highly engineered contaminated data to the training set of the model. Through the learning process with this contaminated data, the model later adopts erroneous patterns. It can be conditioned to associate harmless actions with a specific damaging signature, e.g. This compromises the integrity of the model both internally and externally and causes systemic and long-term problems which are extremely difficult to detect and remedy once in place.
- **Explainability and the Black Box Problem:** Many advanced types of AI models, particularly deep learning models, are black boxes, which is why it is difficult to understand how they reached a specific decision. This is an important operational hindrance in cybersecurity because it cannot be explained. Given what is known as the why, security analysts need to understand the reasoning behind an alert generated by an AI so that they can respond accordingly when investigating the matter. Since teams struggle to decide whether an alert represents a true positive or a weird false positive, a black box model compromises confidence and makes operations of responding more complex, which may result in the dismissal of actual threats.
- **Privacy and Bias in Training Data:** AI models applied in cybersecurity often require being trained on large amounts of data, some of which include sensitive user information, which is a serious privacy concern. Also, the model will also adopt and possibly even intensify existing biases in case the training data is non-representative. As an example, the actions of specific user groups or geographical locations can be unproportionately labeled as malicious (Kolhar & Sridevi, 2025).

4. ETHICAL CONSIDERATIONS IN AI FOR CYBERSECURITY

The integration of AI into cybersecurity raises deep ethical issues that extend beyond the mere technological effectiveness. Algorithms being biased towards certain ideas is one of the biggest problems, in which algorithms being trained on past or non-representative data strengthen their initial perceptions. This may result in unjustified penalties and loss of trust by discriminatory monitoring like incorrect labelling of behaviors by specific user groups or geographical locationThis collection and processing of personal data must be highly controlled to prevent the so-called creep of functions the repurposing of data originally intended to be used in security. Ultimately, such challenges require a system founded on accountability, equity and transparency. The same tools which are designed to protect us also risk to create an environment of bigotry, immunity, and low privacy without deliberate moral boundaries (Sharma, 2025).

4.1 Bias and Fairness in Threat Detection

A system that produces systematically inequitable outcomes, which disproportionately target or filter out threats belonging to specific groups will be considered biased in AI-based threat detection. This bias is often the source of the training data. The model will get to know how to associate malice with attributes in case the attacks by certain user group or geographic area make up the majority of past data. Traffic in one branch of an office of a particular country e.g. may be brought to prominence simply because it was over-represented in a prior attack log but not necessarily because it is a more dangerous traffic. This results in a high number of false positives for that group, squandering resources and fostering discrimination. Blind spots are also produced because threats from underrepresented sources could go unnoticed. In order to guarantee fair and accurate protection for the entire business, it is necessary to actively identify and mitigate these biases using strategies like diverse data sampling, fairness-aware algorithms, and ongoing monitoring of model outputs across all segments.

Figure 4. The cycle of bias in threat detection

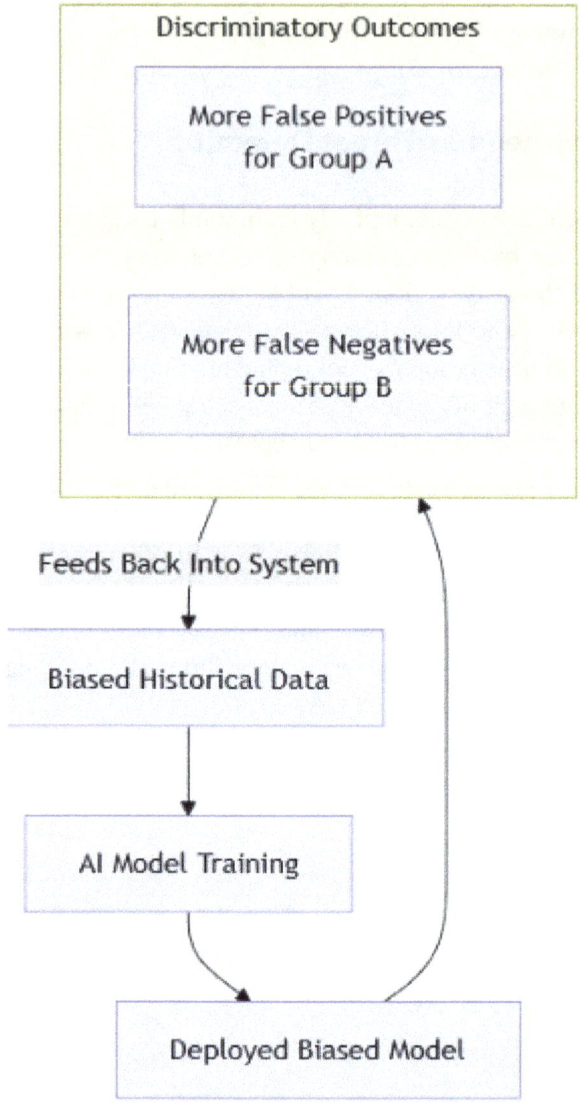

This flowchart visualizes the self-reinforcing cycle of bias in AI-driven threat detection.

- Biased Historical Data: Biased historical data is where the cycle starts. The data presented here is not indicative of the actual environment. For instance, because of previous targeted operations, it may include:

- More assault examples from a single geographic area.
- Logs that underrepresent activity from some departments (like HR) and represent activity from others (like engineering).
- Labels created by humans that carry prejudices, whether intentional or unintentional.

- **Model Training (AI Model Training):** An AI model is trained using this skewed data. All of the data's patterns, including skewed correlations, are learned by the model. It discovers that specific IP address ranges, user behaviors, or linguistic patterns are "high-risk," not because they are malicious per such, but rather because the skewed dataset linked them to malice.
- **Deployment (Deployed Biased Model):** Predictions are made using fresh, real-world data by the now-trained and implemented model. It functions as a Deployed Biased Model since it was trained on biased data. All incoming network traffic, user actions, and emails are subject to its learnt, distorted rules.
- **Outcomes (Discriminatory Outcomes):** The model's bias manifests in two primary types of discriminatory outcomes:
    - More False Positives for Group A: The model incorrectly labels as harmful lawful activity from a particular group (such as users from a given region). This results in a prejudiced experience by causing pointless alerts, locked accounts, and wasted analyst time.
    - The model may simultaneously under-flag activity from other groups that were under-represented in the training data, resulting in more False Negatives for Group B. As a result, actual attacks from these sources can go unnoticed, creating severe blind spots (Sridevi & Kolhar, 2025).

Breaking the Cycle: Interventions are required in multiple phases to ensure there is no inequality: training datasets should be balanced, algorithmic tools to find and eliminate bias in the training process, and to verify the model performance differences among groups, the feedback loop must not be allowed to worsen the situation.

4.2 Privacy-Preserving AI Techniques

Figure 5. A taxonomy of privacy-preserving AI techniques

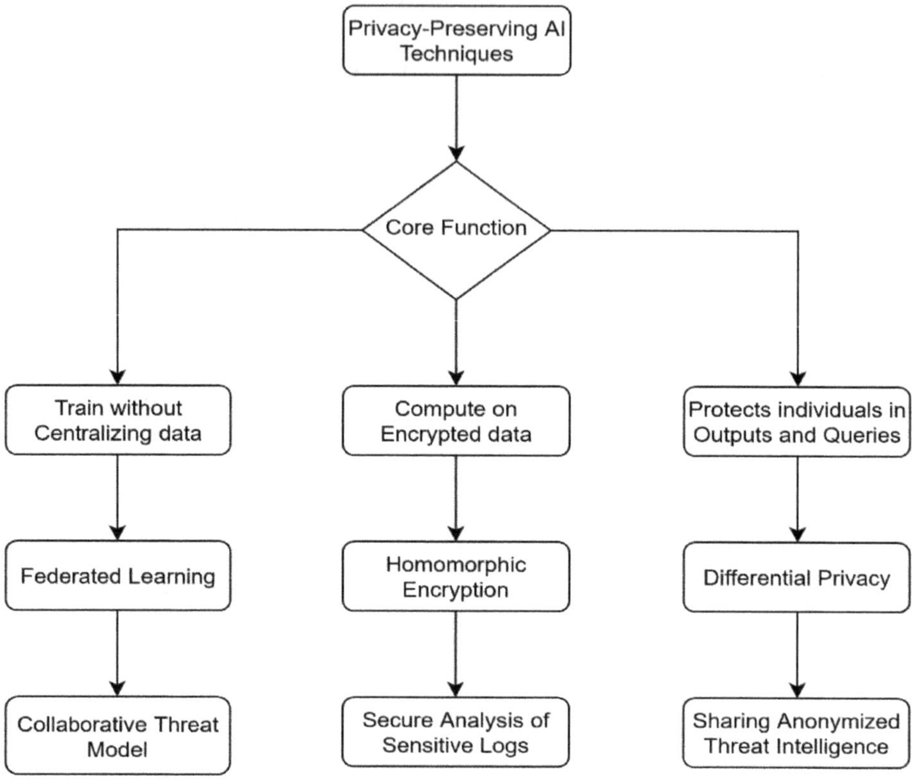

This diagram provides a structured overview of the three primary privacy-preserving AI techniques, linking their core function to a practical cybersecurity application.

- **The diagram starts with the main objective**: AI Techniques That Protect Privacy. All of these techniques allow for the extraction of insights from data while maintaining the privacy of the people or organizations that are represented in it. Fundamental Operations (The "How"): Three primary strategic functions are used to classify the techniques.
  - Train without Centralizing Data: By doing this, the privacy risk associated with storing sensitive data in one place is avoided

- Protect People in Outputs & Queries: This strategy focuses on making sure that the analysis's findings cannot be reverse-engineered to reveal personal data (Scrivano, 2025).

- **Specific Techniques (The "What"):** Each core function is realized by a specific, well-known technique:
  - The "decentralized training" function is carried out by Federated Learning. The model is supplied to the data sources (e.g., user devices, edge servers) rather than to a central server. Only the model updates (weights/gradients) are transmitted back and averaged to enhance the global model once local models have been trained on-device. This preserves local storage and the privacy of raw user data.
  - A feature of homomorphic encryption is "computation on encrypted data." Encrypted data is maintained throughout the processing pipeline. This ciphertext can be subjected to computations by an AI model, and the final encrypted result that is decoded is identical to the outcome of the same operations on the plaintext. For outsourcing analysis to unreliable cloud settings, this is perfect.
  - Differential privacy offers mathematical assurances on output privacy. It functions by adding precisely measured amounts of statistical noise to data or query output. While reliable aggregate patterns can still be learned, this makes it hard to say for sure whether any particular person's data was included in the dataset (Olafuyi, 2023).
- **Cybersecurity Applications (The "Why"):** The diagram finally connects each technique to a concrete use case:
  - A Collaborative Threat Model is made possible by Federated Learning. Without ever exposing their internal data or proprietary network logs, several businesses can work together to train a better malware detection model by sharing what their local models have learnt.
  - Sensitive log analysis can be done securely thanks to homomorphic encryption. A government organization might encrypt its logs and forward them to an outside analytics company. Without ever being able to decrypt or view the sensitive data underneath, the company may use its AI models to identify hazards straight on the encrypted logs.
  - Differential privacy makes it easier to share threat intelligence that has been anonymized. Differential privacy can be employed when sharing attack patterns or indicators of compromise (IoCs) with other companies. This ensures that the shared data cannot be used to infer other sensitive information about the targeted organization or be linked back to the original victim (Çakır, 2024).

4.3 Regulatory and Compliance Frameworks (GDPR, AI Act)

- **General Data Protection Regulation:** The General Data Protection Regulation, sometimes known as the GDPR, is a comprehensive EU statute that has radically changed the global data privacy scene. Its principles place stringent requirements on any AI system that handles the personal data of EU individuals, even if it is not only an AI policy. Its use in artificial intelligence is based on the ideals of lawfulness, fairness, and transparency. Legal justification must be provided for AI choices, and data subjects must be able to see how their data is processed. Importantly, the GDPR gives people the "Right to Explanation," which allows them to contest decisions made by automated systems, including artificial intelligence, and request meaningful human participation., which requires enterprises to show compliance through documentation and strong data security measures, and data minimization and purpose limitation, which states AI systems should only use the bare minimum of personal data required for a clear, defined purpose.
- **EU Artificial Intelligence Act (AI Act)**: The EU AI Act, which uses a risk-based approach to regulate AI systems according to their potential for harm, is the first comprehensive horizontal legal framework for AI in history. It divides uses of AI into four different risk categories. Applications that pose unacceptable risk, such as government social scoring, are prohibited. Prior to and following market placement, high-risk AI systems, which include thorough risk assessments, superior datasets, thorough documentation, human oversight, and high levels of accuracy and robustness. Chatbots and other limited risk AI are subject to certain disclosure requirements; users must be informed that they are communicating with an AI. Lastly, even though voluntary sets of behavior are encouraged, Minimal Risk AI like AI-powered spam filter is largely unregulated. The AI Act directly relates to cybersecurity by mandating that the high-risk AI systems be resistant to efforts by the bad actors to alter their usage or operation.
- Interplay and Global Impact: AI Act and GDPR collaborate in order to create a powerful regulatory landscape in the EU. The AI Act regulates the AI systems themselves, whereas GDPR regulates the data that is supplied into them. For example, they both require transparency and robustness, which frequently overlap and support one another. Similar to the "Brussels Effect," which occurs when multinational corporations adopt these strict standards as a global baseline to streamline operations, these frameworks have a large global impact. This means that in order for cybersecurity AI systems to meet both the GDPR's data protection principles and the AI Act's cybersecurity resilience criteria, they must be built with Privacy-by-Design and Fairness-

by-Design, be technically interpretable, and be resilient to adversarial attacks (Adewale & Samuel, 2024).

4.4 Pipeline for Secure and Ethical AI Model Development

Figure 6. Pipeline for secure and ethical AI model development

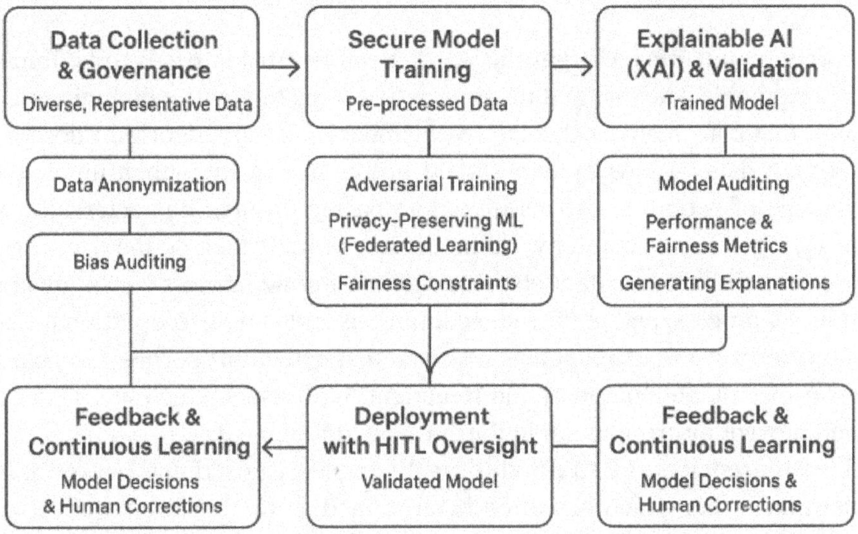

The following diagram represents a design cycle of the proposed development of the Secure and Ethical AI in Cybersecurity with a focus on the continuous lifecycle. The process will start with Data Collection & Governance, in which various and representative data is curated and processed beforehand with anonymization and bias auditing to create a just and private basis. This verified data is then inputted into the Secure Model Training stage where the model is defended against manipulation by adversarial training, privacy protecting measures such as federated learning, and algorithmic fairness policies. The trained model is then carefully Explainable AI (XAI) & Validated with the trained model being audited to check its performance, biased results and functions to give an explanation to the decisions it makes. After being validated, the model will proceed to Deployment with HITL (Human-in-the-Loop) Oversight, where critical alerts or low-confidence decisions in the real world are checked by a human expert. Lastly, the results of this deployment, such as model choices and human correction, are re-invested into the system as Feedback

Continuous Learning, and the model is able to use new data and human feedback to learn and evolve over time, and respond to the changing threat (Sridevi & Kolhar, 2025; Toya, 2025).

5. PROPOSED FRAMEWORK FOR SECURE AND ETHICAL AI IN CYBERSECURITY

5.1 Trustworthy AI Design Principles

- **Fairness and Bias Mitigation**: AI that can be trusted needs to be impartial and equitable This method requires active steps to identify and minimize biases that can manifest themselves in model outputs, algorithm design and training data. An AI system should not create or strengthen unfair disadvantage of people or groups of people basing on their characteristics, such as age, gender, or ethnicity. Some of the methods include the use of representative and diverse datasets, placing algorithmic fairness constraints in the training process, and performing continuous audits of disproportional effects. Whether it is the loan applications or threat detection scoring, the goal is to ensure equitable outcomes and treatment to all users which will foster trust and prevent discrimination in the automated judgments.
- **Transparency and Explainability:** When an organisation is not open, it undermines trust which has often been termed as the black box problem. As per this concept, the stakeholders should be in a position to understand AI systems and understand the logic behind their moves. This involves the creation of Explainable AI (XAI) models that can be used to explain the reason behind their outputs. It offers clarity to the users and regulators on when and how they engage with artificial intelligence. This transparency is necessary to accountability since it helps individuals to prove findings, trouble-shoot problems, and to trust the functionality of the system particularly in high stakes industries such as cybersecurity or healthcare.
- **Robustness and Reliability:** A competent and reliable system of AI should include strong, dependable, and secure features. In normal conditions, it is expected to be faithful and accurate. Nevertheless, it is expected to work safely and securely in case of unexpected inputs, aggressive attacks, or evil manipulation. This involves the implementation of mechanisms to prevent data poisoning and evasion attacks, checking models on diverse data, and extensive checking of edge cases. In other words, the system should be strong. Users should believe that the AI cannot fail disastrously nor can it be easily

deceived, ensuring that it delivers consistent things that can fulfill its purpose throughout its entire existence.

- **Accountability and Human Oversight**: An effective accountability system should be in place. Under this concept, individuals and organizations have the responsibility of developing, implementing, and the outcomes of their AI systems. It demands properly defined supervisory processes, including human-in-the-loop (HITL) of any significant decisions. Auditing system processes, measures to counteract negative impacts, and provision of solutions need to be put in place, along with well-defined points of responsibility. Accountability also ensures that there is a human being who will be constantly checking on the actions of the AI to ensure they are in control and have a backup plan in case something goes wrong (Nnamani, 2024).

5.2 Governance and Accountability Mechanisms

Multi-layered systems referred to as AI Governance and Accountability Mechanisms ensure that AI systems are designed and implemented in a proper way. This structure incorporates not only the specialized and internal technical checks but also the external legal environment in general. The External Layer of legal and regulatory frameworks The GDPR and the EU AI Act set obligatory requirements of data privacy, fairness, and openness. Next, to transform the external laws into an internal policy, companies formulate an Internal Governance Layer through their own formulation of their own policies, code of ethics and internal monitoring organizations (e.g. an AI Ethics Board). A certain set of procedures is conducted through an Operational Layer to conduct necessary risk assessment, model audits, and documentation on all AI projects. Finally, the Technical Layer employs the tools that allow explainability, recording decisions and monitoring model drift, which directly involve accountability into the AI system. This multi-layered approach will ensure that the responsibility is a part of the organizational and technology fabric and not an afterthought (Kolhar & Sridevi, 2026).

Figure 7. The multi-layered pillars of AI governance

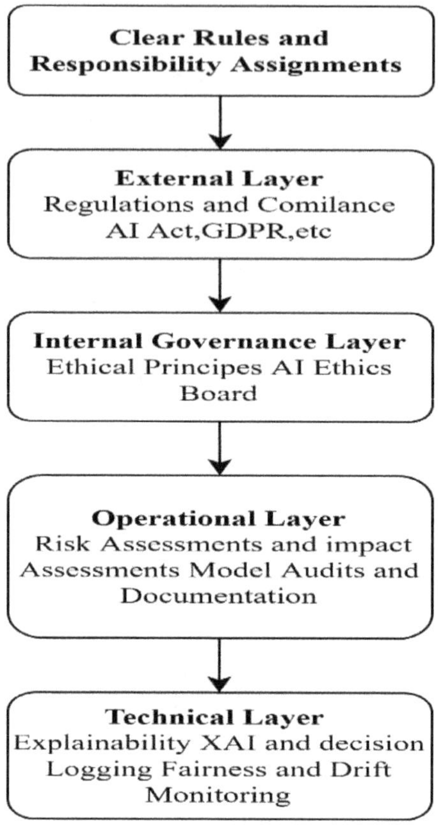

This diagram demonstrates that AI governance is presented as a stack of four mutually dependent layers with the bottom of the structure being the responsibility of human beings.

- External Layer (Regulatory Compliance): This is the upper layer that signifies the external legal environment. It includes the GDPR and EU AI Act. These are uncompromising conditions that develop the minimum requirements of the system. They "set the rules of the road."
- **Internal Governance Layer (Corporate Policy):** This is the level in which the corporation develops its own cultural rules and interpretations of the laws externally. It consists of an AI Ethics Board / group that provides supervision and guidance, and the internal Ethical Principles of the company (like commitment to justice). At this layer, external law is translated into internal policy.

- **Operational Layer (Processes & Controls):** Here, high-level policies are turned into actionable, repeatable processes. This includes concrete activities like:
    - o All new AI projects should be subject to risk and impact assessment so as to identify the risks that may arise.
    - o Model Audits and Documentation: In order to show compliance, and encourage transparency, independent checks and maintenance of comprehensive records (including model cards) are needed (Sridevi & Kolhar, 2026).
- **Technical Layer (Tools & Systems):** This is the implementation layer, in which accountability is integrated into the technology. It entails technical equipment like:
    - o **Explainable AI (XAI) & Audit trails**: Systems that can explain AI choices and can keep audit trails that are not editable.
    - o **Fairness & Drift Monitoring**: Automated systems that continuously examine the model with bias results or deterioration in production.
- **Foundation (Clear Roles and Responsibility):** The entire structure should be supported by the clear assignment of Roles and Responsibility (e.g. Data Owner, Model Owner, AI Ethics Officer). This makes each layer and each process responsible to a particular individual or group, making the overall governance model both feasible and implementable (Sridevi & Kolhar, 2026).

5.3 Human-in-the-Loop Approaches in Points

- **Enhanced Accuracy and Error Correction**: Human-in-the-Loop solutions greatly increase AI accuracy by utilizing human judgment. The AI is a force multiplier since it filters through gigantically huge pieces of data to indicate the most significant or unclear data to be assessed by humans. In the threat detection domain, e.g. the AI may identify a potentially dangerous connection in the network, but a human analyst makes a final judgment depending on the circumstances that the AI lacks. Such collaborative approach provides continuous feedback of corrected data to improve the performance of the model in future and allows to correct AI mistakes in real-time, so that false positives and false negatives are not harmful.
- **Uncertainty and Trust:** HITL has the ability to handle uncertainty cases where the AI is not sure of itself, which can be seen as one of the key strengths of the model. The methodology emphasizes the low-confidence predictions that should be reviewed by humans instead of autonomously making the possibly erroneous judgment. This is necessary when making a poor decision

could have catastrophic consequences, such as the case of responding to an incident of cybersecurity. The approach will strengthen the trust of the AI system because it will ensure that a human expert reviews the most unclear outcomes. A tool that is aware of its weaknesses and when necessary, yields to human judgment is more acceptable and will be used by the users.

- **Strategic Resource Allocation and Workflow Augmentation**: The allocation of human resources is essentially optimized using HITL techniques. Artificial intelligence (AI) frees up human experts to concentrate on difficult, strategic, and creative problem-solving by automating routine, high-volume analysis. For example, at a Security Operations Center (SOC), the AI filters thousands of alarms and only shows analysts the most advanced threats. By preventing alert fatigue, improving job happiness, and ensuring that precious human expertise is deployed where it has the greatest impact, this augmentation of human workflow eventually results in a more successful and efficient human-machine collaboration (Akhtar & Rawol, 2024).

6. CASE STUDIES AND REAL-WORLD APPLICATIONS

Case Study 1: Microsoft AI-Driven Threat Intelligence

Microsoft is able to use its global telemetry of Windows and Azure to drive threat intelligence using AI. The most important of them is phishing defense, in which its models process billions of emails each month to detect malicious sender patterns and links. This can be correlated with such indicators as newly-registered domains and enable such phishing campaigns to be blocked in advance. This scalability system helps to safeguard millions of users against new threats that human analysts could not have been able to monitor manually

Critical Analysis: Microsoft is highly scalable but is based on massive centralized telemetry data which is very problematic to privacy. Such large models can also be black-box and thus not easy to justify the reason behind blocking a particular email, which may contradict regulatory requirements of the right to explanation. Moreover, the model will rely on the variety of the training data, which can be subject to bias in case some of the user groups or areas are over-represented in the telemetry (Kolhar & Sridevi, 2026).

Case Study 2: The Enterprise Immune System of Darktrace

Darktrace applies unsupervised machine learning to model the pattern of life that is unique to each user, device, and network in an organization and creates dynamic baseline of normal behavior. This technique has worked well on a real-life case of insider threat in a manufacturing company whereby its AI was capable of identifying a senior engineer whose device was taking time to exfiltrate confidential CAD files to a rival company. This was a non-malware-based, non-obvious attack bypassing the conventional signature tools that demonstrates the power of AI in detecting something unusual that can be a danger

Critical Analysis: Although an effective tool in identifying new threats, the unsupervised learning mechanism of Darktrace is very sensitive and may produce significant numbers of false positives which will cause fatigue to the analyst. Moreover, the status of the model as the normative activity can be gradually poisoned by the constant attacker who changes his or her behavior subjectively as time advances. The proprietary aspect of the model is another cause of the black box problem and the cost of solution can be quite high making it unaffordable to small and medium-sized enterprises (Jothishri et al., 2024).

Case Study 3: Project Zero and Vulnerability Detection of Google

The Project Zero staff of Google uses machine learning to improve in its detection of zero-day vulnerabilities in software. The AI is trained with the history data of vulnerabilities to discover potentially dangerous patterns of code in new software. It is a force multiplier, as millions of lines of code are scanned by this system to signal the most suspicious areas to be viewed by a human expert. This human-in-the-loop process helps to identify and fix the major security vulnerabilities faster and reinforces the digital ecosystem as a whole.

Critical Analysis: This method is by nature limited to its training data, the known types of vulnerabilities in the past. It might thus have trouble detecting radically new types of security vulnerabilities (unknown unknowns). This is also because the output of the AI is purely subject to further human validation, i.e. it is not a replacement of profound knowledge in security. The computing power required to train and run such models on a large codebase is also high and less-resourceful organisations are therefore less likely to access it.

7. FUTURE DIRECTIONS AND CHALLENGES

- **Granted, there are some specific trends in the future of AI and adversarial AI**: There are several major trends in the future of defensive and offensive AI: To poison or bypass AI defensive implementations, attackers will continue to use AI to develop polymorphic malware, automate complex social engineering attacks, and even perform direct adversarial attacks. The primary issue is to develop powerful AI that will be immune to such manipulations. It is important to build stronger architectures that will detect and filter malicious input without reducing their core detection capabilities, and to come up with new strategies in adversarial training, where models are constantly tested by simulated attacks.

- **Explainable AI (XAI) to Trust and Actionability**: To the future, Transparent AI should dominate black box AI. Security analysts should be aware of the reason why an AI detected a threat in order to properly assess and develop credibility. The first challenge is that the most complex ones like deep neural networks are inherently difficult to comprehend. Striking a balance between explainable and high-accuracy is difficult and there is a risk that providing a simpler explanation may obscure the real and potentially incorrect reasoning behind the model leading to the perception of confidence.
- **Automated Goverance and ethical Compaliance**: The production of automated governance tools is an important direction to move in as regulations such as the AI Act evolve. This is comprised of systems of continuous bias detection, compliance auditing, and real-time enforcement of ethical boundaries. It is not an easy task to translate high level moral ideals into some codified laws that are legally binding. Justice and appropriate human supervision in dynamic danger environments is hard to define. Extremely rigid systems that hamper defensive processes or conversely, systems so complicated that the control of their functioning is inexplicable elicit the possibility of creating more risks and burdens on companies.
- **The Scalability and Environmental Cost**: Developed AI is increasingly more costly in terms of computational power. The future is more effective models and the control of other AIs using AI. One of the key concerns that will influence the overall safety of the digital ecosystem is ensuring that the search of secure AI is only feasible and accessible to all organizations and not only the well-funded ones. This may create the disparity between individuals who are able to afford state of the art protection and those who cannot (Gundoor, 2022; Shree et al., 2024).

8. CONCLUSION

Introducing Artificial Intelligence into cybersecurity is not a technological advancement but a complete paradigm shift. The chapter has proposed that the way to truly have a resilient defense in digital is the inseparable combination of technical resilience and ethical governance. Our suggestion was to have a multi-layered governance structure with adversarial resistant AI models coupled with an integrated pipeline to ensure security and ethics are co-engineered throughout the process. The pragmatic suggestion of the reading is a vivid plan of action among the professionals-a reminder that AI equipment expenditures must be accompanied by mechanisms to provide control, auditing, and human-in-the-loop partnership. In the future, various significant research directions will be important in the development of this field. To begin with, better and practical XAI techniques should be deployed to promote confidence and expedite incident response. Second, homomorphic encryption along with scaling PETs to allow use in the real time will enable collaborative defense to be used in a secure manner. Lastly, automated tools will be required to enable non-stop compliance and bias tracking to ensure that the alignment of ethics is achieved in the dynamic threat environment. Through taking the initiative to meet these technical and moral demands, we can define the future of AI in cybersecurity, which is not only more safe but also fair, reliable, and trustworthy.

REFERENCES

Adewale, S., & Samuel, S. V. (2024). *The intersection of Artificial Intelligence and cybersecurity: Challenges and opportunities*. World Journal Of Advanced Research and Reviews., DOI: 10.30574/wjarr.2024.21.2.0607

Akhtar, Z. B., & Rawol, A. T. (2024). *Harnessing artificial intelligence (AI) for cybersecurity: Challenges, opportunities, risks, future directions. 2*(2), 1485. DOI: 10.59400/cai.v2i2.1485

Anwar, N., Rahaman, M., Widodo, A. M., Sekti, B. A., Erzed, N., Tangkudung, R., Muchlis, M., Yuhefizar, Y., & Budhisantosa, N. (2025). Sustainable Cybersecurity in the AI Era. *Advances in Computational Intelligence and Robotics Book Series*, 603–620. DOI: 10.4018/979-8-3693-8034-5.ch030

Çakır, A. M. (2024). AI Driven Cybersecurity. *Human-Computer Interaction, 8*(1), 119. DOI: 10.62802/jg7gge06

George, S. (2024). Artificial Intelligence-Powered Cybersecurity. *Advances in Information Security, Privacy, and Ethics Book Series*, 247–276. DOI: 10.4018/979-8-3373-1102-9.ch008

Gundoor, T. K. (2022). IoT-Enabled 5G Networks for Secure Communication. In *Information Security Practices for the Internet of Things, 5G, and Next-Generation Wireless Networks* (pp. 1-29). IGI Global.

Gundoor, T. K. (2024). Artificial Intelligence on Knowledge Management and Industry Revolution 4.0.

Gundoor, T. K. (2025). Identifying Nobel Features in Non-Portable Executable Malware Files. *IAENG International Journal of Computer Science, 52*(1).

Gundoor, T. K., & Sridevi, D. (2024). Optimized Feature Selection and classification for Non-Portable Executable Malware. [IJCNIS]. *International Journal of Communication Networks and Information Security, 16*(4), 546–552.

Jagli, D. (2024). The Role of Artificial Intelligence in Cyber Security. *Deleted Journal, 20*(3), 5283–5291. DOI: 10.52783/jes.6327

Jana, S., Biswas, R., Banerjee, C., Patra, T., Pal, M., & Pal, K. (2024). Leveraging Artificial Intelligence for Enhancing Cybersecurity: A Comprehensive Review and Analysis. *International Journal of Advanced Research in Science. Tongxin Jishu*, •••, 173–183. DOI: 10.48175/IJARSCT-19030

Jothishri, S., Upender, T., Ravikumar, R., Sailaja, Y., Yuvabharathi, E., & Agnestreesa, J. (2024). *AI Cyber Security: Enhancing Network Security with Deep Learning for Real-Time Threat Detection and Performance Evaluation*. 1–6. DOI: 10.1109/ICONAT61936.2024.10774912

Kolhar, A. & Sridevi. (2025). Future Trends and Innovation in Machine Intelligence for Cyber Risk Management. In M. Almaiah & Y. Maleh (Eds.), *Machine Intelligence Applications in Cyber-Risk Management* (pp. 415-438). IGI Global Scientific Publishing. DOI: 10.4018/979-8-3693-7540-2.ch018

Kolhar, A. & Sridevi. (2026). Cybersecurity in Smart Devices. In M. Amin (Ed.), *Cybersecurity and Privacy in the Era of Smart Technologies* (pp. 31-62). IGI Global Scientific Publishing. DOI: 10.4018/979-8-3373-2282-7.ch002

Kumar, N. (2023). *AI in Cybersecurity: Threat Detection and Response with Machine Learning*. DOI: 10.52783/tjjpt.v44.i3.237

Mishra, M., Pradhan, R. C., Agrawalla, K., & Bokka, R. (2025). *AI for Cybersecurity Threat Detection: A Machine Enabled Computing Perspective*. 1–5. DOI: 10.1109/ASSIC64892.2025.11158640

Nnaka, K. I., Mbamalu, P. O., Nwaigbo, J. C., Ozo-ogueji, P. C., Njoku, V. I., & Ekechi, C. C. (2025). AI-powered threat detection: Opportunities and limitations in modern cyber defense. *World Journal Of Advanced Research and Reviews*, *27*(2), 210–223. DOI: 10.30574/wjarr.2025.27.2.2854

Nnamani, C. C. (2024). Exploiting AI Capabilities: An in-Depth Analysis of Artificial Intelligence Integration in Cybersecurity for Threat Detection and Response. *International Journal of Education. Management and Technology*, *2*(3), 268–286. DOI: 10.58578/ijemt.v2i3.3904

Olafuyi, B. A. (2023). *Artificial Intelligence in Cybersecurity: Enhancing Threat Detection and Mitigation*. International Journal of Scientific and Research Publications., DOI: 10.29322/IJSRP.13.12.2023.p14419

Pardhi, N., Gundewar, S., Chute, T., & Adithyan, S. (2025). *Ethical and Strategic Implications of AI in Cybersecurity*. 1–6. DOI: 10.1109/IC2E365635.2025.11166708

Rahman, M., Uddin, I., Das, R., Saha, T., Haque, M. R., Shatu, N. R., & Shafiq, S. I. (2025). Application of Artificial Intelligence in Detecting and Mitigating Cyber Threats. *International Research Journal of Innovations in Engineering and Technology*, *09*(01), 17–26. DOI: 10.47001/IRJIET/2025.901003

Scrivano, A. (2025). *The Impact of AI on Cybersecurity: Threats and Solutions*. DOI: 10.21203/rs.3.rs-7550421/v1

Sharma, S. K. (2024). AI-Enhanced Cyber Threat Detection and Response Systems. *AI-Enhanced Cyber Threat Detection and Response Systems.*, *1*(2), 43–48. DOI: 10.36676/ssjaiml.v1.i2.14

Sharma, S. K. (2025). AI-Powered Cybersecurity: The Future of Threat Detection. *Indian Scientific Journal Of Research In Engineering And Management*, *09*(04), 1–9. DOI: 10.55041/IJSREM45943

Shree, S. R. A., J., A., N., & Saranya, V. (2024). *Leveraging Artificial Intelligence for Cybersecurity* (pp. 29–43). IGI Global. DOI: 10.4018/979-8-3693-4159-9.ch003

Sissodia, R., Rauthan, M. S., Barthwal, V., & Dwivedi, V. (2025). Artificial Intelligence (AI) in Cybersecurity. *Advances in Computational Intelligence and Robotics Book Series*, 121–152. DOI: 10.4018/979-8-3373-0583-7.ch005

Sridevi & Kolhar. A. (2025). Energy-Efficiency Strategies for Wireless Sensor Networks in IoT. In A. Sathio, M. Rind, S. Awan, & A. Junejo (Eds.), *Energy-Efficient Deep Learning Approaches in IoT, Fog, and Green Blockchain Revolution* (pp. 167-192). IGI Global Scientific Publishing. DOI: 10.4018/979-8-3373-0300-0.ch006

Sridevi & Kolhar. A. (2026). Fundamentals of 6G Networks. In R. Shaikh (Ed.), *6G Networks and AI-Driven Cybersecurity* (pp. 1-32). IGI Global Scientific Publishing. DOI: 10.4018/979-8-3373-0568-4.ch001

Thapaliya, S. (2025). Artificial Intelligence and Cybersecurity: Pioneering Next-Generation Protection Strategies. *SADGAMAYA*, *2*(1), 61–65. DOI: 10.3126/sadgamaya.v2i1.80334

Toya, H. (2025). Artificial Intelligence and Security: Enhancing Cyber Defense Mechanisms. *Oriental Journal of Computer Science and Technology*, *17*(01), 23–25. DOI: 10.13005/ojcst17.01.07

Wang, W. (2025). *AI-Driven Cybersecurity Solutions Enhancing Threat Detection in Healthcare and Airlines*. DOI: 10.20944/preprints202501.1352.v1

Compilation of References

Aayog, N. I. T. I. (2018). *National Strategy for Artificial Intelligence# AIForAll*. Government of India.

Abolaji, E. O., & Akinwande, O. T.Elijah Oluwatoyosi AbolajiOladayo Tosin Akinwande. (2024). AI powered privacy protection: A survey of current state and future directions. *World Journal of Advanced Research Reviews*, *23*(3), 2687–2696. DOI: 10.30574/wjarr.2024.23.3.2869

Achuthan, K., Ramanathan, S., Srinivas, S., & Raman, R. (2024). Advancing cybersecurity and privacy with artificial intelligence: Current trends and future research directions. *Frontiers in Big Data*, *7*, 1497535. DOI: 10.3389/fdata.2024.1497535 PMID: 39703783

Adamson, G., Havens, J. C., & Chatila, R. (2019). Designing a value-driven future for ethical autonomous and intelligent systems. *Proceedings of the IEEE*, *107*(3), 518–525. DOI: 10.1109/JPROC.2018.2884923

Adewale, S., & Samuel, S. V. (2024). *The intersection of Artificial Intelligence and cybersecurity: Challenges and opportunities*. World Journal Of Advanced Research and Reviews., DOI: 10.30574/wjarr.2024.21.2.0607

Adeyeye, O. J., Akanbi, I., Emeteveke, I., & Emehin, O. (2024). Leveraging secured AI-driven data analytics for cybersecurity: Safeguarding information and enhancing threat detection. *International Journal of Research and Publication and Reviews*, *5*(10), 3208–3223. DOI: 10.55248/gengpi.5.1024.2911

Aggarwal, A., & Gaur, S. (2024). Applying artificial intelligence to explore online harassment and cyberbullying prevention. In *Impact of AI on Advancing Women's Safety* (pp. 104–120). IGI Global Scientific Publishing.

Akhtar, Z. B., & Rawol, A. T. (2024). *Harnessing artificial intelligence (AI) for cybersecurity: Challenges, opportunities, risks, future directions*. 2(2), 1485. DOI: 10.59400/cai.v2i2.1485

Alasiry, S., Wong, K., & Ibrahim, T. (2025). Privacy-preserving multimodal federated GANs for neurodegenerative disease prediction. *Frontiers in Artificial Intelligence in Medicine, 6*, Article 88.

Alexander, S. (2025). *Deepfakes reshape cyberbullying, TCU expert calls for action*. Texas Christian University.

Ali, A., Hussain, F., & Khan, S. (2022). Assistive AI for low-resource communities: Ethical and cultural perspectives. *Journal of Inclusive Technology*, *8*(3), 45–61.

Alipour, N., Burke, T., & Courtney, J. (2024). Skin type diversity in skin lesion datasets: A review. *Current Dermatology Reports*, *13*(3), 198–210. DOI: 10.1007/s13671-024-00440-0 PMID: 39184010

Ali, W. N. H. W., Mohd, M., & Fauzi, F. (2018). Cyberbullying detection: An overview." in *2018 Cyber Resilience Conference (CRC);* November 13–15, 2018; 1–3.

Alketbi, K. S., & Mehmood, A. (2025). A Comprehensive Survey of Explainable Artificial Intelligence Techniques for Malicious Insider Threat Detection. *IEEE Access : Practical Innovations, Open Solutions*.

Alkhodair, A. J. (2025). *FairAI: Distributed Ledger Technology (DLT) Based Ethical Artificial Intelligence (AI) Training Framework.* Paper presented at the 2025 4th International Conference on Computing and Information Technology (ICCIT).

Allahrakha, N. (2024). *UNESCO's AI ethics principles: Challenges and opportunities*. International Journal of Law and Policy., DOI: 10.59022/ijlp.225

Almheiri, S. J., Shah, A. A., Abbas, S., Ahmad, M., & Khan, M. A. (2025). Smart sustainable cyber security: Modelling an interpretable and transparent threat detection with explainable artificial intelligence. *Discover Sustainability*, *6*(1), 442. DOI: 10.1007/s43621-025-01280-z

Altaf, F., Israr, M., & Khan, S. H. (2024). Counter Financing of Terrorism and Challenges for the government of Pakistan. *The Journal of Research Review*, *1*(04), 360–370.

Alzoubi, M. M. (2024). Investigating the synergy of Blockchain and AI: enhancing security, efficiency, and transparency. *Journal of Cyber Security Technology*, 1-29.

Amann, A., Blasimme, M., Vayena, E., Frey, A., & Madai, V. (2020). Explainability for artificial intelligence in healthcare: A multidisciplinary perspective. *BMC Medical Informatics and Decision Making*, *20*(1), 310. Advance online publication. DOI: 10.1186/s12911-020-01332-6 PMID: 33256715

Ameen, A. H., Mohammed, M. A., & Rashid, A. N. (2023). Dimensions of artificial intelligence techniques, blockchain, and cyber security in the Internet of medical things: Opportunities, challenges, and future directions. *Journal of Intelligent Systems, 32*(1), 20220267. DOI: 10.1515/jisys-2022-0267

Amir Latif, R. M., Hussain, K., Jhanjhi, N., Nayyar, A., & Rizwan, O. (2020). A remix IDE: Smart contract-based framework for the healthcare sector by using Blockchain technology. *Multimedia Tools and Applications*, •••, 1–24.

Amugongo, L. M., Kriebitz, A., Boch, A., & Lütge, C. (2023). Operationalising AI ethics through the agile software development lifecycle: A case study of AI-enabled mobile health applications. *AI and Ethics*, •••, 1–18.

Anwar, N., Rahaman, M., Widodo, A. M., Sekti, B. A., Erzed, N., Tangkudung, R., Muchlis, M., Yuhefizar, Y., & Budhisantosa, N. (2025). Sustainable Cybersecurity in the AI Era. *Advances in Computational Intelligence and Robotics Book Series*, 603–620. DOI: 10.4018/979-8-3693-8034-5.ch030

Arreche, O., Guntur, T., & Abdallah, M. (2024). Xai-ids: Toward proposing an explainable artificial intelligence framework for enhancing network intrusion detection systems. *Applied Sciences (Basel, Switzerland), 14*(10), 4170. DOI: 10.3390/app14104170

Arrieta, A. B., Díaz-Rodríguez, N., Del Ser, J., Bennetot, A., Tabik, S., Barbado, A., García, S., Gil-López, S., Molina, D., & Benjamins, R. (2020). Explainable Artificial Intelligence (XAI): Concepts, taxonomies, opportunities and challenges toward responsible AI. *Information Fusion, 58*, 82–115. DOI: 10.1016/j.inffus.2019.12.012

Artificial Intelligence (AI) Coined at Dartmouth. (n.d.). Dartmouth College. Retrieved September 24, 2025, from https://home.dartmouth.edu/about/artificial-intelligence-ai-coined-dartmouth

Artificial Intelligence Act. (2024). *Article 6: Classification rules for high-risk AI systems. Regulation (EU) 2024/1689.* https://artificialintelligenceact.eu/article/6

Asif, R., Hassan, S. R., & Parr, G. (2023). Integrating a blockchain-based governance framework for responsible AI. *Future Internet, 15*(3), 97. DOI: 10.3390/fi15030097

Awasthi, S., Shanmugam, R., Jena, S. R., & Srivastava, A. (2020). Review of techniques to prevent fake accounts on social media. *International Journal of Advanced Science and Technology, 29*(4), 8350–8365.

Badawy, W., Zinhom, H., & Shaban, M. (2025a). Navigating ethical considerations in the use of artificial intelligence for patient care: A systematic review. *International Nursing Review, 72*(3), e13059. DOI: 10.1111/inr.13059 PMID: 39545614

Bainbridge, W. S. (2006). Cognitive technologies. In *Managing nano-bio-info-cogno innovations* (pp. 203–226). Springer Netherlands. DOI: 10.1007/1-4020-4107-1_14

Baldimtsi, F., Burkhart, M., Damgård, I., & Orlandi, C. (2013). Anonymous biometric access control. In *International Conference on Financial Cryptography and Data Security*. Springer.

Baniecki, H., & Biecek, P. (2024). Adversarial attacks and defenses in explainable artificial intelligence: A survey. *Information Fusion*, *107*, 102303. DOI: 10.1016/j.inffus.2024.102303

Banks, G. (1986). Artificial intelligence in medical diagnosis: The INTERNIST/CADUCEUS approach. *Critical Reviews in Medical Informatics*, *1*(1), 23–54. PMID: 3331578

Baqar, M. (2024). Balancing Innovation and Ethics in AI-Driven Software Development. *arXiv preprint arXiv.10252.*

Barnett, G. O., Cimino, J. J., Hupp, J. A., & Hoffer, E. P. (1987). DXplain: An evolving diagnostic decision-support system. *Journal of the American Medical Association*, *258*(1), 67–74. DOI: 10.1001/jama.1987.03400010071030 PMID: 3295316

Barocas, S., Hardt, M., & Narayanan, A. (2020). Fairness and machine learning. *Recommender systems handbook, 1*, 453-459.

Beauchamp, T. L., & Childress, J. F. (1994). Principles of biomedical ethics. Edicoes Loyola. Oxford University Press, New York.

Belkacem, A. N., Jamil, N., Palmer, J. A., Ouhbi, S., & Chen, C. (2020). Brain Computer Interfaces for Improving the Quality of Life of Older Adults and Elderly Patients. *Frontiers in Neuroscience*, *14*, 692. DOI: 10.3389/fnins.2020.00692 PMID: 32694979

Benaloh, J. (2013). End-to-end verifiable elections: Public evidence from secret ballots. *USENIX Journal of Election Technology and Systems*, *1*(1), 18–37.

Benaloh, J., & Tuinstra, D. (1994). Receipt-free secret-ballot elections. In *Proceedings of the Twenty-Sixth Annual ACM Symposium on Theory of Computing*. DOI: 10.1145/195058.195407

Benčević, M., Habijan, M., Galić, I., Babin, D., & Pižurica, A. (2024). Understanding skin color bias in deep learning-based skin lesion segmentation. *Computer Methods and Programs in Biomedicine*, *245*, 108044. DOI: 10.1016/j.cmpb.2024.108044 PMID: 38290289

Bennett, C. L., & Rosner, D. K. (2019). The promise of assistive technology design. *ACM Transactions on Accessible Computing*, *12*(4), 1–32. DOI: 10.1145/3777475

Ben-Sasson, E., Bentov, I., Horesh, Y., & Riabzev, M. (2018). *Scalable, transparent, and post-quantum secure computational integrity*. Cryptology ePrint Archive.

Ben-Sasson, E., Chiesa, A., Genkin, D., Tromer, E., & Virza, M. (2013). SNARKs for C: Verifying program executions succinctly and in zero knowledge. In *Annual Cryptology Conference*. Springer. DOI: 10.1007/978-3-642-40084-1_6

Ben-Sasson, E., Chiesa, A., Genkin, D., Tromer, E., & Virza, M. (2014). Succinct non-interactive zero knowledge for a von Neumann architecture. In *23rd USENIX Security Symposium*.

Bentham, J. (1996). *An introduction to the principles of morals and legislation*. Oxford University Press.

Bhumichai, D., Smiliotopoulos, C., Benton, R., Kambourakis, G., & Damopoulos, D. (2024). The convergence of artificial intelligence and blockchain: The state of play and the road ahead. *Information (Basel)*, *15*(5), 268. DOI: 10.3390/info15050268

Bialkova, S. (2024). AI transforming business and everyday life. In *The rise of AI user applications: Chatbots integration foundations and trends* (pp. 143–165). Springer Nature Switzerland. DOI: 10.1007/978-3-031-56471-0_9

Binns, R. (2022). Human Judgment in algorithmic loops: Individual justice and automated decision-making. *Regulation & Governance*, *16*(1), 197–211. DOI: 10.1111/rego.12358

Bonawitz, K., Ivanov, V., Kreuter, B., Marcedone, A., McMahan, H. B., Patel, S., Ramage, D., Segal, A., & Seth, K. (2017). Practical secure aggregation for privacy-preserving machine learning. In *Proceedings of the 2017 ACM SIGSAC Conference on Computer and Communications Security*. DOI: 10.1145/3133956.3133982

Boston.com. (2024). *Plymouth man allegedly used AI to stalk and harass woman*. https://www.boston.com/news/crime/2024/09/11/plymouth-man-allegedly-used-ai-to-impersonate-stalk-harrass-mass-woman/

Boudi, A. L., Boudi, M., Chan, C., Boudi, F. B., & Boudi, A. (2024). Ethical challenges of artificial intelligence in medicine. *Cureus*, *16*(11), e74495. DOI: 10.7759/cureus.74495 PMID: 39726447

Bowe, S., Gabizon, A., & Miers, I. (2017). *Scalable multi-party computation for zk-SNARK parameters in the random beacon model*. IACR Cryptology ePrint Archive, 2017, 1050.

Brady, W. J., Jackson, J. C., Lindström, B., & Crockett, M. J. (2023). Algorithm-mediated social learning in online social networks. *Trends in Cognitive Sciences, 27*(10), 947–960. DOI: 10.1016/j.tics.2023.06.008 PMID: 37543440

Brooks, R. A. (1991). Intelligence without representation. *Artificial Intelligence, 47*(1-3), 139–159. DOI: 10.1016/0004-3702(91)90053-M

Brown, J. (2018, July 25). *IBM Watson reportedly recommended cancer treatments that were "unsafe and incorrect." Gizmodo.* https://gizmodo.com

Bünz, B., Bootle, J., Boneh, D., Poelstra, A., Wuille, P., & Maxwell, G. (2018). Bulletproofs: Short proofs for confidential transactions and more. In *2018 IEEE Symposium on Security and Privacy (SP)*. IEEE. DOI: 10.1109/SP.2018.00020

Buolamwini, J., & Gebru, T. (2018). Gender shades: Intersectional accuracy disparities in commercial gender classification. *Proceedings of the 2018 Conference on Fairness, Accountability, and Transparency (FAT*) *, 77-91. DOI: 10.1145/3287560.3287584

Çakır, A. M. (2024). AI Driven Cybersecurity. *Human-Computer Interaction, 8*(1), 119. DOI: 10.62802/jg7gge06

Calzarossa, M. C., Giudici, P., & Zieni, R. (2025). An assessment framework for explainable AI with applications to cybersecurity. *Artificial Intelligence Review, 58*(5), 150. DOI: 10.1007/s10462-025-11141-w

Camacho, N. G. (2024). The role of AI in cybersecurity: Addressing threats in the digital age. *Journal of Artificial Intelligence General science (JAIGS) ISSN: 3006-4023, 3*(1), 143-154.

Cámbara, A., Peiró-Lilja, C., Farrús, M., & Luque, J. (2021). *English accent accuracy analysis in a state-of-the-art automatic speech recognition system.* arXiv preprint arXiv:2105.05041.

Camilleri, M. A. (2024). Artificial intelligence governance: Ethical considerations and implications for social responsibility. *Expert Systems: International Journal of Knowledge Engineering and Neural Networks, 41*(7), e13406. DOI: 10.1111/exsy.13406

Capel, T., & Brereton, M. (2023, April). What is human-centered about human-centered AI? A map of the research landscape. In *Proceedings of the 2023 CHI conference on human factors in computing systems* (pp. 1-23). DOI: 10.1145/3544548.3580959

Caselli, T., Basile, V., Mitrović, J., Kartoziya, I., & Granitzer, M. (2020). "I feel offended, don't be abusive! implicit/explicit messages in offensive and abusive language." in *Proceedings of the 12th Language Resources and Evaluation Conference;* May 13–15, 2020; (European Language Resources Association), 6193–6202.

Cavoukian, A. (2009). Privacy by design: The 7 foundational principles. *Information and privacy commissioner of Ontario, Canada, 5*(2009), 12.

Chakraborty, S. (2025). *Human values, ethics, and dignity in the age of artificial intelligence*. IGI Global. DOI: 10.4018/979-8-3693-9035-1

Chan, C. Y. S. (2020). The multi-dimensions of social participation of older adults in Hong Kong.

Chandler, P., & Sweller, J. (1991). Cognitive load theory and the format of instruction. *Cognition and Instruction, 8*(4), 293–332. DOI: 10.1207/s1532690xci0804_2

Chase, M., Meiklejohn, S., & Zaverucha, G. (2014). Password systems with perfect security properties. In *2014 IEEE Symposium on Security and Privacy*. IEEE.

Chatelain, P., Delmaire, G., Alboody, A., Puigt, M., & Roussel, G. (2021). Semi-automatic spectral image stitching for a compact hybrid linescan hyperspectral camera towards near field remote monitoring of potato crop leaves. *Sensors (Basel), 21*(22), 7616. DOI: 10.3390/s21227616 PMID: 34833696

Chatzakou, D., Kourtellis, N., Blackburn, J., De Cristofaro, E., Stringhini, G., & Vakali, A. (2017, April). Measuring# GamerGate: A tale of hate, sexism, and bullying. In *Proceedings of the 26th international conference on world wide web companion* (pp. 1285-1290). DOI: 10.1145/3041021.3053890

Chen, L., Zhang, C., & Wilson, C. (2013). "Tweeting under pressure: analyzing trending topics and evolving word choice on sina weibo." in *Proceedings of the first ACM conference on Online social networks* COSN'13; October 7–8, 2013; (New York, NY, USA: Association for Computing Machinery), 89–100. DOI: 10.1145/2512938.2512940

Chen, Y., Clayton, E. W., Novak, L. L., Anders, S., & Malin, B. (2023). Human-centered design to address biases in artificial intelligence. *Journal of Medical Internet Research, 25*, e43251. DOI: 10.2196/43251 PMID: 36961506

Chevuri, N. (2025). *Data protection in social services: A comprehensive guide to HIPAA and GDPR implementation*. International Journal of Scientific Research in Computer Science, Engineering and Information Technology., DOI: 10.32628/CSEIT25112369

Choi, E., Bahadori, M. T., Schuetz, A., Stewart, W. F., & Sun, J. (2016). Doctor AI: Predicting clinical events via recurrent neural networks. In *Proceedings of the Machine Learning for Healthcare Conference* (pp. 301–318). PMLR.

Chouraik, C. (2025). Morocco's Financial Renaissance: Embracing Digital Innovation with Visionary Regulation. *Journal of Economics Business Issues*, *5*(1), 58–68.

Chowdhury, A. R., Campanelli, M., Ganesh, C., Gailly, N., & Shikhelman, C. (2024). *SoK: Privacy-preserving computing in the blockchain era*. IACR Cryptology ePrint Archive. https://eprint.iacr.org/2023/727

Christou, G., Meyer, T., & Fanni, R. (2025). The European union: Assessing global leadership through actorness in artificial intelligence. *Journal of European Integration*, *47*(3), 383–401. DOI: 10.1080/07036337.2024.2377200

Clegg, A., Bates, C., Young, J., Ryan, R., Nichols, L., Teale, E. A., Mohammed, M. A., Parry, J., & Marshall, T. (2016). Development and validation of an electronic frailty index using routine primary care electronic health record data. *Age and Ageing*, *45*(3), 353–360. DOI: 10.1093/ageing/afw039 PMID: 26944937

Coeckelbergh, M. (2020). Artificial intelligence, responsibility attribution, and a relational justification of explainability. *Science and Engineering Ethics*, *26*(4), 2051–2068. DOI: 10.1007/s11948-019-00146-8 PMID: 31650511

Collins, B. X., Bélisle-Pipon, J.-C., Evans, B. J., Ferryman, K., Jiang, X., Nebeker, C., Novak, L., Roberts, K., Were, M., Yin, Z., Ravitsky, V., Coco, J., Hendricks-Sturrup, R., Williams, I., Clayton, E. W., & Malin, B. A. (2024). Addressing ethical issues in healthcare artificial intelligence using a lifecycle-informed process. *JAMIA Open*, *7*(4), ooae108. Advance online publication. DOI: 10.1093/jamiaopen/ooae108 PMID: 39553826

Conway, B., Nolan, K., & Quille, K. (2024, December). HCAI Block Model: A competence model for Human Centred Artificial Intelligence at K-12. In *Proceedings of the 2024 Conference on Human Centred Artificial Intelligence-Education and Practice* (pp. 22-28). DOI: 10.1145/3701268.3701273

Couture, V., Roy, M.-C., Dez, E., Laperle, S., & Bélisle-Pipon, J.-C. (2023). Ethical implications of artificial intelligence in population health and the public's role in its governance: Perspectives from a citizen and expert panel. *Journal of Medical Internet Research*, *25*, e44357. DOI: 10.2196/44357 PMID: 37104026

Cumming, D., Saurabh, K., Rani, N., & Upadhyay, P. (2024). Towards AI ethics-led sustainability frameworks and toolkits: Review and research agenda. *Journal of Sustainable Finance Accounting*, *1*, 100003. DOI: 10.1016/j.josfa.2024.100003

Dandotiya, A. S., Gupta, S. K., Dandotiya, N., & Sharma, M. P. (2024). *AI in everyday life: transforming society*. Navi International Book Publication house.

Dankwa-Mullan, I. (2024). Health equity and ethical considerations in using artificial intelligence in public health and medicine. *Preventing Chronic Disease*, *21*, E64. DOI: 10.5888/pcd21.240245 PMID: 39173183

Das, A., Cuzzocrea, A., Gkoulalas-Divanis, A., Shams, T., Islam, M. S., Pentyala, Y., & Hashem, G. (2020). *Anonymizing data for privacy-preserving federated learning. arXiv preprint arXiv:2002.09096.* https://arxiv.org/abs/2002.09096

Das, S. R., Jhanjhi, N., Asirvatham, D., Rizwan, F., & Javed, D. (2025). Securing AI-Based Healthcare Systems Using Blockchain Technology. In *AI Techniques for Securing Medical and Business Practices* (pp. 333–356). IGI Global.

de Freitas, M. P., Piai, V. A., Farias, R. H., Fernandes, A. M. R., de Moraes Rossetto, A. G., & Leithardt, V. R. Q. (2022). Artificial Intelligence of Things Applied to Assistive Technology: A Systematic Literature Review. *Sensors (Basel)*, *22*(21), 8531. DOI: 10.3390/s22218531 PMID: 36366227

de Visser, E. J., et al. (2021). Transparency in human–robot interaction: A review. *Frontiers in Robotics and AI, 8*, 646402. https://doi.org/DOI: 10.3389/frobt.2021.646402

Devarapu, K. (2020). Blockchain-Driven AI Solutions for Medical Imaging and Diagnosis in Healthcare. *Technology Management Review*, *5*(1), 80–91.

Dinakar, K., Reichart, R., & Lieberman, H. (2011). Modeling the detection of textual cyberbullying. In *Proceedings of the International AAAI Conference on Web and Social Media* (Vol. 5, No. 3, pp. 11-17).

Ding, H., Wu, J., Zhao, W., Matinlinna, J. P., Burrow, M. F., & Tsoi, J. K. (2023). Artificial intelligence in dentistry—A review. *Frontiers in Dental Medicine*, *4*, 1085251. DOI: 10.3389/fdmed.2023.1085251 PMID: 39935549

Dwork, C., Roth, A., & others. (2014). The algorithmic foundations of differential privacy. *Foundations and Trends in Theoretical Computer Science*, *9*(3–4), 211–407.

Eden, C. A., Chisom, O. N., & Adeniyi, I. S. (2024). Integrating AI in education: Opportunities, challenges, and ethical considerations. *Magna Scientia Advanced Research and Reviews, 10*(2), 006-013.

El-Assy, A. (2024). Federated multimodal AI for Alzheimer's early detection across diverse hospitals. *Journal of Medical AI Research*, *7*(2), 112–124.

Elbaz, G. (2025). *AI security risks in 2025: 6 threats & 6 defensive measures.* Oligo Security. https://www.oligo.security/academy/ai-security-risks-in-2025-6-threats-6-defensive-measures

Elendu, C., Amaechi, D. C., Elendu, T. C., Jingwa, K. A., Okoye, O. K., Okah, M. J., Ladele, J. A., Farah, A. H., & Alimi, H. A. (2023). Ethical implications of AI and robotics in healthcare. *Revista de Medicina (São Paulo)*, *102*(50), e36671. DOI: 10.1097/MD.0000000000036671 PMID: 38115340

Elyoseph, Z., Refoua, E., Asraf, K., Lvovsky, M., Shimoni, Y., & Hadar-Shoval, D. (2024). Capacity of generative AI to interpret human emotions from visual and textual data: Pilot evaluation study. *JMIR Mental Health*, *11*, e54369. DOI: 10.2196/54369 PMID: 38319707

Encyclopaedia Britannica. (n.d.). *Alan Turing: Biography, facts, computer & machine.* In *Encyclopaedia Britannica*. Retrieved September 22, 2025, from https://www.britannica.com/biography/Alan-Turing

Ernstberger, J., Chaliasos, S., Zhou, L., Jovanovic, P., & Gervais, A. (2024). Do you need a zero knowledge proof? *Cryptology ePrint Archive*.

Esposito, E. (2022). *Artificial communication: How algorithms produce social intelligence*. MIT Press. DOI: 10.7551/mitpress/14189.001.0001

European Commission. (2024). *EU Artificial Intelligence Act*. Official Journal of the European Union.

European Commission. *Proposal for a Regulation on Artificial Intelligence (AI Act)*, 2021. [Online]. Available: https://digital-strategy.ec.europa.eu/en/library/proposal-regulation-artificial-intelligence-ai-act

European Commission. S. (2019). Ethics guidelines for trustworthy AI. *Publications Office*.

European Parliament and Council of the European Union. (2024). *Regulation (EU) 2024/1689 of the European Parliament and of the Council of 13 June 2024 laying down harmonised rules on artificial intelligence* (L, 2024/1689). EUR-Lex.https://eurlex.europa.eu/eli/reg/2024/1689/oj/eng

European Union. (2024). *Regulation (EU) 2024/1689 of the European Parliament and of the Council of 13 June 2024 laying down harmonised rules on artificial intelligence (Artificial Intelligence Act).* Official Journal of the European Union.

Farhud, D. D., & Zokaei, S. (2021). Ethical issues of artificial intelligence in medicine and healthcare. *Iranian Journal of Public Health, 50*(11), i–v. DOI: 10.18502/ijph.v50i11.7600 PMID: 35223619

Feige, U., Fiat, A., & Shamir, A. (1987). Zero-knowledge proofs of identity. In *Proceedings of the Nineteenth Annual ACM Symposium on Theory of Computing*. ACM. Bünz, B., Bootle, J., Boneh, D., Poelstra, A., Wuille, P., & Maxwell, G. (2018, May). Bulletproofs: Short proofs for confidential transactions and more. In *2018 IEEE symposium on security and privacy (SP)* (pp. 315-334). IEEE.

Ferrag, M. A., Ndhlovu, M., Tihanyi, N., Cordeiro, L. C., Debbah, M., Lestable, T., & Thandi, N. S. (2024). Revolutionizing cyber threat detection with large language models: A privacy-preserving bert-based lightweight model for iot/iiot devices. *IEEE Access : Practical Innovations, Open Solutions, 12*, 23733–23750. DOI: 10.1109/ACCESS.2024.3363469

Fjeld, J., Achten, N., Hilligoss, H., Nagy, A., & Srikumar, M. (2020). *Principled artificial intelligence: Mapping consensus in ethical and rights-based approaches to principles for AI* (Berkman Klein Center Research Publication No. 2020-1). Harvard University. DOI: 10.2139/ssrn.3518482

Fleisig, R., Smith, E., Bossi, D., Rustagi, N., Yin, D., & Klein, D. (2024). *Linguistic bias in ChatGPT: Language models reinforce dialect discrimination*. arXiv preprint arXiv:2406.08818. https://arxiv.org/abs/2406.08818 DOI: 10.18653/v1/2024.emnlp-main.750

Floridi, L. (2019). Establishing the rules for building trustworthy AI. *Nature Machine Intelligence, 1*(6), 261–262. DOI: 10.1038/s42256-019-0055-y

Floridi, L., & Cowls, J. (2022). A unified framework of five principles for AI in society. *Machine learning and the city: Applications in architecture and urban design*, 535-545.

Floridi, L. (2024). Introduction to the special issues: The ethics of artificial intelligence: Exacerbated problems, renewed problems, unprecedented problems. *American Philosophical Quarterly, 61*(4), 301–307. DOI: 10.5406/21521123.61.4.01

Floridi, L., Cowls, J., Beltrametti, M., Chatila, R., Chazerand, P., Dignum, V., Luetge, C., Madelin, R., Pagallo, U., Rossi, F., Schafer, B., Valcke, P., & Vayena, E. (2018). AI4People—An ethical framework for a good AI society: Opportunities, risks, principles, and recommendations. *Minds and Machines, 28*(4), 689–707. DOI: 10.1007/s11023-018-9482-5 PMID: 30930541

Food and Drug Administration. (2025). *Predetermined change control plan (PCCP) for AI/ML-enabled devices: Guidance for industry and Food and Drug Administration staff.* U.S. Department of Health and Human Services.

Fredrikson, M., Jha, S., & Ristenpart, T. (2015). Model inversion attacks that exploit confidence information and basic countermeasures. In *Proceedings of the 22nd ACM SIGSAC Conference on Computer and Communications Security*. ACM. DOI: 10.1145/2810103.2813677

Friedman, B., & Hendry, D. (2019). *Value sensitive design: Shaping technology with moral imagination*. MIT Press. DOI: 10.7551/mitpress/7585.001.0001

Frost, E. K., Bosward, R., Aquino, Y. S. J., Braunack-Mayer, A., & Carter, S. M. (2022). Public views on ethical issues in healthcare artificial intelligence: Protocol for a scoping review. *Systematic Reviews, 11*(1), 142. DOI: 10.1186/s13643-022-02012-4 PMID: 35841073

Gabriel, O. T. (2023). *Data privacy and ethical issues in collecting health care data using artificial intelligence among health workers.* Center for Bioethics and Research, Göksal, Ş. İ., & Solarte Vasquez, M. C. (2024). The Blockchain-Based Trustworthy Artificial Intelligence Supported by Stakeholders-In-The-Loop Model. *Scientific Papers of the University of Pardubice. Series D, Faculty of Economics Administration, 32*(2).

Gabriela, G., Cerasela, S. E., & Alina, C. A. (2018). The EU general data protection regulation implications for Romanian small and medium-sized enterprises. [Economic Sciences Series]. *Ovidius University Annals, 18*(1), 88–91.

Gammelgård-Larsen, A., Van Berkel, N., Skov, M. B., & Kjeldskov, J. (2024, May). Designing for human-AI interaction: Comparing intermittent, continuous, and proactive interactions for a music application. In *Extended Abstracts of the CHI Conference on Human Factors in Computing Systems* (pp. 1-8).

General Data Protection Regulation (GDPR). (n.d.). *GDPR Information Portal.* Retrieved October 26, 2025, from https://gdpr-info.eu/

Gennaro, R., Gentry, C., & Parno, B. (2013). Quadratic span programs and succinct NIZKs without PCPs. In *Annual International Conference on the Theory and Applications of Cryptographic Techniques*. Springer. DOI: 10.1007/978-3-642-38348-9_37

Gentry, C. (2009). Fully homomorphic encryption using ideal lattices. In *Proceedings of the Forty-First Annual ACM Symposium on Theory of Computing*. DOI: 10.1145/1536414.1536440

George, S. (2024). Artificial Intelligence-Powered Cybersecurity. *Advances in Information Security, Privacy, and Ethics Book Series*, 247–276. DOI: 10.4018/979-8-3373-1102-9.ch008

Gerke, S., Minssen, T., & Cohen, G. (2020). Ethical and legal challenges of artificial intelligence-driven healthcare. In *Artificial intelligence in healthcare* (pp. 295–336). Elsevier. DOI: 10.1016/B978-0-12-818438-7.00012-5

Gillespie, T. (2018). *Custodians of the Internet: Platforms, content moderation, and the hidden decisions that shape social media*. Yale University Press.

Goldreich, O. (2019). *Foundations of cryptography: Volume 1, basic tools*. Cambridge University Press.

Goldwasser, S., Micali, S., & Rackoff, C. (2019). The knowledge complexity of interactive proof-systems. In *Providing sound foundations for cryptography: On the work of Shafi Goldwasser and Silvio Micali*. DOI: 10.1145/3335741.3335750

Google Health, & DeepMind. (. (2020). AI for breast cancer screening: Results from multi-site validation. *Nature*, *577*, 89–94. DOI: 10.1038/s41586-019-1799-6

Gorelik, A. J., Li, M., Hahne, J., Wang, J., Ren, Y., Yang, L., Zhang, X., Liu, X., Wang, X., Bogdan, R., & Carpenter, B. D. (2025). Ethics of AI in healthcare: A scoping review demonstrating applicability of a foundational framework. *Frontiers in Digital Health*, *7*, 1662642. DOI: 10.3389/fdgth.2025.1662642 PMID: 41000336

Groth, J. (2016). On the size of pairing-based non-interactive arguments. In Fischlin, M., & Coron, J.-S. (Eds.), Lecture Notes in Computer Science: Vol. 9666. *Advances in Cryptology – EUROCRYPT 2016, Part II* (pp. 305–326). Springer. DOI: 10.1007/978-3-662-49896-5_11

Guan, H., Yap, P. T., Bozoki, A., & Liu, M. (2024). Federated learning for medical image analysis: A survey. *Pattern Recognition*, *151*, 110424. DOI: 10.1016/j.patcog.2024.110424 PMID: 38559674

Gundoor, T. K. (2022). IoT-Enabled 5G Networks for Secure Communication. In *Information Security Practices for the Internet of Things, 5G, and Next-Generation Wireless Networks* (pp. 1-29). IGI Global.

Gundoor, T. K. (2024). Artificial Intelligence on Knowledge Management and Industry Revolution 4.0.

Gundoor, T. K. (2025). Identifying Nobel Features in Non-Portable Executable Malware Files. *IAENG International Journal of Computer Science*, *52*(1).

Gundoor, T. K., & Sridevi, D. (2024). Optimized Feature Selection and classification for Non-Portable Executable Malware. [IJCNIS]. *International Journal of Communication Networks and Information Security*, *16*(4), 546–552.

Gunning, D., & Aha, D. (2019). DARPA's explainable artificial intelligence (XAI) program. *AI Magazine, 40*(2), 44–58. DOI: 10.1609/aimag.v40i2.2850

Gupta, N., Jati, A., & Chattopadhyay, A. (2025). Ai attacks ai: Recovering neural network architecture from nvdla using ai-assisted side channel attack. *ACM Transactions on Embedded Computing Systems*, *24*(5), 1–29. DOI: 10.1145/3731560

Gupta, S. (2025). Zero-Knowledge Proofs For Privacy-Preserving Systems: A Survey Across Blockchain, Identity, And Beyond. *Engineering Technology Journal*, *10*(07), 5755–5761.

Haggenmüller, S., Schmitt, M., Krieghoff-Henning, E., Hekler, A., Maron, R. C., Wies, C., Utikal, J. S., Meier, F., Hobelsberger, S., Gellrich, F. F., Sergon, M., Hauschild, A., French, L. E., Heinzerling, L., Schlager, J. G., Ghoreschi, K., Schlaak, M., Hilke, F. J., Poch, G., & Brinker, T. J. (2024). Federated learning for decentralized artificial intelligence in melanoma diagnostics. *JAMA Dermatology*, *160*(3), 303–311. DOI: 10.1001/jamadermatol.2023.5550 PMID: 38324293

Halder, S. (2021). Violence Against Women in Bangladesh: Uprising Scenario and Safeguards in Cyberspace (Doctoral dissertation, Khulna university).

Han, H. (2022). *The impact of Artificial Intelligence (AI) and blockchain adoption in corporate governance: ethical perspectives.* Brunel University London, Joseph, S., Kolade, T. M., Obioha Val, O., Adebiyi, O. O., Ogungbemi, O. S., & Olaniyi, O. O. (2024). AI-powered information governance: Balancing automation and human oversight for optimal organization productivity. *Asian Journal of Research in Computer Science, 17*(10), 10.9734.

Hanna, M. G., Pantanowitz, L., Jackson, B., Palmer, O., Visweswaran, S., Pantanowitz, J., Deebajah, M., & Rashidi, H. H. (2025). Ethical and bias considerations in artificial intelligence/machine learning. *Modern Pathology*, *38*(3), 100686. DOI: 10.1016/j.modpat.2024.100686 PMID: 39694331

Han, S., Kelly, E., Nikou, S., & Svee, E.-O. (2022). Aligning artificial intelligence with human values: Reflections from a phenomenological perspective. *AI & Society*, *37*(4), 1383–1395. DOI: 10.1007/s00146-021-01247-4

Hariyanti, E., Janeswari, M. B., Moningka, M. M., Aziz, F. M., Putri, A. R., Hapsari, O. S., Sutha, N. A. A. D., Sinaga, Y. A. A., & Bendesa, M. P. (2023). Implementations of Artificial Intelligence in Various Domains of IT Governance: A Systematic Literature Review. *Journal of Information Systems Engineering & Business Intelligence*, *9*(2), 305–319. DOI: 10.20473/jisebi.9.2.305-319

Heidari, A., Navimipour, N. J., Dag, H., Talebi, S., & Unal, M. (2024). A novel blockchain-based deepfake detection method using federated and deep learning models. *Cognitive Computation*, *16*(3), 1073–1091. DOI: 10.1007/s12559-024-10255-7

Hermosilla, P., Berríos, S., & Allende-Cid, H. (2025). Explainable AI for Forensic Analysis: A Comparative Study of SHAP and LIME in Intrusion Detection Models. *Applied Sciences (Basel, Switzerland)*, *15*(13), 7329. DOI: 10.3390/app15137329

Herrmann, T. (2025, May). AI as a Sparring Partner–An HCAI Approach to Promote Human Capabilities. In *International Conference on Human-Computer Interaction* (pp. 162-176). Cham: Springer Nature Switzerland. DOI: 10.1007/978-3-031-93415-5_10

Holzinger, A., et al. (2020). Measuring the quality of explanations: The System Causability Scale (SCS). *KI – Künstliche Intelligenz, 34*(2), 193–198. https://doi.org/.DOI: 10.1007/s13218-019-00635-0

Huang, X., Khetan, A., Cvitkovic, M., & Karnin, Z. (2020). TabTransformer: Tabular data modeling using contextual embeddings. arXiv. https://arxiv.org/abs/2012.06678

Ibrar, M., Nahom, H., Mohammed, A., Márquez-Sánchez, S., Fernandez, J. H., Corchado, J. M., & Erbad, A. 2024, June. An Explainable AI-Based Demand Response Optimization Framework for Smart Buildings. In *International Symposium on Distributed Computing and Artificial Intelligence* (pp. 88-98). Cham: Springer Nature Switzerland.

IEEE. (2022). *Ethically aligned design: A vision for prioritizing human well-being with autonomous and intelligent systems*. IEEE Global Initiative on Ethics of Autonomous and Intelligent Systems.

ISIC – International Skin Imaging Collaboration. (n.d.). *ISIC Archive*.

Jabeen, M., Hussain, M., & Rana Hassam Ahmed, H. A. (n.d.). A blockchain-based IPFS augmented distributed information sharing paradigm for secure communication in networked environment.

Jabeen, M., Ahmad, M., Qasim, M., & Hasnain, M. (2024). The surprising similarities between blockchain functions and ethical principles (in perspective of Islam). *International Research Journal of Management and Social Sciences*, *5*(1), 657–669.

Jabeen, M., Ibrar, M., Hussain, M., & Hassan, M. A. S. (2025). Blockchain-based explainable AI for secure and privacy-preserving automated machine learning in IoT-edge for smart medical healthcare. In *AI and blockchain applications for privacy and security in smart medical systems* (pp. 59–80). IGI Global Scientific Publishing. DOI: 10.4018/979-8-3373-0593-6.ch003

Jagli, D. (2024). The Role of Artificial Intelligence in Cyber Security. *Deleted Journal*, *20*(3), 5283–5291. DOI: 10.52783/jes.6327

Jahan, M. S., & Oussalah, M. (2023). A systematic review of hate speech automatic detection using natural language processing. *Neurocomputing*, *546*, 126232. DOI: 10.1016/j.neucom.2023.126232

Jana, S., Biswas, R., Banerjee, C., Patra, T., Pal, M., & Pal, K. (2024). Leveraging Artificial Intelligence for Enhancing Cybersecurity: A Comprehensive Review and Analysis. *International Journal of Advanced Research in Science. Tongxin Jishu*, •••, 173–183. DOI: 10.48175/IJARSCT-19030

Jansen, C., & Jeschke, S. (2018). Mitigating risks of digitalization through managed industrial security services. *AI & Society*, *33*(2), 163–173. DOI: 10.1007/s00146-018-0812-1

Jedličková, A. (2025). Ethical approaches in designing autonomous and intelligent systems: A comprehensive survey towards responsible development. *AI & Society*, *40*(4), 2703–2716. DOI: 10.1007/s00146-024-02040-9

Jia, W., Xie, T., & Wang, B. (2024). A privacy-preserving scheme with multi-level regulation compliance for blockchain. *Scientific Reports*, *14*, 438. DOI: 10.1038/s41598-023-50209-x

Jia, H., Yaghini, M., Choquette-Choo, C. A., Dullerud, N., Thudi, A., Chandrasekaran, V., & Papernot, N. (2021). Proof of learning: Definitions and practice. In *IEEE Symposium on Security and Privacy (S&P)*. https://arxiv.org/abs/2103.05633

Jobin, A., Ienca, M., & Vayena, E. (2019). The global landscape of AI ethics guidelines. *Nature Machine Intelligence*, *1*(9), 389–399. DOI: 10.1038/s42256-019-0088-2

Joshi, G., Jain, A., Araveeti, S., Adhikari, S., Garg, H., & Bhandari, M. (2024). FDA-approved artificial intelligence and machine learning (AI/ML)-enabled medical devices: An updated landscape. *Electronics (Basel)*, *13*(3), 498. DOI: 10.3390/electronics13030498

Jothishri, S., Upender, T., Ravikumar, R., Sailaja, Y., Yuvabharathi, E., & Agnestreesa, J. (2024). *AI Cyber Security: Enhancing Network Security with Deep Learning for Real-Time Threat Detection and Performance Evaluation.* 1–6. DOI: 10.1109/ICONAT61936.2024.10774912

Kakish, D. R. K., AlSamhori, J. F., Fajardo, A. N. R., Qaqish, L. N., Jaber, L. A., Abujudeh, R., Al-Zuriqat, M. H. M., Mohammed, A. Y., & Nashwan, A. J. (2025). Transforming dermatopathology with AI: Addressing bias, enhancing interpretability, and shaping future diagnostics. *Dermatological Reviews*, *6*(1), e70018. DOI: 10.1002/der2.70018

Kaletski-Maisel, G., & Jowallah, R. (2025). Empowering Citizens: Preparing for the Future of Digital Literacy and AI in Education. In Digital Citizenship and the Future of AI Engagement, Ethics, and Privacy (pp. 133-150). IGI Global Scientific Publishing.

Kang, O., & Hirschi, K. (2025). Bias and stereotyping: Human and artificial intelligence (AI). *Annual Review of Applied Linguistics*, 1-16. Das, A., & Rad, P. (2020). Opportunities and challenges in explainable artificial intelligence (xai): A survey. *arXiv preprint arXiv:2006.11371.*

Katz, J., & Lindell, Y. (2007). *Introduction to modern cryptography: Principles and protocols.* Chapman & Hall/CRC. DOI: 10.1201/9781420010756

Kaul, V., Enslin, S., & Gross, S. A. (2020). History of artificial intelligence in medicine. *Gastrointestinal Endoscopy*, *92*(4), 807–812. DOI: 10.1016/j.gie.2020.06.040 PMID: 32565184

Kempt, H. (2023). *Ethical investigations of AI in medical diagnostics.* Dissertation, Rheinisch-Westfälische Technische Hochschule Aachen, 2023, Kulothungan, V. (2024). *A Blockchain-Enabled Approach to Cross-Border Compliance and Trust.* Paper presented at the 2024 IEEE 6th International Conference on Trust, Privacy and Security in Intelligent Systems, and Applications (TPS-ISA).

Keshk, M., Koroniotis, N., Pham, N., Moustafa, N., Turnbull, B., & Zomaya, A. Y. (2023). An explainable deep learning-enabled intrusion detection framework in IoT networks. *Information Sciences*, *639*, 119000. DOI: 10.1016/j.ins.2023.119000

Khalkhali, V., Lee, H., Nguyen, J., Zamora-Erazo, S., Ragin, C., Aphale, A., Bellacosa, A., Monk, E. P., & Biswas, S. K. (2025). MST-AI: Skin Color Estimation in Skin Cancer Datasets. *Journal of Imaging*, *11*(7), 235. DOI: 10.3390/jimaging11070235 PMID: 40710621

Khan, M. S. H., Ahmad, M., Akhtar, K., Jabeen, M., Begum, U., & Ikram, N. (2023). Shanghai Cooperation Organization (SCO): An emerging power block. *Russian Law Journal, 11*(5), 1084–1088.

Khan, M., Tan, S., & Abdullah, F. (2024). AIoT-based remote patient monitoring for diabetes management: A case study from Singapore. *Health Informatics Journal, 30*(1), 56–70.

Kiayias, A., & Zacharias, T. (2017). End-to-end verifiable elections. In *European Symposium on Research in Computer Security*. Springer.

Kim, B.-S., Jin, Y., Lee, J., & Kim, S. (2022). FMCW radar estimation algorithm with high resolution and low complexity based on reduced search area. *Sensors (Basel), 22*(3), 1202. DOI: 10.3390/s22031202 PMID: 35161947

Kim, J., Maathuis, H., & Sent, D. (2024). Human-centered evaluation of explainable AI applications: A systematic review. *Frontiers in Artificial Intelligence, 7*, 1456486. DOI: 10.3389/frai.2024.1456486 PMID: 39484154

Koenecke, A., Nam, A., Lake, E., Nudell, J., Quartey, M., Mengesha, Z., Toups, C., Rickford, J. R., Jurafsky, D., & Goel, S. (2020). Racial disparities in automated speech recognition. *Proceedings of the National Academy of Sciences of the United States of America, 117*(14), 7684–7689. DOI: 10.1073/pnas.1915768117 PMID: 32205437

Kolhar, A. & Sridevi. (2025). Future Trends and Innovation in Machine Intelligence for Cyber Risk Management. In M. Almaiah & Y. Maleh (Eds.), *Machine Intelligence Applications in Cyber-Risk Management* (pp. 415-438). IGI Global Scientific Publishing. DOI: 10.4018/979-8-3693-7540-2.ch018

Kolhar, A. & Sridevi. (2026). Cybersecurity in Smart Devices. In M. Amin (Ed.), *Cybersecurity and Privacy in the Era of Smart Technologies* (pp. 31-62). IGI Global Scientific Publishing. DOI: 10.4018/979-8-3373-2282-7.ch002

Koren, Y., Bell, R., & Volinsky, C. (2009). Matrix factorization techniques for recommender systems. *Computer, 42*(8), 30–37. DOI: 10.1109/MC.2009.263

Koutsoubis, N., Yilmaz, Y., Ramachandran, R. P., Schabath, M., & Rasool, G. (2024). Privacy-preserving federated learning and uncertainty quantification in medical imaging. *Radiology. Artificial Intelligence*. Advance online publication. DOI: 10.1148/ryai.240637 PMID: 40366260

Krippendorff, K. (2019). The cybernetics of design and the design of cybernetics. In *Design Cybernetics: Navigating the New* (pp. 119–136). Springer International Publishing. DOI: 10.1007/978-3-030-18557-2_6

Krizhevsky, A., Sutskever, I., & Hinton, G. E. (2012). ImageNet classification with deep convolutional neural networks. *Advances in Neural Information Processing Systems*, •••, 25.

Kukul, B. (2023). Personal data and personal safety: Re-examining the limits of public data in the context of doxing. *International Data Privacy Law*, *13*(3), 182–193. DOI: 10.1093/idpl/ipad011

Kumar, N. (2023). *AI in Cybersecurity: Threat Detection and Response with Machine Learning*. DOI: 10.52783/tjjpt.v44.i3.237

Kumar, N., Singh, P., & Jain, R. (2020). Smart assistive systems: A survey of AI-driven accessibility. *ACM Computing Surveys, 53*(6), 1–34. DOI: 10.1145/3406093

Kumari, R., Das, S., & Singh, R. K. (2025). Ethical considerations in AI powered diagnosis and treatment. In *Responsible and Explainable Artificial Intelligence in Healthcare* (pp. 25–53). Elsevier. DOI: 10.1016/B978-0-443-24788-0.00002-9

Kumar, P., Chauhan, S., & Awasthi, L. K. (2023). Artificial intelligence in healthcare: Review, ethics, trust challenges & future research directions. *Engineering Applications of Artificial Intelligence*, *120*, 105894. DOI: 10.1016/j.engappai.2023.105894

Kurtansky, N. R., D'Alessandro, B. M., Gillis, M. C., Betz-Stablein, B., Cerminara, S. E., Garcia, R., Girundi, M. A., Goessinger, E. V., Gottfrois, P., Guitera, P., Halpern, A. C., Jakrot, V., Kittler, H., Kose, K., Liopyris, K., Malvehy, J., Mar, V. J., Martin, L. K., Mathew, T., & Rotemberg, V. (2024). The SLICE-3D dataset: 400,000 skin lesion image crops extracted from 3D TBP for skin cancer detection. *Scientific Data*, *11*(1), 884. DOI: 10.1038/s41597-024-03743-w PMID: 39143096

Kuznetsov, O., Sernani, P., Romeo, L., Frontoni, E., & Mancini, A. (2024). On the integration of artificial intelligence and blockchain technology: A perspective about security. *IEEE Access : Practical Innovations, Open Solutions*, *12*, 3881–3897. DOI: 10.1109/ACCESS.2023.3349019

Lacity, M. C., & Lupien, S. C. (2022). *Blockchain Fundamentals for Web 3.0*. University of Arkansas Press.

Laskar, P. (2025). Cryptographic Provenance and the Future of Media Authenticity: Technical Standards and Ethical Frameworks for Generative Content. *Journal of Computer Science and Technology Studies*, *7*(6), 967–972.

Latif, R. M. A., Asghar, M. I., Umer, M., & Hussain, K. (2023). Blockchain-based secure and efficient ride sharing system. In *Handbook of research on cybersecurity issues and challenges for business and FinTech applications* (pp. 364–387). IGI Global Scientific Publishing.

Latif, R. M. A., Farhan, M., Ahmad, J., Mostarda, L., & Cacciagrano, D. (2025). Blockchain-Based Medicine Supply Chain for Transparent Healthcare Tracking. In *AI and Blockchain Applications for Privacy and Security in Smart Medical Systems* (pp. 81–106). IGI Global Scientific Publishing. DOI: 10.4018/979-8-3373-0593-6.ch004

Latif, R. M. A., Farhan, M., Rizwan, O., Hussain, M., Jabbar, S., & Khalid, S. (2021). Retail level Blockchain transformation for product supply chain using truffle development platform. *Cluster Computing*, *24*(1), 1–16. DOI: 10.1007/s10586-020-03165-4

Latif, R. M. A., & Riaz, M. U. (2023). A Secure Distributed System for the Electronic Voting System Using Blockchain Technology. In *Handbook of Research on Cybersecurity Issues and Challenges for Business and FinTech Applications* (pp. 338–363). IGI Global Scientific Publishing.

Lavin, R., Liu, X., Mohanty, H., Norman, L., Zaarour, G., & Krishnamachari, B. (2024). A survey on the applications of zero-knowledge proofs. *arXiv preprint arXiv.00243.*

Lazar, J., Goldstein, D. F., & Taylor, A. (2017). Ensuring digital accessibility through user participation. *Human–Computer Interaction, 32*(4), 265–292. https://doi.org/ DOI: 10.1080/07370024.2016.1180939

Lee, S., Ko, H., Kim, J., & Oh, H. (2023). vCNN: Verifiable convolutional neural network based on zk-SNARKs. *IEEE Transactions on Dependable and Secure Computing*. https://arxiv.org/abs/2210.08718

Lenat, D. B., & Guha, R. V. (1990). *Building Large Knowledge-Based Systems.* Addison-Wesley.

Leung, T.-H., Leung, S.-C., & Wong, C.-K. G. (2020). The effectiveness of an emergency physician–led frailty unit for the living-alone elderly: A pilot retrospective cohort study. *Hong Kong Journal of Emergency Medicine*, *27*(3), 162–167. DOI: 10.1177/1024907919825674

Li, J., Monroe, J., & Jurafsky, D. "Understanding neural networks through human feedback," *Proceedings of the 2018 Conference on Empirical Methods in Natural Language Processing*, pp. 1–11, 2018.

Lin, D., Xu, X., & Liu, J. (2025). Chinese High School Students AI Competency Survey: Based on the UNESCO Students' AI Competency Framework. *Journal of Educational Technology and Innovation*, *7*(1). Advance online publication. DOI: 10.61414/0y6gsj74

Lindell, Y. (2017). How to simulate it–A tutorial on the simulation proof technique. In *Tutorials on the foundations of cryptography* (pp. 277–346). DOI: 10.1007/978-3-319-57048-8_6

Lindsay, R. K., Buchanan, B. G., Feigenbaum, E. A., & Lederberg, J. (1993). DENDRAL: A case study of the first expert system for scientific hypothesis formation. *Artificial Intelligence*, *61*(2), 209–261. DOI: 10.1016/0004-3702(93)90068-M

Litjens, G., Kooi, T., Bejnordi, B. E., Setio, A. A. A., Ciompi, F., Ghafoorian, M., van der Laak, J. A. W. M., van Ginneken, B., & Sánchez, C. I. (2017). A survey on deep learning in medical image analysis. *Medical Image Analysis*, *42*, 60–88. DOI: 10.1016/j.media.2017.07.005 PMID: 28778026

Liu, X., Wang, H., Li, Z., & Qin, L. (2021). Deep learning in ECG diagnosis: A review. *Knowledge-Based Systems*, *227*, 107187. DOI: 10.1016/j.knosys.2021.107187

Liu, X., & Yang, X. (2024). Research progress on frailty in elderly people. *Clinical Interventions in Aging*, *19*, 1493–1505. DOI: 10.2147/CIA.S474547 PMID: 39224708

Liu, Y.-K., & Moody, D. (2024). Post-quantum cryptography and the quantum future of cybersecurity. *Physical Review Applied*, *21*(4), 040501. DOI: 10.1103/PhysRevApplied.21.040501 PMID: 38846721

Liu, Z. (2025). Cultural bias in large language models: A comprehensive analysis and mitigation strategies. *Journal of Transcultural Communication*, *3*(2), 224–244. DOI: 10.1515/jtc-2023-0019

Livraga, G. (2019). Privacy in microdata release: Challenges, techniques, and approaches. In Crato, N., & Paruolo, P. (Eds.), *Data-driven policy impact evaluation* (pp. 117–139). Springer., DOI: 10.1007/978-3-319-78461-8_5

Li, W. (2020). The language of bullying: Social issues on Chinese websites. *Aggression and Violent Behavior*, *53*, 101453. DOI: 10.1016/j.avb.2020.101453

Li, Y., Rao, S., Solares, J. R. A., Hassaine, A., Ramakrishnan, R., Canoy, D., Zhu, Y., Rahimi, K., & Salimi-Khorshidi, G. (2020). BEHRT: Transformer for electronic health records. *Scientific Reports*, *10*(1), 7155. DOI: 10.1038/s41598-020-62922-y PMID: 32346050

London, A. J. (2019). Artificial intelligence and black-box medical decisions: Accuracy versus explainability. *The Hastings Center Report*, *49*(1), 15–21. DOI: 10.1002/hast.973 PMID: 30790315

Lo, S. K., Liu, Y., Lu, Q., Wang, C., Xu, X., Paik, H.-Y., & Zhu, L. (2022). Toward trustworthy ai: Blockchain-based architecture design for accountability and fairness of federated learning systems. *IEEE Internet of Things Journal, 10*(4), 3276–3284. DOI: 10.1109/JIOT.2022.3144450

Lucas, G. M., et al. (2016). It's only a computer: The impact of human-like avatars on counseling outcomes. *Computers in Human Behavior, 52*, 331–338. .DOI: 10.1016/j.chb.2015.06.008

Luk, J. K., & Chan, D. K. (2022). Medical practice CME: Frailty and sarcopenia—From theory to practice. *Hong Kong Medical Journal, 28*(5), 392–395. DOI: 10.12809/hkmj219411 PMID: 38232963

Lu, Q., Zhu, L., Xu, X., Whittle, J., Zowghi, D., & Jacquet, A. (2024). Responsible AI pattern catalogue: A collection of best practices for AI governance and engineering. *ACM Computing Surveys, 56*(7), 1–35. DOI: 10.1145/3626234

Lyu, Y., Dost, M., Koh, S., & Wicker, J. (2024). Regional bias in monolingual English language models. *Machine Learning, 113*(7), 2541–2560. DOI: 10.1007/s10994-024-06555-6

Maccaro, A., Stokes, K., Statham, L., He, L., Williams, A., Pecchia, L., & Piaggio, D. (2024). Clearing the fog: A scoping literature review on the ethical issues surrounding artificial intelligence-based medical devices. *Journal of Personalized Medicine, 14*(5), 443. DOI: 10.3390/jpm14050443 PMID: 38793025

Mahama, H., Rana, T., Marjoribanks, T., & Elbashir, M. Z. (2023). Principles-based risk regulatory reforms and management control practices: A field study. *Accounting, Auditing & Accountability Journal, 36*(3), 773–800. DOI: 10.1108/AAAJ-10-2020-4983

Maldonado-Ruiz, D., Torres, J., & Madhoun, N. E. (2022). Fundamentals of blockchain technology. In *Principles and Practice of Blockchains* (pp. 3–25). Springer.

Mazzi, F. (2025). Evaluating the normative implications of national and international artificial intelligence policies for Sustainable Development Goal 3: Good health and well-being. *Health Affairs Scholar, 3*(6), qxaf108. Advance online publication. DOI: 10.1093/haschl/qxaf108 PMID: 40584023

McCarthy, J., Minsky, M. L., Rochester, N., & Shannon, C. E. (1955). A Proposal for the Dartmouth Summer Research Project on Artificial Intelligence.

McCarthy, J., Minsky, M. L., Rochester, N., & Shannon, C. E. (2006). A proposal for the dartmouth summer research project on artificial intelligence, august 31, 1955. *AI Magazine, 27*(4), 12–12.

Mennella, C., Maniscalco, U., De Pietro, G., & Esposito, M. (2024). Ethical and regulatory challenges of AI technologies in healthcare: A narrative review. *Heliyon, 10*(4), e09540. DOI: 10.1016/j.heliyon.2024.e26297 PMID: 38384518

Mergen, A., Çetin-Kılıç, N., & Özbilgin, M. F. (2025). Artificial intelligence and bias towards marginalised groups: Theoretical roots and challenges. In *AI and Diversity in a Datafied World of Work: Will the Future of Work be Inclusive?* (Vol. 12, pp. 17–38). Emerald Publishing Limited. DOI: 10.1108/S2051-233320250000012004

Mienye, I. D., Swart, T. G., Obaido, G., Jordan, M., & Ilono, P. (2025). Deep convolutional neural networks in medical image analysis: A review. *Information (Basel), 16*(3), 195. DOI: 10.3390/info16030195

Millar, M. (2011). Patient rights and healthcare-associated infection. *The Journal of Hospital Infection, 79*(2), 99–102. DOI: 10.1016/j.jhin.2011.04.031 PMID: 21798627

Miller, R. A. (1984). INTERNIST-1/CADUCEUS: Problems facing expert consultant programs. *Methods of Information in Medicine, 23*(1), 9–14. DOI: 10.1055/s-0038-1635320 PMID: 6374372

Miller, R. A., Pople, H. E.Jr, & Myers, J. D. (1982). Internist-I, an experimental computer-based diagnostic consultant for general internal medicine. *The New England Journal of Medicine, 307*(8), 468–476. DOI: 10.1056/NEJM198208193070803 PMID: 7048091

Miller, T. (2019). Explanation in artificial intelligence: Insights from the social sciences. *Artificial Intelligence, 267*, 1–38. DOI: 10.1016/j.artint.2018.07.007

Milosevic, T. (2022). *Artificial intelligence to address cyberbullying, harassment, and misinformation*. National Institutes of Health.

Milosevic, T., Van Royen, K., & Davis, B. (2022). Artificial intelligence to address cyberbullying, harassment and abuse: New directions in the midst of complexity. *International Journal of Bullying Prevention : an Official Publication of the International Bullying Prevention Association, 4*(1), 1–5. DOI: 10.1007/s42380-022-00117-x PMID: 35233506

Minsky, M., & Papert, S. (1969). *Perceptrons: An Introduction to Computational Geometry*. MIT Press.

Mishra, M., Pradhan, R. C., Agrawalla, K., & Bokka, R. (2025). *AI for Cybersecurity Threat Detection: A Machine Enabled Computing Perspective*. 1–5. DOI: 10.1109/ASSIC64892.2025.11158640

Mittelstadt, B. D., Allo, P., Taddeo, M., Wachter, S., & Floridi, L. (2016). The ethics of algorithms: Mapping the debate. *Big Data & Society, 3*(2), 1–21. DOI: 10.1177/2053951716679679

Moghadam, M. P., Moghadam, Z. A., Qazani, M. R. C., Pławiak, P., & Alizadehsani, R. (2024). Impact of artificial intelligence in nursing for geriatric clinical care for chronic diseases: A systematic literature review. *IEEE Access : Practical Innovations, Open Solutions*, *12*, 122557–122587. DOI: 10.1109/ACCESS.2024.3450970

Mohassel, P., & Zhang, Y. (2017). SecureML: A system for scalable privacy-preserving machine learning. In *2017 IEEE Symposium on Security and Privacy (SP)*. IEEE. DOI: 10.1109/SP.2017.12

Mollahosseini, A., Chan, D., & Mahoor, M. H. (2016, March). Going deeper in facial expression recognition using deep neural networks. In *2016 IEEE Winter conference on applications of computer vision (WACV)* (pp. 1-10). IEEE. DOI: 10.1109/WACV.2016.7477450

Montayre, J., Kuo, K., & Leung, K. M. C. (2024). Social frailty prevalence among older people in Hong Kong. *Journal of Ageing and Longevity*, *4*(3), 225–233. DOI: 10.3390/jal4030016

Montoya, L. N., Roberts, J. S., & Hidalgo, B. S. (2025, March). Towards fairness in AI for melanoma detection: systemic review and recommendations. In *Future of information and communication conference* (pp. 320–341). Springer Nature Switzerland. DOI: 10.1007/978-3-031-84460-7_21

Munawar, M., Singh, T. M., & Hanafiah, M. M. (2025). The Future of AI in Cyberbullying Prevention: Trends and Technologies. In *Combating Cyberbullying With Generative AI* (pp. 237–278). IGI Global Scientific Publishing. DOI: 10.4018/979-8-3373-0543-1.ch009

Murdoch, T. B. (2021). Privacy and artificial intelligence: Challenges for protecting health information in a new era. *BMC Medical Ethics*, *22*(1), 76. Advance online publication. DOI: 10.1186/s12910-021-00687-3 PMID: 34525993

Murphy, K., Di Ruggiero, E., Upshur, R., Willison, D. J., Malhotra, N., Cai, J. C., Malhotra, N., Lui, V., & Gibson, J. (2021). Artificial intelligence for good health: A scoping review of the ethics literature. *BMC Medical Ethics*, *22*(1), 14. DOI: 10.1186/s12910-021-00577-8 PMID: 33588803

Namvarpour, M., Pauwels, H., & Razi, A. (2025). AI-induced Sexual Harassment: Investigating Contextual Characteristics and User Reactions of Sexual Harassment by a Companion Chatbot. *Proceedings of the ACM on Human-Computer Interaction*, *9*(7), 1–28. DOI: 10.1145/3757548

Nassif, S. A. (2024). Algorithm Literacy among Youth: Understanding and Navigating Social Media Algorithms. *The Egyptian Journal of Media Research*, *2024*(89), 33–72.

Natale, S., & Ballatore, A. (2020). Imagining the thinking machine: Technological myths and the rise of artificial intelligence. *Convergence (London)*, *26*(1), 3–18. DOI: 10.1177/1354856517715164

National Institute of Standards and Technology. (2023). *Artificial Intelligence Risk Management Framework (AI RMF 1.0)* (NIST AI 100-1). U.S. Department of Commerce. DOI: 10.6028/NIST.AI.100-1

Nebeker, C., et al. (2019). Digital health research and the ethics of data privacy. *NPJ Digital Medicine, 2*(1), 1–5. https://doi.org/DOI: 10.1038/s41746-019-0166-3

Neupane, S., Mitra, S., Fernandez, I. A., Saha, S., Mittal, S., Chen, J., Pillai, N., & Rahimi, S. (2024). Security considerations in ai-robotics: A survey of current methods, challenges, and opportunities. *IEEE Access : Practical Innovations, Open Solutions*, *12*, 22072–22097. DOI: 10.1109/ACCESS.2024.3363657

Newell, A., & Simon, H. A. (1961). GPS, a program that simulates human thought. In Billing, H. (Ed.), *Lernende Automaten*. Oldenbourg.

Nilsson, N. J. (1983). Artificial intelligence prepares for 2001. *AI Magazine*, *4*(4), 7–7.

Nithin, G. N., Pradhan, A. K., & Swain, G. (2024). zkHealthChain – Blockchain enabled supply chain in healthcare using zero knowledge. In D. Puthal et al. (Eds.), *IFIP Advances in Information and Communication Technology*: Vol. 684. *Internet of Things* (pp. 133–148). Springer. DOI: 10.1007/978-3-031-45882-8_10

Nnaka, K. I., Mbamalu, P. O., Nwaigbo, J. C., Ozo-ogueji, P. C., Njoku, V. I., & Ekechi, C. C. (2025). AI-powered threat detection: Opportunities and limitations in modern cyber defense. *World Journal Of Advanced Research and Reviews*, *27*(2), 210–223. DOI: 10.30574/wjarr.2025.27.2.2854

Nnamani, C. C. (2024). Exploiting AI Capabilities: An in-Depth Analysis of Artificial Intelligence Integration in Cybersecurity for Threat Detection and Response. *International Journal of Education. Management and Technology*, *2*(3), 268–286. DOI: 10.58578/ijemt.v2i3.3904

Nobata, C., Tetreault, J., Thomas, A., Mehdad, Y., & Chang, Y. (2016). "Abusive language detection in online user content." in *Proceedings of the 25th International Conference on World Wide Web WWW'16. (Republic and Canton of Geneva, CHE: International World Wide Web Conferences Steering Committee)*, 145–153. DOI: 10.1145/2872427.2883062

Noble, S. U. (2018). *Algorithms of oppression: How search engines reinforce racism*. New York University Press. DOI: 10.18574/nyu/9781479833641.001.0001

Nussbaum, M. (2006). *Frontiers of justice: Disability, nationality, species membership*. Harvard University Press.

Odezuligbo, I., Alade, O., & Chukwurah, E. F. (2024). Ethical and regulatory considerations in AI-driven medical imaging: A perspective overview. *Medical AI Ethics*, *8*(2), 156–174. DOI: 10.30574/ijsra.2024.13.1.1739

OECD. (2019). *F. T. C. A. N.* Principles on Artificial Intelligence.

Olafuyi, B. A. (2023). *Artificial Intelligence in Cybersecurity: Enhancing Threat Detection and Mitigation*. International Journal of Scientific and Research Publications., DOI: 10.29322/IJSRP.13.12.2023.p14419

Ozmen, B. (2025). Navigating FDA regulations for development of artificial intelligence technologies in plastic surgery. *Aesthetic Surgery Journal*, *45*(8), 865–868. Advance online publication. DOI: 10.1093/asj/sjaf051 PMID: 40181519

Packer, M., Hoffer, E. P., Barnett, G. O., Famiglietti, K., Kim, R. J., McLatchey, J., Elkin, P. L., Cimino, C., & Studney, D. (1989). Evolution of DXplain: A decision support system. *Proceedings of the Annual Symposium on Computer Applications in Medical Care,* 949–951.

Palanica, A., et al. (2022). Edge AI and privacy in assistive health monitoring. *Sensors, 22*(14), 5171. DOI: 10.3390/s22145171

Pardhi, N., Gundewar, S., Chute, T., & Adithyan, S. (2025). *Ethical and Strategic Implications of AI in Cybersecurity*. 1–6. DOI: 10.1109/IC2E365635.2025.11166708

Pariser, E. (2011). *The filter bubble: What the Internet is hiding from you*. Penguin Press.

Parno, B., Howell, J., Gentry, C., & Raykova, M. (2013). Pinocchio: Nearly practical verifiable computation. In *2013 IEEE Symposium on Security and Privacy*. IEEE. DOI: 10.1109/SP.2013.47

Patchin, J. W., & Hinduja, S. (2015). Measuring cyberbullying: Implications for research. *Aggression and Violent Behavior*, *23*, 69–74. DOI: 10.1016/j.avb.2015.05.013

Pati, R., Gupta, H., & Lee, M. (2024). Differential privacy-enhanced federated learning for genomics. *Nature Communications, 15*, 1456.

Pei, W. (2025). AI can be cyberbullying perpetrators: Investigating the role of artificial intelligence in cyberbullying. *Technology in Society, 70*, 102217.

Pennebaker, J. W., Francis, M. E., & Booth, R. J. (2001). *Linguistic Inquiry and Word Count: LIWC*. Lawrence Erlbaum Associates.

Peters, D., Vold, K., Robinson, D., & Calvo, R. A. (2020). Responsible AI—Two frameworks for ethical design practice. *IEEE Transactions on Technology and Society, 1*(1), 34–47. DOI: 10.1109/TTS.2020.2974991

Pina, E., Ramos, J., Jorge, H., Váz, P., Silva, J., Wanzeller, C., Abbasi, M., & Martins, P. (2024). Data privacy and ethical considerations in database management. *Journal of Cybersecurity and Privacy, 4*(3), 494–517. DOI: 10.3390/jcp4030024

Poelstra, A. (2016). Confidential transactions. *Ledger*, *1*, 1–19.

Polygon Labs. (2023, March 27). Ethereum scalability with zkEVM performance and security. https://polygon.technology/polygon-zkevm

Ptaszynski, M., Masui, F., Nitta, T., Hatakeyama, S., Kimura, Y., Rzepka, R., & Araki, K. (2016). Sustainable cyberbullying detection with category-maximized relevance of harmful phrases and double-filtered automatic optimization. *International Journal of Child-Computer Interaction, 8*, 15–30. DOI: 10.1016/j.ijcci.2016.07.002

Rahman, A., Debnath, T., Kundu, D., Khan, M. S. I., Aishi, A. A., Sazzad, S., Sayduzzaman, M., & Band, S. S. (2024). Machine learning and deep learning-based approach in smart healthcare: Recent advances, applications, challenges and opportunities. *AIMS Public Health, 11*(1), 58–109. DOI: 10.3934/publichealth.2024004 PMID: 38617415

Rahman, M., Uddin, I., Das, R., Saha, T., Haque, M. R., Shatu, N. R., & Shafiq, S. I. (2025). Application of Artificial Intelligence in Detecting and Mitigating Cyber Threats. *International Research Journal of Innovations in Engineering and Technology, 09*(01), 17–26. DOI: 10.47001/IRJIET/2025.901003

Rahmati, M., & Pagano, A. (2025). Federated Learning-Driven Cybersecurity Framework for IoT Networks with Privacy Preserving and Real-Time Threat Detection Capabilities. Informatics, Rane, N., Choudhary, S. and Rane, J., 2024. Artificial intelligence for enhancing resilience. *Journal of Applied Artificial Intelligence, 5*(2), 1–33.

Ramos, G. (2023). *Ethics of artificial intelligence*.

Rane, N., Choudhary, S., & Rane, J. (2023). Blockchain and Artificial Intelligence (AI) integration for revolutionizing security and transparency in finance. *Available at SSRN* 4644253. DOI: 10.2139/ssrn.4644253

Ratti, E., Morrison, M., & Jakab, I. (2025). Ethical and social considerations of applying artificial intelligence in healthcare—A two-pronged scoping review. *BMC Medical Ethics*, *26*(1), 68. DOI: 10.1186/s12910-025-01198-1 PMID: 40420080

Regehr, K., Shaughnessy, C., Zhao, M., & Shaughnessy, N. (2024). *Safer scrolling: How algorithms popularise and gamify online hate and misogyny for young people*. University College London & University of Kent. https://www.ascl.org.uk/ASCL/media/ASCL/Help%20and%20advice/Inclusion/Safer-scrolling.pdf

Rezvan, M., Shekarpour, S., Alshargi, F., Thirunarayan, K., Shalin, V. L., & Sheth, A. (2020). Analyzing and learning the language for different types of harassment. *PLoS One*, *15*(3), e0227330. DOI: 10.1371/journal.pone.0227330 PMID: 32218569

Rheingold, H. (2000). *Tools for thought: The history and future of mind-expanding technology*. MIT press.

Ribeiro, M. T., Singh, S., & Guestrin, C. (2016, August). " Why should i trust you?" Explaining the predictions of any classifier. In *Proceedings of the 22nd ACM SIGKDD international conference on knowledge discovery and data mining* (pp. 1135-1144). DOI: 10.18653/v1/N16-3020

Rong, Y., Leemann, T., Nguyen, T. T., Fiedler, L., Qian, P., Unhelkar, V., Seidel, T., Kasneci, G., & Kasneci, E. (2023). Towards human-centered explainable ai: A survey of user studies for model explanations. *IEEE Transactions on Pattern Analysis and Machine Intelligence*, *46*(4), 2104–2122. DOI: 10.1109/TPAMI.2023.3331846 PMID: 37956008

Ross, C., & Swetlitz, I. (2018). IBM's Watson supercomputer recommended "unsafe and incorrect" cancer treatments, internal documents show. *STAT*, *25*, 1–10. https://www.statnews.com/2018/07/25/ibm-watson-recommended-unsafe-incorrect-treatments

Rumelhart, D. E., Hinton, G. E., & Williams, R. J. (1986). Learning representations by back-propagating errors. *Nature*, *323*(6088), 533–536. DOI: 10.1038/323533a0

Russell, S., & Norvig, P. (2021). *Artificial intelligence: A modern approach* (4th ed.). Pearson.

Saengprang, S., & Gadavanij, S. (2021). Cyberbullying: The case of public figures. *LEARN J. Lang. Educ. Acquis. Res. Netw.*, *14*, 344–369.

Sah, C. P., Kaur, M., & Singh, G. (2024). *Efficiency of zero-knowledge proofs: A through review and analysis.* Paper presented at the 2024 IEEE International Conference on Public Key Infrastructure and its Applications (PKIA). DOI: 10.1109/PKIA62599.2024.10729195

Sakurai, Y. (2025). Advance decision-making for future disability in East Asia: Addressing challenges in end-of-life medical care for older adults. *IEEE Access : Practical Innovations, Open Solutions.*

Salako, A. O., Fabuyi, J. A., Aideyan, N. T., Selesi-Aina, O., Dapo-Oyewole, D. L., & Olaniyi, O. O. (2024). Advancing information governance in AI-driven cloud ecosystem: Strategies for enhancing data security and meeting regulatory compliance. *Asian Journal of Research in Computer Science, 17*(12), 66–88. DOI: 10.9734/ajrcos/2024/v17i12530

Salem, A. H., Azzam, S. M., Emam, O. E., & Abohany, A. A. (2024). Advancing cybersecurity: A comprehensive review of AI-driven detection techniques. *Journal of Big Data, 11*(1), 105. DOI: 10.1186/s40537-024-00957-y

Sarker, I. H. (2023). Multi-aspects AI-based modeling and adversarial learning for cybersecurity intelligence and robustness: A comprehensive overview. *Security and Privacy, 6*(5), e295. DOI: 10.1002/spy2.295

Sawyer, B. D., Miller, D. B., Canham, M., & Karwowski, W. (2021). Human factors and ergonomics in design of a 3: automation, autonomy, and artificial intelligence. *Handbook of human factors and ergonomics*, 1385-1416. Holzinger, A., Biemann, C., Pattichis, C. S., & Kell, D. B. (2017). What do we need to build explainable AI systems for the medical domain? *arXiv preprint arXiv:1712.09923.* Doshi-Velez, F., & Kim, B. (2017). Towards a rigorous science of interpretable machine learning. *arXiv preprint arXiv:1702.08608.*

Schilke, O., & Reimann, M. (2025). The transparency dilemma: How AI disclosure erodes trust. *Organizational Behavior and Human Decision Processes, 188*, 104405. DOI: 10.1016/j.obhdp.2025.104405

Schuessler-Lenz, M., Herberts, C., Reischl, I., Ruiz, S., Celis, P., Beuneu, C., . . . Timón, M. (2023). Marketing regulatory oversight of advanced therapy medicinal products in Europe. *Regulatory Aspects of Gene Therapy Cell Therapy Products: A Global Perspective*, 1-21.

Scrivano, A. (2025). *The Impact of AI on Cybersecurity: Threats and Solutions.* DOI: 10.21203/rs.3.rs-7550421/v1

Sen, A. (1999). *Development as freedom.* Oxford University Press.

Shafin, S. S. (2025). An explainable feature selection framework for web phishing detection with machine learning. *Data Science and Management*, *8*(2), 127–136. DOI: 10.1016/j.dsm.2024.08.004

Shahzad, M. F., Xu, S., Lim, W. M., Yang, X., & Khan, Q. R. (2024). Artificial intelligence and social media on academic performance and mental well-being: Student perceptions of positive impact in the age of smart learning. *Heliyon*, *10*(8), e29523. Advance online publication. DOI: 10.1016/j.heliyon.2024.e29523 PMID: 38665566

Shamsujjoha, M., Lu, Q., Zhao, D., & Zhu, L. (2024). *Towards AI-safety-by-design: A taxonomy of runtime guardrails in foundation model-based systems. arXiv preprint arXiv:2408.12345.*

Sharma, B., Sharma, L., Lal, C., & Roy, S. (2024). Explainable artificial intelligence for intrusion detection in IoT networks: A deep learning based approach. *Expert Systems with Applications*, *238*, 121751. DOI: 10.1016/j.eswa.2023.121751

Sharma, S. K. (2024). AI-Enhanced Cyber Threat Detection and Response Systems. *AI-Enhanced Cyber Threat Detection and Response Systems.*, *1*(2), 43–48. DOI: 10.36676/ssjaiml.v1.i2.14

Sharma, S. K. (2025). AI-Powered Cybersecurity: The Future of Threat Detection. *Indian Scientific Journal Of Research In Engineering And Management*, *09*(04), 1–9. DOI: 10.55041/IJSREM45943

Shibata, T., & Wada, K. (2011). Robot therapy: A new approach for mental healthcare. *Current Psychiatry Reviews, 7*(3), 180–188. https://doi.org/DOI: 10.2174/157340011796391202

Shimo, S. (2020, November). Risks of bias in AI-based emotional analysis technology from diversity perspectives. In *2020 IEEE International Symposium on Technology and Society (ISTAS)* (pp. 66-68). IEEE. DOI: 10.1109/ISTAS50296.2020.9462168

Shin, Y. (2025). Toward human-centered artificial intelligence for users' digital well-being: Systematic review, synthesis, and future directions. *JMIR Human Factors*, *12*(1), e69533. DOI: 10.2196/69533 PMID: 40928842

Shneiderman, B. (2022). *Human-Centered AI*. Oxford University Press. DOI: 10.1093/oso/9780192845290.001.0001

Shortliffe, E. H. (1974). A rule-based computer program for advising physicians regarding antimicrobial therapy selection. *Proceedings of the 1974 ACM Annual Conference* - Volume 2, 739–744. DOI: 10.1145/1408800.1408906

Shree, S. R. A., J., A., N., & Saranya, V. (2024). *Leveraging Artificial Intelligence for Cybersecurity* (pp. 29–43). IGI Global. DOI: 10.4018/979-8-3693-4159-9.ch003

Simonsen, J., & Robertson, T. (Eds.). (2013). *Routledge international handbook of participatory design* (Vol. 711). Routledge.

Sissodia, R., Rauthan, M. S., Barthwal, V., & Dwivedi, V. (2025). Artificial Intelligence (AI) in Cybersecurity. *Advances in Computational Intelligence and Robotics Book Series*, 121–152. DOI: 10.4018/979-8-3373-0583-7.ch005

Sporner, M. L., et al. (2020). User-driven design of AI-enabled wheelchair navigation systems. *Disability and Rehabilitation: Assistive Technology, 15*(5), 527–536. https://doi.org/DOI: 10.1080/17483107.2019.1571119

Sridevi & Kolhar. A. (2025). Energy-Efficiency Strategies for Wireless Sensor Networks in IoT. In A. Sathio, M. Rind, S. Awan, & A. Junejo (Eds.), *Energy-Efficient Deep Learning Approaches in IoT, Fog, and Green Blockchain Revolution* (pp. 167-192). IGI Global Scientific Publishing. DOI: 10.4018/979-8-3373-0300-0.ch006

Sridevi & Kolhar. A. (2026). Fundamentals of 6G Networks. In R. Shaikh (Ed.), *6G Networks and AI-Driven Cybersecurity* (pp. 1-32). IGI Global Scientific Publishing. DOI: 10.4018/979-8-3373-0568-4.ch001

Stangl, A.. (2020). AI-powered visual assistance for blind users: A field study. **Proceedings of the 2020 CHI Conference on Human Factors in Computing Systems (CHI '20)**. DOI: 10.1145/3313831.3376689

Stroud, A. M., Anzabi, M. D., Wise, J. L., Barry, B. A., Malik, M. M., McGowan, M. L., & Sharp, R. R. (2025). Toward safe and ethical implementation of health care artificial intelligence: Insights from an academic medical center. *Mayo Clinic Proceedings. Digital Health*, *3*(1), 100189. DOI: 10.1016/j.mcpdig.2024.100189 PMID: 40206995

Subías-Beltrán, P., Unceta, I., & de Lecuona, I.. (2025). Asking the right questions: A governance approach to uphold human autonomy in artificial intelligence. *AI & Society*. Advance online publication. DOI: 10.1007/s00146-025-02611-4

Tadesse, G. A., Cintas, C., Varshney, K. R., Staar, P., Agunwa, C., Speakman, S., Jia, J., Bailey, E. E., Adelekun, A., Lipoff, J. B., Onyekaba, G., Lester, J. C., Rotemberg, V., Zou, J., & Daneshjou, R. (2023). Skin tone analysis for representation in educational materials (STAR-ED) using machine learning. *NPJ Digital Medicine*, *6*(1), 151. DOI: 10.1038/s41746-023-00881-0 PMID: 37596324

Tan, K. H. (Ed.). (2019). Stop Cyberbullying. Malaysia: Penerbit Universiti Kebangsaan malasia.

Tang, L., Li, J., & Fantus, S. (2023). Medical artificial intelligence ethics: A systematic review of empirical studies. *Digital Health*, *9*, 20552076231186064. DOI: 10.1177/20552076231186064 PMID: 37434728

Tasdelen, A. (2024). Fundamentals of Blockchain. In *Exploring Blockchain Applications* (pp. 6–25). CRC Press. DOI: 10.1201/9781003389552-2

Taylor, R. R., O'Dell, B., & Murphy, J. W. (2024). Human-centric AI: Philosophical and community-centric considerations. *AI & Society*, *39*(5), 2417–2424. DOI: 10.1007/s00146-023-01694-1

Teo, R., Singh, P., & Chen, L. (2024). Federated learning for breast cancer detection across Asia and Europe: Preserving privacy in cross-border healthcare. *IEEE Journal of Biomedical and Health Informatics*, *28*(5), 1901–1912.

Thanasi-Boçe, M., & Hoxha, J. (2025). Blockchain for Sustainable Development: A Systematic Review. *Sustainability (Basel)*, *17*(11), 4848. DOI: 10.3390/su17114848

Thapaliya, S. (2025). Artificial Intelligence and Cybersecurity: Pioneering Next-Generation Protection Strategies. *SADGAMAYA*, *2*(1), 61–65. DOI: 10.3126/sadgamaya.v2i1.80334

Thellman, E., & Ziemke, T. (2023). Empathy and emotional engagement in human–AI interaction. *AI & Society*, *38*, 477–488.

Tilala, M. H., Chenchala, P. K., Choppadandi, A., Kaur, J., Naguri, S., Saoji, R., Devagup-tapu, B., & Tilala, M. (2024). Ethical considerations in the use of artificial intelligence and machine learning in health care: A comprehensive review. *Cureus*, *16*(6). Advance online publication. DOI: 10.7759/cureus.62443 PMID: 39011215

Topol, E. (2019). Deep medicine: How artificial intelligence can make healthcare human again. Hachette UK.

Torfi, A., Fox, E. A., & Reddy, C. K. (2022). Differentially private synthetic medical data generation using convolutional GANs. *Information Sciences*, *586*, 485–500. DOI: 10.1016/j.ins.2021.12.018

Torre, D., Chennamaneni, A., Jo, J., Vyas, G., & Sabrsula, B. (2025). Toward enhancing privacy preservation of a federated learning cnn intrusion detection system in iot: Method and empirical study. *ACM Transactions on Software Engineering and Methodology*, *34*(2), 1–48. DOI: 10.1145/3695998

Toya, H. (2025). Artificial Intelligence and Security: Enhancing Cyber Defense Mechanisms. *Oriental Journal of Computer Science and Technology*, *17*(01), 23–25. DOI: 10.13005/ojcst17.01.07

Tronto, J. (2020). *Moral boundaries: A political argument for an ethic of care*. Routledge. DOI: 10.4324/9781003070672

Tronto, J. C. (2013). *Caring democracy: Markets, equality, and justice*. NYU Press.

Turing, A. M. (1950). Computing Machinery and Intelligence. *Mind*, *LIX*(236), 433–460. DOI: 10.1093/mind/LIX.236.433

Tyagi, A. K. (2024). Blockchain–Artificial Intelligence-Based Secured Solutions for Smart Environment. *Digital Twin Blockchain for Smart Cities*, 547-577.

Tybjerg, K. (2003). Wonder-making and philosophical wonder in Hero of Alexandria. *Studies in History and Philosophy of Science*, *34*(3), 443–466. DOI: 10.1016/S0039-3681(03)00053-0

U.S. Food and Drug Administration. (2025). *Artificial intelligence-enabled device software functions: Lifecycle management and marketing submission recommendations (Draft guidance)*. https://www.fda.gov/media/184856/download

Umucu, E. (2025). Artificial Intelligence and Health Equity for People with Disabilities: An Integrated Framework for Disability-Inclusive AI Design. *Inquiry : a Journal of Medical Care Organization, Provision and Financing*, *62*, 00469580251365472. Advance online publication. DOI: 10.1177/00469580251365472 PMID: 40847466

Unesco. (2022). *Recommendation on the ethics of artificial intelligence*. United Nations Educational, Scientific and Cultural Organization.

Vallor, S. (2016). *Technology and the virtues: A philosophical guide to a future worth wanting*. Oxford University Press. DOI: 10.1093/acprof:oso/9780190498511.001.0001

Van de Poel, I., & Royakkers, L. (2023). *Ethics, technology, and engineering: An introduction*. John Wiley & Sons.

Van Hee, C., Jacobs, G., Emmery, C., Desmet, B., Lefever, E., Verhoeven, B., De Pauw, G., Daelemans, W., & Hoste, V. (2018). Automatic detection of cyberbullying in social media text. *PLoS One*, *13*(10), e0203794. DOI: 10.1371/journal.pone.0203794 PMID: 30296299

van Leersum, C. M., & Maathuis, C. (2025). Human centred explainable AI decision-making in healthcare. *Journal of Responsible Technology*, *21*, 100108. DOI: 10.1016/j.jrt.2025.100108

Van Wynsberghe, A. (2020). Designing robots for care: Care centered value-sensitive design. In *Machine ethics and robot ethics* (pp. 185–211). Routledge. DOI: 10.4324/9781003074991-17

Vishwakarma, P. (2023). Journal of Internet Commerce: A Bibliometric Overview. *JournalofInternetCommerce,22*(4),567–593.DOI: 10.1080/15332861.2022.2095178

Vocdoni & Aragon. (2022). FC Barcelona Web3 voting https://publish.obsidian.md/refi-barcelona/Ecosystem+Map/Local/Vocdoni

Wadden, J. J. (2023). *Ethics and healthcare artificial intelligence: some problems and solutions for advanced diagnostic systems.* University of British Columbia, Whig, P., Sharma, R., Yathiraju, N., Jain, A., & Sharma, S. (2025). Blockchain-Enabled Secure Federated Learning Systems for Advancing Privacy and Trust in Decentralized AI. *Model Optimization Methods for Efficient Edge AI: Federated Learning Architectures, Frameworks Applications*, 321-340.

Wang, W. (2025). *AI-Driven Cybersecurity Solutions Enhancing Threat Detection in Healthcare and Airlines*. DOI: 10.20944/preprints202501.1352.v1

Wang, Z., Ma, J., Wang, X., Hu, J., Qin, Z., & Ren, K. (2022). Threats to training: A survey of poisoning attacks and defenses on machine learning systems. *ACM Computing Surveys*, *55*(7), 1–36. DOI: 10.1145/3538707

Wan, X., Shen, J., & He, G. (2022). Effects of traditional Chinese exercises on frailty, quality of life, and physical function on frail and pre-frail older people: A systematic review and meta-analysis. *The Journal of Frailty & Aging*, *11*(4), 407–415. DOI: 10.14283/jfa.2022.52 PMID: 36346727

Waseem, Z., Davidson, T., Warmsley, D., & Weber, I. (2017). "Understanding abuse: a typology of abusive language detection subtasks." in *Proceedings of the First Workshop on Abusive Language Online*; July 30–August 4, 2017; 78–84. DOI: 10.18653/v1/W17-3012

Weiner, E. B., Dankwa-Mullan, I., Nelson, W. A., & Hassanpour, S. (2025). Ethical challenges and evolving strategies in the integration of artificial intelligence into clinical practice. *PLOS Digital Health*, *4*(4), e0000810. DOI: 10.1371/journal.pdig.0000810 PMID: 40198594

Wiegand, M., Siegel, M., & Ruppenhofer, J. (2018). Overview of the germeval 2018 shared task on the identification of offensive language.

Winfield, A. F. T., & Jirotka, M. (2018). Ethical governance is essential to building trust in robotics and AI systems. *Philosophical Transactions of the Royal Society A: Mathematical, Physical and Engineering Sciences, 376*(2133), 20180085. DOI: 10.1098/rsta.2018.0085

Wong, A., & Sussman, J. B. (2025). Understanding model drift and its impact on health care policy. *JAMA Health Forum*, *6*(1), e252724. DOI: 10.1001/jamahealth-forum.2025.2724 PMID: 40815525

World Health Organization. (2021). *Ethics and governance of artificial intelligence for health: WHO guidance.* World Health Organization. https://www.who.int/publications/i/item/9789240029200

World Health Organization. (2024). *Ethics and governance of artificial intelligence for health: Guidance on large language models*. World Health Organization.

World Health Organization. (2024). *Ethics and governance of artificial intelligence for health: Large multimodal models. WHO guidance.* World Health Organization. https://www.who.int/news/item/18-01-2024-who-releases-ai-ethics-and-governance-guidance-for-large-multi-modal-models

Xhako, D., Hyka, N., Spahiu, E., & Hoxhaj, S. (2025). Medical image analysis using deep learning algorithms (DLA). *AIMS Biophysics*, *12*(2), 121–143. DOI: 10.3934/biophy.2025008

Xie, X., Ge, Y., Walia, H., Yang, J., & Yu, H. (2023). Leaf-counting in monocot plants using deep regression models. *Sensors (Basel)*, *23*(4), 1890. DOI: 10.3390/s23041890 PMID: 36850487

Xing, H., Sun, R., Ren, J., Wei, J., Feng, C. M., Ding, X., Guo, Z., Wang, Y., Hu, Y., Wei, W., Ban, X., Xie, C., Tan, Y., Liu, X., Cui, S., Duan, X., & Li, Z. (2025). Achieving flexible fairness metrics in federated medical imaging. *Nature Communications*, *16*(1), 3342. DOI: 10.1038/s41467-025-58549-0 PMID: 40199877

Xu, W., & Gao, Z. (2024). Applying HCAI in developing effective human-AI teaming: A perspective from human-AI joint cognitive systems. *interactions, 31*(1), 32-37.

Xu, B., & Yang, G. (2025). Interpretability research of deep learning: A literature survey. *Information Fusion*, *115*, 102721. DOI: 10.1016/j.inffus.2024.102721

Xu, Y. (2021). The invisible aggressive fist: Features of Cyberbullying language in China. *Int. J. Semiot. Law - Rev. Int. Sémiot. International Journal for the Semiotics of Law*, *34*(4), 1041–1064. DOI: 10.1007/s11196-020-09746-1

Yadava, A. (2023). Ethical and regulatory challenges of AI adoption in the financial services sector: A global perspective. *International Journal of Science Research Archive, 10*(13), 10.30574.

Yang, M. (2024). Baltimore teacher accused of using AI to create fake, racist recording of principal. *The Guardian*. Retrieved from https://www.theguardian.com/us-news/2024/apr/27/baltimore-teacher-ai-fake-racist-recording-principal

Yang, F., Abedin, M. Z., Qiao, Y., & Ye, L. (2024). Towards Trustworthy Governance of AI-Generated Content (AIGC): A Blockchain-Driven Regulatory Framework for Secure Digital Ecosystems. *IEEE Transactions on Engineering Management*, *71*, 14945–14962. DOI: 10.1109/TEM.2024.3472292

Yang, J., Zhao, L., & Kim, S. (2024). Bias and generalizability of diagnostic AI across imaging devices and populations. *The Lancet. Digital Health*, *6*(4), e223–e234.

Yang, X., Lupón, J., Vidán, M. T., Ferguson, C., Gastelurrutia, P., Newton, P. J., Macdonald, P. S., Bueno, H., Bayés-Genís, A., Woo, J., & Fung, E. (2018). Impact of frailty on mortality and hospitalization in chronic heart failure: A systematic review and meta-analysis. *Journal of the American Heart Association*, *7*(23), e008251. DOI: 10.1161/JAHA.117.008251 PMID: 30571603

Yaseen, A. (2023). AI-driven threat detection and response: A paradigm shift in cybersecurity. *International Journal of Information and Cybersecurity*, *7*(12), 25–43.

Yasin, A. 2025. Malware analysis in IoT devices and AI. In *Malware analysis in IoT devices and AI*. The institution of Engineering and Technology (IET).

Yi, X., Yang, X., Kelarev, A., Lam, K. Y., & Tari, Z. (2022). *Blockchain foundations and applications*. Springer. DOI: 10.1007/978-3-031-09670-9

Yu, H. (2024). Why isn't composite equity issuance favored by the stock market? A risk-based explanation for the anomaly. *International Review of Financial Analysis*, *94*, 103288. DOI: 10.1016/j.irfa.2024.103288

Zampieri, M., Malmasi, S., Nakov, P., Rosenthal, S., Farra, N., & Kumar, R. (2019). Semeval-2019 task 6: Identifying and categorizing offensive language in social media (offenseval). *arXiv preprint arXiv:1903.08983*. DOI: 10.18653/v1/S19-2010

Zampieri, M., Nakov, P., Rosenthal, S., Atanasova, P., Karadzhov, G., Mubarak, H., . . . Çöltekin, Ç. (2020). SemEval-2020 task 12: Multilingual offensive language identification in social media (OffensEval 2020). *arXiv preprint arXiv:2006.07235*. DOI: 10.18653/v1/2020.semeval-1.188

Zeng, L., Ying-Chao, L. I., Humanities, S. O., & Polytechnic, S. (2019). The classification and modal sense of implicit violent speech acts. *J. Nanchang Univ. Soc. Sci.*, *50*, 117–124.

Zhang, J., Fang, Z., Zhang, Y., & Song, D. (2020). Zero-knowledge proofs for decision tree predictions and accuracy. In *ACM Conference on Computer and Communications Security (CCS)*. https://eprint.iacr.org/2020/1266

Zhang, Z., Sun, J., & Yang, Y. (2023). *zkFL: Zero-knowledge proof-based gradient aggregation for federated learning*. arXiv preprint. https://arxiv.org/abs/2310.02554

Zhang, L., Howard, S., Montpool, T., Moore, J., Mahajan, K., & Miranskyy, A. (2023). Automated data validation: An industrial experience report. *Journal of Systems and Software*, *197*, 111573. DOI: 10.1016/j.jss.2022.111573

Zhang, S., Wu, L., Zhao, Z., Masso, J. F., & Chen, M. (2024). Artificial intelligence in gerontology: Data-driven health management and precision medicine. *Advances in Gerontology*, *14*(3), 97–110. DOI: 10.1134/S2079057024600691

Zhang, Z., Al Hamadi, H., Damiani, E., Yeun, C. Y., & Taher, F. (2022). Explainable artificial intelligence applications in cyber security: State-of-the-art in research. *IEEE Access : Practical Innovations, Open Solutions*, *10*, 93104–93139. DOI: 10.1109/ACCESS.2022.3204051

Zhong, J., Qiu, J., Sun, M., Jin, X., Zhang, J., Guo, Y., Qiu, X., Xu, Y., Huang, J., & Zheng, Y. (2022). To be ethical and responsible digital citizens or not: A linguistic analysis of cyberbullying on social media. *Frontiers in Psychology*, *13*, 861823. DOI: 10.3389/fpsyg.2022.861823 PMID: 35572339

Zhou, J., Chen, S., Wu, Y., Li, H., Zhang, B., Zhou, L., Hu, Y., Xiang, Z., Li, Z., Chen, N., Han, W., Wang, D., & Gao, X. (2024). PPML-Omics: A privacy-preserving federated machine learning method protects patients' privacy in omic data. *Science Advances*, *10*. https://www.science.org/doi/10.1126/sciadv.adh8601

Zhou, N., Zhang, C.-T., Lv, H.-Y., Hao, C.-X., Li, T.-J., Zhu, J.-J., Zhu, H., Jiang, M., Liu, K.-W., Hou, H.-L., Liu, D., Li, A.-Q., Zhang, G.-Q., Tian, Z.-B., & Zhang, X.-C. (2019). Concordance study between IBM Watson for Oncology and clinical practice for patients with cancer in China. *The Oncologist*, *24*(6), 812–819. DOI: 10.1634/theoncologist.2018-0255 PMID: 30181315

Zhou, S. K., Greenspan, H., Davatzikos, C., Duncan, J. S., van Ginneken, B., Madabhushi, A., Prince, J. L., Rueckert, D., & Summers, R. M. (2021). A review of deep learning in medical imaging: Imaging traits, technology trends, case studies with progress highlights, and future promises. *Proceedings of the IEEE*, *109*(5), 820–838. DOI: 10.1109/JPROC.2021.3054390 PMID: 37786449

Zuboff, S. (2023). The age of surveillance capitalism. In *Social theory re-wired* (pp. 203–213). Routledge. DOI: 10.4324/9781003320609-27

About the Contributors

Affan Yasin is an Assistant Professor at the School of AI and Advanced Computing, Xi'an Jiaotong-Liverpool University (XJTLU), China. He holds a PhD in Software Engineering from Tsinghua University, China, where he studied under Prof. Wang Jianmin. Following his PhD, he completed postdoctoral fellowships at Tsinghua University, Northwestern Polytechnical University, and Universitas Airlangga, Indonesia. Dr. Yasin's research interests encompass empirical software engineering, requirements engineering, human factors in security, social engineering, phishing attacks, education, game design, agent-based modeling, natural language processing, and interdisciplinary studies. He has published over 30 research papers in esteemed journals and conferences, including Information and Software Technology, Journal of Software: Process and Evolution, and IET Software. He has also contributed to Computer Fraud & Security and authored a book chapter published by Springer. In addition to his research, Dr. Yasin has served as a lead guest editor for journals such as Applied Sciences, Electronics, AI, and Computers, Materials & Continua (CMC). His research collaborations extend globally, involving researchers at institutions like the University of Hertfordshire (UK), Hamad Bin Khalifa University (Qatar), Mälardalen University (Sweden), Tsinghua University (China), Emerson University (Pakistan), and Universitas Airlangga (Indonesia).

Farhan Ullah is an Associate Research Professor at the Cybersecurity Center of Prince Mohammad Bin Fahd University (PMU) in Saudi Arabia. He earned his Ph.D. in Computer Science from Sichuan University, Chengdu, China, in 2020. Prior to his current role, he served as an Associate Professor at Northwestern Polytechnical University (NPU) in Xi'an, China, and as a visiting research fellow at the University of Camerino, Italy. He has also held a lecturing position at COMSATS University Islamabad, Pakistan. Dr. Ullah's research interests encompass cybersecurity, malware analysis, data science, deep learning, and Explainable AI. He has published extensively in reputable journals and conferences, including IEEE,

Springer, Elsevier, and Wiley. His work has garnered over 2,600 citations, reflecting his significant contributions to the field. Additionally, he has been invited as a keynote speaker and has delivered courses at international conferences and summer schools. He has also contributed as a guest editor for renowned journals such as the IEEE Journal of Biomedical and Health Informatics and KSII Transactions.

Rubia Fatima is an Assistant Professor and Coordinator of the Information Technology program at Emerson University, Multan, Pakistan. She earned her Ph.D. in Software Engineering from Tsinghua University, Beijing, China, under the supervision of Prof. Jianmin Wang and Associate Prof. Lin Liu. Prior to her doctoral studies, she completed her Master's degree in Information Technology from Bahauddin Zakariya University, Multan, Pakistan. Dr. Fatima's research interests encompass empirical software engineering, AI, social engineering, human factors in security, game-based education, and serious games. She has published over 28 research papers in reputable international journals and conferences. Her work has contributed significantly to the fields of software security and educational technology. Her work reflects a strong commitment to advancing knowledge in both theoretical and applied aspects of software engineering. She actively collaborates on interdisciplinary projects and engages in mentoring students and early-career researchers. With a passion for academic excellence and innovation, she continuously contributes to the growth of research culture in Pakistan. Dr. Fatima also plays an active role in curriculum development and educational quality enhancement at her institution. She is committed to bridging the gap between academia and industry through impactful research and community engagement.

***

Muhammad Shafqat Ali received the B.S. degree in Computer Science from the University of Central Punjab, Lahore, Pakistan, in 2021, and the M.S. degree in Computer Science from COMSATS University Islamabad, Sahiwal Campus, Pakistan, in 2024. From 2024 to 2025, he served as a Lecturer in the Department of Computer Science at Government College University, Faisalabad, Pakistan. He is currently pursuing an M.Sc. in Management with Data Analytics at BPP University Limited, United Kingdom. His research interests include machine learning, deep learning, and computer vision.

Amara Hafeez is a researcher and academic specializing in software engineering, artificial intelligence, and cybersecurity. She holds a MS in Software Engineering from University of Agriculture, Faisalabad, where her work has focused on the ethical and practical applications of AI in modern software systems. Her research interests include explainable AI, machine learning applications in security, and sustainable software engineering practices.

Iram Hanif is a researcher and academic specializing in software engineering, artificial intelligence, and cybersecurity. Hanif holds a degree of MS in Software Engineering from The University of Agriculture Faisalabad, where their work has focused on the ethical and practical applications of AI in modern software systems.

Nazeef Ul Haq is a Lecturer in the Department of Computer Science at the University of Engineering and Technology (UET), Lahore, Pakistan. He received his Master's degree in Computer Science from the National University of Sciences and Technology (NUST), Islamabad, and is currently pursuing a PhD in Computer Science at UET Lahore. His research focuses on advancing the fields of computer vision, natural language processing, and generative AI, with an emphasis on developing intelligent systems that can analyze and interpret complex data. He has contributed to several research projects exploring the integration of machine learning and deep learning techniques in real-world applications. His work aims to bridge the gap between theoretical advancements and practical solutions in AI-driven technologies.

Majid Hussain is currently serving as the Dean of the Department of Information Technology at The University of Faisalabad, Faisalabad. With a distinguished academic and professional career spanning over many years, he has contributed extensively to the fields of information technology, software engineering, cybersecurity, and artificial intelligence. He holds a Ph.D. and has led numerous initiatives to advance research, innovation, and education in IT.

Muhammad Ibrar is an Assistant Professor in Computer Science with a strong academic and research background in Computer Networking and the Internet of Things (IoT). He has completed his Postdoctoral research in the area of advanced communication networks and intelligent connected systems, where his work focused on improving network performance, security, scalability, and energy efficiency in IoT-enabled environments. His research interests include wireless and mobile networks, IoT architectures, network security, edge and cloud computing, smart systems, and next-generation communication technologies. He has published research in reputable journals and conferences and actively contributes to academic and industrial research collaborations. In addition to his research activities, he is dedicated to teaching and mentoring undergraduate and postgraduate students, supervising research projects, and developing modern curricula aligned with emerging technologies. His goal is to advance innovative, secure, and efficient networking solutions for real-world applications such as smart cities, healthcare, and industrial automation.

Farzana Jabeen is Currently serving as Assistant Professor at National University of Sciences and Technology Islamabad Pakistan. She did her PhD from Tsinghua University, Beijing China in HCI. Research areas and interests include UI/UX, Intelligent Interfaces, HCI for health care, Well Being of Neurological Disorders, Assistive Technology for differently abled users.

Muqadsa Jabeen is a Lecturer in Computer Science with research interests in Artificial Intelligence, Machine Learning, and healthcare applications.

Waqas Junaid received the Ph.D. degree from the School of Computer Science and Engineering, Guangxi Normal University, Guilin, Guangxi, China, the MS (CS) degree from the University of Agriculture Peshawar in 2018, and the MCS degree from Abdul Wali Khan University Mardan in 2014. He is currently a postdoctoral researcher at school of software, Northwestern Polytechnical Unviersity, Xian, China. His research interests are problem-oriented requirements engineering, organization problems, microservices, modeling, verifying, testing, validating cyber physical systems based on Problem Frames, human computer interaction, and Auto repair codes using LLM.

Muhammad Khalid is currently working as a Lecturer(Assistant Professor) in the school of computer science, University of Hull. Before this, he worked Post-Doctoral Research Fellow at the University of Lincoln, Lincoln. He was responsible for assuring robot autonomy toward safety aspects in the project called MeSAPro. In this project, he ensured robotic safety through human-robot interaction for the robots used in the strawberry collection. Khalid has completed his PhD from Northumbria University in 2020 on Autonomous parking in intelligent smart cities, where he was awarded a fully funded PhD studentship in 2017 under research development framework.

Amrutha Kolhar obtained the MCA. Degree in Computer Science from the Karnatak University in 2022. she is currently working as a Research Scholar under the guidance of Dr. Sridevi, Professor, Department of Computer Science, Karnatak University, Dharwad. Received research fellowship from Other Backward Classes, (OBC), and Govt. of Karnataka. Area of research is "Network Security". At present working on the research topic: "Development and enhancing inter-operability of API and validating its authentication: X-IoT Devices". and also, IAENG student member (International Association of Engineers)(Member no: 366909)

Saima Anwar Lashari is an Assistant Professor at the College of Computing and Informatics, Saudi Electronic University, Dammam, Saudi Arabia. She earned her PhD in Information Technology from Universiti Tun Hussein Onn Malaysia

(UTHM) in 2016 and completed a postdoctoral fellowship there in 2017. She has published numerous research articles in reputable journals and conference proceedings. Her research interests include machine learning, deep learning, pattern recognition, and image processing.

Sana Anwar Lashari is an Associate Professor in the School of Nursing at Shandong Xiehe University, Shandong, China. She earned her PhD in Educational Psychology and has extensive teaching experience across undergraduate and postgraduate Psychology programs. Her scholarly work centers on adolescent wellbeing, personality development, and pedagogical practices in higher education. She has published widely in Scopus-indexed and refereed journals and is engaged in collaborative research projects that bridge psychology, education, and health sciences.

Tahira Anwar Lashari is an Associate Professor at the School of Electrical Engineering and Computer Science (SEECS), National University of Sciences and Technology (NUST), Islamabad, Pakistan. She holds a PhD in Educational Psychology from Universiti Tun Hussein Onn Malaysia (UTHM). Her academic and research career reflects a strong interdisciplinary focus, bridging psychology, education, and technology. Dr. Lashari's scholarly interests center on educational psychology, engineering education, gamification, technology-enhanced pedagogy, and digital learning environments. Her work includes studies on augmented reality applications, assistive technologies for children with special needs, and sentiment analysis. Dr. Lashari contributes to both research and teaching, emphasizing the role of psychological principles in technology-supported learning and instructional design.

Asad Malik is an assistant research professor at MSU.

Rizwan Riaz Mir is a researcher and data science enthusiast with interests in data analytics, artificial intelligence, and applied computer science. He is pursuing work focused on data-driven decision-making and health informatics. His research emphasizes practical applications of data science to improve medical outcomes, healthcare systems, and digital learning environments.

Mehvish Rashid has considerable professional experience in software industry and in academia. Currently an Assistant Professor, Mehvish has completed her doctorate in Software Engineering from Dublin City University, Ireland. Her Doctorate is specific to incorporating Knowledge Retention (KR) mechanisms in Open Source Software (OSS) projects. She believes that most of OSS projects fail due to the lack of knowledge available to contributors who can perform ongoing maintenance tasks crucial to the evolution of OSS. Furthermore, OSS projects due the transient nature of contributors and the difference in work settings from traditional organisations require a Proactive Knowledge Retention (PKR) mechanisms, while contributors are still active on the project. She has significant number of publications in reputable venues listed under publication section. She completed her Master Thesis in Regression Testing while working with Ericsson AB, Sweden, which further enhanced her technical skills. She also has worked for IBM as an ETL Tester on a project in the telecom sector. The solution she worked on is designed for SQM (Service Quality Management) to gain insight into the performance of organization's telecom network. In the past, she performed testing on web applications utilizing various testing techniques. Her specialties are Web Application Testing, Manual, and Automated Testing (Functional, Regression, Performance). Software Testing is one of her areas of interest, and she keeps adding to her domain.

Ifra Shabbir did their MS in Computer Science from COMSATS University Sahiwal. Currently, they are working as a research writer with a professor. Their research interests include machine learning, artificial intelligence, and data-driven applications.

Rabia Shahid is currently affiliated with the Center of Data Science, Government College University, Faisalabad (GCUF), Punjab, Pakistan. She is pursuing her Ph.D. in Computer Science, with a research focus on Data Science, Artificial Intelligence, and Deep Learning. Her research interests include Generative AI, Machine Learning for Healthcare, and Computer Vision applications. She has contributed to several research projects involving AI-based medical diagnostics, hybrid deep learning models, and automated data analytics systems. Her recent work focuses on Generative Adversarial Networks (GANs) for medical image synthesis and Transformer-based architectures for video summarization and visual analytics.

Sridevi, Professor, Department of Computer Science, Karnatak University, Dharwad. Obtained a PhD from Mangalore University, Mangalore in 2017. Research interest includes Advanced Computer Networks, Mobile and Wireless Communication, Network Security, Cloud Computing and the Internet of Things. At present guiding four research scholars and one M.Phil. awarded. And also, Reviewer for the Journal of Advances in Mathematics and Computer Science. Published more than 30 research papers in a national and international journal.

Djihad Tria is an Assistant Professor in the Department of Management and Social Sciences at Amity University Tashkent. She earned her PhD in Economics from Universiti Utara Malaysia and has extensive teaching experience at both undergraduate and postgraduate levels in quantitative economics, economics and business administration, communication and public relations, and organizational management. Her research focuses on microfinance, labour market policies, macroeconomic assessment, informal employment, modelling methods, and energy economics. She has published extensively in Scopus-indexed and peer-reviewed journals and actively engages in collaborative research projects in the areas of labour economics, macroeconomic policy, microfinance, government expenditure, and the informal economy..

Muhammad Usman Akhtar, completed his Ph.D. in Software Engineering from Wuhan University, Hubei, China in the year 2024. He previously received his MS in Computer Science from the University of Engineering and Technology (UET), Peshawar, Pakistan, in the year 2018, and his BS in Software Engineering from Islamia College, Peshawar, Pakistan, in the year 2013. Then he started his professional career as a Research Assistant at the National Center for Big Data and Cloud Computing at UET, Peshawar. As far as his research publications are concerned, he has eight publications to his credit, with a cumulative impact factor of more than 47.7. In addition, he contributed to one chapter in the book EH-ARCUN: Energy Harvested Analytical Approach Towards Reliability with Cooperation for Underwater WSNs (Chapter 14, 147-157). He has contributed to NetworkX (an open-source Python library) used for creating, analyzing and visualizing complex graphs in various domains such as social networks, biological networks, and more.

Affan Yasin is a researcher at the School of AI and Advanced Computing (AIAC), Xi'an Jiaotong-Liverpool University (XJTLU), Suzhou, Jiangsu, China. His research interests lie at the intersection of artificial intelligence, cybersecurity, and modern software engineering systems, with a particular focus on ethical and explainable AI applications.

Muhammad Naveed Yasir serves as an Assistant Professor at Emerson University, Multan, where he also coordinates the Artificial Intelligence program. He earned an M.S. in Engineering (Control & Automation) from The University of Sheffield, United Kingdom, and later a Ph.D. in the same field from Dongguk University, Seoul, South Korea. His research is focused on the dynamic intersection of artificial intelligence, AI in health systems, robotics, computer vision, and control systems.

Index

A

Adversarial Attacks 212, 277, 302, 319, 327, 334
Agentic AI 245, 251, 254, 255, 257, 258, 271, 272
AI-driven Cybersecurity 305, 319, 338
Algorithmic Bias 12, 41, 81, 156, 192, 194, 223, 239, 276
Algorithmic moderation 68, 84
Anomaly Detection 212, 284, 291, 292, 305, 319
Artificial Intelligence (AI) 1, 2, 9, 12, 14, 20, 26, 32, 33, 34, 35, 37, 38, 40, 41, 44, 47, 49, 59, 61, 62, 63, 64, 65, 67, 68, 73, 74, 77, 83, 86, 87, 88, 89, 90, 94, 98, 102, 114, 118, 119, 120, 121, 124, 126, 130, 151, 152, 153, 155, 156, 157, 159, 160, 162, 163, 165, 166, 168, 169, 171, 176, 177, 179, 180, 181, 182, 183, 193, 199, 203, 209, 213, 214, 215, 216, 217, 218, 219, 222, 226, 229, 231, 234, 235, 241, 242, 243, 251, 253, 273, 274, 276, 277, 278, 279, 281, 283, 284, 291, 302, 303, 304, 305, 306, 326, 328, 332, 334, 336, 337, 338
Assistive Technologies 37, 38, 39, 41, 42, 47, 48, 49, 54, 55, 57, 58, 59, 65

B

Blockchain Governance 102, 156

C

Convolutional Neural Network 152, 314
cyber harassment 67
Cybersecurity 63, 94, 96, 98, 108, 109, 111, 113, 116, 120, 130, 160, 164, 165, 176, 181, 203, 205, 275, 276, 277, 278, 279, 280, 281, 282, 284, 286, 288, 289, 291, 293, 294, 295, 297, 298, 299, 300, 301, 302, 303, 304, 305, 306, 307, 308, 312, 319, 320, 324, 325, 326, 327, 328, 332, 334, 335, 336, 337, 338

D

Data Augmentation 222, 234, 319
Data Privacy 19, 20, 54, 63, 88, 94, 119, 135, 136, 153, 160, 162, 181, 188, 192, 202, 225, 239, 254, 281, 305, 326, 329
Data Sensitivity 155, 156, 158, 172, 173, 178
Decision Support Systems 183
Deep Learning 6, 16, 53, 71, 74, 75, 87, 157, 167, 172, 181, 183, 184, 192, 216, 219, 223, 241, 253, 257, 260, 263, 271, 274, 276, 281, 284, 290, 292, 294, 299, 303, 304, 305, 306, 312, 313, 318, 320, 337, 338

E

Ethical AI 9, 40, 58, 65, 93, 96, 99, 100, 101, 108, 123, 124, 126, 127, 128, 147, 149, 153, 156, 159, 167, 173, 174, 176, 181, 189, 190, 194, 197, 213, 221, 227, 233, 234, 235, 236, 239, 245, 254, 258, 259, 276, 278, 289, 297, 307, 327, 328
Ethical AI Frameworks 65
Ethical AI Governance 93, 96, 99, 100, 101, 239
Explainable AI (XAI) 17, 34, 43, 52, 62, 65, 119, 160, 168, 174, 179, 187, 194, 211, 230, 235, 242, 243, 258, 277, 278, 279, 280, 282, 286, 288, 289, 291, 294, 295, 297, 298, 301, 302, 303, 304, 327, 328, 331, 334

F

Federated Learning 46, 94, 108, 114, 120, 121, 124, 128, 132, 133, 134, 135, 136, 146, 147, 148, 153, 156, 158, 169, 172, 177, 178, 180, 184, 205, 211, 212, 215, 225, 227, 228, 234, 241, 242, 276, 278,

287, 295, 304, 325, 327
Frailty monitoring 245, 251, 254, 255, 257, 258, 262, 271, 272

G

Generative AI 61, 72, 78, 80, 89, 192, 210, 245, 254, 258, 259, 261, 263, 272
Geriatric care 247, 250, 256, 257, 259, 263, 272

H

Health Equity 64, 171, 177, 187, 200, 215
Human-Centered Artificial Intelligence 2, 9, 47, 59, 64, 65
Human Computer Interaction 41
Human Intelligence 2, 68

M

Machine Learning 16, 32, 33, 34, 53, 63, 74, 75, 76, 111, 126, 127, 128, 129, 135, 144, 150, 152, 153, 160, 179, 183, 199, 202, 214, 216, 218, 241, 243, 251, 253, 255, 256, 258, 259, 267, 271, 274, 276, 281, 282, 284, 293, 294, 295, 304, 305, 306, 308, 312, 332, 333, 337

N

Natural Language Processing 16, 34, 49, 74, 87, 253, 281, 316, 317

P

Participatory and Inclusive Design 43, 65
Patient Safety 155, 156, 157, 160, 161, 162, 163, 166, 167, 168, 172, 173, 174, 176, 178, 181, 198, 199, 200, 213, 223, 226
Privacy-preserving systems 119

R

Regulatory Compliance 8, 20, 114, 121, 127, 147, 181, 184, 208, 237, 330
Responsible AI 28, 30, 34, 116, 118, 128, 149, 159, 163, 222, 223, 228, 240, 281, 302, 303

T

Thread detection 286, 289, 297
Transformer models 245, 254, 258, 259
Trustworthy AI 2, 7, 11, 32, 62, 93, 94, 120, 125, 200, 222, 278, 297, 298, 328
Trustworthy AI Systems 93, 125

U

User Experience 14, 16, 18, 25, 43, 49, 148

Z

Zero-Knowledge Proofs 107, 111, 112, 114, 119, 120, 121, 123, 124, 125, 126, 128, 130, 132, 133, 134, 135, 136, 137, 139, 142, 144, 149, 151, 153

www.ingramcontent.com/pod-product-compliance
Lightning Source LLC
LaVergne TN
LVHW060006031026
849161LV00025B/1502
9798337360386